LORD MAHĀVĪRA AND HIS TIMES

LALA SUNDAR LAL JAIN RESEARCH SERIES

Vol. VI

LORD MAHĀVĪRA AND HIS TIMES

KAILASH CHAND JAIN

MOTILAL BANARSIDASS PUBLISHERS PVT. LTD.
DELHI

First Edition: 1974
Revised Edition: Delhi, 1991

ISBN: 81-208-0805-3

Also available at:
MOTILAL BANARSIDASS
41 U.A., Bungalow Road, Jawahar Nagar, Delhi 110 007
120 Royapettah High Road, Mylapore, Madras 600 004
16 St. Mark's Road, Bangalore 560 001
Ashok Rajpath, Patna 800 004
Chowk, Varanasi 221 001

PRINTED IN INDIA
BY JAINENDRA PRAKASH JAIN AT SHRI JAINENDRA PRESS, A-45 NARAINA INDUSTRIAL AREA, PHASE I, NEW DELHI 110 028 AND PUBLISHED BY NARENDRA PRAKASH JAIN FOR MOTILAL BANARSIDASS PUBLISHERS PVT. LTD., BUNGALOW ROAD, JAWAHAR NAGAR, DELHI 110 007

DEDICATED

TO

His Holiness Āchārya Śrī Nana Lalji Mahārāja

FOREWORD

Lord Mahāvira and His Times by Dr. Kailash Chand Jain of the Vikram University (Ujjain)—known for his scholarship, industry and devotion to Jaina studies—is a timely and valuable publication. I offer my congratulations to Dr. Jain. The author has drawn upon an extensive range of material in the preparation of the book. It should be of wide interest.

India's most characteristic and far-reaching contribution to human civilization is, probably, the principle and practice of ahiṁsā. Lord Mahāvīra stands as its supreme embodiment, personification.

Ahiṁsā has been always central to man's progress, but at no time its need and relevance has been more than today. Man's very survival in the atomic age depends on science and ahiṁsā. And ahiṁsā is not, and cannot be, in the very nature of things a static doctrine. On the contrary (like science) it is an exploration where every sincere effort and practice opens new possibilities and new horizons.

In the deeply inspiring words of Mahatma Gandhi—who can speak about ahiṁsā with greater insight, experience and faith than Gandhiji : "By reason of Life-long practice of ahiṁsā, I claim to be an expert in it, though very imperfect. Speaking in absolute terms, the more I practise it the clearer I see how far I am from the full expression of ahiṁsā in my life. It is his ignorance of this, the greatest duty of man in the world, which makes him say that in this age, non-violence has little scope in the face of violence, whereas I make bold to say that in this age of the Atom Bomb unadulterated non-violence is the only force that can confound all the tricks put together of violence."

Dr. Jain's book is a very welcome and significant addition to the literature on Lord Mahāvīra and ahiṁsā.

D.S. KOTHARI

Delhi
22 August 1974

PREFACE

The work entitled 'Lord Mahāvīra And His Times' deals with the history and culture of India during the age of Mahāvīra in the sixth century B.C. This age is marked by outstanding achievements in different spheres—political, religious, social, economic, artistic, and literary. It saw the beginning of the political unification of India under the hegemony of Magadha, and the propagation of Buddhism, Jainism, and other heterodox religious sects. A social code for the observance of the people was prescribed. Because of commerce and trade flourishing during this period, there was all-round prosperity. Besides, development in language, literature, and arts was no less marked.

Many an attempt was made from time to time to write India's history concerning one or the other aspect of this age. Of these attempts, T.W. RHYS DAVIDS was the first to describe ancient India during the period of the Buddha from the Buddhist point of view, in his work 'Buddhist India' (1903). Being a pioneer work on this subject, it is indeed invaluable, though it was written at a time when materials indispensable to the author of such a work were scanty.

'The Social Organization in North India in Buddhist Time', written by R. FICK, in 1920 A.D., comes next and is based on the *Jātakas* of the Pāli Buddhist canon. This work throws a flood of light on the social life of northern India during the Buddha's time. Based as it is on only one type of sectarian evidence and being concerned only with the social organization of this period, it does not, indeed, give a comprehensive picture.

J.C. JAIN tried to include in *Life in Ancient India as Depicted in the Jaina Canons* (1945), all the available materials of the Jaina Canon for the first time in the real sense with reference to social life. This is only an one-sided picture.

Similarly, B.C. LAW's *India as Described in the early texts of Buddhism and Jainism* does not make much use of Brahmanical sources.

M.M. SINGH's work *Life in North-Eastern India in Pre-Mauryan Times*, however, incorporates both the Buddhist as well as the Brahmanical sources, and the author has tried to give a picture of social, religious, and economic life of that period. The political and cultural history of India of this period has been discussed in *The age of Imperial Unity* edited by R.C. MAJUMDAR. In both these works, the Jaina sources have not been given the treatment they deserve in comparison with the Brahmanical and the Buddhist ones. Besides, the recent archaeological material discovered in the excavations has not been fully utilised.

Lord Mahāvīra is closely related to his age in which he lived and propagated his religion. One cannot understand his life and teachings unless one looks into the circumstances in which he was brought up. Such an attempt has been made by giving a panorama of the cultural history of that period in this work.

A number of works dealing with Mahāvīra's life and teachings have been written. Most of them do not seem to be historically authentic as they are based on late sources. The most reliable work, it appears to me, is *Mahāvīra—His Life and Teachings* by B.C. LAW who has taken help from both the Buddhist and the Jaina texts in the original. He has made a comparative study of both the texts in elucidating some knotty points of Mahāvīra's life and his doctrine. In his work *Some Jaina Canonical Sūtras*, he has presented a critical account of the principal Jaina canonical texts which, along with his articles published in different research journals, have been utilised in this work.

The present study has been divided into ten chapters. In Chapter I some legendary accounts, given in Jaina scriptures, have been critically examined in the light of archaeological evidence. It appears, both from the Buddhist and the Jaina texts, that Pārśvanātha is a historical figure, and the history of Jainism can be extended to his times. In Chapter II, the different sources which have been drawn upon for the writing of this work have been critically discussed.

Chapter III gives an account of the 'Life of Mahāvīra' from his childhood to *Nirvāṇa*. Some controversial questions like his birthplace and the year of *Nirvāṇa* have been discussed.

Chapter IV deals with his teachings based on the original texts. Early Buddhist texts have been used as collateral evidence, in writing this chapter.

In Chapter V, the different sects contemporaneous with Lord Mahāvīra have been enumerated and some interesting light has been thrown on the life and teachings of some of their founders.

Chapter VI describes the sixteen great states *Solasamahājanapadas*. How the political unification of India was gradually brought about under Bimbisāra and Ajātaśatru, both rulers of Magadha, has been pointed out here. The administrative machinery and the constitution of the republics especially of the Lichchhavīs, have also been described.

Chapter VII throws light on the social conditions of the age under consideration. The duties and responsibilities of the individuals as regards the *varṇas* and *āśramas* have been fixed. Some old social customs like *Niyoga* have disappeared and the new ones, in harmony with the new set-up of the society, have come into existence. Such topics as family, marriage, position of woman, dress, ornaments, festivals, and games have also been examined.

Chapter VIII deals with economic conditions. The village was considered to be the basis of social economy. A large number of professions and industries came into existence and were organized into guilds which became a special feature of the economic life of the time. The increased use of iron started and the coined money came into vogue.

Chapter IX is devoted to art and architecture. The noteworthy feature of this age is the revival of urban life when the use of kiln bricks started. The North Black Polished Ware, of de luxe quality, is the gift of this age.

Chapter X demonstrates how this period can be regarded as one of the most creative epochs in the spheres of education, literature, and science.

An idea of writing this work arose in my mind while discussing with NARENDRA BHANAWAT on the occasion of the XXVI session of All India Oriental Conference held at Ujjain from 26th to 28th Oct. 1972. I thought of writing it in commemoration of the auspicious occasion of the 25th centenary of Lord Mahāvīra which falls in the year 1974-75. I am grateful to NARENDRA BHANAWAT who placed this idea before the Akhila Bhāratīya Sādhu Mārgīya Jain Saṁgha. I am extremely thankful to the Saṁgha and its office bearers who became ready for financial assistance to this project. I am highly obliged to SARDAR MAL KANKARIA who gave final shape to this project. I owe an immense debt to GANPAT RAJ BOHARA who constantly inspired me for writing this work. My sincere thanks are also due to GUMAN MAL CHORADIA, JUGRAJ SETHIA, BHANWAR LAL KOTHARI and GOKUL CHAND SURYA who took keen interest in publication of this work.

I am also indebted to H.V. TRIVEDI, DALSUKH BHAI MALVANIA, H.B. JAIN, M.L. DALAL and S.M. PAHADIA who helped me in one way or other. I also wish to thank my student PRAMOD GANAPATYA for preparing maps. In conclusion, I want to express my extreme gratefulness to D.S. KOTHARI, former Chairman of the University Grants Commission, for writing a foreword to this work.

KAILASH CHAND JAIN

Mohan Niwas, Dewas Road,
Ujjain (M.P.)
10th October, 1974.

ABBREVIATIONS

ABORI.	Annals of the Bhandarkar Oriental Research Institute, Poona.
Āchā.	*Āchārāṅga.*
AIHT.	Ancient Indian Historical Tradition by F.E. Pargiter.
Ait. Br.	*Aitareya Brāhmaṇa.*
Aṅgu.	*Aṅguttara Nikāya.*
Anta.	*Antagaḍadasāo.*
Anu.	*Anuyogadvāra.*
Āp. Dh. S.	*Āpastamba Dharma-sūtra.*
APJLS.	*Arbudāchala Prāchīna Jaina Lekha Saṁdoha.*
Ās. G. Sū.	*Āśvalāyana Gṛihya-sūtra.*
ASI.	Archaeological Survey of India, Annual Reports.
Āva.	*Āvaśyaka.*
Āva. Chū.	*Āvaśyaka Chūrṇi.*
Bau. Dh. S.	*Baudhāyana Dharma Sūtra.*
Bhag.	*Bhagavatī.*
Bhāgavata.	*Bhāgavata Purāṇa.*
Bhā.	*Bhāshya.*
BHPIP.	A History of Pre-Buddhistic Indian Philosophy by Benimadhab Barua.
Brahma.	*Brahmajāla Sutta.*
Bṛi. Up.	*Bṛihadāraṇyaka Upanishad.*
Bṛih.	*Bṛihatkalpa.*
CAG.	Cunningham's Ancient Geography of India, Ed. by S.N. Majumdar.
CAH.	The Cambridge History of India, Ed. by E. Rapson (Ancient India).
Chhānd.	*Chhāndogya Upanishad.*
Chū.	*Chūrṇi.*

Chv.	*Chullavagga* (of *Vinaya Piṭaka*).
CL.	Carmichael Lectures by D. R. Bhandarkar.
Com.	Commentary.
Das.	*Dasaveyāliya.*
Dhp.	*Dhammapada.*
Dh. S.	*Dharma Sūtra.*
Dia.	Dialogues of the Buddha.
Digha.	*Dīghanikāya.*
DPPN.	Dictionary of Pali Proper Names.
ERE.	Encyclopaedia of Religion and Ethics, Ed. by J. Hastings.
FSONB.	The Social Organization in North-East India in Buddha's Time by R. Fick.
Gau. Dh. S.	*Gautama Dharma Sūtra.*
GEB.	Geography of Early Buddhism by B.C. Law.
Gop. Br.	*Gopatha Brāhmaṇa.*
GS.	The Book of Gradual Sayings.
HBSJY.	*Bhāratīya Saṁskṛiti me Jaina Dharma Kā Yogadāna* by H. L. Jain.
HTB.	*Si-yu-Ki.* Buddhist Records of the Western World. Translated from the Chinese of Hiuen Tsang (A.D. 629) by Samuel Beal 2 Vols. London, 1884.
I. Ar.—A Review.	Indian Archaeology—A Review.
IHQ.	Indian Historical Quarterly, Calcutta.
IP.	Indian Prehistory, 1964.
Jā.	*Jātaka.*
JASB.	Journal of the Asiatic Society of Bengal, Calcutta.
Jayadh.	*Jayadhavalā.*
JBORS.	Journal of the Bihar and Orissa Research Society, Patna.
JDL.	Journal of the Department of Letters, Calcutta University.
JIH.	Journal of Indian History.

Jīvā.	*Jīvābhigama.*
JLAIDJC.	Life in Ancient India as Described in the Jain Canons by J. C. JAIN.
JNSI.	Journal of the Numismatic Society of India, Banaras.
Kalpa.	*Kalpasūtra.*
Kau. Up.	*Kaushitaki Upanishad.*
KHDS.	History of Dharmaśāstra by P.V. KANE.
KMA.	Malwa Through the Ages by K.C. JAIN.
KS.	The Book of Kindred Sayings.
KVSBM.	*Śramaṇa Bhagavān Mahāvīra* by KALYANA VIJAYA.
LMLT.	Mahāvīra : His Life and Teachings by B. C. LAW.
Mahā. Ni.	*Mahāniśitha.*
Maitra. Sam.	*Maitrāyaṇī Saṁhitā.*
Majjh.	*Majjhima Nikāya.*
Matsya.	*Matsya Purāṇa.*
Mbh.	*Mahābhārata.*
ME.	Mahāvīra Era.
Milinda.	*Milindapañho.*
Moh. Ind.	Mohenjo-dāro and the Indus Civilization by J. MARSHALL.
Mv.	*Mahāvagga* (of *Vinaya Piṭaka*).
NATA.	*Āgama Aura Tripiṭaka Eka Anuśīlana* by NAGRAJ.
Nāyā.	*Nāyādhammakahā.*
NDGDAMI.	The Geographical Dictionary of Ancient and Medieval India by N. L. DEY.
Nir.	*Niryukti.*
Niryā.	*Nirayāvaliyāo.*
Niśī.	*Niśītha.*
NPP.	*Nāgarī Prachāriṇī Patrikā*, Banaras.
NS.	Numismatic Supplementary.
Ogha.	*Ogha Nijjutti.*
Ovā.	*Ovavāiya.*
Pā.	*Ashṭādhyāyī* of Pāṇini.
Pā. G. S.	*Pāraskara Gṛihyasūtra.*

Panna.	*Paṇṇavaṇā.*
Pari.	*Pariśishṭaparvan* of Hemachandra.
Peta.	*Petavatthu.*
PHAI.	Political History of Ancient India by H. C. RAYCHAUDHURI.
Piṇḍa.	*Piṇḍanijjutti.*
PSOB.	Studies in the Origins of Buddhism by G.C. PANDEY.
Rāya.	*Rāyapaseṇaiya.*
RBI.	Buddhist India by T. W. RHYS DAVIDS.
RV.	*Ṛigveda.*
Saṁ.	*Saṁyutta Nikāya.*
Sama.	*Samavāyāṅga.*
Sāmañña.	*Sāmaññaphala Sutta.*
Śat. Br.	*Śatapatha Brāhmaṇa.*
SBB.	Sacred Books of the Buddhists, London.
SBE.	Sacred Books of the East, Oxford.
SSHJ.	The Heart of Jainism by S. STEVENSON.
Sthānā or *Ṭhā.*	*Sthānāṅga* or *Ṭhāṇāṅga.*
Sū.	*Sūtra.*
Su. Ni.	*Sutta-Nipāta.*
Sūtra.	*Sūtrakṛitāṅga* (*Sūyagaḍāṅga*).
Taitt. Saṁ.	*Taittirīya Saṁhitā.*
Tandula.	*Tandulaveyāliya.*
Theragā.	*Theragāthā.*
Ṭi.	*Ṭikā.*
Tri. pu. Cha.	*Trishashṭiśalākā Purusha Charita* of Hemachandra.
Uttarā.	*Uttarādhyayana.*
Uvā.	*Uvāsagadasāo.*
Vas. Dh. S.	*Vasishṭha Dharma Sūtra.*
Vin.	*Vinaya Piṭaka.*
Vṛi.	*Vṛitti.*
VTM.	*Tirthaṅkara Mahāvīra* by VIJAYENDRA SURI.
Vya.	*Vyavahāra.*

CONTENTS

CHAPTER IX

CHAPTER X

CHAPTER 1

JAINISM BEFORE LORD MAHĀVĪRA

The history of Jainism before Lord Mahāvīra is shrouded in considerable obscurity. Materials which can reconstruct it are scanty, dubious and capable of different interpretations. Scholars have, therefore, come to widely divergent conclusions. The Jainas themselves believe that their religion is eternal and that before Mahāvīra (C. 600 B.C.), there lived twentythree Tīrthaṅkaras who appeared at certain intervals to propagate true religion for the salvation of the world. Some scholars[1] hold that there are traces of the existence of *Śramaṇa* culture even in pre-Vedic times. H. JACOBI[2] tried to prove, both from the Buddhist and the Jaina records, that Pārśvanātha, the immediate predecessor of Mahāvīra, who is said to have flourished some 250 years before him, is a historical personality.

JAINA RELIGION AS ETERNAL

According to the traditions preserved in the scriptures, Jaina religion is eternal, and it has been revealed again and again in every cyclic period of the world by innumerable Tīrthaṅkaras. The whole span of time is divided into two equal cycles, *Utsarpiṇi Kāla* and *Avasarpiṇi Kāla*. Each *Utsarpiṇi* and *Avasarpiṇi Kāla* extends over ten *Koṭā-Koṭi Sāgaropama* years which are sub-divided into six parts known as *aras*. The

1. H. ZIMMER : Philosophies of India, pp. 217-227;
   J.G.R. FORLONG : Short Studies in the Science of Comparative Religions, pp. 243-244;
   PSOB : p. 260;
   TULSI : Pre-Vedic Existence of *Śramaṇa* Tradition.
2. SBE, XLV, pp. xx-xxiii.

six divisions of *Avasarpiṇi* are known as *Sushamā-Sushamā*, *Sushamā*, *Sushamā-Duhshamā*, *Duhshamā-Sushamā*, *Duhshamā* and *Duhshamā-Duhshamā*. The six divisions of *Utsarpiṇi* are *Duhshamā Duhshamā*, *Duhshamā*, *Duhshamā-Sushamā*, *Sushamā-Duhshamā*, *Sushamā* and *Sushamā-Sushamā*. During each successive *ara* of *Avasarpiṇi Kāla*, the age, height, strength and happiness of the *Yugalikas* gradually declined. In all, fourteen *Kulakaras* (*Manus*) are said to have flourished during this period.

After the *Kulakaras*, twentyfour Tīrthaṅkaras appeared at certain intervals and preached the true religion for the salvation of the world. Their names are: (1) Ṛishabha, (2) Ajita, (3) Sambhava, (4) Abhinandana, (5) Sumati, (6) Padmaprabha, (7) Supārśva, (8) Chandraprabha, (9) Suvidhi or Pushpa, (10) Sītala, (11) Śreyāṁśa, (12) Vāsapūjya, (13) Vimala, (14) Ananta, (15) Dharma, (16) Śānti, (17) Kunthu, (18) Ara, (19) Malli, (20) Munisuvrata, (21) Nami, (22) Nemi, (23) Pārśva, and (24) Vardhamāna or Mahāvīra.

All Tīrthaṅkaras were Kshatriyas; Munisuvrata and Nami belonged to Harivaṁśa, and the remaining twentytwo to the Ikshvāku race. Malli, according to the Śvetāmbaras, was a woman, but this the Digambaras deny, for according to them no female can attain liberation. The interval in years between one Tīrthaṅkara and the other has been calculated. Pārśva's predecessor, Arishṭanemi, is stated to have died 84,000 years before Mahāvīra's *Nirvāṇa*. Nami died 500,000 years before Arishṭanemi, Munisuvrata 11,00,000 years before Nami; the next intervals are 65,00,000 and 10,000,000 or a *crore*; the following intervals cannot be expressed in definite number of years, but are given in *Palyopamas* and *Sāgaropamas*, the last interval being one *crore* of *crores* of *Sāgaropamas*. The length of the life and height of the Tīrthaṅkaras are in proportion to the length of the interval.

Besides twelve Universal monarchs[1] (*Chakravartīs*), nine

1. (1) Bharata, (2) Sagara, (3) Madhavā, (4) Sanatakumāra, (5) Śānti, (6) Kunthu, (7) Araha, (8) Subhauma, (9) Padma, (10) Harisheṇa, (11) Jayasena, and (12) Brahmadatta.

Vāsudevas,[1] nine *Baladevas*[2] and nine *Prativāsudevas*[3] lived within the period ranging from the first to the twenty-second Tīrthaṅkara. Together with the twentyfour Tīrthaṅkaras, there are sixtythree great personages (*Trishashṭiśalākāpurushacharita*) of Jaina history.

From such statements and descriptions of the blissful state of the world at its initial stages, it is evident that the Jainas, like the Hindus, attributed to the first race of man a longer life and greater strength and happiness than what fall to the share of his offspring in the present age. We know that the Greeks and Romans also held similar views. The world has grown worse and worse, and the life of man shorter and shorter, so that the twentythird Tīrthaṅkara, Pārśva, is said to have lived only for a hundred years, and died 250 years before his more celebrated successor, Mahāvīra, who lived only for seventytwo years.

ARCHAEOLOGICAL EVIDENCE TO ASCERTAIN THE TRUTHFULNESS OF THE LEGENDS

This legendary account of the existence of Jainism in such an early period on the basis of Jaina scriptures is not reliable, as it is not consistent with archaeological facts. The archaeologists tell a different story. The earliest man of Early Palaeolithic Culture lived in India in the Middle Pleistocene Period, i.e., some 200,000 years ago. Economically, man was then a savage and a hunter, and with the help of stone tools, he subsisted largely on fruits, roots and grubs, and on the chase with the help of his bow and arrow. The Middle Stone Age Culture is assigned to the later half of the Pleistocene (25,000 years before), and the tools are of typical flake

1. (1) Achala, (2) Vijaya, (3) Bhadra, (4) Suprabha, (5) Sudarśana, (6) Ānanda, (7) Nandana, (8) Padma, and (9) Rāma.
2. (1) Triprishṭha, (2) Dviprishṭha, (3) Svayambhū, (4) Purushottama, (5) Purushasiṁha, (6) Purushapuṇḍarīka, (7) Datta, (8) Nārāyaṇa, and (9) Krishṇa.
3. (1) Aśvagrīva, (2) Tāraka, (3) Meraka, (4) Madhu, (5) Niśumbha, (6) Bali, (7) Prahlāda, (8) Rāvaṇa, and (9) Jarāsandha.

   The legends of their lives form the subject of Hemachandra's great epic, the *Trishashṭiśalākāpurushacharita* based on older sources, probably the *Vāsudevahiṇḍi*.

nature, smaller than those of the Early Stone Age Culture. Up to the Mesolithic stage of culture of the Early Holocene Age, man was still a hunter and used tiny stone tools called microliths, which are non-geometric. Pottery did not come into existence till then.

If the evidence of the lowest levels of Langhraj in Gujarat is taken to be a general feature, the geometric element seems to have made its appearance in the microlithic industry. It was followed by the appearance of pottery. There is also some evidence, though inconclusive, regarding agriculture and domestication of animals at this stage. A picture of people using pottery and geometric microliths is also afforded by the cave-shelters of Madhya Pradesh. None of these stages has been dated with reasonable approximation.

The carbon-14 datings for the pre-pottery village culture of Kili Ghul Mohammad, near Quetta in Pakistan, confined to the Baluchi hills (Period I viz. 3690 ± 85 B.C. and 3510 ± 515 B.C.), are of great value. They provide evidence for the domestication of animals and for agriculture but not for the use of pottery. Kili Ghul Mohammad III marks the infiltration of copper. Kalibangan and Kotdiji cultures (3000 B.C.) are famous for pre-Harappan deposits, such as pottery, and structures. The Harappan civilization with many metropolitan centres, such as Rupar in the East Punjab, Kalibangan in North Rajasthan, Alamgirpur in Uttara Pradesh, and Rangpur, Lothal, and Somanatha in Gujarat, is the last and most elaborate phase of long cultural evolution (2500-1800 B.C.). It was followed by the various Chalcolithic cultures (1800-600 B.C.)—of the Ganga Yamuna basin, of Madhya Pradesh and the Deccan, the Neolithic Cultures of the North West, etc. It is in the light of the material furnished by these different cultures that we should study Jainism before Mahāvīra. The archaeological evidence does not prove such an antiquity of Jainism as is revealed by the Jaina scriptures.

THE THEORY OF TWENTYFOUR TĪRTHAṄKARAS

The *Kalpasūtra* ascribed to Bhadrabāhu (3rd century B.C.) shows the early stages of the development of Jainism when the tradition of four Tīrthaṅkaras or Jinas was cherished by the Jaina community. The four Jinas, whose life history is presented in the *Kalapasūtra*, are Ṛishabhadatta, Arishṭanemi, Pārśva and Mahāvīra. The conception of the former Buddhas was current even in Buddhism as early as the third century B.C. because some of them were worshipped in their own *stūpas*. Both in Jainism and Buddhism, the number gradually increased from four to seven, and from seven to twentyfour Tīrthaṅkaras. The tradition of twenty-four Tīrthaṅkaras became well established among the Jainas in about the first or second century A.D.[1] It might have risen earlier in Jainism, as the Nirgranthas were never spoken of, in Buddhist writings, as a newly risen sect nor was Nātaputta referred to as their founder. Accordingly, the Nirgranthas were, probably, an old sect at the time of Buddha, and Nātaputta only a reformer of the Jaina Church which might have been founded earlier by Pārśvanātha.

ṚISHABHA AS FOUNDER OF JAINISM

According to the Jaina tradition, Ṛishabha, who belonged to the Ikshvāku family of Ayodhyā, was the founder of Jainism. His parents were Nābhirāja and Marudevī. The son's name was Bharata after whom India is said to be named. He was the first Jina and the first Tīrthaṅkara who was born in an age when people, primitive and illiterate, did not know any art. He is said to have taught the arts of cooking, writing, pottery, painting and sculpture for the first time. It was during his time that the institution of marriage, the ceremony of cremating the dead, building of the mounds and the festivals in honour of Indra and the Nāgas came into existence. We may, thus, look upon him as a great pioneer in the history of human progress.

1. Even in the *Bhagavatī Sūtra* of the Jainas, the Ājīvika saint Gośāla is said to have claimed for himself the status of the twentyfourth and last Tīrthaṅkara of current *Avasarpiṇi* age The terminology of the phrase is distinctly Jaina. This is not true because before Gośāla, only two previous Ājīvika leaders. namely, Nandavachchha and Kisa Saṅkichcha, are known.

It is often said that there is a reference to Lord Ṛishabha in the Vedic literature. Some Vedic preceptors paid reverence to Lord Ṛishabha, and regarded him as the Lord of Lords. In the Ṛigveda,[1] and in the *Taittirīya Āraṇyaka*,[2] Vātaraśanas have been used in the sense of *Śramaṇas*. Vātaraśana has also been mentioned, and in the same context an excellent tribute has been paid to Keśī.[3] This Keśī alludes to Ṛishabha because in Jaina literature, there is a tradition that Lord Ṛishabha was called Keśī. Even on the ancient images of Lord Ṛishabha, locks of hair are noticed. In the *Rigveda*,[4] Keśī has been mentioned along with Vṛishabha. It is more probable that the reference to Lord Ṛishabha in *Vrātyakhaṇḍa* of the *Atharvaveda* is only metaphorical. From this it is argued that Vṛishabha lived before the Vedic times and was the first fountain head of *Śramaṇa* culture. It is from the context of the *Ṛigveda* that Lord Ṛishabha has been depicted as one who sponsored Vātaraśana *Śramaṇas* in the *Bhāgavata Purāṇa*[5] of the eighth century A.D.

Against this, it may be argued that though in the *Ṛigveda* and in other Vedic writings, 'Ṛishabha' has been mentioned many times, its meaning has been controversial and susceptible of different interpretations. There is no evidence of Ṛishabha being mentioned as the founder of Jainism in Vedic literature. Even in the days of Mahāvīra, Ṛishabha was not known as the founder of Nirgrantha sect from any contemporary source. From about the fourth or third century B.C., it seems that Ṛishabha became popular as the first Jina, the first Tīrthaṅkara, and the founder of Jainism. Like the imaginary Manu of Brahmanical literature, he has been described as the first ruler and founder of the new Social Order.

ARISHṬANEMI OR NEMINĀTHA AS TĪRTHAṄKARA

Besides Ṛishabhadeva, Arishṭanemi or Neminātha has also been mentioned as the Tīrthaṅkara of the Jainas in the

1. *RV*, X, 11.139.2-3.
2. *Taitt*. Ar, 2.7.1, p. 137.
3. *RV*, X, 11, 136-1.
4. *Ibid*., X. 9, 102-6.
5. *Bhāgavata*, V, 3, 20.

Kalpasūtra. He is said to be the twenty-second Tīrthaṅkara. He was the son of a king named Samudravijaya of Śauripura, a big town on the bank of the Yamunā. His mother's name was Śivādevī. He was named Arishṭanemi because his mother saw in a dream a *nemi*, the outer rim of a wheel, which consisted of *rishṭa* stones flying up to the sky. Giranara or Raivataka hill is considered to be his nirvāṇa-place.

Neminātha is connected with the legend of Śrīkṛishṇa as his relative. According to the *Trishashṭiśalākāpurushacharita*, he was a cousin of Lord Kṛishṇa who negotiated his marriage with Rājamatī, daughter of Ugrasena, ruler of Dvārikā, but Neminātha, taking compassion on the animals which were to be slaughtered in connection with the marriage feast, left the marriage procession suddenly and renounced the world. He then left Dvārikā and proceeded to a garden called Sahasambhavana on the mount Raivataka, where he practised asceticism and attained salvation. According to the *Kalpasūtra*, he lived up to the age of 1,000 years.

The *Chhāndogya Upanishad*[1] refers to Kṛishṇa, son of Devakī, as a disciple of Ghora Aṅgirasa who instructed him about *tapas* (asceticism), *dāna* (charity), *ārjava* (simplicity or piety), *ahiṁsā* (non-injury) and *satyavāchana* (truthfulness)—virtues which are extolled by Kṛishṇa in the *Gītā*. As Jaina tradition makes Vāsudeva-Kṛishṇa a contemporary of Tīrthaṅkara Arishṭanemi who preceded Pārśvanātha, some scholars identify Ghora Āṅgirasa with Neminātha. Neminātha is also known to have instructed Śrīkrishṇa, but his identification with Ghora Aṅgirasa is by no means correct as he is not known by this name in Jaina literature.

The age when Vāsudeva-Kṛishṇa flourished cannot be determined with certainty. The reference in the *Chhāndogya Upanishad* seems to point to a date in the sixth or seventh century B.C. The *Mahābhārata* war, in which Kṛishṇa is known to have participated, was, according to H.C. Ray Chaudhuri, fought either in the 14th century B.C. or in the 9th century B.C.[2]

1. Chhānd, III, 17, 6.
2. Phai, pp. 31-36.

The curious Jaina version of Kṛishṇa legend along with that of Arishṭanemi having some points of similarity between itself on the one hand and the Brahmanical and Buddhistic versions on the other, was invented with the obvious purpose of gaining popularity for the Jaina faith in Western India by making the local people believe that the whole of the Yādava race attained salvation under the influence and guidance of the 22nd Tīrthaṅkara, Neminātha. Actually, Neminātha is not a historical figure at all and the same is probably the case with Lord Kṛishṇa also.

JAINISM AS A PRE-VEDIC RELIGION

It has been pointed out by some scholars that Jainism is a pre-Vedic religion. G.C. PANDEY[1] has tried to show that the anti-ritualistic tendency, within the Vedic fold, is itself due to the impact of an asceticism which antedates the *Vedas*. Jainism represents a continuation of this pre-Vedic stream. Some of the relics,[2] recovered from the excavations at Mohenjo-dāro and Harappa, are related to *Śramaṇa* or Jaina tradition. The nude images in *Kāyotsarga*, i.e., the standing posture lost in meditation, closely resemble the Jaina images of the Kushāṇa period. *Kāyotsarga* is generally supposed to belong to the Jaina tradition. There are some idols even in *Padmāsana* pose. A few others, found at Mohenjo-dāro, have heads of serpents. They probably belonged to pre-Vedic Nāga tribe. The image of the seventh Tīrthaṅkara, Lord Supārśva, has a canopy of serpent-heads.

Even after the destruction of the Indus civilization, the straggling culture of the *Śramaṇas*, most probably going back to pre-Vedic and pre-Aryan times, continued even during the Vedic period as is indicated by some such terms as *Vātaraśana*, *Muni*, *Yati*, *Śramaṇa*, *Keśi*, *Vrātya*, *Arhan* and *Śiśnadeva*. The *Keśi Sūkta* of the *Ṛigveda* delineates the strange figure of the *Muni* who is described as long-haired, clad in dirty, tawny-coloured garments, walking in the air, drinking poison,

1. PSOB, p. 317.
2. Moh. Ind, plate xii,
Figs. 13. 14, 15, 19, 22.

delirious with *Mauneya* and inspired. There can hardly be any doubt that the *Muni* was to the Ṛigvedic Culture an alien figure. The *Taittirīya-Āraṇyaka*[1] speaks of *Śramaṇas* who were called *Vātaraśanāḥ*. They led a celibate life and could disappear at will and teach the Brāhmaṇas the way of righteousness.

The word *Śramaṇa* occurs in the *Upanishads*,[2] although the *Muṇḍakopanishad* has various references to the shaven-headed ascetics who revile the *Vedas*. All the passages of Vedic literature,[3] taken together, suggest that the *Yatis* were the people who had incurred the hostility of Indra the patron of the Aryas, and whose bodies were, therefore, thrown to the wolves.

The *Pañchaviṁśa Brāhmaṇa*[4] describes some peculiarities of the Vrātyas. They did not study the *Vedas*; they did not observe the rules regulating the Brahmanical order of life. They called an expression difficult to pronounce when it was not difficult to pronounce at all and spoke the tongue of the consecrated though they themselves were not consecrated. This proves that they had some Prakritic form of speech. The Prakrit language is especially the language of the canonical works of the Jainas. K.P. JAYASWAL[5] states that they had traditions of the Jainas current among them.

In the *Ṛigveda*,[6] *Arhan* has been used for a *Śramaṇa* leader: 'Oh Arhan, you fed compassion for this useless world.' The mention of *Śiśnadevas* (naked gods) in the *Ṛigveda*[7] is also noteworthy.

As a matter of fact, however, there is no definite evidence for the existence of Jainism in pre-Vedic times. The images representing *Kāyotsarga* excavated at Mohenjo-dāro, cannot be ascribed to Jainism unless there is some evidence for it. Even from the various terms mentioned in the *Ṛigveda*, no definite

1. *Taitt. Ār*, I, pp. 87, 137-8.
2. *Bṛi. Up*. 4. 3. 22.
3. *Taitt. Sam*, VI, 2, 75; *Kāṭhaka Saṁhitā*, VIII, 5; *Ait Bṛ*. 35. 2; *Kau Up*, III. 1; *AV*, II, 53, *Tāṇḍya Mahā-Brāhmaṇa*, VIII, 1-4.
4. *Pañch. Br*, XVII, 4, 1-9.
5. JBORS, XIV, p. 26.
6. RV, II, 33, 10.
7. *Ibid.*, VII, 21, 5; x, 99, 3,

conclusion can be drawn regarding the existence of Jainism in those days.

Jainism it appears, was not extant in so early a period, but the primitive currents of religious and philosophical speculation of the pre-Vedic period along with Sāṅkya-Yoga and Buddhism considerably influenced this religion. All the three shared a kind of pessimism, a conclusion that human life is full of misery. No trace of this attitude is to be found in the optimistic outlook of the Vedic Aryans. The doctrine of transmigration, unknown to the early Brāhmaṇas, suddenly emerges in the *Upanishads* and forms an essential element in these three systems. What is more important is the fact that this doctrine assumes its peculiarly Indian form by its association with the doctrine of Karman, and we know that some of the most primitive ideas of Karman are found in Jaina Metaphysics as well. An atheistic attitude and a kind of dualism between spirit and matter characterize all the three systems of thought. To the same primitive influence of pre-Vedic times may also be attributed the introduction of the practice of image-worship. From early times, the cult of symbols and images seems to have been current among the Jainas who continued the traditional religious practices of the pre-Aryan settlers of the Sindhu Valley region.

H. JACOBI[1] noticed some marks of antiquity in the character of Jaina philosophy. Such a mark is the animistic belief that nearly everything is possessed of a soul; not only have plants their own souls, but particles of earth, cold water, fire and wind too. This theory of primitive animism in Jaina philosophy indicates that this religion originated at a very early time when higher forms of religious beliefs and cults had not taken hold of the Indian mind. Another mark of antiquity in Jainism is that in the development of metaphysics, the category of quality is not yet clearly and distinctly conceived, but it is just evolving, as it were, out of the category of substance.

In the Vedic period, there existed two distinct religious cultural traditions—the strictly orthodox and Aryan tradition

1. SBE, XLV, p. xxxiii.

of the Brāhmaṇas and the straggling culture of the *Munis* and *Śramaṇas*, most probably going back to pre-Vedic and pre-Aryan times. During the later Vedic period, the two streams tended to mingle, and the result was the great religious ferment from which Jainism appears to have originated. Jainism and other Śramika religious sects grew up among the imperfectly Aryanised Communities of the East in response to the cultural atmosphere and social needs. These sects spread out, flourished and became highly popular there. On the other hand, Brahmanical religion had its stronghold in the North and the West.

PĀRŚVANĀTHA AS AN HISTORICAL FIGURE

H. JACOBI[1] and others have tried to prove on the authority of both the Jaina and the Buddhist records that Pārśva was a historical personage. Their arguments are as follows:

1. In the Buddhist scriptures, there is a reference to the four vows (*Chāturyāma Dharma*) of Pārśva in contradiction to the five vows of Mahāvīra. The Buddhists could not have used the term *Chāturyāma Dharma* for the Nirgranthas unless they had heard it from the followers of Pārśva. This proves the correctness of the Jaina tradition that the followers of Pārśva, in fact, existed at the time of Mahāvīra.

2. The Nirgranthas were an important sect at the time of the rise of Buddhism, as may be inferred from the fact that they are frequently mentioned in the *Piṭakas* as opponents of Buddha and his disciples This is further supported by another fact. Maṅkhali Gośāla, a contemporary of Buddha and Mahāvīra, divided mankind into six classes, and of these, the third class contained the *Nirgranthas*. Gośāla, probably, would not have ranked them as a separate class of mankind if they had recently come into existence. He must have regarded as members of a very important and at the same time an old sect.

3. The *Majjhima Nikāya* records a dispute between

1. SBE, XLV, pp. xx-xxiii.

Buddha and Sakdāl, the son of a Nirgrantha. Sakdāl was not himself a Nirgrantha. Now, when a famous controversialist, whose father was a Nirgrantha, was a contemporary of Buddha, the Nirgrantha sect could scarcely have been founded during Buddha's life-time.

4. The existence of Pārśva's Order in Mahāvīra's time is proved by the reported disputes between the followers of Pārśva and those of Mahāvīra. The followers of Pārśva, who did not fully recognize Mahāvīra as their spiritual guide, existed during Mahāvīra's life-time. A sort of compromise was effected between the two sections of the Jaina Church.

These arguments clearly show that Pārśvanātha was a real historical figure. Very few facts of his life are, however, known. The *Kalpasūtra* informs us that Pārśva was the son of king Aśvasena of Vārāṇasī (Banaras) and queen Vāmā, belonging to the Ikshvāku race of the Kshatriyas. No such person as Aśvasena is known, from Brāhmaṇa records, to have existed. The only individual of that name, mentioned in epic literature, was a king of the Snakes (Nāgas), and he cannot in any way be connected with the father of the Jaina prophet 'Pārśva'. Pārśva is said to have been born in 877 B.C. It is evidently impossible to prove the correctness of this date as we do not have a single definite date in Indian history before the time of Buddha.

Many legends have gathered round Pārśva. Throughout his life he was connected with snakes in one way or the other. In his childhood, for instance, while he lay by the side of his mother, a serpent was seen crawling about there When he grew up, he saved a serpent from the grave danger it was in. He also saved a poor terrified snake which had taken shelter in a log of wood to which a Brāhmin ascetic, Kamaṭha, was setting fire. After its death, the snake became God Dharaṇendra who spread a serpent's hood over Pārśva.

Pārśva was married to Prabhāvati, the daughter of Prasenajit the king of Kuśasthala. He must have been a man of genial nature, as he is always given the epithet *Purishādānīya*,[1]

1. *Kalpa*, 149, 155.

'beloved of men'. He lived for thirty years in great splendour and happiness as a householder, and then, forsaking all his wealth, became an ascetic. After 84 days of intense meditation, he attained the perfect knowledge of a prophet, and from that time, he lived for about seventy years in the state of most exalted perfection and sainthood. At last, he attained *Nirvāṇa*[1] (liberation) in 777 B.C. on the summit of Mount *Sammedaśikhara*, now named Pārsvanātha hill after him.

A man of practical nature, Pārśva was remarkable for his organizing capacity. He organized the *Saṁgha* (Organization) efficiently for the propagation of Jainism. He had eight *gaṇas* and eight *gaṇadharas*, namely, Subha and Āryaghosha, Vaśishṭha and Brahmachārin, Saumya and Śrīdhara, Vīrabhadra and Yaśas. He had an excellent community of 16,000 *Śramaṇas* with Āryadatta at their head; 38,000 nuns with Pushpachūlā at their head; 164,000 lay votaries with Suvrata at their head; 372,000 female lay votaries with Sunandā at their head;[2] 350 sages who knew the four *Pūrvas*; 1,400 sages who were possessed of the *avadhi* knowledge; 1,000 kevalins; 1,100 sages who could transform themselves; 600 sages possessing correct knowledge; 1,000 male and 2,000 female disciples who had reached perfection; 750 sages, each gifted with a mighty intellect; 600 professors and 1,200 sages in their last birth.[3] Here the Digambara texts differ. According to them, there were ten *gaṇas* and ten *gaṇadharas* among whom Svayambhū was the chief apostle. They also differ in giving the number of nuns, laymen and female lay votaries which, according to them, was twentysix thousand, one lac and three lacs respectively. The numbers given above seem to have been exaggerated, but the division of Jaina *Saṁgha* in different branches proves the great organizing capacity of Pārśva. He is said to have visited many cities, the most important of which for the dissemination of Jainism are Ahichchhatrā, Āmalakappā, Śāvatthī, Kāmpillapura, Sāgeya, Rāyagiha, and Kosambī.

According to the Jaina tradition, the sacred literature descending from the time of Pārśva was known as *Puvvas*

1. *Kalpa*, 168-169.
2. *Ibid.*, 160-164.
3. *Ibid.*, 166.

(*Pūrvas*). These 'Earlier' compositions were called *Puvvas* (*Pūrvas*) evidently because they existed prior to the *Aṅgas*. They are said to have formed a common basis of Jaina and Ājīvika canon. It is from these *Pūrvas* that Gośāla Maṅkhaliputta, the leader of the Ājīvikas drew inspiration. It is said that the Ājīvika canon, consisting of eight *Mahāṇimittas* and two *Mārgas*, was atleast partially based upon these *Pūrvas*.[1]

The fourteen *Pūrvas* were reckoned as constituting a twelfth *Aṅga* called *Dṛishṭivāda*. The knowledge of the fourteen *Pūrvas* remained up to *Sthūlabhadra*, the eight patriarch after Mahāvīra. For some time, only ten *Pūrvas* were known and then the remaining *Pūrvas* were gradually lost. H.L. JAIN thinks that in the *Shaṭkhaṇḍāgama* of Pushpadanta and Bhūtabali, we have not only an important canonical book of the Digambaras but also a later representation of the *Dṛishṭivāda* which contained the original fourteen *Pūrvas*.[2]

The Jaina *Sūtras* and the early Buddhist texts enlighten us about the doctrines and followers of Pārśva who was merely an ascetic of the ancient hermit type, and not a philosopher like Mahāvīra. The religious order founded by him had a reputation for a high and rigid standard of conduct. He made four moral precepts binding upon his followers, precepts which were later enforced by Mahāvīra and Buddha among their followers. His rules were not confined only to these four precepts but they embraced many other rules laid down for the practical guidance of the fraternity and laity. All the fundamental rules of the Nigaṇṭha community were due to Pārśva and his followers. B.M. BARUA[3] points out that Pārśva,

1. B.M. BARUA interprets the word *Puvva* in the text not in the specialised Jaina sense, but merely as "past traditions". (See JDL, II, p. 41). His view is perhaps strengthened by the fact that the eightfold *Mahāṇimitta* of the Ājivikas bears no resemblance to the titles of the fourteen lost *Pūrvas* of the Jaina tradition.

2. *Sama*. 147 fol. 128. *Utpāda-pūrva, Agravāṇīya-pūrva, Vīryapravāda-pūrva, Astināsti-pravāda-pūrva, Jñāna-pravāda-pūrva, Satya-pravāda-pūrva, Ātma-pravāda-pūrva, Karma-pravāda-pūrva, Pratyā-khyāna-pravāda-pūrva, Vidyānupravāda-pūrva, Avandhya-pūrva, Prāṇayu-pravāda-pūrva, Kriyāviśāla-pūrva*, and *Lokavindusāra-pūrva*.

3. BHPIP, p. 380.

the philosophic predecessor of Mahāvīra, had rules of conduct which demanded a philosophic justification in order that they might not appear arbitrary or be confused with social conventions.

The *Uttarādhyayana Sūtra* furnishes a dialogue which sheds abundant light on this obscure point. The interlocutors are the two leading representatives of the Nigaṇṭha Orders of the time. Keśī, a follower of Pārśva's rule, asks Gautama, who was one of the chief disciples of Mahāvīra: "When the four precepts promulgated by the great sage Pārśva are held equally binding upon the two orders, what is the cause of difference between us ?" "Wisdom" replies Gautama, "recognizes the truth of the law and the ascertainment of true things. The first saints were simple but slow of understanding, the last saints, prevaricating and slow of understanding, those between the two, simple and wise; hence there are two forms of the Law. The first could only with difficulty understand the precepts of the Law, and the last could only with difficulty observe them, but those between them easily understood and observed them."[1] Here the purport of Gautama's reply is that Pārśva's was mere religious order while Mahāvīra's was not only a religious order, but also a distinct school of thought.

About the teachings of Pārśva, it must be admitted, we have no exact knowledge. His religion was, however, meant for one and all without any distinction of caste or creed. He allowed women to enter his Order. He laid stress on the doctrine of *ahiṁsā*. According to him, strict asceticism was the only way to the attainment of salvation. Fundamentally, the doctrines of Pārśva and Mahāvīra were the same. The only points of difference concerned vows and garments.[2] Pārśva preached four vows instead of five and allowed an under and upper garment. It is interesting to find the monks of the Order of Pārśva practising *Jinakappa*.[3] Pārśva's doctrine of the six

1. SBE, XLV, pp. 122-123.
2. However, the view that the Śvetāmbaras and Digambaras are the followers respectively of Pārśva and Mahāvīra is rejected by most authorities. As a matter of fact, this division took place much later than Mahāvīra.
3. JLAIDJC, p. 27.

classes of living beings served as the basis of Mahāvīra's doctrine of six *leśyās*.[1] According to H. JACOBI, the Order of Pārśva seems to have undergone some changes in the period between the death of Pārśva and the advent of Mahāvīra.

Pārśva enjoined on his followers four great vows: (1) Abstinence from killing living beings; (2) Avoidance of falsehood; (3) Avoidance of theft, and (4) Freedom from possessions. H. JACOBI[2] has clearly perceived that a doctrine attributed to Mahāvīra in the Buddhist *Sāmaññaphala Sutta* properly belonged to his predecessor, Pārśva, insofar as the expression *Chātuyāma Saṁvara* is concerned. The doctrine is that, according to Mahāvīra, the way to self-possession self-command, and imperturbability consists of 'a four-fold self-restraint', such as restraint in regard to all water, restraint in regard to all evil, and restraints imposed for the purification of sin and feeling a sense of ease on that account.[3]

The Jaina writers tell us that Nagnajit, king of Gandhāra, Nimi, king of Videha, Durmukha, king of Pañchāla, Bhīma, king of Vidarbha, and Karakaṇḍu, king of Kaliṅga adopted the faith of the Jainas.[4] As Pārśva (877-777 B.C.) was probably the first historical Jina, these rulers, if they really became converts to his doctrines, have to be placed between 842 B.C. and 600 B.C. They are known to have ruled over their respective kingdoms before the sixth century B.C.

Pārśva had a large number of followers round about Magadha even in the days of Mahāvīra. Mahāvīra's parents, who belonged to the Jñātrī-Kshatriyas, were worshippers of Pārśva.[5] Following the teachings of Pārśva, they peacefully died practising the slow starvation of their senses. The *Uttarādhyayana Sūtra*[6] relates a meeting between Keśī and Gautama

1. The classification of living beings in terms of six colours may be traced in Pārśva's doctrine of six *Jīvanikāyas* (*Āchā*, II, 15, 16).
2. SBE, XLV, pp. xix-xxii.
3. Dia, II, pp. 74-75.
4. SBE, XLV. p. 87.
5. *Āchā*, II, 15.16.
6. *Uttarā*, 23, pp. 119-129.

as representatives of the two Jaina Orders, the old and the new. The *Bhagavatī Sūtra*[1] refers to a dispute between Kālāsavesiyaputta, a follower of Pārśva, and a disciple of Mahāvīra. The *Nāyādhammakahāo*[2] says that Kālī, an old maiden joined Pārśva's order and was entrusted to Pupphachūlā, the head of the nuns. The two sisters of Uppalā joined the order of Pārśva, but being unable to lead the rigid life of the order, they became Brāhmin *parivrājikās* (female wanderers). Munichanda, a follower of Pārśva, lived in a potter's shop in *Kumārāya-Sannivesa* in the company of his disciples. Vijayā and Pagabbhā, two female disciples of Pārśva, saved Mahāvīra and Gośāla in *Kūviya-sannivesa.*[3] The *Bhagavatī Sūtra*[4] refers to Gāṅgeya, a follower of Pārśva in Vāṇiyagāma. He gave up the four vows of Pārśva and adopted the five *Mahāvratas* of Mahāvīra. The *Nāyādhammakahāo*[5] mentions Puṇḍariya who accepted the four vows of Pārśva. The followers of Pārśva moved in the company of five hundred monks into the city of Tuṅgiya.[6] A number of laywomen joined Pārśva's Order.[7] The *Rāyapasenaiyasūya*[8] refers to a follower of Pārśva named Keśī who visited Seyaviyā where a discussion between him and Paesi took place regarding the identity of the soul and body. A follower of Pārśva named Udaka met Gautama, the famous disciple of Mahāvīra. Gautama was successful in winning over Udaka to his side.[9] From the dialogue between Udaka and Gautama, it appears that the followers of Pārśva and the disciples of Mahāvīra were respectively known as the Nigaṇṭha Kumāraputtas and the Nigaṇṭha Nāthaputtas.

1. *Bhag*, I, 76.
2. Nāyā, II. i; p. 222 ff.
3. *Āva*, *chū*, p. 291.
4. *Bhag*, IX. 32.
5. *Nāyā*, 19, p. 218.
6. *Bhag*, 2-5.
7. *Nāyā*, II, 10.
8. *Rāya*, 147 ff.
9. *Sūtra*, II, 7.

CHAPTER II

SOURCES

Since certain very significant changes took place in the political, religious, social, and economic spheres, the age of Lord Mahāvīra may be said to have marked a new epoch in Indian history. Also known as 'The Historic Period', it provides a firm basis for the reconstruction of Indian chronology by furnishing dates of the death of Mahāvīra and Buddha. The sources for the reconstruction of the history of 'Lord Mahāvīra and His Times' may be divided into two main classes: (i) Literature and (ii) Archaeology. The literary evidence is very rich and varied in comparison with the archaeological.

1. *LITERATURE*

The contemporary literature on which this work is generally based remained in the form of oral traditions for a considerable time and was codified much afterwards with certain interpolations and changes. Hence, it has been used after critical examination. The literary evidence is twofold: (a) direct and (b) collateral. The direct evidence is that which is furnished by the Jaina literary works, and the collateral one is gathered from the contemporary Buddhist and Brahmanical literary sources. Collating these sources of information, one cannot only prepare a sketch of the life of Mahāvīra but also draw a fairly vivid picture of India, depicting political, religious, social, economic, and other conditions of the time in which he lived, moved and preached.

The Jaina literary works may be further divided into sub-classes.

(i) *Canonical Literary Works*

These canonical works of the Jainas did not originate at one particular point of time, though their traditions can be traced back to Mahāvīra and his disciples. But afterwards, these works had to undergo considerable changes, as a result of which several works as portions of the works were added to them from time to time. While different names are ascribed to one and the same canon, the number of canons varies considerably. Besides, certain canons or parts of the canons have become totally obsolete.

The important canonical texts are the *Kalpa Sūtra*, *Sūtrakṛitāṅga* (*Sūyagaḍaṁga*), *Uttarādhyayana Sūtra* (*Uttarājjhayaṇa Sūya*), *Āchārāṅga Sūtra* (*Āyārāṁga Sutta*), *Vyākhyā-Prajñapti* (*Bhagavatī Viyāhapaṇṇatti*), *Niryāvalī Sūtra* (*Nirayāvaliya Sūya*), *Upāsakadaśā* (*Uvāsagadasāo*), *Jñātādharmakathā* (*Nāyādhammakahāo*), *Aupapātika Sūtra* (*Ovavāiya Sūya*), *Rājapraśnīya Sūtra* (*Rāyapasenaiya Sūya*), and *Āvaśyaka Sūtra* (*Āvassaya Sūya*). As far as the contents of these Jaina canonical *Sūtras* are concerned, they are traditionally known as the *Pravachanas* of the Jainas, particularly those of Mahāvīra. Their chief interest lies in the clear presentation of various topics relating to the lives of the Jinas and their teachings. Incidentally, they also throw valuable light on the political and cultural aspects of the country.

The major portion of the *Kalpa Sūtra* is devoted to the biography of Mahāvīra, including his birth, lineage, parentage, childhood, marriage, itinerary during asceticism and finally his death. It also refers to the nine Lichchhavis as having formed a league with nine Mallakīs and eighteen clan-lords of Kāśī-Kośala.[1]

The *Sūtrakṛitāṅga*, the *Uttarādhyayana* and the *Āchārāṅga* contain the oldest part of the canon from the linguistic and literary points of view. These are very important as they enlighten us about the original teachings of Mahāvīra. The object of the *Sūtrakṛitāṅga* is to guard young monks against heretical beliefs and to lead them on towards the attainments of the highest knowledge.[2] They are to encounter many trials and tribulations but not to commit sins. The fundamental doctrines of Jainism leading to the final deliverance of man have been discussed. Mahāvīra has been represented as a great teacher and praised for the virtues which have been described. This work also describes the four heretical creeds of the time of Mahāvīra—*Kriyāvāda*, *Akriyāvāda*, *Ajñānavāda*, and *Vinayavāda*

1. SBE, XXII, p. 266.
2. *Ibid*, XLV, p. xxxviii.

—creeds which are known to have given rise to three hundred and sixtythree schools. One passage gives the names of the existing classes, such as Ugras, Bhogas, Aikshvākus, Jñātris, Kauravas, and Lichchhavis.[1]

The intention of *Uttarādhyayana*, as rightly pointed out by H. JACOBI, is to instruct a young monk in his principal duties, to commend to him the ascetic life by precepts and examples, and to warn him against the dangers besetting his religious life.[2] It emphasises the duties of pupils towards their teachers, and their mutual relations. The fundamental principles of Jainism, such as *Triratna*, austerities, *Karma*, *Navatattva*, *Leśyās*, *Samitis*, and *Guptis*, have also been discussed. Instructions regarding the practice of righteousness by Mahāvīra have been given. Ten conditions for the realization of celibacy have been mentioned. Daśārṇabhadra of Daśārṇa, Karakaṇḍu of Kaliṅga and Udāyana of Sauvīra are known to have become Jaina monks after giving up their kingdoms. Śreṇika with his wives, servants and relatives appears to have adopted Jainism. Harikeshabala, born in the family of Chaṇḍālas, became a monk possessing the highest virtues. Vijayaghosha, who was engaged in performing Brahmanical sacrifice, was converted to Jainism by the monk Jayaghosha, who approached him for alms.

The *Āchārāṅga Sūtra* has preserved a sort of religious ballad, an account of the years during which Mahāvīra led a life of rigorous asceticism, thus preparing himself for the attainment of the highest spiritual knowledge. It contains important rules for Jaina monks and nuns. These rules are classified in the *Sūtra* under such general heads as begging, walking, modes of speech, entry into other's possessions, postures, places of study, and attending to the calls of nature.

The *Bhagavatī Sūtra* in its various dialogues gives a vivid picture of the life and work of Mahāvīra, his relationship to his disciples and to the kings and princes of the time, and contains an account of the Jaina dogmas on *Saṁsāra* and *Karma*

1. SBE, XLV, p. 339.
2. *Ibid.*, p. xxxix.

in the form of questions and answers between Mahāvīra and Indrabhūti Gautama. It also embodies a list of sixteen *Mahājanapadas* at the time of Mahāvīra. *Aṅga* was governed as a separate province under Kūṇiya with Champā as its capital. In the wạr with Vaiśālī, Kūṇiya is said to have made use of *Mahāśilākanṭaka* and *Rathamushala*. Udāyana, a ruler of Sauvīradeśa, being influenced by the teachings of Mahāvīra, renounced the world and became a Jaina monk. The work also enlightens us about the life and teachings of Gośāla who lived in the company of Mahāvīra for a period of about six years during which the latter was engaged in his ascetic practices.

The *Nirayāvali Sūtra* refers to the great battle between Kūṇika of Champā and king Cheṭaka of Videha and Vaiśālī, when the eighteen confederate kings are stated to have sided with the latter. The bone of contention was the Magadha State elephant Śreyanāka and a huge necklace of eighteen strings of pearls which were given by Śreṇika to his sons, Halla and Vehalla.

A vivid picture of social life has been presented by the *Uvāsagadasāo*. It contains the stories of pious householders who became lay adherents of Jainism. The wealthy potter named Saddālaputta, for instance, was at first a follower of Makkhali Gośāla, but afterwards went over to Mahāvīra. It informs us about the life and teachings of Gośāla who lived in his company for some time. Bārāṇasī, Kampillapura Palāśapura and Ālabhī were the important towns within the kingdom of Jiyasattu, and Vaiśālī was ruled by Cheṭaka.

The title of the text *Nāyādhammakahāo* may be explained as 'Stories for the dhamma of Nāya' (Jñātṛi), i.e. Mahāvīra, who is also called Jñātṛiputra, Nāya or Nātaputta. The stories found here explain the teachings of Mahāvīra. They indirectly throw light on the economic condition of the people. They describe the sea-faring merchants of Champā, who loaded their waggons with various commodities and proceeded to deep harbour. A merchant named Pālita of Champā is known to have gone on business to the town of Pihuṇḍa or Pithuṇḍa, a sea-coast town. The palaces, described in this text as lofty, had domes, and their floors were richly decorated with various kinds of gems and jewels.

The *Uvavāiya Sūya* (*Aupapātika Sūtra*) contains an account of Mahāvīra's *Samovaśaraṇa* in Champā and the pilgrimage of Kūṇiya to this place. It also speaks of the *Tāpasas* as those *religiex* who adopted the *Vānaprastha* mode of life on the banks of the sacred rivers typified by the Ganges.

The *Rāyapasenaiya* is an *Upāṅga* containing a dialogue between Keśī, a disciple of Pārśva and Paesi, a ruler of Setavyā. Keśī tries to prove to Paesi that the soul is independent of the body. The Pāli counterpart of this *Upāṅga* is known as the *Pāyāsi Suttanta*. This text also describes the celestial mansion of Sūryābhadeva, its beautiful pillars, its opera hall and pavilion. The details of architectural varieties and decorations given here are important and have a bearing on the development of Indian architecture. Corresponding to such a description, we have pictures of various celestial mansions in the Pāli *Vimānavatthu*.

The *Āvaśyaka Sūtra* contains some interesting historical details of the time of Mahāvīra. During the war between Chandanā's father and king Śatānīka, she was taken captive by an army of the enemy and sold in Kauśāmbī to a banker, Dhanāvaha. In due course Chandanā accepted Jainism from Mahāvīra and became a nun. The daughters of king Cheṭaka of Vaiśālī were married to some contemporary rulers. Mṛigāvatī was married to king Śatānīka of Kauśāmbī, Śivā to Chaṇḍapradyota of Ujjayinī, Jyeshṭhā to Nandivardhana, brother of Lord Mahāvīra and ruler of Kuṇḍagrāma, and Sujyesṭhā joined the Order of Mahāvīra's disciples. Mahāvīra during his wanderings as a monk visited Kāśī. Ajātaśatru of Magadha not only humbled Kośala and permanently annexed Kāśī but also absorbed the state of Vaiśālī. Magadha and Avanti were brought face to face with each other. Udāyina was a devout Jaina.

(ii) *Exegeses of the Canons*

The exegetical literature interpreting the canons is very vast. As a matter of fact, it seems to be quite impossible to interpret the canons without the help of the commentaries.

On the whole, this commentarial literature appears to be trustworthy since the commentaries have tried to preserve the old traditions and legends current in those days. While illustrating the tenets of the canons, their authors have referred to old compositions, ancient traditions and ancient explanations. All this proves that they have attempted to make them authentic. This literature includes some of the important commentaries such as the *Bṛihatkalpa Bhāshya* and its *Vṛitti*, the *Vyavahāra Bhāshya* and its *Vivaraṇa*, the *Niśitha Chūrṇi*, the *Āvaśyaka Chūrṇi* and commentaries on the *Āvaśyaka* and *Uttarādhyayana*.

This exegetical literature is undoubtedly a mine of rich treasure in itself. In these works we come across descriptions of various customs and beliefs prevalent in those days in different parts of India, of various feasts and festivals, of religious sects, wandering ascetics, famine, robbers, and dacoits, of inaccessible roads, mountains and deserts, of economic production, industry, trade routes, dress, ornaments, food, and various other matters of importance, which have nothing to do with religion as such, but are of general interest to man.

This exegetical literature consists of four parts (a) *Nijjutti*, (b) *Bhāsa*, (c) *Chuṇṇi*, and (d) *Ṭikā*.

(a) *Nijjutti*

The oldest explanatory literature represented by *Nijjuttis* contains a number of historical or legendary tales elucidating Jaina doctrines and moral or disciplinary rules given in the Jaina canons. The following are the ten *Nijjuttis*: (1) *Āyārāṅga*, (2) *Sūyagaḍāṅga*, (3) *Sūriyapannatti*, (4) *Uttarājjhayana*, (5) *Āvassaya*, (6) *Dasaveyāliya*, (7) *Dasāsuyakkhandha*, (8) *Kappa*, (9) *Vavahāra*, and (10) *Isibhāsiya*. Tradition is unanimous in attributing the authorship of the *Nijjuttis* to Bhadrabāhu who seems to be different from Bhadrabāhu (297 B.C.), the last *Śrutakevalin*.

(b) *Bhāsa*

The next chronological stage of development in the commentarial literature after *Nijjuti* is *Bhāsa*. The eleven

Āgamas seem to have their separate *Bhāsas*. The *Bhāsas* on the *Bṛihatkalpa Sūtra*, *Vyavahāra Sūtra* and *Niśitha Sūtra* are very important as they contain most valuable items of information regarding various topics, especially the life of monks and nuns and the society of those early days.

(c) *Chuṇṇi*

The third category of commentaries is known as *Chuṇṇis*. Most of the *Āgamas* contain *Chuṇṇis*, most of which in their published form are ascribed to Jinadāsagaṇi Mahattara. Out of the extant *Chuṇṇis*, the *Āvassaya* and *Niśiha* are most important as they contain an invaluable treasure of information from the point of Jaina history and culture. The *Āvassaya Chuṇṇi* describes some important incidents of the life of Mahāvīra and also refers to some important kings and princes contemporary to him.

(d) *Ṭikā*

Haribhadra Sūri (705-775 A.D.) was a distinguished and versatile writer who is known to have written his commentaries on the canons in Sanskrit. His commentaries on *Āvassaya*, *Dasaveyāliya*, *Nandi* and *Anuyoga* are famous. Śīlāṅka Sūri (872 A.D.), Vādivetāla Śānti Sūri, Abhayadeva Sūri and others also contributed to exegetical literature in which the commentaries on the *Avassaya*, *Uttarajjhayana*, *Bṛihatkalpa Bhāshya*, *Vyavahāra Bhāshya*, *Ṭhānāṅga*, *Bhagavati*, *Jambudvipa-prajñpti* and *Kalpa Sūtra* are most valuable for the reason that they record various important traditions.

These different types of commentaries on canonical works give detailed information about the life of Mahāvīra, and other political and cultural aspects of his times. Their motive was sometimes to apotheosize Lord Mahāvīra into a superhuman being by describing him in hyperbolic terms. Though based on tradition, these are still late works and cannot be wholly relied upon unless they are not confirmed by some other independent sources. After critical examination of traditions and legends, these works have been utilised.

(iii) *Purāṇas and Charitras*

Like the *Purāṇas* of the Brahmins, Jaina *Purāṇas* too are available. In some Jaina *Purāṇas* and the *Charitras*, accounts of the life of Mahāvīra and of other contemporary rulers have been given. These are not of much importance from the historical point of view as they appeared very late and their descriptions are exaggerated. The main *Purāṇas* concerning the life of Mahāvīra are Jinasena's *Harivaṁśapurāṇa* (783 A.D.) and Guṇabhadra's *Uttarapurāṇa* (9th century A.D.). The *Trishashṭhiśalākāpurushacharitra* of Hemachandra (12th century A.D.) yields some information regarding Lord Mahāvīra and some of his contemporary rulers. The *Mahāvīrachariyam* of Nemichandra, the *Mahāvīrachariyam* of Guṇachandra Gaṇi, the *Vardhamānacharitra* of Asaga (988 A.D.), and the *Vardhamānacharita* of Sakalakīrti (1464 A.D.) are late biographical works on Mahāvīra.

(iv) *Miscellaneous Works*

The *Tiloyapaṇṇati* of Vṛishabha (V.S. 535), the *Daśabhakti* of Pūjyapāda (5th century A.D.), the *Jayadhavalā Ṭikā* of Vīrasena (V.S. 873), the *Trilokasāra* of Nemichandra (973 A.D.), the *Pariśishṭaparvan* of Hemachandra (12th century A.D.) and the *Vichāraśreṇi* of Merutuṅga (1306 A.D.) have been utilised in one way or the other for this work.

(b) *Collateral Evidence*

The collateral evidence supplied by the Buddhist and Brahmanical accounts is to a great extent supplementary to Jaina evidence. There is a good deal of agreement between them. This evidence may be placed under two heads: (i) the Buddhist and (ii) the Brahmanical.

(i) *Buddhist Literature*

Like the Jaina canon, the Buddhist canon was not compiled at one particular time. It is primarily concerned with the early Buddhist doctrines but incidentally throws light on the political and cultural aspects of the society as well. Among the Buddhist canonical texts, the *Vinaya Piṭaka* and *Sutta Piṭaka* are important.

The *Mahāvagga* and the *Chullavagga* of the *Vinayapiṭaka* are noteworthy. The *Mahāvagga* is mainly concerned with the formation of the *Saṁgha* and its rules, but its incidental refereces are valuable in that they throw considerable light on the daily life of the people. The rules of the procedure and debates of the assemblies of the republics during this period seem to be the same as those of the Buddhist *Saṁghas* which were modelled on *Saṁgha* or *Gaṇa* States. While describing the rules for the *Bhikshus*, the *Chullavagga* gives an idea of the articles of furniture, utensils and other amenities of the common dwelling-house.

The *Sutta Piṭaka* comprises the following five collections called *Nikāyas*: (1) *Dīgha*, (2) *Majjhima*, (3) *Saṁyutta*, (4) *Aṅguttara*, and (5) *Khuddaka*. In the *Dīgha*, *Majjhima* and *Aṅguttara*, there are references to Nigaṇṭha Nātaputta, to his teachings and to the Nirgranthas. These parallel references sometimes prove the correctness of the traditions preserved in the Jaina texts, and thus they are valuable for the history of Jainism during the time of Mahāvīra. This also leads us to believe that in the days of Buddha, Mahāvīra was considered to be an important personality and Jainism a strong living religion.

The *Brahmajālasutta* of the *Dīghanikāya* is important for the history, not only of Buddhism but of the entire religious life and thought of ancient India. The *Sāmaññaphala Sutta* is a valuable piece of evidence for the life and thought at the time of Buddha, as it appears from the views of prominent non-Buddhist teachers and founders of sects. From the *Mahāparinibbāṇa Sutta*, it is known that in reply to Varshākāra, the Chancellor of Magadha, Buddha indicated the seven points of excellence of the Vajjis which may be regarded as the directive principles of State policy. In the *Mahāsudassana Sutta* of the *Dīgha Nikāya*, there is a description of the palace of King Mahā-sudassana.

The *Majjhima Nikāya* throws considerable light on the life of Buddhist monks, as also on Brahmanical sacrifices, various forms of asceticism, the relation of Buddha to the Jainas and other systems of the day, the superstitions and the socio-political conditions of the time. The *Aṅguttara Nikāya* gives a list of the sixteen States existing during the time of Buddha.

The *Theragāthā* and *Therigāthā* are very important on account of the pictures of life they portray, pictures that give us a valuable insight into the social conditions of those days, especially into the position of women.

The *Jātakas*, which from a part of the *Khuddaka Nikāya* of the *Sutta-Piṭaka*, are generally concerned with the day-to-day life of the people. Some of the *Jātakas* supply valuable material for the reconstruction of the political, social and economic history of India during the sixth century B.C. They give us valuable information regarding the constitution of the republics, especially of the Lichchhavīs, and king's officers. They throw light on social organization, position of women, festivals and recreations. They mention educational institutions, especially Taxila, the various subjects taught there, the teachers and students. Some of them refer to various professions and industries, trade and commerce, and the guilds in which they were organized. There is also a reference to coins known as *Kārshāpaṇas*. The *Mahā Ummaga Jātaka*[1] gives a vivid account of the palace of the Mahā Ummaga and also a list of motifs illustrating scenes from heavenly life and mythical beliefs depicted on the walls of the great hall of the Mahā-Ummaga palace.

(ii) *Brahmanical Literature*

Since the *Dharma Sūtras* and the *Gṛihya Sūtras* are supposed to have belonged to the sixth century B.C., they have been utilised to corroborate certain important pieces of evidence. Besides throwing a flood of light on the social and economic conditions of the period in question, they sometimes enlighten us about its political and other aspects as well. Baudhāyana in his *Dharma Sūtra* mentions such states as Saurāshṭra, Avanti Magadha, Aṅga, Puṇḍra and Vaṅga. The *Dharma Sūtras* also describe the four *Varṇas* and different castes along with their duties and privileges. They discuss the four *Āśramas* (Stages of life) and emphasize the duties of the individual at every stage.

1. *Mahā Ummaga Jā*, VI, 432.

They insist upon the mutual cordial relations between the teachers and students. A list of holidays in the *Gurukulas* has been given, and it is obvious that interruptions in study were allowed for a variety of causes and circumstances. In these *Sūtras* we also find references to icons. The *Gṛihya Sūtras* are concerned mainly with domestic rituals.

The *Ashṭādhyāyī* of Pāṇini has been used because it supplies valuable political and cultural data of this age. He mentions both classes of states, viz., the republics (*Saṁgha* or *Gaṇa*) and the kingdoms (*Janapadas*). That women followed the profession of teaching is apparent from his work which also embodies certain terms that denote the existence of the art of writing. The author discusses town-planning and also refers to some important towns. His work contains references to images.

The traditions preserved in the *Purāṇas* form an important source of information for the history of Mahāvīra's time. The fifth and the last section known as *Vaṁśānucharita* of some *Purāṇas* gives an account of the kings of the ruling dynasties. The names of some of these kings ruling over Magadha, Avanti, Kāśī, Kośala etc., are accepted as fairly reliable, because they are partially corroborated by both Jaina and Buddhist literatures.

ARCHAEOLOGY

Though no written record of this period is extant, the monuments and antiquities discovered in the archaeological excavations conducted at different places are helpful for the purpose of historical reconstructions. The existence of some early cities such as Rājagṛiha, Vārāṇasī, Mathurā, Śrāvastī, Ujjain and Hastināpura is proved by archaeological findings. City-walls, fortifications and parts of urban settlement have been excavated, giving us a rough idea of town-planning during this period.

The actual remains of the buildings of this period are few because of the perishable nature of the materials used in those days. The existence of the early structures of *Stūpas* along with some other antiquities are known from their archaeological remains discovered at a village, Lauria Nandangarh, in Champaran District of Bihar and Piprahwa (District Basti) of the Nepal border. Wood, mud and mud-bricks were widely used during this period. Small hearths of bamboo and reed have been discovered at Chandraketugarh and Mathura. Structures made of mud and mud-bricks are found at Nagda, Atranjikhara, Hastināpura, Mathura, and Rajaghat. Burnt bricks were used probably for building places of public utility, and their remains have been discovered at Rupar, Hastināpura, and Ujjain. The historic *Jarāsandha-kī Baiṭhaka* built during this period at Rājagṛiha is of stones. Some of the paintings preserved in the rockshelters discovered near Pachmarhi, Mirzapur, and Manikpur may also belong to this period.

No sculptures but the terracottas of this period have been discovered at certain places, such as Hastināpura, Mathurā, Ahichchhatrā, Rajaghat near Vārāṇasī, Śrāvastī and Sonepur. These are made of grey, black, polished, and red ware. Both human and animal figurines are found, but the number of human figurines is larger at this date than that found in the preceding culture. These are better modelled than the specimens of the earlier period, and they are decorated by incision, circles and stamps.

The archaeological excavations carried out at different sites give us an idea of the ceramics used by the people. This period was noteworthy for the introduction of some new fabrics, the most important of them being the North Black Polished Ware, known as a prince among the potteries in India. Black slipped Ware, Red and Black Ware, Grey Ware, and Red Ware were the associate potteries of this age which met the increasing demand of the people. Pottery vessels of different shapes, shades, and colour give an idea of the artistic taste of the people.

Metal objects, such as ornaments, beads, and toilets recovered from the early historical sites in excavations, throw an important light on the material life of the people. The discovery of a large number of iron objects at Ujjain, Nagda, Eran, etc. proves the popularity of iron. Its wide use for different purposes resulted in the surplus of wealth and prosperity during this period.

Coins found at Taxila, Paila, Golakhapur, Patrah, etc. seem to have belonged to this age. These coins are punch-marked because they were being punched by a number of symbols successively by different punches. These punch-marked coins known as *Kārshāpaṇas*, are the earliest coins of India, and are usually made of silver and copper, though silver pieces are certainly more numerous. The vast majority of the silver punch-marked coins follow the standard of 16 *māshakas*. The larger and thinner coins are as a general rule of an earlier date than the small and thick ones. The number of symbols on the obverse is usually five. The popular symbols during this period were the sun, the six arms, a hill above a tank with two fishes, and a peculiar symbol surrounded with five taurines.

Thus with the help of these different sources, an attempt has been made to give a correct picture of Lord Mahāvīra and his times. Certain handicaps have to be experienced by the historian of so early a period because of the paucity and vagueness of the historical material. In fact, the primary source material remained in the shape of traditions for a considerably long time, and then it was codified. This has been utilised only after a thorough critical examination. At the same time, other independent evidences have also been tapped to corroborate it wherever necessary. Still, however, nothing can be said positively on controversial issues in the absence of substantial evidence.

CHAPTER III

LIFE OF LORD MAHĀVĪRA

Lord Mahāvīra, the last Tīrthaṅkara of the Jainas, is described as a supreme personality and acknowledged as 'a great Brāhmaṇa', 'a great guardian', 'a great guide', 'a great preacher', 'a great pilot', and 'a great recluse'.[1] Around his personality there gathered a large number of men and women belonging to different castes and classes. His disciples and followers sincerely believed that their master was, whether walking or sitting, gifted with a supreme knowledge and vision of the *summum bonum*. It is this earnest belief in the greatness of the Teacher that induced them to repose their trust in him and in his words. To them, he stood as a living example of highest human virtue and perfection. His life was to them a perennial source of light and inspiration. His sufferings and forbearance kept them steady in all their trials and tribulations. And his teachings and instructions were for them not ordinary words but utterances of one who saw the light of truth and was able to lead others along the path to enlightenment.

HIS CLAN

'Mahāvīra' or the Great Hero was not the personal name of the religious teacher. He was better known to his contemporaries as Nigaṇṭha, Nāta-putta-Nigaṇṭha of the Nāta or Nāya clan. This name is composed of two separate epithets, Nigaṇṭha and Nātaputta, the first of which is religious and the second secular. He was Nigaṇṭha (Nirgrantha) in a literal as well as in a figurative sense—unclothed without and free from all worldly bonds and ties within. He was called Nātaputta because he was a scion of the Nāya, Nāta[2] or Jñātṛi clan of the Kshatriyas. Just as the Buddha was called Śākyaputta because he was a scion of his clan, so

1. Uvā, VII.
2. SBE, XXII, pp. 80, 248.

was Mahāvīra called Nātaputta because he was a scion of the Nāta Clan.

HIS BIRTH AND PARENTAGE

The Jaina tradition places the birth of Mahāvīra in the year 599 B.C. He belonged to Kāśyapa *gotra*. He was a son of Kshatriya Siddhārtha, also known as Śreyāṁsa and Yaśāṁśa, and of Kshatriyāṇī Triśalā, also known as Videhadattā and Priyakāriṇī of the Vasishṭha *Gotra*.[1] His mother was a sister of Cheṭaka, one of the kings of Vaiśālī. His parents, both lay followers of Pārśva, were pious and chaste, virtuous and strict. They rigorously observed the principles of Jainism.

One incident regarding the birth of Mahāvīra, which has been mentioned by some Śvetāmbara works, cannot be ignored. It is said that Mahāvīra was first conceived in the womb of a Brāhmin lady called Devānandā but was later transferred to the womb of Tiśalā Khattiyāṇī as Tīrthaṅkaras are not born in the Brahmin families.[2] The *Bhagavatī Sūtra* puts this episode into the mouth of Mahāvīra himself. The incident as described there relates to Devānandā and Usabhadatta, the original parents, coming to see Mahāvīra when the latter had become famous as a preacher. On seeing Mahāvīra milk began to flow from the breast of Devānandā due to the strong motherly love she bore towards him. Gotama asked his Master the reason for this upon which the latter admitted that he was the son of Devānandā. The text goes on to say that these original parents of Mahāvīra accepted the order of their Jaina son.[3] This may be one of the causes of his having Brāhmin disciples.

Curiously enough, the tradition about the transfer of the womb goes back to the beginning of the Christian era or even earlier, as it is found depicted in one of the Mathura Sculptures.[4] This story seems to have been borrowed from

1. *Āchā*, II, 15, 15; *Kalpa*, 109, 110.
2. Sbe, XXII, p. 226; *Sama*, p. 89a; *Sthānā*, p. 523b; *Āchā*, II, 15. 4-5 (pp. 190-191).
3. *Bhag*, 9.33 (pp. 457-58).
4. V.A. Smith : The Jain Stūpa and other Antiquities of Mathura, Plate No. 18.

the Puranic story of the transfer of the embryo of Kṛiṣṇa from the womb of Devakī to that of Rohiṇī. This incident regarding the transfer of the womb has been discredited by the Digambaras.

H. JACOBI thinks that Siddhārtha had two wives, the Brāhmaṇī Devānandā, the real mother of Mahāvīra, and the Kshatriyāṇī Triśalā. The name Ṛiṣabhadatta has been invented by the Jainas in order to provide Devānandā with another husband. Siddhārtha was connected with persons of high rank and great influence through his marriage with Triśalā. It was, therefore, profitable, if not probable, to give out that Mahāvīra was the son, and not merely the step-son, of Triśalā, for the reason that he should be entitled to the patronage of her relations. The Jainas' preference for Kshatriyas rather than for Brāhmaṇas is also proved by this curious legend.[1] In the *Bhagavati Sūtra*, there is no mention of the change of Mahāvīra's embryo, and Devānandā has been stated to be the mother of Mahāvīra. It is reasonable to assume that Ṛiṣabhadatta and Devānandā were original parents of Mahāvīra, but they might have given Mahāvīra to Siddhārtha and Triśalā to be adopted by them.

Before birth, Mahāvīra's mother is said to have seen a number of dreams. According to the Śvetāmbaras, they numbered fourteen. These fourteen dreams, according to the *Kalpa Sūtra*, were (1) an elephant; (2) a bull; (3) a lion; (4) the anointing of the goodess Śrī; (5) a garland; (6) the moon; (7) the sun; (8) a flag; (9) a vase; (10) a lotus lake; (11) an ocean; (12) a celestial abode; (13) a heap of jewels and (14) a flame. The Digambaras, who describe sixteen dreams, insert the visions of a throne of diamonds and rubies, and also of a great king of the gods dwelling below the earth. They also assert that she saw the sun before she dreamt about the moon. In place of a flag, they affirm that she saw two fishes. They also assert that she witnessed two vases instead of one, filled with pure water. The interpreters foretold that the child would become either a universal monarch or a prophet possessing all possible knowledge. Since it is a legendary account, it is

1. SBE, XXII, p. xxxi, f. n. 2.

not necessary to believe that the mother of the *Tīrthankara* actually saw all the dreams. The birth of great men has often afterwards been made a theme for some of the most fanciful and superhuman legends[1] the world has known.

BIRTHPLACE

The early scriptures of both the Śvetāmbaras[2] and the Digambaras[3] agree that Kuṇḍapura or Kuṇḍagrāma was the birthplace of Mahāvīra. After examining the evidence contained in the *Āchārāṅga Sūtra*[4], the *Sūtrakṛitāṅga*[5], the *Kalpa Sūtra*[6], the *Uttarādhyayana Sūtra*[7] and the *Bhagavatī-Sūtra-Ṭīka*,[8] it becomes clear that Jainism had a great stronghold in the area of Vaiśālī-Kuṇḍapura of the Videha country during this period and that Mahāvīra was closely associated with this area. The name *Visālie* i.e. *Vaiśālika* was given to Mahāvīra in the *Sūtra-Kṛitāṅga. Vaiśālika* apparently means a native of Vaiśālī, the capital of Videha country. Thus it is clear that Mahāvīra was born at Kuṇḍapura near Vaiśālī in the Videha country.

From the seventh century onwards, the gradual decline of Vaiśālī began and the Jainas came to forget the birthplace of the last Tīrthankara. Some Digambara Jaina works[9] place Vaiśālī under Cheṭaka in Sindhu-Vishaya or Sindhu-deśa.

1. SBE, XXII, pp. 231-238.
2. *Āvaśyaka Niryukti, Kalpa Sūtra, Āvaśyaka Sūtra,* (*Hāribhadrīya-Ṭīkā*), *Mahāvīra Chariyaṁ* of Nemichandra, *Mahāvīra Chariyam* of Guṇachadra Gaṇi, *Paumachariyam* of Vimala Sūri, *Varāṅga-Charitam* of Jaṭāsiṁha Nandi and *Āvaśyaka-Chūrṇi.*
3. Pūjyapāda's *Daśabhakti,* (p. 116); Jinasena's *Harivaṁśapurāṇa* (1.2); Guṇabhadra's *Uttarapurāṇa* (74); Dāmanandi's *Purāṇa Saṁgraha*; Asaga's *Vardhamāma-Charitra* (XVII. 61); Sakalakīrti's *Vardhamāna Charitra* (VII).
4. *Āchā,* II, 15. 15, 17.
5. Sūtra, 1, 2, 3, 22.
6. *Kalpa,* (*Sūtras* 110, 112, 128).
7. *Uttarā*, VI, 17.
8. *Bhagavatī Ṭī*, II, 1, 12, 2.
9. *Uttara-Purāṇa* (75); *Vimala Purāṇa*; *Śreṇika-Charitra* (9); and *Ārādhanā-Kathā-Kosha* (4).

To them Tirabhukti became Sindhu-Vishaya. Evidently, however, Vaiśālī was not situated in Sindhu-Sauvīra. K. P. JAIN[1] suggests two reasons for this confusion. Firstly, it may be that the authors have equated Sindhu-deśa with Vṛijideśa[2], and, secondly, there might have been a confusion especially because Ujjayinī in Avanti, too, was called Viśālā,[3] and there was the Sindhu river in the adjoining territory for which reason it was called Sindhu-deśa in the middle ages (8th to 15th centuries A.D.). Since the Digambara writers, K.P. JAIN adds, lived more in the Ujjayinī region, they appear to have confused Ujjayinī (which was also called Viśālā) with the Viśālā, little knowing that another Viśālā different from their own existed in Eastern India.

Efforts have recently been made to find out the birthplace of Lord Mahāvīra, the son of the Jñātṛika leader of Kshatriya-Kuṇḍapura or Kuṇḍalapura and the maternal son of a Lichchhavi chief. While the Digambara Jainas found a village called Kuṇḍalapura near Nālandā, the Śvetāmbara Jainas found a site called Kshatriyakuṇḍa near the village Lachhwād or Lachhuār in South Monghyr. These came to be regarded as the birthplaces of Lord Mahāvīra by the respective sects. Temples and *Dharmaśālās* were constructed and the Jaina pilgrims began to pour into these places. Thus while the real birthplace was forgotten, other places came to be recognized as such.

The present site, Kshatriyakuṇḍa, near Lachhwād, cannot be the birthplace of Lord Mahāvīra because it formed part of Aṅga, and not of Videha. Modern Kshatriyakuṇḍa is situated on the mountain while there are no references to mountains in connection with ancient Kshatriyakuṇḍa of Kuṇḍapura in the Jaina scriptures. Near the present Kshatriyakuṇḍa, no traces of such ancient places as Vaiśālī, Vāṇijyagrāma,

1. *Jaina Siddhānta Bhāskara*, 3 (Sept. 1936), p. 50, f.n.).
2. *Sindhu-deśa* literally means 'the country of Rivers' and Tirabhukti, too, has a similar meaning, i.e. 'the Province situated on the Banks (of Rivers). From the Gupta period onwards, Videha came to be known as Tirabhukti.
3. *Meghadūta*, 1,30.

Kollāga-Sanniveśa and Karmāragrāma are found. The nullaha near it is not the Gaṇḍakī river.

In the *Mahāvagga* of the Buddhists, it has been said that Buddha, while sojourning at Koṭiggāma, was visited by the courtezan Ambapāli and the Lichchhavis of the neighbouring capital, Vaiśālī. From Koṭiggāma, he went to where the Nātikas lived. There he lodged in the Nātika Brick Hall. From there he went to Vaiśālī where he converted the general-in-chief (of the Lichchhavis), a lay disciple of the Nirgranthas. H. Jacobi has identified Koṭiggāma of the Buddhists with Kuṇḍagāma of the Jainas. Apart from the similarity of the names, the reference to the Nātikas, apparently identical with the Jñātrika Kshatriyas to whose clan Mahāvīra belonged, and to Sīha, the Jaina, points to the same direction. Kuṇḍagrāma, therefore, was probably one of the suburbs of Vaiśālī, the capital of Videha. This conjecture is borne out by the name *Vesālie*, i.e. *Vaiśālika* given to Mahāvīra in the *Sūtrakṛitāṅga*. *Vaiśālika* apparently means a native of Vaiśālī; and Mahāvīra could rightly be called as such when Kuṇḍagrama was a suburb of Vaiśālī. H. Jacobi regards Kuṇḍapura as only an insignificant place and believes that the sovereign of it could at best have been only a petty chief.[1] The identification of Koṭiggāma with Kuṇḍapura seems to be doubtful, and both seem to be independent villages.

A.F.R. Hoernle[2] has clearly shown that Vaiśālī is the birthplace of Mahāvīra. Vāṇiyagāma was another name of the well-known city of Vaiśālī, the capital of the Lichchhavi country. This city, commonly called Vaiśālī, occupied a very extended area, which included within its circuit, besides Veśālī proper, several other places such as Vāṇiyagāma and Kuṇḍagāma. They still exist as villages called Bāniyā and Basukuṇḍa.

The identification of Vaiśālī with the group of remains associated with the village of Basāṛh in Muzaffarpur District, some forty km. to the north of Patna, is conclusively proved by the survival of the ancient name with only slight modifi-

1. SBE, XXII, pp. x-xiii.
2. English translation of *Uvāsagadasāo* (Bibliotheca Indica Series, Calcutta, 1888),

cations; by the geographical bearings taken from Patna and other places; by the topographical details compared with description recorded by Yuan Chwang, the Chinese pilgrim in the seventh century and by the finding on the spot of sealings of letters inscribed with the name *Vaiśālī*[1].

The identification of ancient Vaiśālī and Kuṇḍagāma or Kuṇḍapura with Basāṛh and Basukuṇḍa respectively has been supported by several other scholars such as T. Bloch[2], S. Stevenson,[3] N. L. Dey[4] and B. C. Law[5]. Some of these scholars consider Kuṇḍapura, Vāṇiyagāma, Kollāga Sanniveśa and Karmāragrāma to be the suburbs of Vaiśālī. This view does not seem to be correct. These were independent villages which may be identified with the modern villages of Basukuṇḍa, Baniyā, Koluā and Kūmana Chhaparāgāchhī respectively. Brāhmaṇakuṇḍa and Kshatriyakuṇḍa were the two wards of Kuṇḍapura, and between them was situated Bahuśāla Chaitya. Vaiśālī and Kuṇḍapura were situated on the eastern bank of the Gaṇḍakī river, while Karmāragrāma, Kollāga Sanniveśa,[6] Vāṇijyagrāma and *Dvipalāśa Chaitya* on the west.

CHILDHOOD

There are scriptural anecdotes, myths and miracles connected with the childhood of Mahāvīra. It is stated in them that his birth was celebrated alike by gods and men, and it was received by his parents with the loftiest expectations. On the day of his birth, the prisoners in Kuṇḍapura were released. Festivals kept the whole town bound in mirth and joy for ten days after which many offerings were made to the gods.[7] His parents named him 'Vardhamāna'[8] or the 'Prosper-

1. V.A. Smith : Encyclopaedia of Religion and Ethics, Vol. XII (New York, 1921), pp. 567-68
2. Asi, 1903-4, p. 82.
3. Sshj, pp. 21-22.
4. Ndgdami, p. 107.
5. Lmlt, p. 19.
6. A F.R Hoernle and H. Jacobi interpreted *Sanniveśa* in the sense of ward and suburb respectively but it was also used in the sense of *grāma*. See Vtm, I, p. 98.
7. *Kalpa*, 97-105.
8. Ibid., 91, 106-107; *Āchā*, II, 15, 15.

ous one', because with his birth, the wealth, fame and merit of the family increased.

The two ascetics, Sañjaya and Vijaya, became somehow suspicious about the nature of some object. As their suspicion immediately disappeared at the sight of Lord Mahāvīra soon after his birth, they therefore gave him the name *Sanmati* in devotion.[1]

The scriptures of both the Śvetāmbaras and the Digambaras relate the legends of Mahāvīra's supreme valour and how easily he excelled all his companions in strength and physical endurance during boyhood. One day, playing with his friends in the garden of his father, Mahāvīra saw an elephant, mad with fury and with juice flowing from his temples, rushing towards him. His companions, all boys, shocked and frightened at the sight of this imminent danger, deserted their comrade and ran away. Without losing a moment, Mahāvīra made up his mind to face the danger squarely, went towards the elephant, caught hold of his trunk with strong hands and mounted his back at once.

Another legend tells how, when Māhāvīra was playing with the same children at *Āmbali pipali* (a short of 'tick or 'tig') among the trees, a god disguised as a dreadful snake appeared on a tree. All his companions were alarmed and fled away. Mahāvīra, mustering courage, remained calm. He caught hold of the snake and threw it away. The god again decided to frighten the child by carrying him high up into the sky on his shoulders. Mahāvīra, however, was not in the least alarmed, and seizing this opportunity of showing his superiority over the immortals, whacked the god and pulled his hair so hard that he was only too ready to descend and get rid of his obstreperous burden.[2] As he stood fast in the midst of dangers and fears, patiently enduring all hardships and calamities, adhering to the chosen rules of penance, and as he was wise, indifferent to pleasure and pain alike, rich in self-control and gifted with fortitude, the name *Mahāvīra* was given to

1. *Mahāpurāṇa*, 74.
2. *Tri. pu. Cha*, 10, 2, 217; *Āva. Chu.* I. p. 246.

him. As he was devoid of love and hate, he was called *Śramaṇa*.[1]

In person, Mahāvīra seems to have been handsome and impressive. He was clever and was possessed of a very keen intellect.[2] The *Kalpa Sūtra*[3] mentions that from his very birth, he possessed 'supreme, unlimited and unimpeded knowledge and intuition.' We may assume that he received the usual education and training of a Kshatriya aristocrat in literature and philosophy, in military and administrative sciences, and in music and fine arts.

LIFE OF A HOUSEHOLDER

On the question of Mahāvīra's marriage, there is a fundamental difference of detail between the Digambara and the Śvetāmbara accounts. The Digambara works[4] deny the fact of Mahāvīra's marriage. On the other hand, in the Śvetāmbara accounts,[5] there is an allusion to his marriage. In his youth, Mahāvīra was, however, given to contemplation and had begun to entertain plans of renunciation. His parents tried to solve the problem by marrying him off to a beautiful young woman, Yaśodā, a Kshatriya lady of Kauṇḍinya *Gotra*, who soon presented him with a daughter named Aṇojjā. Aṇojjā was married to Jamālī, a Kshatriya, who after becoming Mahāvīra's follower created a schism. Mahāvīra's grand daughter, who belonged to the Kauśika *Gotra*, had two names : Seshavatī and Yaśovatī.

Mahāvīra's paternal uncle was Supārśva. His elder brother was Nandivardhana and his elder sister Sudarśanā. His parents died when he was thirty years old. Afterwards, his elder brother, Nandivardhana, succeeded his father. With the permission of his brother and other authorities,[6] he carried out his long cherished resolve and became a monk with the usual rites. The Digambara works do not mention the names

1. *Kalpa*, 120; *Āchā*, II, 15. 15.
2. Ibid., 110.
3. Ibid , 112.
4. *Padmapurāṇa*, 20, 67; *Harivaṁśapurāṇa*. 60, 214; *Tiloyapaṇṇati*, 4, 670 etc,
5. *Āchā*, II. 15, 15; *Kalpa*, 109.
6. *Kalpa*. 110.

of his elder brother and elder sister. According to them, Mahāvīra embarked upon his spiritual vocation during the lifetime of their parents. At first his parents were opposed to the idea of their delicately natured child undergoing all the hardships that fall to the lot of a houseless mendicant, but at last they acquiesced.

HIS ASCETIC LIFE : HIS TWELVE YEARS OF PREPARATION

The *Āchārāṅga Sūtra* has preserved a sort of religious ballad giving an account of the years during which Mahāvīra led a life of the hardest asceticism, thus preparing himself for the attainment of the highest spiritual knowledge. The account given in the *Kalpa Sūtra* substantially agrees with that of the *Āchārāṅga Sūtra*. Both the *Āchārāṅga* and the *Kalpa Sūtra* narrate the story of his *Sādhanā* in such a manner as to suggest that he had to make superhuman efforts before he could aspire to obtain the coveted position of a *Kevalin*. It is remarkable that this account of *Mahāvīra Sādhanā* given in the *Āchārāṅga* and the *Kalpa Sūtra* does not bring in Gośāla to form an episode. It is only from the *Bhagavatī Sūtra* and the *Uvāsagadasāo* that we know that the Ājīvika Teacher Gośāla lived in the company of Mahāvīra for a period of about six years during this ascetic period of Mahāvīra's life.

Mahāvīra renounced the world at the age of thirty. It seems that he joined the order of Pārśva of which his parents were lay followers. Whereas the Digambaras believe that Mahāvīra abandoned clothes at the time of his initiation, the Śvetāmbaras hold that he abandoned them after thirteen months. The *Āchārāṅga Sūtra* gives the following account of his ascetic life.

For a year and a month since he renounced the world Mahāvīra did not discard his clothes. Thereafter, he gave up his garments and became naked.[1] Even when he used his robe, he used it only in winter.[2] For more than four months,

1. *Āchā.* I, 8, 1, 3.
2. Ibid., I, 8, 1, 1.

many living beings gathered on his body, crawled about it, and caused him pain.[1] Then he meditated, walking with his eye fixed on a square space before him of the length of a man. Many people assembled, shocked at the sight; they struck him and cried. He renounced the company of the female sex and of all householders. When asked, he gave no answer; when saluted he gave no reply. He was beaten with sticks, and struck by sinful people.[2]

For more than a couple of years, he led a religious life without using cold water; he lived in solitude, guarded his body, had intuition, and was calm. He carefully avoided injuring the meanest form of life. He did not use what was expressly prepared for him. He consumed clean food. He did not use another's robe, nor did he eat out of another's vessel. Disregarding contempt, he went with indifference to places where food was prepared. He was not desirous of eating delicious food, nor had he any longing for it. He neither rubbed his eyes nor scratched his body.[3]

Mahāvīra sometimes lodged in workshops, assembling places, wells or shops; sometimes in manufactories or under a shed of straw. He sometimes took shelter in travellers' halls, garden-houses or towns; sometimes in a cemetery, in relinquished houses, or at the foot of a tree. At these places, he spent thirteen long years meditating day and night, exerting himself, undisturbed strenuously. He did not seek sleep for the sake of pleasure; he would wake up himself and sleep only a little, free from cares and desires. Waking up again, he would lie down exerting himself; going outside for once in a night, he would walk about for an hour. In these resting places, he had to face manifold calamities. Crawling or flying animals attacked him. Bad people, the guard of the village, or lance-bearers assaulted him. Always a master of himself, he endured these hardships as he wandered about, speaking but little. Ill treated by the wanderers, he engaged himself in

1. Āchā, I, 8, 1, 2.
2. Ibid., I, 8, 1, —4, 5, 6, 7.
3. Ibid., I, 8, 1, —10, 11, 12, 17, 18. 19.

his meditations, free from resentment.[1] Always calm and cool-headed, he patiently bore the pains caused by grass, cold, fire, flies and gnats.[2]

Mahāvīra travelled in the pathless country of Rāḍha, in Vajrabhūmi and Śvabhrabhūmi, where he used most comfortless beds and seats. The rude natives of the place attacked him and unleashed their dogs to bite him, but he never used his sticks to keep them off. Being perfectly enlightened he endured the abusive language of the rustics. Sometimes when he did not reach the village, the inhabitants met him on the outskirts and attacked him, saying 'Get away from here.' He was struck with a stick, fist, or lance; he was hit with a fruit, a clod, and a potsherd. When once he sat without moving his body, they cut his flesh, tore his hair or covered him with dust. They disturbed him in his religious meditation. Abandoning the care of his body, he endured all pains free from desire.[3]

Mahāvīra was able to abstain from the indulgence of the flesh, though he was never attacked by any illness. Whether wounded or not, he never had any desire for any medical treatment. Purgatives and emetics, anointing of the body and bathing, shampooing and cleaning of the teeth did not behove him, after he learned that the body is something unclean. In the cold season, he meditated in the shade, and in summer, he exposed himself to the heat. He lived on rough food : rice, pounded jujube, and beans. Using these three kinds of food, he sustained himself eight months. Sometimes he ate only the sixth meal, or the eighth, the tenth and the twelfth. Sometimes he ate stale food. He committed no sin himself, nor did he induce others to do so, nor did he consent to the sins of others. He meditated persevering in some posture, without any motion whatsoever; he meditated in mental concentration on the things above, below, beside, free from desires. He meditated free from sin and desire, not

1. Āchā I, 8, 2-2 3, 4, 5, 6, 7, 8, 10, 11.
2. Ibid., I, 8, 3, 1.
3. Ibid., I, 8, 3-2, 3, 4, 7, 8, 9, 10, 11, 12.

attached to sounds or colours ; though still an erring mortal, he never acted carelessly.[1]

Thus, like a hero at the head of a battle, he bore all hardships, and, remaining undisturbed, proceeded on the road to deliverance. Understanding what truth is and restraining his impulses for the purification of his soul, he finally liberated himself.[2]

The account of Mahāvīra's ascetic life given in the *Kalpa Sūtra* is as follows. When the moon was in conjunction with the asterism *Uttaraphalguni*, he, after fasting two and a half days without drinking water, put on a divine robe, and, quite alone, nobody else being present, tore out his hair and, abandoning his house, entered the state of houselessness.[3] For more than a year he wore clothes. Afterwards, he walked about naked, and accepted the alms in the hollow of his hand. Fore more than twelve years, he neglected his body and took no care of it. With exemplary equanimity he bore, experienced and suffered all pleasant or unpleasant occurrences arising from divine powers, men or animals.[4]

Henceforth, the ascetic Mahāvīra remained circumspect in speech, movement, begging, accepting anything, and carrying his outfit and drinking vessel. He guarded his thoughts, words, acts, senses and chastity. He moved without wrath, pride, deceit and greed. He remained calm, tranquil, composed, liberated, free from temptations, without egoism, and without property. In short, he had cut off all earthly ties, and was not stained by any worldliness. As water does not adhere to a copper vessel, so sins found no place in him. His course was unobstructed like that of Life. Like the firmament, he wanted no support, and like the wind he knew no obstacles. His heart was pure like the water in autumn. He remained unsoiled like leaf of a lotus. His senses were well protected like those of a tortoise. He lived single and alone like the horn of a rhinoceros. He was free like a bird. He was always

1. *Āchā*, I, 8, 4,—1, 2, 3, 4, 5, 6, 7, 8, 14, 15.
2. Ibid., I, 8, 4, 16.
3. *Kalpa*, 116.
4. Ibid., 117.

waking like the fabulous bird, Bhāruṇḍa. He was valorous like an elephant, strong like a bull, unassailabe like a lion, steady and firm like Mount Mandāra, deep like the ocean, mild like the Moon, refulgent like the Sun and pure like excellent gold. Like the earth, he patiently bore everything and like a well-kindled fire, he shone in his splendour.[1]

Out of all the eight months of summer and winter taken together, Mahāvīra spent only a single night in villages and only five nights in towns. He was indifferent alike to the smell of ordure and of sandal, to straw and jewels, dirt and gold, and pleasure and pain. He was attached neither to this world nor to the world beyond. He desired neither life nor death. He arrived at the other shore of the *Saṁsāra*, and exerted himself for the suppression of the defilement of *Karma*.[2]

With supreme knowledge, intuition, conduct, valour, uprightness, mildness, dexterity patience, freedom from passions, control, contentment, and understanding, Mahāvīra meditated on himself for twelve years on the supreme path to final liberation which is the fruit of veracity, control, penance and good conduct.[3]

The *Kalpa Sūtra* gives a list of forty-two rainy seasons spent by Mahāvīra since he renounced the life of a householder. He stayed the first rainy season in Asthikagrāma, three rainy seasons in Champā and Pṛishṭichampā, twelve in Vaiśālī and Vāṇijyagrāma, fourteen in Rājagṛiha and Nālandā, six in Mithilā, two in Bhadrikā, one in Ālabhikā, one in Panitabhūmi, one in Śrāvastī and the last one in the town of Pāpā in king Hastipāla's office.[4]

B.C. Law[5] thinks that the *Kalpa Sūtra* list of places is worded according to the idea of succession and chronology. The idea of succession is suggested by two expressions : 'the first rainy season in Asthikagrāma' and 'the last rainy season in Pāpā or Pāvā'. Accordingly he suggests the names of places

1. *Kalpa*, 117.
2. Ibid , 119.
3. Ibid., 120.
4. Ibid., 122.
5. LMLT, p. 32.

where Mahāvīra spent the twelve rainy seasons of his ascetic life.[1] He stayed the first rainy season in Asthigrāma, three rainy seasons in Champā and Pṛishṭichampā and eight in Vaiśālī and Vāṇijyagrāma. This view does not appear to be correct. Except the first and the last, the other places have not been mentioned in chronological order but in groups.

According to a commentary on the *Kalpa Sūtra*, Asthigrāma was formerly called Vardhamāna. It would perhaps be more correct to say that Asthigrāma was the earlier name of Vardhamāna (modern Burdwan). But none need be surprised if Asthigrāma was the same place as Hatthigāma (Hastigrāma) which lay on the high road from Vaiśālī to Pāvā (probably modern Kasiā).[2] Champā was the capital of Aṅga which was conquered in Mahāvīra's time by Śreṇika Bimbisāra and permanently annexed to Magadha. Its actual site is probably marked by two villages of Champānagara and Champāpura near Bhagalpur. Pṛishṭichampā must have been a place near Champā. Vaiśālī is identified with modern Basārah in Vaiśālī, a district of Bihar. It was the chief seat of government of the Vṛiji-Lichchavīs in Mahāvīra's time. Vāṇiyagāma is the same as modern Bania, a village near Basārah.[3] Rājagṛiha (modern Rājgir) was the capital of Magadha in Mahāvīra's time. Nālandā is identified with modern Bargaon, 10 km. to the north-west of Rājgīr in the district of Nālandā near Bihar (Bihar-sharif).[4] Mithilā was the capital of the prosperous kingdom of Videha. It is identified with Janakapur, a small town within the Nepal border, north of which the districts of Muzaffarpur and Darbhanga meet.[5] Badrikā, which is the same name as the Pāli Bhaddiya, was an important place in the kingdom of Aṅga.[6] It was visited by Buddha and is identified with modern Monghyr.[7]

1. LMLT, 29.
2. Ibid., p. 33.
3. GEB, p. 6.
4. AGI, p. 537.
5. Ibid., p. 718.
6. Dhammapada Commentary, I, p. 384.
7. R. SANKRITYAYANA : *Vinaya Piṭaka*, p. 248n.

Ālabhikā, which is the same as the Pāli Ālavi, is identified by A. CUNNINGHAM and A. F. R. HOERNLE with Newal or Nawal in Unao District in U. P., and by N.L. DEY with Aviwa, 40 km. north-east of Eatwah.[1] It lay between Sāvatthi and Rājagiha.[2] Paṇitabhūmi, which is the same as Paṇiyabhūmi, was a place in Vajrabhūmi, a division of the pathless country of Rāḍha.[3] Śrāvastī was the flourishing capital of the kingdom of Kośala in Mahāvīra's time. It is identified with Sahet-Mahet on the bank of the Rapti.[4] Pāpā, which is the same name as the Pāli Pāvā, was one of the chief seats of government of the Mallas. It was in Mahāvīra's time one of the halting stations on the highway from Vaiśālī to Kuśīnārā and Kapilavastu.[5] A. CUNNINGHAM took it for the modern village, Padaraona, 18 km. to the N. N. E. of Kasiā.[6] It is identified with a place located at a distance of ten km. from Biharsharif in Patna District.[7]

One important event of this period of Mahāvīra's life was his meeting with Gośāla Maukhaliputta, the head of the Ājīvika sect. From the account given in the *Bhagavatī Sūtra*, it is known that during the second year of his ascetic life, Mahāvīra stayed at Nālandā during the rainy season. At this time, Gośāla, who was then wandering about in the country showing pictures to the people at large, happened to arrive and put up there. Owing to Mahāvīra's extraordinary self-restraint, his impressive habits of meditation, his capacity to prophesy things correctly and to the fact a rich householder Vijaya, of Rājagṛiha had shown respect and hospitality to him, Gośāla was attracted, and wanted to be his disciple, but Mahāvīra declined his request. His prayer was not granted on two successive occasions even though the Master was entreated by the rich householders, Ānanda and Sudarśana.

1. GEB, p. 24.
2. PBAI, p 160.
3. SBE, XXII, p. 264, f. n. 4; also p. 84.
4. AGI, p. 469.
5. GEB, p. 15.
6. Ibid., p. 498.
7. HSBJY, p. 24.

In the meantime, Mahāvīra went to the settlement of Kollāga, at some distance from Nālandā, where he was hospitably greeted by the Brāhmin Bahula. (Kollāga is identified with the modern village Kolhuā.) Gośāla proceeded towards Rājagṛiha and its suburbs to find out Mahāvīra but in vain. He came back to the weaver's shed of Nanda where he gave away his cloths, vessels, shoes, and pictures to a Brāhmin of the place, shaved off his hair and beard, and in despair departed in search of the Master. On his way, he came across Kollāga where he saw people praising Bahula's liberality towards Mahāvīra.[1]

Gośāla continued his search of Mahāvīra and at last succeeded in finding him out at Paṇiyabhūmi. He again requested him with greater earnestness to make him his disciple. This time his request was granted, and both Mahāvīra and his disciple Gośāla lived together for six years in Paṇiyabhūmi, practising asceticism. Afterwards, they started from Paṇiyabhūmi to Kūrmagrāma, and on from Kūrmagrāma to Siddhārthagrāma. Siddhārthagrāma is probably the same as Siddhangrām in the Birbhum District.[2] While at Kūrmagrāma, they met an ascetic named Vesayana who remained seated with upraised arms and upturned face in the glare of the Sun, while his body was swarming with lice. Gośāla enquired whether he was a sage or a bed of lice. Vesayana became very angry and attempted to strike Gośāla with his supernormal powers. Mahāvīra explained to him the severe ascetic discipline by which such powers could be obtained.

While at Siddhārthagrāma, Gośāla uprooted sesame shrub and threw it away. Owing to a lucky fall of rain, the shrub came to life again. From this, he jumped to the conclusion that all plants were capable of reanimation. He drew even further conclusion that not only plants, but in fact all living beings were capable of reanimation. His theory of reanimation and other doctrines did not find favour with

1. HBSJY, p. 23.
2. History of Bengal, Vol. I, p. 22.

Mahāvīra who believed in the freedom of the will. Henceforth Gośāla severed his connection with Mahāvīra and established a separate sect known as Ājīvika.[1]

B.M. Barua[2] is of the opinion that the Jaina account of Gośāla is biased and that it cannot therefore be relied upon. It is equally possible that Mahāvīra in the beginning of his ascetic career might have become a disciple of Gośāla. Gośāla was recognised as a teacher at least two years before Mahāvīra. He predeceased Mahāvīra by some sixteen years. There is a discrepancy between the accounts of the *Bhagavatī* and the *Kalpa Sūtra*. According to the former, Mahāvīra spent six years in Paṇiyabhūmi in the company of Gośāla, while the latter gives him only one year in that place, but six years in Mithilā. The inference from these two somewhat contradictory accounts seems to be this—that in the second year of his monkhood, Mahāvīra left the religious order of Pārśvanātha, and joined the School of Gośāla. And when six years afterwards the difference of opinion led Mahāvīra to leave that school, he founded a new school of his own and organized a religious order mainly after the model of Pārśvanātha. This view of B.M. Barua's appears to be only imaginary and is not supported by any solid dependable evidence. There are clear proofs that from the beginning of his ascetic life, Mahāvīra became a Jaina monk and that he did not join any religious order afterwards.

The incidental enumeration of the places visited by Mahāvīra in the *Bhagavatī Sūtra* during his ascetic life does not tally with those given in the *Kalpa Sūtra*. The *Bhagavatī Sūtra* associates Nālandā, Rājagṛiha, Paṇiyabhūmi, Siddhārthagrāma and Kūrmagrāma with his early wanderings. The *Uvāsaga-dasāo* mentions Vāṇijyagrāma, Champā, Bārāṇasī, Ālabhi (Pāli Alavi), Kampilyapura, Polāsapura, Rājagṛiha, and Śrāvastī as the places that were visited by Mahāvīra. Both the *Bhagavatī Sūtra* and the *Uvāsaga-dasāo* would have us believe that he received extraordinary respect from certain rich householders even long before his Jinahood. Bārāṇasī is no other

1. *Uvā*, Tr. by A. F. R. Hoernle, App. I.
2. Bhpip, p. 374.

than modern Benaras. Kampillapura is identified with Kampil in the Farrukabad District.[1] Polāsapura has not been identified, but at the time of Mahāvīra, it was within the kingdom of king Jiyasattu, the ruler of Kośala.

The *Āvaśyaka Niryukti*,[2] the *Āvaśyaka Chūrṇi*,[3] the *Āvaśyaka Bhāshya*,[4] the *Āvaśyaka Ṭīkā*, the *Kalpa Sūtra Ṭīkā*,[5] and the *Mahāvīra Charitras* written by Nemi Chandra, Guṇa Chandra and Hema Chandra somehow give us a detailed account, with chronological succession of Mahāvīra's itinerary. Though based on tradition, these are still very late works and cannot be wholly relied upon. Their motive was sometimes to glorify Lord Mahāvīra and present him as a superhuman being, rather than as an ordinary mortal. One important conclusion may be drawn that Jainism had penetrated to far-flung areas so that at the time of composition of these works. their authors expressly mention the visit of Lord Mahāvīra to these places in order to impress the masses, but actually the spread of Jainism during the time of Mahāvīra there seems to be quite impossible.

When Mahāvīra was thirty years old, he renounced the world with the permission of his elder brother, Nandivardhana, and his relatives. With people pursuing him, he set out from Kuṇḍagrāma in the dark of *Mārgasirsha* on the tenth day in winter by simply putting on a divine garment (*Devadussa*). He came to the garden of Nāyasaṇḍavaṇa situated in the north-east direction on the outskirts of Kuṇḍaggāma. At this place, the renunciation ceremony of Mahāvīra was celebrated with great rejoicings. He is said to have given the first half of his garment to a Brāhmaṇa.

FIRST YEAR

In the evening of the same day, Mahāvīra left Nāyasaṇḍa for Kumāragāma. There were two routes by which this journey was performed, one by water and the other by

1. GEB, p. 18.
2. *Āva. Nir*, 458-527.
3. *Āva, Chū*, pp. 268-333.
4. *Āva, Bhā*, III.
5. *Kalpa, Ṭī*, 5.121.

land. Mahāvīra preferred the latter and reached Kumāragāma. Now this village is famous by the name of Kammana-Chhaparā.[1] Here, Mahāvīra stood in meditation but was harassed by a cowherd who took him for a thief and wanted to hit him. Next day, Mahāvīra proceeded to Kollāga Sannivesa where he broke his fast. From there, he started for Morāga Sannivesa and reaching there, stayed in a hermitage. Next day, he left Morāga Sannivesa but again came back to this place after eight months. Then he proceeded to Aṭṭhiyagāma, where he put up in the shrine of Sūlapāṇī. Here Sūlapāṇī Jakkha is said to have caused Mahāvīra many troubles but the latter bore them with his wonted equanimity and patience. Thus Mahāvīra spent his first rainy season at Aṭṭhiyagāma.

SECOND YEAR

From Aṭṭhiyagāma, Mahāvīra again came to Morāga Sannivesa where lived an ascetic named Achchhandaka. Then he started for Vāchāla, which was divided into Uttaravāchāla and Dakkhinavāchāla, and between them flowed the rivers Suvannakūlā and Ruppakūlā. When Mahāvīra was going from Dakkhiṇavāchāla to Uttaravāchāla, the remaining half of his garment got entangled in the thorns on the bank of Suvannakūlā. From this time onwards, Mahāvīra became a naked monk. There were two routes to Uttaravāchāla, one through the hermitage named Kanakakhala and another from outside it. Mahāvīra chose the former one which was more difficult. At Uttaravāchāla, he had to face a poisonous snake named Ḍrishṭivisha. From Kanakakhala, he travelled to Seyaviyā where he was received by King Paesi. T. W. Rhys Davids identifies this place with Satiabia and Vost with Basedita, twenty five km. from Sahet-Mahet and ten km. from Balarampur.[2] Mahāvīra arrived at Surabhipura from Seyaviyā after crossing the Ganges, and afterwards proceeded to Thūṇāka Sannivesa where he stood in meditation. The place was situated in the country of Mallas to the north-west of Patna on the right bank of the Gaṇḍakī.[3] From here, Mahāvīra proceeded to

1. Hbsjy, p. 23.
2. Ndgdami, p. 184.
3. Juphs, Vol XV. Pt. II.

Rāyagiha and sojourned in a weaver's shed in Nālandā where he passed the second rainy season. Here Gośāla met him and the two left for Kollāga together.

THIRD YEAR

From Kollāga, Mahāvīra and Gośāla came to Sunnakhālaya and then to Bambhaṇagāma. This Bambhaṇagāma lay in a route from Rājagṛiha to Champī.[1] From this place, they reached Champī where Mahāvīra spent the third rainy season.

FOURTH YEAR

From Champā, Mahāvīra and Gośāla arrived at Kālāya Sannivesa and thence to Pattakālaya. At both these places, Gośāla was insulted for his misbehaviour. Then, both came to Kumārāya Sannivesa where Mahāvīra practised meditation in the garden, Champaramaṇijja. Then they proceeded to Chorāga Sannivesa where they were taken to be spies and were taken prisoners. Chorāga Sannivesa may be identified with Choreya in Lohardugga District in Bengal.[2] From this place, they travelled to Piṭṭhichampā where Mahāvīra passed the fourth rainy season.

FIFTH YEAR

From Piṭṭhichampā, Mahāvīra and Gośāla proceeded to Kayaṅgalā, now identified with Kaṅkajol in Santhal *Parganā* in Bihar.[3] At this place, some ascetics were staying with their families. Gośāla is known to have misbehaved with them and was therefore punished. Then both came to Sāvatthi and, later, to Haledduga. Here under a big turmeric tree Mahāvīra stood in meditation. His feet are said to have been burnt by fire. Meditation over, both proceeded to Naṅgala where Mahāvīra stood in meditation again in the Vāsudeva temple. Gośāla was punished once again for his misdemeanour. Then, they arrived at Avattagāma where Mahāvīra spent his time in meditation in the Baladeva temple and Gośāla was taken to task for his misbehaviour. Continuing their travels in this

1. VTM I, p. 194
2. GEB, p 40.
3. R SANKRITYAYANA: *Vinaya Piṭaka*, p. 248 n.

region, they reached Chorāya Sannivesa from where they journeyed to Kalambuka Sannivesa. Here both were tied by Kālahasti and were beaten; later on, they were set at liberty by Kālahasti's brother, Megha, who recognized Mahāvīra. Then they journeyed to the country of Lāḍha where Mahāvīra had to endure various kinds of painful sufferings. Lāḍha or Rāḍha comprises the modern districts of Hooghly, Howrah, Bankura, Burdwan, and the eastern part of Midnapore.[1] From this place, they moved on towards punnakalasa where some robbers made a dastardly attempt on Mahāvīra's life. Undaunted, they travelled to the city of Bhaddiya where Mahāvīra passed the fifth rainy season.

SIXTH YEAR

From Bhaddiya, both Mahāvīra and Gośāla travelled to Kayalisamāgama, and then onward to Jambusaṇḍa and Tambāya Sannivesa. Jambusaṇḍa was located between Ambagāma and Bhoganagara on a route from Vaiśālī to Kuśīnārā.[2] Then they arrived at Kūiya Sannivesa where, suspected of being spies, they were kept as prisoners, but were later released at the intercession of two sisters, Vijayā and Pragalbhā. Kūiya or Kūpiya is identified with a place located at a distance of ten km. from the Khalīlābāda Mehadāvala road in Khalīlābad Tehsil of Ḍhūhabastī District.[3]

Now Gośāla and Mahāvīra parted with each other. Mahāvīra left for Vaiśālī where he stood in a blacksmith's shed. The blacksmith, seeing Mahāvīra naked, ran to hit him. Afterwards, Mahāvīra proceeded to Gāmāya Sannivesa where he was honoured by Vibhelaka Jakkha. From this place, he travelled to Sālisīsayagāma where the demoness Kaṭapūtanā caused him much trouble. After six months, Gośāla again joined Mahāvīra at this place. Finally, Mahāvīra visited Bhaddiya in order to spend the sixth rainy season there.

SEVENTH YEAR

Then Mahāvīra and Gośāla travelled together in the country of Magadha. In the course of the journey, Mahāvīra

1. AGI, p. 732.
2. VTM, I, p. 203, f.n. 1.
3. *Ibid.*, p. 204. f.n.1.

decided to spend the seventh rainy season at Ālabhiyā.

EIGHTH YEAR

From Ālabhiyā, Mahāvīra and Gośāla set out for Kuṇḍāga Sannivesa. At this place, Mahāvīra stood in meditation in the temple of Vāsudeva. Gośāla was again beaten for his bad manners. Then they visited Maddanagāma and stayed in the Baladeva temple. Afterwards they came to Bahusālagagāma where Mahāvīra was harassed by Sālejjā Vāṇamāntarī. From this place, they proceeded to the capital Lohaggalā where the royal servants suspected them to be spies and caught them. Later on they were set free at the intercession of Uppala who is said to have arrived there from Aṭṭhiyagāma. Lohaggalā may be identified with Lohardagā situated in the region which forms the central and north-western portion of the Chhota Nagpur Division.[1] From Lohaggalā, they went to Purimatāla where Mahāvīra stood in meditation in the garden of Sagaḍamuha. Purimatāla may be identified with Purulia in Bihar.[2] From there, they travelled to Unnāga and on to Gobhūmi. At last they reached Rāyagiha in order to pass the eighth rainy season.

NINTH YEAR

From Rāyagiha, Mahāvīra and Gośāla again set out for a Lāḍha country which is non-Aryan. In the course of this journey, they passed through Vajjabhūmi and Subbhabhūmi, where Mahāvīra had to endure all sorts of tortures. Sometimes people surrounded him and set their dogs upon him. Mahāvīra got no shelter in this region. He passed the ninth rainy season in this country.

TENTH YEAR

Mahāvīra and Gośāla then travelled to Siddhatthapura and Kummagāma. Soon they returned to Siddhatthapura. It may be the same as Siddhangrāma in Birbhum District.[3] Severing his relations with Mahāvīra again, Gośāla now went to Sāvatthi while Mahāvīra visited Vaiśālī where the republi-

1. Imperial Gazetteers, Vol. VIII, p. 475.
2. JLAIDJC. p. 324.
3. History of Bengal. Vol. I. p. 22.

can chief Saṅkha saved him from the trouble caused by the local children. From here, Mahāvīra crossed the river Gaṇḍai by boat and reached Vāṇiyagāma. He then proceeded to Sāvatthi where he passed the tenth rainy season.

ELEVENTH YEAR

From Sāvatthi, Mahāvīra set out for Sānulaṭṭhiyagāma, which may be identified with Dalabhum in Singhbhum District in Bengal.[1] He then went to Peḍhālagāma and stood in meditation in the garden of Peḍhāla in the shrine of Polāsa. In this region of the Mlechchhas, Mahāvīra had to suffer much. He travelled later to Vāluyagāma, Subhoma, Suchchhettā, Malaya and finally on to the Hatthisīsa. At all these places, apparently located in the north-west part of Orissa, Mahāvīra had to undergo extreme physical torture. Afterwards he reached Tosali where he was suspected to be a robber and hit hard. The place is now identified with Dhauli and some neighbouring places in Orissa. Then he travelled to Mosali where he was caught under the suspicion of a dacoit and brought before the king, but he was soon released. Mahāvīra again returned to Tosali and found himself in great troubles. He was actually to be hanged here but was luckily rescued by Tosali Kshatriya. Then he arrived at Siddhatthapura from where he proceeded to Vayaggāma. For a period of six months, he had to bear great hardship at all these places. From Vayaggāma, he proceeded to Ālabhiyā and then to Seyaviyā and Sāvatthi. At last, passing through Kośāmbī, Vānārasi, Rāyagiha and Mithilā he spent the eleventh rainy season at Vaiśālī.

TWELFTH YEAR

From Vaiśālī, Mahāvīra came to Suṁsgumārapura which is identified with a hilly place near Chunar in Mirzapur District.[2] He proceeded thence to Bhogapura, which lay between Pāvā and Vaiśālī,[3] and to Nandiggāma, from where he travelled to Meṇḍhiyagāma. Afterwards he proceeded to Kośāmbī, where he received his alms after a period of four

1. JLAIDJC, p. 278.
2. R. SANKRITYAYANA: *Majjhima*, p. 61 n.
3 *Suttanipāta*, V. 1.38

months. From Kośāmbī, he set out for Sumaṅgalgāma and then for Pālayagāma. Finally, he reached Champā for spending the twelfth rainy season.

THIRTEENTH YEAR

From Champā Mahāvīra came to Jambhiyagāma. Kalyana Vijaya identifies it with Jambhigaon near the river Damodar in the Hazaribagh District,[1] but it must be located somewhere near modern Pāvāpurī in Bihar.[2] From this place, he reached Meṇḍhiyagāma. Then he visited Chhamāṇigāma where a cow-herd is said to have thrust iron nails into his ears. In this condition, Mahāvīra is said to have reached Majjhima Pāvā where the nails were removed from his ears.

MAHĀVĪRA'S PENANCE IN A CEMETERY AT UJJAIN

According to the Śvetāmbaras, Mahāvīra was born with three kinds of knowledge: *Matijñāna*, *Śrutajñāna* and *Avadhijñāna*. He also gained the fourth kind of knowledge, *Manaḥparyāyajñāna*, by which he knew the thoughts of all sentient beings possessing the five senses in the two and a half continents till some time after his initiation to asceticism. According to the Digambaras, Mahāvīra failed to gain it, though he performed meditation for six months, sitting absolutely motionless. At the end of the six months, he went to Kulapura where its ruler, Kulādhipa, came and did him honour, washed his feet with his own hands, and, having walked round him three times, offered him rice and milk. These Mahāvīra took as his first meal (*Paraṇum*) after fasting for six months. He returned to the forest and wandered about in it performing twelve kinds of penance, but still the knowledge was withheld from him. At last he visited Ujjayinī and did penance in a cemetery there when Rudra and his wife tried in vain to interrupt him. It was only after overcoming this temptation and again embarking upon his forest life of meditation that, according to the Digambara belief, he obtained *Manaḥparyāyajñāna*.[3]

KEVALAJÑĀNA

The period of twelve years spent in penance and medita-

1. Kvsbm, pp. 357, 370.
2. Jlaidjc, p. 289.
3. Sshj, p. 33.

tion was not fruitless, for in the thirteenth year, Mahāvira at last attained supreme knowledge and final deliverance from the bonds of pleasure and pain. The Jainas themselves have described this most important moment of the prophet's life:

"During the thirteenth year, in the second month of summer, in the fourth fortnight, the light (fortnight) of *Vaiśākha*, on its tenth day, called *Suvrata*, while the moon was in conjunction with the asterism *Uttara-Phalguni*, when the shadow had turned towards the east, and the first wake was over, outside of the town Jṛimbhikagrāma on the northern bank of the river Ṛijupālikā, in the field of the householder Sāmāga, in a north-eastern direction from an old temple, not far from a *Sāl* tree, in a squatting position with joined heels exposing himself to the heat of the Sun, with the knees high and the head low, in deep meditation, in the midst of abstract meditation, he reached *Nirvāṇa*, the complete and full, the unobstructed, unimpeded, infinite and supreme, best knowledge and intuition, called *Kevala*."

When the venerable Mahāvira had become an *Arhat* and a *Jina*, he was a *Kevalin*, omniscient and comprehending all objects; he knew all the conditions of the world, of gods, men and demons; whence they come, where they go, whether they are born as men or animals, or become gods or hell-beings; their food, drink, doings, desires, open and secret deeds, their conversation and gossip and the thoughts of their minds; he saw and knew all the conditions in the whole world of all living beings.[1]

At this time, Mahāvira (the great hero) or Jina (the conqueror) was forty-two years old; and from this age, he entered upon a new stage of life. that of a religious teacher and the head of a sect called the Nirgranthas, 'free from fetters'. He went from place to place for the propagation of his doctrine, and for making converts. His first declaration about himself aroused confidence among his followers and urged them to follow his example in their own life. The Buddhist texts give us an idea of his first declaration which is as follows:

I am all-knowing and all-seeing, and possessed of an infinite knowledge. Whether I am walking or standing still,

1- *Āchā*, II, 15, 25-26; *Kalpa*, 120, 121.

whether I sleep or remain awake, the supreme knowledge and intuition are present with me—constantly and continuously. There are, O Nirgranthas, some sinful acts you have done in the past, which you must now wear out by this acute form of austerity. Now that here you will be living restrained in regard to your acts, speech, and thought, it will work as the non-doing of *Karma* for future. Thus, by the exhaustion of the force of past deeds through penance and the non-accumulation of new acts, (you are assured) of the stoppage of the future course, of rebirth from such stoppage, of the destruction of the effect of *Karma*, from that, of the destruction of pain, from that, of the destruction of mental feelings, and from that, of the complete wearing out of all kinds of pain."[1]

FIRST SERMON

When Mahāvīra attained kevalahood, a *Samavaśaraṇa* (religious conference) was held on the bank of the river Ujjuvāliyā, but it is said that the first discourse of Mahāvīra remained unsuccessful. Then after traversing twelve *yojanas*, he is said to have returned to Majjhima Pāvā where the second *Samavaśaraṇa* was convened in the garden of Mahāsena. Here after a long discussion on various religious and philosophic points, Mahāvīra converted to Jainism the eleven learned Brāhmaṇas who had gone there to attend the great sacrifice performed by a rich Brāhmaṇa named Somila.

According to the Digambara scriptures, even after obtaining *Kevalajñāna* (Enlightenment) at Jṛimbhikagrāma, Mahāvīra did not break his vow of silence taken from the time of *Pravrajyā*, and wandering continuously for sixtysix days in silence, reached Rājagṛiha, the capital of Magadha. Outside the city of Rājagṛiha, at Vipulāchala where he settled, a *Samavaśaraṇa* was held for his first sermon. First of all he converted eleven learned Brāhmaṇas, including Indrabhūti Gautama, who were known as his disciples (*Gaṇadharas*). King Śreṇika with the members of the royal family, including his queen Chetanā, and the whole army came to the *Samavaśaraṇa* to pay homage to Mahāvīra as well as to listen to his first sermon. It is said that the king asked him several questions

1. *Majjh.* I, pp. 92-93.

concerning the faith and all of them were satisfactorily answered.

ELEVEN DISCIPLES (GAṆADHARAS)

First of all, Mahāvīra by his preaching converted to Jainism the eleven learned Brāhmaṇas who became his disciples, his eleven *Gaṇadharas*. They listened to Mahāvīra's discourses and heard the gentle, thoughtful answers he gave to all questions. Finally, being convinced of the truth of his views, they became his disciples or *Gaṇadharas*. The eldest was Indrabhūti, then followed Agnibhūti, Vāyubhūti, Vyakta, Sudharmā, Maṇḍikata, Mauryaputra, Akampita, Achalabhrātā, Metārya and Prabhāsa. The first three Gaṇadharas were brothers and belonged to the Gautama *Gotra*, and were residents of Gobbaragāma. The fourth belonged to the Bhāradvāja *Gotra* and was the resident of Kollāga Sannivesa; the fifth belonged to the Agni Veśyāyana *Gotra* and was the resident of Kollāga Sannivesa; the sixth belonged to the Vasishṭha *Gotra* and was the resident of Moriya Sannivesa; the seventh belonged to the Kāśyapa *Gotra* and was the resident of Moriya Sannivesa; the eighth belonged to the Gautama *Gotra* and was the resident of Mithilā; the ninth belonged to the Hārīta *Gotra* and was resident of Kośala; the tenth belonged to the Kauḍinya *Gotra* and was the resident of Tuṅgika Sannivesa; and the eleventh belonged to the same *Gotra* and was the resident of Rājagṛiha. These Gaṇadharas were all Brāhmaṇa teachers, and all except Indrabhūti and Sudharmā, died during the life-time of Mahāvīra. They are said to have been versed in the twelve *Aṅgas*, the fourteen *Pūrvas* and the whole *Gaṇipiḍaga* (the basket of the Gaṇis).[1]

The Digambaras have some different names for these *Gaṇadharas* and give a different account of Gautama's conversion. According to Guṇabhadra[2] the eleven names are as follows: Indrabhūti, Vāyubhūti, Agnibhūti, Sudharmā, Maurya, Maundra, Putra, Maitreya, Akampana, Andhavela or Anvachela and Prabhāsa. Indrabhūti became a very learned

1. *Āva. Nir.* 658-660.
2. *Uttara Purāṇa*, 24, 373-374.

pandita and grew extremely vain of his learning. One day, however, an old man appeared and asked him to explain a certain verse to him. Mahāvīra had, the old man said, repeated the *Śloka* to him, but had immediately afterwards become so lost in meditation that he could get no explanation of it from the saint, and yet he felt that he could not live unless he knew the meaning. The verse contained references to *Kāla* and *Dravya, Pañcha Astikāya, Tattva* and *Leśyā*, not one of which could Gautama understand, but being too true a scholar to pretend to a knowledge which he did not possess, he sought out Mahāvīra to ask for an explanation. The moment he was in the presence of the great ascetic, all his pride in his fancied learning fell from him, and he besought Mahāvīra to teach him. He not only became a convert himself, but took over with him his five hundred pupils and his three brothers.[1] In the Digambara Jaina *Paṭṭāvalis*, Sudharmā comes after Indrabhūti, and Sudharmā was also known by the name of Lohārya.

One significant fact about these *Gaṇadharas* is that all of them were Brahmins , which proves that among the Brahmins also an ideological revolution was taking place and compelling them to give up their traditional grooves of thoughts advocating ritualism. Further, it was this intelligentsia that predominantly included the Brahmins who helped him spread his faith.

FOUR ORDERS OF THE JAINA COMMUNITY (*SAṀGHA*)

Mahāvīra possessed a unique power of organization. By his wonderful personality and organizational skill, he attracted a large number of people, both men and women, to be his disciples. From them therefore grew the four orders of his community: monks, nuns, laymen, and laywomen.

The chief among his followers were the fourteen thousand monks placed under the charge of Indrabhūti Gautama. Mahāvīra resolved to combat by regulations and organization those special temptations and dangers which beset ascetics in their wandering life. For this purpose, he divided fourteen

1. SSHJ, pp. 61-62.

thousand monks into nine regular schools called *Gaṇas*, placing each school under the headship of one of his chief disciples or *Gaṇadharas*. The leading *Gaṇadhara* had five hundred monks under him, but some of the others had only three hundred or two hundred and fifty. These *Gaṇadharas* were to guide and instruct separate groups of Nirgranthas.

Besides the fourteen thousand monks, a great multitude of women followed Mahāvīra, and of these some thirtysix thousand actually renounced the world and became nuns. At their head was Chandanā, a first cousin of Mahāvīra's, or, as other accounts have it, his aunt.

Mahāvīra's third Order consisted of laymen numbering about one hundred and fiftynine thousand with Śaṅkha Śataka at their head. These laymen were householders who could not actually renounce the world but they at least could observe the five small vows called *aṇuvrata*. The similarity of their religious duties, differing not in kind but in degree, brought about the close union of laymen and monks. Most of these regulations meant to govern the conduct of laymen were intended apparently to make them participate, in a measure and for some time, in the merits and benefits of monastic life without obliging them to renounce the world altogether. "The genius for organization which Mahāvīra possessed". S. STEVENSON rightly observes, "is shown in nothing more clearly than in the formation of this and the order of laymen. These two organizations gave the Jaina a root in India that the Buddhists never obtained, and that root firmly planted amongst the laity enabled Jainism as we have seen, to withstand the storm that drove Buddhism out of India."[1]

Their fourth and last Order consisted of devout laywomen or *Śrāvikās* numbering about three hundred and fiftyeight thousand with Sulasā and Revatī as their heads. Their household duties prevented their becoming nuns but still they served the ascetics in many ways. The number of members in the four Orders of the Jaina Community is exaggerated, but these is little doubt that Mahāvīra converted a large number of people to Jainism.

1. SSHJ. p. 67.

The Digambaras believe that Mahāvīra did not travel alone but that wherever he went he was accompanied by all monks and nuns who had entered his Order. He preached in a language which they call *An-aksharī*, which was unintelligible to the common people; so Gautama acted as his interpreter and translated all he said into Ardha-Māgadhī.[1]

PLACES OF RAINY SEASONS (CHATURMĀSA)

The Jaina *Kalpasūtra* gives the names of the places where Mahāvīra spent one or more rainy seasons since he became an ascetic after renouncing the world. He stayed the first rainy season in Aṣṭhikagrāma, three rainy seasons in Champā and Pṛishṭichampā, twelve in Vaiśālī and Vaṇija-grāma, fourteen in Rājagṛiha and Nālandā, six in Mithilā, two in Bhadrikā, one in Ālabhikā, one in Paṇitabhūmi, one in Śrāvastī and the last one in the town of Pāpā in king Hastipāla's office.[2] This list is neither exhaustive nor chronological though it covers broadly the fortytwo years of his itinerary. It is rather difficult to distinguish the places he visited during and after the period of his ascetic life merely on the basis of the list supplied by the *Kalpa Sūtra*. There is no doubt that the *Kalpa Sūtra's* authority on the itinerary of Mahāvīra is ancient and fairly reliable. It gives us a fair idea of the area over which he wandered propagating his faith. When the places are correctly identified, we come to know that this area roughly covered the modern state of Bihar and some parts of Bengal and U.P.

The Jain tradition which mentions Mahāvīra's visit to Vītibhaya, the capital of Sindhu Sovīra, to preach to King Uddāyana, is of very doubtful veracity. The earliest reference to this visit is found in the *Bhagavatī*[3] and later on in certain *Chūrṇis* which perpetuate the tradition. It is quite possible that in later times, when Jainism spread to Western India, the Jainas, in order to impress the masses of this region, wanted to

1. SSHJ, p. 41.
2. *Kalpa*, 122.
3. *Bhag*, pp. 5-6 ff.

point out that their association with them was not new. In order to trace the beginning of this association from the earliest times they concocted the story of Mahāvīra's visit to King Uddāyana.

The late Jaina works describe Mahāvīra's itinerary exhaustively and chronologically, but the description does not seem to be fully reliable. After attaining *Kevalajñāna*, Mahāvīra spent no less than thirty rainy seasons at the following places yearwise—(1) Rājagṛiha, (2) Vaiśālī, (3) Vāṇijyagrāma, (4) Rājagṛiha, (5) Vāṇijyagrāma, (6) Rājagṛiha, (7) Rājagriha, (8) Vaiśālī, (9) Vaiśālī, (10) Rājagṛiha, (11) Vāṇijyagrāma, (12) Rājagṛiha, (13) Rājagṛiha, (14) Champā, (15) Mithilā, (16) Vānijyagrāma, (17) Rājagṛiha, (18) Vāṇijyagrāma, (19) Vaiśālī, (20) Vaiśālī, (21) Rājagṛiha, (22) Nālandā, (23) Vaiśālī, (24) Vaiśālī, (25) Rājagṛiha, (26) Nālandā, (27) Mithilā, (28)Mithilā, (29) Rājagṛiha, and (30) Āpāpāpurī.[1]

INFLUENCE ON LAY FOLLOWERS (ŚRĀVAKAS)

First of all, Mahāvīra seems to have tried to attract those householders who formed a large body of lay disciples by laying down certain rules of conduct. Gautama Indrabhūti was taken to task by the Master when he sought to claim a difference in degree in this respect between a recluse and a lay disciple.[2] The gift of supernormal vision was no monopoly of any Order or caste or sex. In this matter, Mahāvīra made no distinction between men and men, or between men and women. He did not enjoin one set of rules for male recluses and another for those of the fair sex, one set of rules for male lay disciples and another for female lay disciples. When he wandered about in the country, he was accompanied by male as well as female recluses.

Mahāvīra not only taught his followers to observe penances and live a life of restraint in all possible ways but also watched how they had been progressing. He also encouraged them in the study of the *Pūrvas* and in developing their power of reasoning and arguing. The Buddhist records themselves attest that there were some able and powerful disputants among

1 NATA, pp. 396-400.

2. *Uvā*, 1.

the Nirgrantha recluses and disciples.[1]

The lay disciples of Mahāvīra and the lay supporters of his Order, both male and female, are all mentioned as persons of opulence and influence. At the same time, they were noted for their piety and devotion. Their contemporaries, including kings and princes, consulted them on many affairs and matters. Among them, Ānanda and his wife Śivanandā from Vāṇijagrāma, Kāmadeva and his wife Bhadrā from Champā, Chūlanipriya and his wife Śyāmā, Sūradeva and his wife Dhanyā from Bārāṇasī, Chullasataka and his wife Pushyā from Kampilyapura, Kundakolita and his wife from Kampilyapura, Sardalaputra and his wife Agnimitrā from Polāsapura and Mahasataka from Rājagṛiha and Nandinīpriya and his wife Aśvinī, and Salatipriya and his wife Phālguni were the most well-known lay disciples of Mahāvīra.

The Pāli *Upāli Sūtra*[2] introduces us to the rich householder Upāli of Balakagrāma, near Nālandā, who was a lay disciple of Mahāvīra and a liberal supporter of the recluses of his Order, both male and female. We are indeed told that a very large number of the inhabitants of Balakagrāma, headed by Upāli, became lay disciples of Mahāvīra. The banker Mṛigāra or Mṛigadhara of Śrāvastī, father-in-law of the Buddhist lady Visākhā, is mentioned as a lay disciple of Mahāvīra and a lay supporter of the Nirgrantha recluses.

The Jaina *Bhagavatī Sūtra* speaks of two other rich householders Vijaya and Sudarśana, among the lay disciples of Mahāvīra. Of these the former was a citizen of Rājagṛiha.

ROYAL PATRONAGE

Not only the rich bankers and merchants, but even kings, queens, princes, and ministers became lay disciples of the Jaina Tīrthaṅkara Mahāvīra. His personal connections with the various rulers were through his mother, Triśalā, the Lichchhavi princess, and his maternal uncle, Cheṭaka, the king of Vaiśālī. According to Jaina traditions, kings like Śreṇika,[3] Kūṇika,[4] Cheṭaka,[5] Pradyota,[6] Śatānīka, Dadhivā-

1. *Majjh*, I. p. 227.
2. *Majjh*, I, 371-387.
3. *Nāyā*, p. 146; *Sthānā*, p. 458, 6; *Uttarā*, XX.
4. *Aup*, 44-46.
5. *Āva*, *Chū*, II, p. 164.
6. *Bhag*, 442.

hana,[1] Udāyana,[2] Vīangaya, Vīrajasa, Śañjaya, Śaṅkha, Kāsivaddhaṇa[3] and others are said to be his followers. Queens like Prabhāvatī of Udāyana,[4] Mṛigāvatī and Jayantī of Kośāmbī,[5] queens of king Śreṇika and Pradyota,[6] and princesses like Chandanā,[7] the daughter of the king of Champā followed Jainism. Princes called Atimukta,[8] Padma,[9] grandsons of Śreṇika, Megha, Abhaya and others[10] are said to have joined the Order of Jainism. The royal patronage must have facilitated the spread of Jainism.

Both Jainism and Buddhism claim most of the contemporary rulers of this period as followers of their respective religions. It seems that it was the general policy of the rulers of this and even of later times to show reverence to the teachers of different sects. As Śreṇika's father is said to be a follower of the Pārśvanātha sect[11] which had also its stronghold at Rājagṛiha, it is natural that Bimbisāra was inclined towards Jainism. The *Uttarādhyayana Sūtra*[12] relates how Bimbisāra, 'the lion of the kings' with the greatest devotion visited the other 'Lion of homeless ascetics' (*Aṇagāra-Siham*) at a *chaitya* with his wives, servants and relations, and became a staunch believer in the Law. R.K. Mookerji and other historians[13] have identified this ascetic with Mahāvīra because of the expression *Aṇagāra Siham*, while others[14] consider him to be a different ascetic, Anāthi of the Nirgrantha sect. His Jaina leanings

1. *Āva, Chū*, II, p. 207.
2. *Bhag*, pp. 556 ff.
3. *Sthānā*, p. 430 b.
4. *Āva*, p. 299.
5. *Bhag*, 12. 2.
6. *Āva, Chū*, p. 91. *Anta*, 7, p. 43
7. *Bhag*, p. 458, 6.
8. *Anta*, III.
9. *Nāyā*, p. 32.
10. *Ibid.*, p 33; *Nāyā*. Chapt. 1; *Āva. Chū*, p. 115.
11. *Trī, Pu*. Cha, x, 6, 8.
12. *Uttarā*, xx, 58.
13. Hindu Civilization, The Age of Imperial Unity, p. 21.
14. Nata, p. 313.

may have been due to his wife Chellanā, who was a daughter of Cheṭaka of Vaiśālī. Hemachandra tells the story that "when the country was under a blight of cold, the king accompanied by Devī Chellanā went to worship Mahāvīra".[1] The fact that Mahāvīra passed fourteen rainy seasons at Rājagṛiha is sufficient to prove that he exercised some influence over both Śreṇika and Kūṇika, the rulers of Magadha. According to the Jaina texts,[2] Mahāvīra was always treated by them and other members of the royal family with the utmost respect. On one occasion, Śreṇika is said to have issued a proclamation promising financial support to the relatives of those who enter the Jaina holy order.[3]

Śreṇika's son Kūṇika is represented in the Jaina texts as a Jaina. These texts[4] are partial in freeing him from the charge the Buddhist texts level against him. The *Aupapātika Sūtra* throws special light on the cordial relations between Kūṇika and Mahāvīra. Kūṇika is known to have appointed a special officer known as *Pravṛitti Vāduka Purusha* to inform him about the wanderings and daily routine of Mahāvīra. It contains an account of Mahāvīra's *Samośaraṇa* in Champā and Kūṇika's pilgrimage to this place. He was a frequent visitor to Mahāvīra with his queens and royal retinue. He had an intimate connection with him both at Vaiśālī and Champā, and openly declared before Mahāvīra and his disciples his faith in him as the true teacher who had made clear the true path of religion based on renunciation and non-violence. Kūṇika was succeeded by his son Udayabhadra, who in the lifetime of his father served him as the Viceroy at Champā. He was a devout Jaina, fasting on the 8th and 14th *tithis*.[5] He is also known to have built a Jaina shrine (*chaityagṛiha*) at the centre of the town, Pāṭaliputra.

In the Buddhist texts, Śreṇika and Kūṇika are known by the names of Bimbisāra and Ajātaśatru and both were devot-

1. *Tri. Pu. Cha*, X, 6. 10, 11.
2. *Daśāśrutaskandha, Anuttaropapātika Daśāṁga* and *Jñātādharmakathā*.
3. *Bihar* through the Ages, p. 127.
4. *Aup*, 12, 27, 30; Hemachandra's *Pariśishṭaparvan*, canto IV; *Āva. Sū*, pp. 684, 687.
5. *Āva, Sū*, p. 690.

ed to the Buddha. Bimbisāra accepted Buddhism, and his conversion was celebrated by inviting the Buddha and his disciples to meals which he himself served at the palace, and then by announcing his donation of the park, Veluvana, to the Buddha and the *Saṁgha*.[1] At another time, when the Buddha had no money with which to pay the ferry-man who carried him across the Gaṅgā, the emperor granted remission of these ferry charges to all ascetics out of his regard for the Master. After the murder of his father, Ajātaśatru paid a visit to the Buddha in his Mango-grove. He also erected a *stūpa* over the relics of the Lord Buddha. He gave full facilities for the holding of the General Council of the Buddhists in the Saptaparṇī cave at Rājagṛiha shortly after the Buddha's death.

At the time of Mahāvīra, Udāyana was a very powerful monarch of Sindhu Sauvīra. He is said to have been related to Mahāvīra through his wife Prabhāvatī, a daughter of king Cheṭaka. It is said that once Udāyana thought of paying a visit to Mahāvīra, who was in Champā at that time, and that the latter knew his thoughts and came down to his capital Vītabhaya in order to ordain him. Udāyana anointed Keśīkumāra, his sister's son, on the throne and joined the order under Mahāvīra.[2] He is known to have attained perfection.[3] The Buddhist scriptures[4] describe Udrāyaṇa or Rudrāyaṇa of Sindhu Sauvīra, with Roruka as his capital, as a Buddhist. It is said that an image of the Buddha was sent by king Bimbisāra to king Udāyana to acquaint him with the Buddhist religion. In course of time, he gave his throne to his son Śikhaṇḍī and joined the Buddhist order under the influence of his queen Chandraprabhā.

According to Jaina traditions, Pradyota, a follower of Mahāvīra, tried all he could for the propagation of Jainism. Mahāvīra was related to Pradyota, because Śivā, the daughter of his maternal uncle Cheṭaka was married to him. Pradyota is said to have installed the *Jīvanta* (life-time) *Svāmī* images of

1. *Vinaya*, I, 39.
2. *Bhag*, 13. 6.
3. *Uttarā*, XVIII, 48.
4. *Avadānakalpalatā*, 40; *Divyāvadāna*, 37.

Mahāvīra at Ujjain, Daśapura and Vidiśā.[1] According to the Buddhists, Pradyota was converted to Buddhism by Mahākachchāyana.[2]

Cheṭaka, the ruler of Vaiśālī, was a follower of Mahāvīra. It was only due to his influence that Vaiśālī became a stronghold of Jainism and that Mahāvīra visited this place from time to time. Cheṭaka had seven daughters, the eldest of whom was married to king Udayana of Vatsa and the youngest to King Śreṇika Bimbisāra of Magadha. One joined the religious Order of Mahāvīra and the other four were married to the members of the royal family. There may be some truth in the suggestion made by C.J. SHAH that these princesses were instrumental in the propagation of Jainism in Northern India.[3]

It is significant that Buddhist books do not mention Cheṭaka at all, though they tell us about the constitutional government of Vaiśālī. Buddhists took no notice of him as his influence was used in the interest of their rivals. Siṁha, a Lichchhavi general, was among the lay disciples of the Jaina Tīrthaṅkara.[4]

Looking at the great importance of Champā in the Jaina annals, there is nothing strange if one assumes that its ruler, Dadhivāhana, followed Jainism and held Mahāvīra in high esteem. His daughter Chandanā or Chandanabālā was the first woman who embraced Jainism shortly after Mahāvīra had attained the *Kevala*.[5] As Champā became a great centre of Jainism, Mahāvīra spent three of the rainy seasons at this place.

The ruler of Kauśāmbī was king Śatānīka to whom was married Mṛigāvatī, the third daughter of Cheṭaka.[6] Both the king and the queen were devotees of Mahāvīra and followers of the Jaina Order. The Jaina tradition also affirms that the king's Minister (*Amātya*) and his wife were Jainas by faith.

1. KMA, p. 119.
2. *Ibid*, p 115.
3. Jainism in Northern India, pp. 88 f.
4. *Vin*, vi, 4, 8.
5. *Āva. Nir*, 520 ff; *Āva. Ṭī*. p. 294 f.
6. *Bhag*. 12, 2.

Śatānīka's son and successor was Udayana. The Jaina literature claims him to be a follower of the Jaina Order. On the other hand, the Buddhist scriptures tell us that Udayana was at first not favourably inclined towards Buddhism, but later, however, he became a devotee of the Buddha.

Sāvatthi, Bārāṇasī, Kampillapura, Mithilā, Polāsapura and Ālabhia were all important towns visited by Mahāvīra within the kingdom of king Jiyasattu.[1] Jiyasattu (*Jita-śatru*, conqueror of enemies) seems to be a title of the king like the epithet *Devānampiya* of Aśoka. Jiyasattu seems to be no other than Pasenadi or Prasenajit of Kośala. The *Rāyapaseṇiya Sutta*[2] records a dialogue between Keśī and Paesi, when the latter, being influenced by the teachings of the former, became a *Samaṇovāsaga*. Keśī, a follower of Pārśva, was a Jaina recluse who is represented in the *Uttarādhyayana Sūtra* as the contemporary of Mahāvīra and Gautama Indrabhūti. Paesi or Pradeśī may be identified with Pasenadi or Prasenjit of Kośala.[3] From the Buddhist texts, it is known that Prasenajit was a great admirer of the Buddha though he was not converted to Buddhism.

After giving up his flourishing kingdom of Daśārṇa, Daśamabhadra, who was the contemporary of Mahāvīra, became a monk.[4] Daśamabhadra is not known from any other source. Daśārṇa is identified with Vīdiśā or Bhilsa region in Madhya Pradesh.[5] The early association of Jainism with

1. *Uvā*, pp. 84-5, 90, 95, 105, 160 and 163.
2. B.C. Law: Some Jaina canonical *Sūtras*, p. 74; 162-204. The Pali counterpart of this Jaina *Sūtra* is undoubtedly the dialogue known as the *Pāyāsī Suttanta* in the *Dīgha* Nikāya. In the Pāli *Suttanta*, the dialogue is put into the mouth of the Buddhist recluse, Kumārakassapa, the Flower-Talker (*Chitra kathi*) and the Chieftain Pāyāsi of Setavyā, a town within the kingdom of Pasenadi of Kośala.
3. Nata, p 369. According to the *Dīghanikāya*, Pradeśi was a vassal of Presenajit while on the evidence of the *Rāyapaśeṇiya Śutta*, Jitaśatru was the ruler under Pradeśī. It seems more reasonable to say that Pradeśī and Jitaśatru are one and the same ruler who may be identified with Prasenajit of Kośala.
4. *Uttarā*, XVIII, 44.
5. Geb, p. 26.

this area is clear even from the Jaina traditions which aver that Vajrasvāmī and other Jain pontiffs obtained liberation in the hills, Kuñjarāvarta and Rathāvarta, in the neighbourhood of Vidiśā.[1]

Karakaṇḍu, king of Kaliṅga, is known to have adopted the faith of the Jinas, and, after placing his son on the throne, exerted himself as 'Śramaṇa'.[2] This proves the existence of Jainism in this Province from very early times, but it is very difficult to say when Karakaṇḍu lived in Kaliṅga. It was a Jaina stronghold, at least from the time of Lord Mahāvīra. The Jaina *Harivaṁśa Purāṇa* informs us that Lord Mahāvīra had preached his faith in Kaliṅga. The *Haribhadrīya Vṛitti* on *Āvaśyaka* confirms Mahāvīra's visit to the country of Kaliṅga and adds that the king of that country was a friend (or relation) of his father's.[3] The reference to Nandarāja as having taken away the image of Jina from Kaliṅga in the inscription of Khāravela is very interesting as it proves the existence of image-worship among the Jainas even in the fifth century B.C.

There are traditions even of Mahāvīra's visit to South India. From the *Jīvandhara Charita* of Bhāskara, it is known that Jīvandhara, who was the ruling chief of this region at this time, was a Jaina. He cordially received Mahāvīra and became an ascetic after obtaining *dīkshā* from him.[4] Jīvandhara seems to be an imaginary name. Actually speaking, there was no such ruler whose kingdom extended to and comprised Southern India during this period.

Mahāvīra is known to have converted to Jainism a prince named Ārdraka who became a monk.[5] He was so much influenced by the teachings of Mahāvīra that he always supported Jainism in his disputations with the teachers of different religions. This Ārdraka is identified with the prince of the Persian emperor Kurusha (558-530 B.C.). Both the emperor and the prince are believed to have sent presents to the king

1. Kma, p. 121.
2. *Uttarā*, XVIII, 45, 47.
3. A.C. Mittal: Early History of Orissa, p. 136.
4. Karnatak through the Ages.
5. *Sūtra*, II, 6.

Śreṇika and his son Abhayakumāra of Magadha who also in return despatched their presents to them. It is said that first of all Abhayakumāra enlightened Ārdraka with the teachings of Mahāvīra. In course of time, Ārdraka joined the Order of Mahāvīra.[1]

On the basis of an evidence furnished by a very late period, Mahāvīra is known to have propagated his message even in the region now known as Rajasthan. There is an inscription of 1276 A.D. which begins with a verse which tells us that Mahāvīra in person came to Śrīmāla.[2] This is supported by the *Śrīmālamāhātmya*, a work of *c.* the thirteenth century A.D., which gives an account of the dissemination of Jainism in Śrīmāla. Disgusted with the behaviour of the Brāhmaṇas of Srīmāla, Gautama Gaṇadhara went to Kashmir where he was converted to Jainism by Mahāvīra. After his return to Srīmāla, he converted the Vaiśyas to Jainism and composed the *Kalpa Sūtra*, the *Bhagavatī Sūtra*, *Mahāvīra Janmasūtra* and other works.[3] An inscription of 1369 A.D., found on the door of the chief shrine in Jīvantasvāmī Śrī Mahāvīra Jaina temple at Mungusthala Mahātīrtha, 7 km. west of Ābū Road, shows that Lord Mahāvīra visited Arbudabhūmi, and an image was consecrated by Śrī Keśī Gaṇadhara during the 37th year of the life of Mahāvīra.[4] These statements are of a very late date and, therefore, cannot be easily relied on. But from them it can be legitimately deduced that in the 13th century A.D., Jainism was considered to be a very old religion in Rajasthan.[5]

Not only the rulers but also several contemporary clans[6] were the followers of the religion of Mahāvīra. There are many stray references in the Jaina *Sūtras* which prove that the Lichchhavīs followed the Jaina faith. Their capital, Vaiśālī, formed one of the headquarters of the Jaina community during the days of Mahāvīra. Out of the fortytwo rainy seasons of

1. J.P. Jain: *Bhāratīya Itihāsa—eka Dṛishṭi*, pp. 67-68.
2. Pras. Wc., 1907, p. 35.
3. *Śrīmālapurāṇa*, pp. 633-663.
4. Apjls, No. 48.
5. Jainism in Rajasthan, p. 8.
6. Sbe, XLV, p. 339.

his ascetic life, Mahāvīra spent twelve at Vaiśālī. Like the Lichchhavīs, the Vajjis, who in fact cannot be strictly differentiated from the Lichchhavīs, came under the influence of Lord Mahāvīra, for Vaiśālī seems to have been regarded also as the metropolis of the entire Vajji Confederacy. The Jñātṛikas of Kuṇḍagrama, who formed one of the most important clans included in the Vajjian confederacy, were also his followers. The other clans of the Vajjian confederacy must have been naturally affected by the doctrines of Nātaputta. It is among these confederate Kshatriyas that Mahāvīra was born and found strong supporters of his religion. The Mallas also seem to have cherished a feeling of respect and sympathy for the great prophet and his doctrines. The Ugras and the Bhogas are repeatedly mentioned in several of the oldest sacred books as being among the most prominent of the earliest converts.

It is clear from the above discussion that though only a few of these kings can definitely be identified, the late tradition without much historical support brings nearly all the kings of North India in those days under the spiritual sway of Mahāvīra in one way or the other. While some of the names of these rulers seem to be imaginary, others might have flourished long after Mahāvīra. From this evidence only one significant conclusion can be drawn, namely, that in course of time, Jainism spread in different parts of India and received royal patronage. During the period of Mahāvīra, its influence seems to have been confined only to the modern states of Bihar and some parts of Bengal and U.P. and it is probable that most of the ruling chiefs of this area patronized Jainism.

MAHĀVĪRA AND THE BUDDHA

The evidence of Buddhist literature is adequate enough to prove that Mahāvīra was a contemporary of the Buddha. Although they had not personally met each other, there were occasions when they felt interested in knowing and discussing each other's views through some intermediaries. Dīrghatapasvī and Satyaka (Pāli Sachchaka) among the Nirgrantha recluses, and Abhaya, the prince, Upāli, the banker, and Simha, the Lichchhavī General among the Jaina laity, loom large among those intermediaries. While they are said to have halted at Nālandā, Vaiśālī and Rājagṛiha at one and the same time, they are not known to have seen each other.[1] Mahāvīra was senior in age to Buddha, the former predeceasing the latter by a few years.

That Mahāvīra and the Buddha were contemporaneous is proved by the synchronization of certain historical facts. When they had started their career as religious teachers and reformers, Śreṇika Bimbisāra and Ajātaśatru were powerful kings of Magadha; Aṅgā was annexed to the kingdom of Magadha, and the Vṛijji-Lichchhavīs of Vaiśālī and the Mallas of Kuśīnāra and Pāvā formed two powerful confederacies. Prasenjit was the monarch of Kośala, and Kāśī was annexed to the kingdom of Kośala.

It is not without reason that Mahāvīra has been represented in the *Abhayarājakumāra Sutta* as personally interested in the welfare of Devadatta who fomented a schism within the Buddhist Order of the time.[2] B.M. Barua suggests that Devadatta was a man with Jaina leaning.[3] It is probably under the influence of Mahāvīra's teaching that Devadatta insisted on having the five special rules introduced in the Buddhist Order.

SCHISMS

Even in the life-time of Mahāvīra, there arose schimatic tendencies in the Jaina Church. In the fourteenth year of Mahāvīra's becoming a prophet, his nephew and son-in-law, Jamāli, headed an opposition against him. Similarly, two years later, a holy man in the Jaina community, Tisagutta, made an attack on certain points in Mahāvīra's doctrine. Both of these schisms were, however, concerned with mere trifles, and seem to have caused no great trouble, as they were speedily stopped by the authority of the prophet himself. Jamāli, however, persisted in his heretical opinions until his death. The Digambaras seem to be ignorant of the earlier schisms.

NIRVĀṆA

Mahāvīra attained *Nirvāṇa* at the age of 72 at Pāvā. It

1 *NATA*. p. 402.
2. *Majjh*, I, pp 392-393.
3. Lmlt p. 17.

is said in the *Kalpasūtra*[1] that when Mahāvīra died, the eighteen confederate kings of Kāśī and Kośala, the nine Mallakīs and the nine Lichchhavīs instituted an illumination, saying "since the light of intelligence is gone, let us make an illumination of material matter."

There is a persistent Jaina tradition that Mahāvīra attained *Nirvāṇa* in 527 B.C. but this seems to have become controversial by an incorrect statement of Hemachandra's (1078-1172 A.D.) to the effect that 155 years after the *Nirvāṇa* of Mahāvīra, Chandragupta became king.[2] The whole problem was made more complicated and controversial by connecting it with Buddha's *Nirvāṇa*, the date of which has not yet been fully and authoritatively ascertained.[3] Scholars are therefore not unanimous about the date of the *Nirvāṇa* of Mahāvīra as they still hold different views.

In order to solve this problem of the date of Mahāvīra's *Nirvāṇa*, one should take a comprehensive view. It is well known from the different sources that Mahāvīra flourished in the age of Śreṇika (Bimbisāra) and Kūṇika (Ajātaśatru) of Magadha, Prasenajit of Kośala, Udayana of Vatsa, Pradyota of Avanti and Pushkarasārin of Taxila. It is also certain that he lived in the days of Maṅkhali Gośāla and Buddha. Maṅkhali Gośāla was his senior contemporary and died sixteen and a half years earlier, while Buddha was his junior contemporary and died afterwards. A Jaina tradition states that Mahāvīra attained *Nirvāṇa* in the 16th year of the reign of Kūṇika and the Buddhist tradition places the Buddha's *Nirvāṇa* in that king's 8th regnal year. The date of Mahāvīra's *Nirvāṇa* is said to have coincided with the date of the coronation at Ujjayinī of Pālaka, the son of Chaṇḍa Pradyota, the king of Avanti. We can be successful in determining the date of Mahāvīra's

1. *Kalpa*, 128.
2. *Pari.* VIII, 339.
3. The different Buddhist traditions place the date of the Buddha differently; the Ceylonese in 544 B.C., the Burmese in 501 B.C.; the Tibetan in 488 B.C. and the Cantonese in 486 B.C. (Some scholars have suggested even 477 B.C. or 453 B.C.) The recently advocated view is 483 B.C. See D.R. Bhandarkar Vol. I. pp. 329-330.

Nirvāṇa if we depend not only on the Buddhist but also on the Jaina and Brahmanical sources to fix up the dates of Mahāvīra's contemporary rulers and religious teachers.

THE THEORY OF MAHĀVĪRA'S NIRVĀṆA IN 467 B.C.

The theory that Mahāvīra's *Nirvāṇa* occurred in 467 B.C. was suggested long ago by H. JACOBI[1] and strongly supported by J. CHARPENTIER.[2] K.A. SASTRI,[3] who subscribes to the same opinion, supports this theory with almost the same arguments which are as follows.

1. This date is based on a tradition recorded by the great Jaina author, Hemachandra, namely, that there was a gap of 155 years between the death of Mahāvīra and the accession of Chandragupta Maurya. According to the Jaina tradition, the accession of Chandragupta Maurya at Ujjain took place in 312 B.C. Hence, the year of the *Nirvāṇa* is 467 B.C. Here the year 312 B.C. probably indicates the date of extension of the Mauryan rule over Ujjayinī in the reign of Chandragupta Maurya.

2. J. CHARPENTIER believed the year of Mahāvīra's *Nirvāṇa* to be 467 B.C. on the presumption that the Buddha's death definitely occurred in 477 B.C. According to the Buddhist texts, Mahāvīra and the Buddha were both contemporaries, and they flourished in the reign of Ajātaśatru.

3. He believed that no person of the name of Vikrama ever existed about 57 B.C. and further that there was discrepancy of 60 years between the account of other Jaina sources and that of Hemachandra who stated that Chandragupta Maurya came to the throne 155 years after Mahāvīra's death. Hence by deducting 60 years from the traditional period of 527 years before Christ, he arrived at the year 467 B.C.

4. According to the Jaina tradition, the Jaina Pontiff Sambhūtivijaya died exactly in the year following Chandragupta's accession, or 156 after Vīra. Bhadrabāhu, the succe-

1. Introductions to SBE, xxii and XLV, on Mahāvīra and his Predecessors, I, A, IX, pp. 156 ff.
2. IA, XLIII, pp. 118 ff; also see CAH, Vol. I, p. 156.
3. History of India. Pt. I, pp. 39-40.

ssor of Sambhūtivijaya; died fifteen years later. All Jaina traditions from Hemachandra downwards give 170 after Vīra as the year of Bhadrabāhu's death. This would be 297 B.C. if the date 467 B.C. is accepted as the year of Mahāvīra's death. The Jaina tradition also brings Bhadrabāhu into the closest connection with Chandragupta in whose reign the date 297 B.C. falls.

5. The *Kalpasūtra* in its present form is a compilation made 980 years after the passing away of Mahāvīra during the reign of Dhruvasena, king of Gujarat, but in another recension the number is 993. King Dhruvasena is known to have ruled from 526 to 540 A.D. From this, the date 467 B.C. is fixed as the year of Mahāvīra's *Nirvāṇa*.

While discussing the date of Gośāla's death, A.L. Basham[1] fixes the date of Mahāvīra's death in 468-467 B.C., which agrees with the date suggested by H. Jacobi on the basis of Hemachandra's *Pariśishṭaparvan* and supported by J. Charpentier. Prof. Basham accepts 483 B.C. as the date of the Buddha's *Nirvāṇa*. On the basis of the *Mahāvaṁśa* synchronism, the accession of Ajātaśatru must have occurred in the year 491 B.C. and the second campaign against the Vajjis in 481-480 B.C. There are two synchronisms for the date of Gośāla's death, the first being the tradition of its occurrence sixteen and a half years before that of Mahāvīra, and the second that of its taking place during the war between Magadha and Vaiśālī in the reign of Ajātaśatru-Kūṇiya. Of the two, the latter seems the more reliable. There were two campaigns of the war called *Mahāśilākaṇṭae* and *Rahamusale* respectively. A.L. Basham suggests that the first campaign, soon after which Gośāla died, must have taken place at some time between the date of Ajātaśatru's accession and the year preceding the Buddha's death. He held the view that the first campaign occurred in 485 B.C. and the death of Gośāla in 484 B.C., if a year is allowed for the news of the 'Battle of Great Stones' to spread to Sāvatthi and to become fixed in the popular consciousness. With regard to the death of Mahāvīra as taking place at Pāvā during the Buddha's lifetime and as mentioned

1. A.L. Basham: *History and Doctrines of the Ājīvikas*. pp. 66-78.

in the Pali scriptures, he considers it to be that of Gośāla at Sāvatthi, which the *Bhagavatī Sūtra* also mentions as having been accompanied by quarrel and confusion. The *Mahā-parinibbāna Sutta* records that the preparations for the campaign against the Vajjis were made in the last year of the Buddha's life while Mahāvīra was still alive during the course of war.

477 B.C.

JAMES HASTING[1] tries to fix the date of Mahāvīra's *Nirvāṇa* in *c.* 477 or 476 B.C. He comes to this conclusion by combining the Jaina date of Chandragupta's accession to the throne 155 years after the *Nirvāṇa* with the historical date of the same event in 322 B.C.

484 B.C.

In his attempt to discuss the date of Gośāla's death, A.F.R. HOERNLE[2] also fixed the date of Mahāvīra's *Nirvāṇa*. He accepts 482 B.C. as the 'practically certain' date of the Buddha's *Nirvāṇa*. King Bimbisāra, the father and predecessor of Ajātaśatru, was murdered by his son eight years before the *Nirvāṇa* or in 490 B.C. A.F.R. HOERNLE believes that for some years before this, Ajātaśatru was the *de facto* ruler, and that the war took place, not in the year of his legal, but of his *de facto* accession, which cannot have been long before the murder of Bimbisāra. H. JACOBI's theory of the later date of Mahāvīra's death he now rejects, in order to devise a chronological scheme according to which Mahāvīra may predecease the Buddha; but the *Bhagavatī* tradition of the sixteen years interval between the deaths of Mahāvīra and Gośāla he accepts without question. He therefore suggests 484 B.C. for the death of Mahāvīra and 500 B.C. for that of Gośāla and for the war and the *de facto* accession of Ajātaśatru.

486 B.C.

H.C. RAYCHAUDHURI[3] suggests 478 B.C. or 486 B.C. and 536 B.C. as the probable dates of Mahāvīra's *Nirvāṇa*, according

1. ERE, Vol. vii, p. 467.
2. *Ibid.*, Vol. I. pp. 260-61.
3. *An Advanced History of India*, p. 73.

to the Cantonese reckoning which places the death of the Buddha in 486 B.C., or according to the Ceylonese one which places it in 544 B.C., whichever is accepted as the basis. Between 478 B.C. and 486 B.C., the first date is said to be in conformity with Hemachandra's who is said to have placed Chandragupta's accession in M.E. 155, that is 323 B.C. in this case, which cannot be far from the truth, but that would be at variance with the clear evidence of the Buddhist canonical texts which make the Buddha survive his Jñātṛika rival. Hence he considers 486 B.C. to be a more likely date as it is also in keeping with the year of Ajātaśatru's accession. The Jaina statement that their Tīrthaṅkara dies some sixteen years after the accession of Kūṇika (Ajātaśatru) can be reconciled with the Buddhist tradition about the death of the same teacher before the eighth year of Ajātaśatru, if we assume that the Jainas, who refer to Kūṇika as the ruler of Champā, begin their reckoning from the accession of the prince to the viceregal throne of Champā while the Buddhists make the accession of Ajātaśatru to the royal throne of Rājagṛiha the basis for their calculation.

C.D. CHATTERJEE[1] also favours 486 B.C., because for him 483 B.C. is definitely the correct year of the Buddha's death and because he believes, on the basis of 'clear evidence of the Buddhist tradition on this question' that Mahāvīra predeceased the Buddha.

488 B.C.

H.C. SETH[2] suggests 488 B.C. as the date of Mahāvīra's death on the basis of the Buddhist tradition, assuming 487 B.C. as the date of the Buddha's death. The great difficulty in accepting 468 B.C. according to him is that it will place Mahāvīra's death several years after that of the Buddha. On the other hand, the tradition preserved in the Buddhist Pāli canon clearly says that Nigaṇṭha Nātaputta, i.e. Mahāvīra, died at Pāvā a little before the Buddha.

1. B.C. Law Volume, Pt. I, pp. 606-607, f.n. 30,
2. *Bhārata-Kaumudī*, Part II, pp. 817-838.

The traditional chronology given in Merutuṅga's *Vichāraśreṇī* puts Mahāvīra's *Nirvāṇa* 470 years before the Vikrama era All the Jaina traditions assign 40 years of reign to Nahavāṇa between the period of Mahāvīra's *Nirvāṇa* and Vikrama. This Nahavāṇa is generally identified with Nahapāṇa, the Mahākshatrapa of Kshaharāta family, who lived after the commencement of the Vikrama era. If we take out 40 years of Nahavāṇa from 470 years, the interval given in these traditions between Mahāvīra *Nirvāṇa* and the commencement of the Vikrama era, the difference between these two important events will be 430 years. This will give 488 B.C. as the date of Mahāvīra *Nirvāṇa*. This will place Mahāvīra's death about a year before that of the Buddha who died in 487 B.C. These two dates will reconcile most of the Buddhist as well as the Jaina traditions about these two great religious teachers.

490 B.C.

Y. Mishra[1] presupposes 487 B.C. as the date of Buddha's death, and then, by comparing the details of the lives of the Buddha and Mahāvīra, especially the places where they spent their rainy seasons, he comes to the conclusion that Mahāvīra died in 490 B.C. In order to find out the date of that specific rainy season when Mahāvīra died, he consulted the lives of the Buddha and Mahāvīra, *viz. Buddhacharyā* (in Hindi) by Rahula Sankrityayana and *Śramaṇa Bhagvān Mahāvīra* by Ratnaprabha Vijaya. In the *Buddhacharyā*, it is stated that Lord Buddha spent the 17th rainy season at Rājagṛiha, further in the *Mahāsakuludāyi Sutta*,[2] it is said that on that particular occasion, both Buddha and Nigaṇṭha Nātaputta were present. Taking 567 B.C. as the date of the birth of the Buddha, this comes to 516 B.C. By taking 561 B.C. as the date of the birth of Mahāvīra, it becomes clear that he spent his 16th rainy season in 516 B.C. at Rājagṛiha. In the rainy season of 513 B.C. also, both the Buddha and Mahāvīra were at Rājagṛiha.

1. Y. Mishra: An Early History of Vaiśālī, pp. 202-212.
2. *Majjh*, II. 3. 7.

The *Sāmaññaphala Sutta* tells us how king Ajātaśatru of Magadha paid visits to one after another of the six heretical teachers to hear their doctrines, and at last discontented with them all, he took refuge with the Buddha. This visit of Ajātaśatru to the Buddha took place in 491 B.C. The rainy season of 491 B.C., which was his forty-second rainy season, was passed by the Buddha at Śrāvastī. This Buddhist reference therefore means that sometime in the last month of the *Chāturmāsya*, the Buddha came to Rājagṛiha. Coming to Mahāvīra, it is known that he lived at Rājagṛiha in 491 B.C. during the rainy season of the forty-first year of his ascetic life. Thus it was possible for Ajātaśatru to meet the Buddha at Rājagṛiha after having met Mahāvīra. Mahāvīra passed his forty-second rainy season in 490 B.C. at Madhyamā Pāvā where he died.

Both from the Buddhist and the Jaina traditions, it is clear that both the Buddha and Mahāvīra were at Vaiśālī in 519 B.C. and that the conversion of Sīha to Buddhism also took place at the same time. The *Upālisutta* is also important, because the event took place at Nālandā when both the teachers were there in 491 B.C.

So the year 490 B.C. as the year of Mahāvīra's death is able not only to show that Buddha survived Mahāvīra but also to make both the teachers spend the same rainy season at Rājagṛiha, Vaiśālī and Nālandā.

498 B.C.

B.C. Law[1] advocated another theory when he postulated 498 B.C. as the date of Mahāvīra's *Nirvāṇa*. According to him, 527 B.C. and 544 B.C. as the dates of the demise of Mahāvīra and Buddha respectively cannot he harmonized with the historical facts connected with the lives of the two great teachers of India. Two things, he says, may be taken as certain: (1) that Mahāvīra predeceased the Buddha by 5 or 6, 7 or 8 or even 14 or 15 years; and (2) that Mahāvīra passed as a Jina before the Buddha. The authenticity of

1. LMLT, p. 53.

B.C. 544 or 543 as the date of Buddha's demise has been questioned by modern scholars who propose either 486 B.C. or 484 B.C. as the correct date. The figure 544 or 543 is accounted for as the date of the accession of Śreṇika Bimbisāra. Similarly, the figure 527 is accounted for as the date of the attainment of Jinahood by Mahāvīra. Accepting this date of Mahāvīra's Kevalīship, one has to compute the date of his birth as B.C. 570, and that of his demise as B.C. 498.

545 B.C.

K.P. Jayaswal fixed the date of Mahāvīra's *Nirvāṇa* in 545 B.C. His main argument was that since according to some Jaina *Paṭṭāvalīs*, it was the interval between Mahāvīra's *Nirvāṇa* and Vikrama's birth, and not his accession, which is said to have been 470 years, and since Vikrama ascended the throne and started his era at the age of 18 in 57 B.C., Mahāvīra's date should be pushed further back by 18 years. He tried to corroborate his theory by a statement of some of the other *Paṭṭāvalīs* which give 219 years as the interval between Mahāvīra and the accession of Chandragupta Maurya, which according to him is otherwise fixed in 325 B.C. He also tried to reconcile his chronology based upon the Jaina sources with the Purāṇic traditions, identified Vikrama with King Pulumāvi, the son of Gautmīputra Sātakarṇi, and fixed the Buddha's *Nirvāṇa* in 544 B.C.[1]

437 B.C.

S.V. Venkatesvara puts forth 437 B.C. as the date of Mahāvīra's *Nirvāṇa*. Believing that the Buddha died sometime between 485 and 453 B.C., and that he could not have died after Mahāvīra, this scholar surmises that 470 years' tradition relates to the Ānanda Vikrama era of 33 A.D.[2]

CRITICISM OF THE ABOVE THEORIES

Although some of the theories set forth above are well reasoned and convincing, they present some serious difficulties.

1. JBORS, 1, Pt. I, pp. 99-104.
2. JRAS, 1917, pp. 122-130.

The greatest defect of some of the above theories is that their advocates, H. JACOBI, J. CHARPENTIER, J. HASTING and A.L. BASHAM, based them on the statement of Hemachandra (12th Century A.D.). Chandragupta Maurya ascended the throne in M.E. (Mahāvīra era) 155. His statement is the solitary instance of this view and is at variance with all other Jaina sources, Digambara or Śvetāmbara, earlier or later than himself, that give this date as M.E. 210 or 215. This caused confusion and has misled these scholars. The *Tiloyapaṇṇati* of *Yativṛishabha* (5th century A.D.), the *Harivaṁśa* of Jinasena (783 A.D.), *Trilokasāra* of Nemichandra (973 A.D.), *Vichāraśreṇi* of Merutuṅga (1306 A.D.) and others mention 215 years.

That Pālaka mentioned in the lists was the son of King Chaṇḍa Pradyota of Ujjayinī and that during the period of 60 years allowed to Kūṇika and Udāyī he was ruling at Pāṭaliputra, are facts corroborated by some other sources. In connection with these dynastic chronologies, it may, however, be noted that it is not correct to treat them as referring to the kings of Magadha. All kings and dynasties mentioned in them are definitely known to be connected with Ujjayinī in Malwa or Western India. Of course, some of them ruled over a big empire covering other parts of India, including Magadha as well.

Curiously enough, even Hemachandra[1] in another context of the same work has admitted that the Nanda dynasty began in M.E. 60 and in another work of his[2] he gives the traditional date 527 B.C. when he mentions that Kumārapāla became a ruler 1669 years after Mahāvīra's *Nirvāṇa*. The year of Kumārapāla's accession to the throne is known to be 1143 A.D.

Another serious defect of these theories is that their advocates attempted to determine the date of Mahāvīra's *Nirvāṇa* on the basis of that of the Buddha's which itself is full of controversy. That has resulted in divergent conclusions. H. JACOBI and J. CHARPENTIER believed the date of Mahāvīra's

1. *Pari*, VI, 243.
2. *Tri. Pu. Ch*, X, 12, 45-46.

Nirvāṇa to be 467 B.C. on the assumption that the Buddha's death occurred definitely in 477 B.C. A.L. BASHAM and A.F.R. HOERNLE accepted 483 B.C. as the date of the Buddha's *Nirvāṇa*, and then attempted to fix the dates of Gośāla and Mahāvīra. H.C. RAYCHAUDHURI, B.C. LAW, H.C. SETH, and Y. MISHRA first presupposed 486-487 B.C. as the date of Buddha's death, and then attempted to fix Mahāvīra's death. K.P. JAYASWAL, by accepting the Buddha's death in 544 B.C., fixed Mahāvīra's *Nirvāṇa* in 545 B.C. The proper approach to the problem is that one should settle the date of the Buddha's *Nirvāṇa* by accepting that of Mahāvīra in 527 B.C. as it is not controversial.

H. JACOBI, J. CHARPENTIER, A.L. BASHAM H.C. SETH and K.P. JAYASWAL wrongly think that the Buddha predeceased Mahāvīra. From the study of the early Buddhist texts, it is clear that Mahāvīra was the senior contemporary of the Buddha ; that he attained *Kevalajñāna* earlier and that he predeceased the Buddha by 5, or 6, 7 or 8, even 14 or 15 years. These Buddhist texts record the death of Mahāvīra or Nigaṇṭha Nātaputta as taking place at Pāvā during the Buddha's life time and as being accompanied by serious confusion and quarrelling among his supporters.

The view held by some scholars that there are irregularities in the list of kings and dynasties ruling from the period of the *Nirvāṇa* of Mahāvīra to 57 B.C. or 78 A.D. is not wholly correct. On the other hand, many scholars also believe that the Jaina traditions have definite historical background. In spite of minor discrepancies in dates, the general account given in them is fully in keeping with the known facts of history.[1] Here the question does not relate to the verification of individual dynasty and king but to the determination of the general correctness of the date of Mahāvīra's *Nirvāṇa* given in the Jaina traditions.

All the Jaina traditions assign forty years of reign to Naḥavāṇa before Vikrama. H.C. SETH thinks that this Nahavāṇa or Nahapāṇa, the Mahākshatrapa of Kshaharāta

1. R.C. MAJUMDAR, *The Age of Imperial Unity*, pp. 155-156.

family, lived after Vikrama, and by taking 40 years out of 470, he considers 430 years to be the difference between the date of Mahāvīra's *Nirvāṇa* and the commencement of the Vikrama era. Against this, it may be suggested that *Nahavāṇa* here means the Śaka rule in Ujjayinī before Vikrama in the second or first century B.C. This Jaina tradition is supported even by numismatic evidence.[1] Copper coins of five rulers, viz., Hamugama, Valāka, Mahu, Dāsa and Sauma, have been scooped out from Ujjain and from the neighbouring region. With the help of palaeography, the historian can place these rulers in the second and first century B.C. K.D. BAJPAI tried to prove that the rulers who issued the coins were Śakas, the predecessors of the two well known dynasties of Bhūmaka and Chashṭana. The names on the coins resemble those of the Śaka chiefs already known from inscriptions and other coins. On the reverse, there are figures such as those of frog, moon on hill, tree within railing; or a double-orbed Ujjain symbol.

J. K. MUKHTAR[2] attempts a refutation of the theory propounded by J. CHARPENTIER as also by K.P. JAYASWAL by trying to prove that Vikrama era started neither with the birth nor with the coronation of Vikrama but with his death, and that therefore no addition or reduction in the traditional interval of 470 years was needed.

Y. MISHRA came to the conclusion that the death of Mahāvīra occurred in 490 B.C. when he compared the details of the lives of the Buddha and Mahāvīra, especially the places where they spent their rainy seasons. For this, he consulted *Buddhacaryā* (in Hindi) by R. SANKRITYAYANA and *Śramaṇa Bhagvān Mahāvīra* by RATNA PRABHA VIJAYA. In the very early Jaina and Buddhist scriptures, no chronological description of the rainy seasons spent by Lord Mahāvīra and the Buddha have been given. Both R. SANKRITYAYANA and RATNAPRABHA VIJAYA have based the account of rainy seasons on very late works which cannot be relied upon.

As regards S.V. VENKATESWARA's theory to the effect that Mahāvīra died in 437 B.C., there is absolutely no tradi-

1. KMA, p. 156.
2. *Jaina Sāhitya Aura Itihāsa Para Viśada Prakāśa*, pp. 26 f.

tion which can support it. Moreover, as the late G.H. OJHA[1] showed in his article 'On the conception of an Ananda Vikrama Era', no such era was ever started or gained currency, nor does it find any mention in the *Pṛithvīrāja-rāso* of poet Chanda as is alleged.

THE THEORY OF MAHĀVĪRA'S NIRVĀṆA IN 527 B.C.

There are scholars[2] who maintain that Mahāvīra's *Nirvāṇa* took place in 527 B.C. The following arguments may be advanced in support of this theory.

1. There is a continuous Jaina tradition from the fifth century A.D. onwards about the date of Mahāvīra's *Nirvāṇa* in 527 B.C. Yativṛishabha (5th century A.D.) seems to have been the first to record this tradition in the *Tiloyapaṇṇati*, and it is corroborated by Jinasena (783 A.D.) in the *Harivaṁśa*, by Nemichandra (973 A.D.) in the *Trilokasāra*, by Merutuṅga (1306 A.D.) in the *Vicāraśreṇi*, and by others. The Jaina writers, whenever they expressed the date of Mahāvīra, did it either straight away in the Mahāvīra Era, or in terms of either the Vikrama or the Śaka era. The Vikrama era and the Śaka era are known to have started in 57 B.C. and 78 A.D. respectively with the well-known interval of 135 years between them. The Jainas have never had any difference of opinion regarding the date of Tīrthaṅkara Mahāvīra, as, for instance, the Buddhists had regarding the date of the Buddha. The reason is that there was no cultural break. Jainism continued to live in India while Buddhism disappeared. In spite of schismatic tendencies and the predominance of particular sects in particular regions, it remained in constant touch with its coreligionists wherever they were or to whichever sub-sect they belonged. Thus the Jainas were able to preserve their cultural traditions.

1. *NPPI*, pp. 377-454, pp. 377-454.
2. G.C. OJHA : *Bhāratīya Prāchina Lipimālā* ; V.S. AGRAWALA : *Tīrthaṅkara Bhagavān Mahāvīra*, II *Bhūmikā*, p. 19 ; H.L. JAIN : *Tattva Samuchchaya*, p. 6, KALYANA VIJAYA : *Vīra Nirvāṇa Saṁvat Aura Jaina Kāla Gaṇanā. VMT*; *NATA*, p. 87.

2. In the *Vicāraśreṇī* of Merutuṅga, there are some old *gāthās* containing references to hisorical and chronological events taking place between the Mahāvīra era and the Vikrama and Śaka eras. The substance of this information may be submitted in the following chronological table.

Mahāvīra died	527 B.C.
Pālaka, acc.	527 B.C.
Nandas established supremacy	467 ,,
Mauryas established supremacy	312 ,,
Pushpamitra, acc.	204 ,,
Balamitra, acc.	174 ,,
Nabhovāhana, acc.	114 ,,
Gardabhilla, acc.	74 ,,
Gardabhilla expelled by the Śakas	61 ,,
Vikramāditya recovers Ujjayinī	57 ,,
Four successors of Vikramāditya	3-78 A.D.
Śaka era commences	78 A.D.

There is nothing in this general chronological scheme which, on the face of it, appears to be absurd or even unworthy of belief. In point of details also, this account is in fair accordance with known historical facts. This chronological scheme must be regarded, on the whole, as transmitting an old historical tradition, which, though not acceptable in all its details without further corroborative evidence, cannot be thrown out as worthless or contradicted by positive testimony of reliable character. Hence, the date of Mahāvīra's *Nirvāṇa*, which is the foundation of this chronological scheme, cannot be wrong.

3. The Jainas have tried to preserve the traditions relating to the *Śrutāvatāra* (i.e. the reduction of the canon). In this connection, some Jaina works[1] give the genealogy of 28 immediate successors of Mahāvīra, divided into five groups with the periods taken by each group. These works tell us at

1. *Tiloyapaṇṇati* (5th century); *Jambudvīpa-prajñapti Saṁgraha* (700 A.D.); *Dhavalā* (780 A.D.), *Harivaṁśa* (783 A.D.) *Jayadhavalā* (837 A.D.), *Kalpasūtra Therāvali*, *Pariśishṭaparvan* and *Prabhāvakacarita*, *Paṭṭāvalis* of Nandi, Sena and Kāshṭhā Saṁghas.

the end that 'by deducting 77 years and 7 months from this period of 683 years, we get 605 years and 5 months, which is the exact interval between Mahāvīra's death and the commencement of the Śaka era. All these sources are in perfect agreement as to the fact that this succession lasted till 683 years after Mahāvīra's *Nirvāṇa*, that up to this time, the direct canonical knowledge, though gradually declining in volume, continued to be preserved in the memory of these *Gurus*, and that it was about this time that the redaction of the surviving canonical knowledge was undertaken and the Jaina canons for the first time appeared in book form.

The slight differences one notices in these various sources, relate only to certain names. Some sources also differ in the extent of knowledge preserved by groups V and VI. The *Paṭṭāvalīs* of the Nandi *Saṁgha*, particularly its Prakṛit *Paṭṭāvalī*, which is quite an old document, gives the total period for the 5 *Gurus* of group IV as 123 years, whereas the other sources give it as 220 or 222 years; and while this *Paṭṭāvalī* allots 99 years to group V, they allot 118 years to it. According to the Jaina traditions, Bhadrabāhu was the contemporary of Chandragupta Maurya (324-300 B.C.), but in the genealogy of the Pontiffs, he is allotted 365 B.C. K.C. SASTRI[1] has tried to rectify this mistake of sixty years in the genealogical table of the Pontiffs.

4. There are also traditions which relate to Kalki who is believed to have flourished at about the close of the first millennium after Mahāvīra's death.[2] In this connection, chronological lists of the ruling dynasties, particularly of Ujjayinī, have been preserved for these one thousand years ending with Kalki's tyrannical rule. Kalki is identified with either Yaśodharman of the Aulikara dynasty of Mandsor or with Mihirakula of the Hūṇa dynasty.[3] It is more likely that he was Mihirakula.

5. Another tradition, which further conforms this date relates to the great schism in the Jaina Saṁgha. According

1. *Jaina Sāhitya Kā Itihāsa*, pp. 356-369.
2. *Tiloyapaṇṇati, Harivaṁśa, Trilokasāra*, etc.
3. N R. PREMI: *Jaina Sāhitya Aura Itihāsa*, p. 20.

to the Śvetāmbara sources, the schism took place in M.E. 609, and according to the Digambara ones, in V.E. 136, thus giving the date as A.D. 82 or 79.[1]

6. The date of the redaction of the Śvetāmbara canon is another instance. Tradition places this event in M.E. 980 or 993 (i.e. A.D. 453 or 466) which seems to be quite correct since Bhadrabāhu III, who wrote the *Niryuktis* on the redacted *Āgamasūtras*, was an elder brother of Várāhamihira, the astronomer (427 S.E. or 505 A.D.).

7. Pushkarasārin, who was a contemporary of Pradyota of Avanti and Bimbisāra of Magadha, was the ruler of Gandhāra with its capital at Taxila. Pradyota was engaged in hostilities with Pushkarasārin the cause of which is not known. Pushkarasārin is said to have sent an ambassador and a letter to king Bimbisāra of Magadha. But Bimbisāra was in no mood to alienate Pradyota. Pradyota was unsuccessful in his war, but was saved from disaster by the outbreak of hostilities between Pushkarasārin and the Pāṇḍavas. The Pāṇḍavas appear to have settled in the Punjab.

This area of Gandhāra seems to have become a part of the Persian empire from about 550 B.C. It is generally held that the eastern conquest of Cyrus (558-530 B.C.) included the Districts of Drangiana, Sattagydia and Gandaritis (Gandhāra). The two later inscriptions of Persepolis (518-515 B.C.) and of Naksh-i-Rustam (515 B.C.) mention Hi(n)du or the northern Punjab as a part of the domain of Darius, the successor of Cyrus. These references indicate that probably it was Cyrus who conquered Gandhāra which was inherited by Darius as a part of his empire, while for himself he pushed his Indian conquest farther into the region called Sindhu.

As Gandhāra became a part of the Persian empire from 550 B.C., its ruler Pushkarasārin must be placed earlier. Bimbisāra and Pradyota, who were the contemporaries of Pushkarasārin, were ruling in about 550 B.C. As Mahāvīra is known to be a contemporary of Bimbisāra and Pradyota, the date of

1. *Āvaśyaka Mūlabhāshya* (609 A.D.), *Darśanasāra* (933 A.D.)

his *Nirvāṇa* in 527 B.C. as recorded in the Jaina scriptures is not improbable.

8. If we assume this date of Mahāvīra's death to be correct, it does not conflict with the known facts of history. Chaṇḍa Pradyota, king of Avanti, died on the same night of 527 B.C. as Tīrthaṅkara Mahāvīra, and he was succeeded by his son Pālaka. Chaṇḍa Pradyota is known to have ruled for 23 years, which implies that he became a ruler in about 550 B.C. Pradyota is known to be one of the contemporaries of both Bimbisāra and his son Ajātaśatru. According to the Jaina tradition, Mahāvīra died sixteen years after the coronation of Ajātaśatru, and this period might have included some years of his Viceroyalty over Champā. It seems that he started his rule from about 535 B.C. His father Bimbisāra, is known to have ruled 28 (or 38) years according to the *Purāṇas*, and 52 years according to the Sinhalese chronicles. Hence his accession to the throne may be placed either in 587 B.C. or in 563 B.C. Since Gośāla is known to have died sixteen and a half years before Mahāvīra, his date of death may be presumed to be 543 B.C. As Buddha was a junior contemporary of Mahāvīra, he might have attained *Nirvāṇa* a few years after Mahāvīra.

PERSONALITY

Mahāvīra was one of the great religious teachers of mankind. He recognized the need for the perfection of self and prescribed certain practical rules of conduct for the attainment of this aim. He did not preach to others what he did not practise himself. For the realization of such an aim, he believed in the blissfulness of the entire being. This happy state, he said, cannot be bought by the wealth, pomp, and power of the world but can certainly be realized through patience, forbearance, self-denial, forgiveness, humanity, compassion, suffering and sacrifice. For this purpose, he inculcated the doctrine of *Ahiṁsā* or non-violence in thought, word and action. Those who came under the influence of his personality, gave up the eating of meat and fish and took to vegetarian diet. This principle was at the back of many philanthropic and humanitarian deeds and institutions which he encouraged.

For Mahāvīra distinctions of caste, creed or sex did not matter. According to him, salvation is the birthright of everyone, and it is assured if one follows the prescribed rules of conduct. His doctrine of *Karma* (action) made the individual conscious of his responsibility for all actions. It also awakened the consciousness that salvation was not a gift or favour but an attainment within the reach of human beings.

Mahāvīra was tolerant in religious matters. As there were different conflicting religious and philosophical views current in his time, he formulated the scheme of *Syādvāda* in which there is room for the consideration of them all. This attitude in religious matters produced an atmosphere of mutual harmony among the followers of different sects, who began to appreciate the views of their opponents as well.

Mahāvīra was a great *Māhaṇa*[1] who possessed fully formed knowledge and insight, who was adored and worshipped by the three worlds, and who was furnished with a wealth of meritorious works. He was known to be a great Guardian[2] because he protected and guarded, with his staff of the Law, all those numerous living beings that in the wilderness of the world were straying or perishing, being devoured or cut as under or pierced through or mutilated or castrated, and with his own hand brought them to the great fold of the *Nirvāṇa*. He was a great preacher[3] because by means of many discourses and explanations he delivered them from evil and with his own hand saved all those numerous living beings that were straying or perishing, and because, overwhelmed by the power of falsehood and overcast by the dense darkness of the eightfold kinds of works, they had lost the true path and were brought back to the right road. He was a great pilot[4] because by means of the boat of Law, with his own hands brought them straight to the shore of the *Nirvāṇa* and delivered all those numerous living beings that, on the great

1. *Upāsakadaśā-Sutram*, ed. by A.F.R. Hoernle, p. 141.
2. Ibid. 3. Ibid. 144. 4. Ibid. 145.

sea of the world, were straying or perishing by sinking or drowning or floating.

Mahāvīra, who was the wisest sage the world has known possessed infinite knowledge and faith. This wise man had explored all beings, mobile or immobile, high or low, eternal or transient. Like a lamp, he saw the Law in a true light.[1] He knew this world and the world beyond.[2] His knowledge was inexhaustible like the water of the sea. As he had mastered all philosophical systems, he understood the doctrines of the Kriyāvādins, of the Akriyāvādins, of the Vainayikas, and of the Ajñānavādins.[3] His perception was infinite.[4]

He endured severe tortures and penances in his life in order to annihilate his *karmans.* He bore everything like the earth. Having conquered the passions which defile the soul : wrath, pride, deceit, greed, the great sage did not commit any wrong, nor did he cause any wrong to be committed by others. He observed the chastity, the highest type of austerity, by abstaining from women. He practised the highest contemplation, which is the purest of the pure—pure without a flaw. He granted protection to all and was the most vigorous. He wandered about without a home and crossed the flood of the *Saṁsāra*. He renounced everything because he had broken away from all ties.[5]

Mahāvīra was a great reformer. Since many abuses had crept into Jainism, he did his utmost to remove them. For this, he had to bring about some changes even in the traditional religion coming from Pārśva. He added the vow of chastity and emphasized the importance of nudity. Though his teachings were based on the old religion, he made a more systematic arrangement of its philosophical tenets. All these point to his great reforming zeal.

Mahāvīra possessed a great organizing capacity, and he made the laity participate in the *Saṁgha* along with the monks. He encouraged a close union between laymen and monks by advocating similar religious duties for both, duties that differed not in kind but in degree.

1. *Sūtra*, I, 6, 4.
2. Ibid, I, 6, 28.
3. Ibid, I, 6, 27.
4. Ibid, I, 6, 25.
5. Ibid, I, 6, 6.

CHAPTER IV

TEACHINGS OF MAHĀVĪRA

Mahāvīra was not the founder but only a reformer of the existing faith of Jainism. His teachings are partly based on the religion of his predecessor, Pārśvanātha, and partly independent. He appears to be a religious philosopher who gave a philosophic justification for the rules of conduct propounded by Pārśvanātha. He was responsible for the codification of an unsystematic mass of beliefs inhering the earlier religion of his predecessor into a set of rigid rules of conduct for monks and laymen. Besides, he had to introduce changes in the existing religion in order to meet the needs of the time. There were several orthodox and heretical sects with their well-known teachers going strong during his time. He understood and mastered the doctrines of the current philosophical systems such as the Kriyāvādins, the Akriyāvādins, the Vinayavādins and the Ajñānavādins. Sometimes he borrowed certain ideas from others in order to bring them into harmony with his own system. He also formulated his own doctrines under the influence of the controversies endlessly going on with his religious contemporaries. Some of his teachings also arose as a natural reaction against corrupt practices current in the society of this period.

No direct evidence regarding the teachings of Mahāvīra has been preserved. Originally, they are supposed to have been embodied in the Fourteen *Pūrvas* and the Eleven *Aṅgas*. These original texts are, however, according to the Digambaras, lost without a trace, but the Śvetāmbaras do not subscribe to this view. According to them, an attempt was made for the compilation of the Eleven *Aṅgas* at the Council of Pāṭaliputra after a famine of twelve year's duration in about the third century B.C., and the *Pūrvas* were considered to be the twelfth *Aṅga* under the name of *Dṛṣṭivāda*. This type of *Āgama* literature grew up by stages during the ten centuries following the death of Mahāvīra. The final redaction of this Āgamika literature with several alterations took place at the council of Valabhī under the presidency of Ārya Devarddhi in 454 (or 467 A.D.).

It seems that the teachings of Jainism underwent some changes in the interval between the time of Mahāvīra and the final composition of the Jaina canon. Older parts of the *Āchār-āṅga* and the *Sūtrakṛtāṅga* may well claim to preserve much original matter, and the same may be true to some extent of some portion of the *Bhagavatī Sūtra* and the *Uttarādhyayana Sūtra*. The earliest Buddhist texts, known as the Pāli *Nikāyas*, also refer to the beliefs and teachings of Mahāvīra. Though we cannot expect them to give a fair and honest exposition of the tenets of their opponents, they somehow corroborate the evidence of the Jaina texts. In the light of both these evidences, an estimate of the teachings of Mahāvīra should be made.

The teachings of Mahāvīra were simple, practical and ethical, but gradually they developed into a complicated system with considerable emphasis on details. Because of conservatism, the evolution was more or less in a straight line, and there are no dissensions on fundamentals in Jainism. Mahāvīra and his disciples propounded not only the doctrinal side of Jainism relating to the nature of the truth and the ideal but also mapped out the practical and disciplinary path leading to the realization of both. It was chiefly in and through the life of monks or mendicants that the ideal of conduct was sought to be fulfilled.

NIRVĀṆA

The ultimate object of Jainism as taught by Mahāvīra is *Nirvāṇa* which consists in the attainment of peace and infinite bliss.[1] *Nirvāṇa* is just another name for *Mokṣa* or liberation, *Mukti* or deliverance, salvation or beatitude. Gautama, a disciple of Mahāvīra, explained *Nirvāṇa* to Keśī, a disciple of Pārśva : "It is a safe, happy, quiet and eternal place in view of all but difficult of approach where there is no old age, nor death, nor sorrow, nor pain, nor disease. It is a state of

1. *Sūtra*, I, 11, 11.

perfection which is obtained by putting an end to the stream of existence."[1] It is liberation from a state of bondage brought on by *karman*. It is deliverance from old age, disease, death, and all that constitutes the self.

This highest goal is to be attained through annihilating the old *Karmans* (*Nirjarā*) lying heavy on the soul by the practice of austerities (*Tapas*), and to stop the influx (*Āśrava*) of new *Karmans* by the practice of self-restraint, called *Saṁvara*, with regard to the body, speech and mind.

Even in a Pāli *Sutta*,[2] the main aim of Mahāvīra's teaching has been mentioned as *Sukha* or infinite bliss which is not reachable through the finite happiness of even so fortunate among men as the reigning monarchs ; it is reachable only through *dukkha* or pain of foregoing and forsaking all finite happiness. Had it been possible to attain beatitude through mundane happiness, king Śreṇika Bimbisāra of Magadha would certainly have attained it. In the Pāli *Sutta*, *Dukkha* or painful and difficult path meant *Dukkarakārika*, or a rigorous practice of penances. It was to be resorted to by us as a means of wearing out and ultimately destroying the effects of sinful deeds (*pāpakamma*) committed in a former existence. The practice of the threefold self-restraint was to be taken recourse to by the aspirant as a means of not giving effect to a new *karman*.

RIGHT FAITH (DARŚANA), *RIGHT KNOWLEDGE* (JÑĀNA), *AND RIGHT CONDUCT* (CĀRITRA)

Right Faith, Right Knowledge, and Right Conduct are the three essential points in Mahāvīra's teachings which lead to perfection by the destruction of *Karmans*. Without Right Faith, there is no Right Knowledge; without Right Knowledge there is no Virtuous Conduct; without virtues, there is no deliverance and without deliverance (*Moksha*), there is no perfection.[3]

1. *Uttarā*, XXIII, 81-84.
2. *Majjh*, I, pp. 93-94.
3. *Uttarā*, XXVIII, 30.

The excellence of one's faith depends on the following points : that one has no doubts about the truth of the tenets ; that one has no preference for the tenets of others ; that one does not doubt the saving qualities of one's own faith ; that one is not shaken in the right belief ; that one practises piety, that one encourages the weak ; that one supports and loves the confessors of the law, and that one endeavours to exalt one's own faith.[1]

Faith is produced by nature (*Nisarga*), instruction (*Upadeśa*), command (*Ājñā*), study of the *Sūtras*, suggestion (*Bija*), comprehension of the meaning of the sacred lore (*Abhigama*), complete course of study (*Vistāra*), religious exercise (*Kriyā*), brief exposition (*saṁkshepa*), and law (*Dharma*).[2]

He who truly understands by a spontaneous effort of his mind the nature of soul, inanimate things, merit and demerit, and who puts an end to sins (*Āśramasaṁvara*), believes by nature. He who believes the four truths taught by the Jinas believes by nature. He who believes these truths having learnt them from somebody else believes by instructions. He who has got rid of love, hatred, delusion and ignorance believes by command. He who obtains righteousness by the study of the *Sūtras* believes by the study of the Sūtras. He who knows the sacred lore believes by the comprehension of the sacred lore. He who understands the true nature of all substances believes by a complete course of study. He who sincerely performs all duties by Right Knowledge, Faith, etc. believes by religious exercise. He who is not versed in the sacred doctrines believes by brief exposition. He who believes in the truth of the realities, believes by the law. There is no right conduct without right belief; it must be cultivated for obtaining Right Faith ; righteousness and right conduct originate together or righteousness precedes right conduct.[3]

There are different kinds of obstruction to right faith, such as sleep, activity, very deep sleep, a high degree of activity, and a state of deep-rooted greed. *Vedanīya* is two-fold : pleasure and pain, *Mohanīya* is twofold : faith and conduct.

1. Uttarā, XXVIII, 31.
2. Ibid, 16.
3. Ibid, 17-29.

The three kinds of *Mohanīya* concerning faith are right faith, wrong faith, and faith, partly right and partly wrong.[1]

The *Uttarādhyayana Sūtra* speaks of five kinds of knowledge : (1) *Śruta* or knowledge derived from the study of sacred books ; (2) *Ābhinibodhika* or knowledge obtained from one's own experience, thought, or understanding ; (3) *Avadhi* or supernatural knowledge; (4) *Manaḥparyāya* or knowledge of the thoughts of other people, and (5) *Kevala*, the highest knowledge.[2]

The *Avadhi-Jñāna* is also employed in the sense of knowledge co-extensive with the object. The *Kalpa Sūtra*,[3] for instance, says : "He viewed the whole Jambudvīpa with his knowledge called *Avadhi*." Here *Avadhi* means that which is limited by the object, that which is just sufficient to survey the field of observation.

The *Manaḥparyāya-jñāna* is defined in the *Āchārāṅga Sūtra* as a knowledge of the thoughts of all sentient beings.[4] The *Kevala-jñāna* according to the same text, is omniscience enabling a person to comprehend all objects, to know all conditions of the world of gods, men, and demons : whence they come, where they go, where they are born, etc.[5]

The first kind of knowledge in Jainism corresponds to the Buddhist *Sutamaya paññā*; the second kind to *Chintāmaya paññā*; the third kind to *Vilokana*; the fourth kind to *Chetopariyāñāṇa*; and the fifth kind to *Sabbaññutā* or omniscience involving the three faculties. One of the Buddhist texts refers to limited knowledge (*Antavanta Jñāna*) as propounded by Mahāvīra. Knowledge which is confined to the limited world is itself limited in its character.[6] The Pāli *Antavanta Jñāna* is evidently the same term as the Jaina *Avadhi Jñāna*.

Knowledge of substances, qualities and all developments (*Dravya*, *Guṇa* and *Paryāya*) has also been imparted by the Jinas. Substance is the substratum of qualities ; qualities are inherent in a substance, but a characteristic feature of developments is that they inhere in substances or qualities.

1. *Uttarā*, XXXIII, 5-9.
2. Ibid, XXVIII, 4.
3. *Kalpa*, I, 15; SBE, XXII, p. 223.
4. *Āchā*, II, 15, 23.
5. Ibid, II, 15, 25.
6. *Aṅgu*, IV, p. 428.

Dharma, *Adharma*, space, time, matter, and souls are the six kinds of substances. Insofar as *Dharma*, *Adharma*, and space are concerned, each of them is a substance, but time, matter, and souls form an infinite number of substances. The distinctive feature of *Dharma* is motion, that of *Adharma* is immobility, and that of space (*Ākāśa*) is room. The distinguishing mark of time is duration, that of the soul the realization of knowledge, faith, conduct, austerities, energy and its manifestations. The characteristic mark of matter is sound, darkness, lustre, etc., that of development is singleness.[1]

Right conduct, which destroys *Karma*, is the avoidance of everything sinful (*Sāmāyika*), the initiation of the novice (*Khedopasthāpanā*), purity produced by peculiar austerities (*Parihāraviśuddhi*), reduction of desire (*Sūkshma samparāya*), and annihilation of sinfulness (*Akashāya yathākhyāta*).[2]

Virtue consists in right conduct. But there is no right conduct without right belief, and no right belief without the right perception of truth.[3] Right conduct is achieved by threefold restraint, the restraint of the body, the restraint of speech and the restraint of mind.[4] The first step towards virtue lies in the avoidance of sins. There are various ways of committing sins, directly and indirectly, through physical acts or through spoken words or even through thoughts.[5] Thus to avoid sins, one must guard oneself by the *Samitis* and *Guptis*.

Not to kill anything, to live according to the rules of conduct and without greed, to take care of the highest good, to control oneself always while walking, sitting and lying down, and in the matter of food and drink, to shake off pride, wrath, deceit and greed, to possess the *Samitis*, to be protected by the five *Saṁvaras*, and to attain perfection by remaining unfettered among the fettered—these, in short, are the cardinal principles of *Cāritra* as taught by Mahāvīra.[6]

1. *Uttarā*, XXVIII, 5-12.
2. Ibid, 32-33.
3. Ibid, 28-29.
4. *Sūtra*, I, 1, 2, 27.
5. Ibid, I, 1, 2, 26.
6. Ibid, 1, 1, 4, 10-13.

Austerities

The road to final deliverance also depends on austerities which destroy the bad *Karmans*. These austerities are of two kinds : external and internal.[1] The external austerities are of six kinds—(1) fasting (*Anaśana*), (2) abstinence (*Avamodarikā*) (3) collecting alms (*Bhikshācharyā*), (4) abstention from dainty food (*Rasaparityāga*), (5) mortification of the flesh (*Kāyakleśa*), and (6) taking care of one's limb (*Saṁlīnatā*).

Fasting is of two kinds (1) temporary (*Itvara*) and (b) fasting which precedes and ends with death (*Maraṇakāla*). Temporary fasting is either that in which a desire (for food) is present, or that in which no such desire exists. Temporary fasting is briefly of six kinds : (1) in the form of a line,[2] (2) in the form of a square, (3) in the form of a cube, (4) of a sixth power, (5) of a twelfth power, and (6) of any arrangement. Fasting, which is to precede death, is of two kinds with regard to the motions of the body : with change (of position) and without change. And, again, it is twofold : admitting relief or not admitting relief; one may either leave the place (which one has chosen to die in) or not leave it ; in both cases one may not take any food.

Abstinence is briefly of five kinds : with regard to (a) substance, (b) place, (c) time, (d) state of mind, and (e) development. He who takes less food than he usually does performs abstinence with regard to substance. Place signifies a village, a capital, a mine, settlement of a wild tribe, a poor town, a town with a harbour, a large town, an isolated town, a hermitage, a halting place, a resting place, a garden, a house, etc. Abstinence with regard to time is observed by him who goes about in the time of the four *Paurūshīs* (3 hours) of the day. If he collects alms in a part of the third *Paurūshī* or in its last quarter, he observes abstinence with reference to time. Abstinence with regard to the state of mind is observed by him who accepts alms from a man or a woman, from a person richly ornamented or plain, if that person does not change his disposition or condition. A monk who observes abstinence according to the particulars which have been enumerat-

1. *Uttarā*, XXX, 7-36.
2. *Ibid*., p. 175, f.n. 4.

ed with regard to substance, place, time, and state of mind, observes abstinence with regard to development too.

With regard to collecting alms, there are eight principal ways of collecting them : the seven *Eshaṇās* (or modes of begging) and other self-imposed restrictions. Abstention from dainty food means abstention from such highly nourishing food and drink as milk, curd, ghee, etc. Mortification of the flesh consists in such different postures as *Vīrāsana*, etc. which benefit the soul, and which are difficult to perform. Using unfrequented lodgings and beds consists in living and sleeping in separate and unfrequented places where there are neither women nor cattle.

Internal austerities are of six types—(1) *Prāyaśchitta* or expiration of sins, (2) *Vinaya* or politeness, (3) *Vaiyāvṛtya* or serving the *Guru*, (4) *Svādhyāya* or study, (5) *Dhyāna* or meditation, and (6) *Vyutsarga* or abandoning the body. Expiration of sins is tenfold, what must be confessed, etc. This is to be strictly observed by a monk and is called expiration of sins. Politeness consists in rising (from one's seat), folding of the hands, offering a seat, loving the *Guru*, and cordial obedience. There are ten kinds of service, such as serving the *Ācārya*, etc. ; doing service consists in giving one's assistance as well as one is able to give. Study is fivefold: (1) learning one's lesson, (2) questioning the teacher about it, (3) repetition, (4) pondering, and (5) religious discourse. To abstain from meditation is to abstain from meditating on painful and sinful things; one should, rather, meditate on the Law with a collected mind. If a monk remains motionless while lying down, sitting or standing upright, this is called abandonment of the body, which is one of the internal austerities.

Five Vows (Vratas) for the ascetics

While Pārśva taught only four vows for the realization of absolute happiness, Mahāvīra taught five in all, making chastity a separate vow altogether. These five vows are *Ahiṁsā* (not to kill), *Satya* (not to lie), *Asteya* (not to steal), *Brahmacarya* (to abstain from sexual intercourse), and *Apratigraha* (to renounce all interest in worldly things, especially in property).

The first great vow of the Jaina is abstinence from killing living beings. In thoughts, words and acts, he should do nothing injurious to beings who people the world, whether they move or not.[1] A Jaina is wary in his walk. He searches into his mind and speech. He is careful in laying down his utensils of begging. He eats and drinks after proper inspection.

The visible effect of *Ahiṁsā* was sought to be proved by a practical demonstration. Already in Mahāvīra's time, the righteous kings of India made it a point of duty to vouchsafe lawful protection to all forms of life within the sacred precincts of a religious establishment.[2] This principle of causing no harm to any being had a salutary effect on man's habitual diet. Those who came under the influence of Mahāvīra's personality and teaching gave up the eating of meat and fish for good, and adhered to a strictly vegetarian diet.

The second great vow is the avoidance of falsehood. A Jaina speaks after deliberation. He comprehends and renounces anger, greed, fear, and mirth. The third great vow is the avoidance of theft. A Jaina begs after deliberation for a limited space. He consumes his food and drink with the permission of his superiors. A Jaina who has taken possession of some space should always take possession of a limited part of it and for a fixed time. He should constantly have his grant renewed. He may beg for a limited ground for his co-religionists after deliberation.

The next vow is the avoidance of sexual pleasure. A Jaina should desist from continually discussing topics relating to women. He should not regard and contemplate the lovely forms of women. He should not recall to his mind the pleasures and amusements he formally had with women. He should not eat and drink too much. He should not drink liquor or eat highly seasoned food. He should not occupy a bed or a couch belonging to women.

The last great vow is freedom from possessions. If a living being with his ears open hears agreeable or disagreeable

1. *Uttarā*, VIII, 10.
2. *Majjh*, II, p. 101, etc.

sounds, he should not be attached to them. If he with his eyes sees agreeable or disagreeable forms, he should not be attached to them. If he with his nose smells agreeable or disagreeable smells, he should not be attached to them. If he with his tongue tastes agreeable or disagreeable things, he should not be attached to them. If he with his organs of feeling feels agreeable or disagreeable things, he should not be attached to them.[1]

The explanation offered by the Jaina texts in support of the addition of the vow of celibacy is as follows. The *Uttarādhyayana*[2] says that "the first saints were simple but slow of understanding, the last saints prevaricating and slow of understanding, those between the two, simple and wise : hence there are two forms of the Law. The first could but with difficulty understand the precepts of the Law, and the last could only with difficulty observe them, but those between them easily understood and observed them."

It is however wrong to suppose that Pārśva did not advocate celibacy. What he did was that in the vow of *Aparigraha* (non-possession) he included the vow of celibacy. This indirect implication of non-possession could easily be understood by the followers of Pārśva who were 'simple and wise'. Mahāvīra's disciples, on the other hand, being prevaricating and slow of understanding could only with difficulty observe 'the vow of non-possession'. He had therefore to add the fifth vow of abstinence from all sexual acts in clear terms.

On this H. Jacobi remarks, "As the vow of chastity is not explicitly mentioned among Pārśva's four vows, but was understood to be implicitly enjoined by them (i.e. Pārśva's followers), it follows that only such men as were of an upright disposition and quick understanding would not go astray by observing the four vows literally, i.e., by not abstaining from sexual intercourse, as it was not expressly forbidden. The argumentation in the text presupposes a decay of morals of the monastic order to have occurred between Pārśva and Mahāvīra, and this is possible only on the assumption of a sufficient interval of time having elapsed between the last

1. *Achā*, II, 15-i-v.
2. *Uttarā*, XXIII, 26-27.

two Tīrthaṅkaras. And this perfectly agrees with the common tradition that Mahāvīra came 250 years after Pārśva."[1]

It is on the basis of the number of vows observed that the sect of Pārśva was known as *Cāturyāma*[2] and that of Mahāvīra as *Pañchayāma*. These vows were strictly observed by monks who took them on entering the order. In their case, the vows were called the five great vows (Mahāvrata). Lay people, however, observed these vows as far as their worldly situation permitted. The five vows of the lay people were, of course, *aṇuvrata* or small vows.

A correct representation of the 'fourfold self-restraint', even in the sense of which the followers of Pārśva understood it, is not wanting in Buddhist literature. Just then a separate vow of chastity was added to the 'fourfold self-restraint' to complete the list of five great vows (*pañcamahāvratas*) promulgated by Mahāvīra. These have been enumerated as abstinence from the idea of killing, the idea of theft, the idea of unchastity, the idea of lying, and some such *tapoguṇa* or virtue of an ascetic.[3] It is interesting indeed to note that even some of the Jaina phrases have been reproduced in the Buddhist text.

As celibacy and nudity are closely related from the point of view of controlling the senses and the non-attachment to bodily pleasures and external needs, Mahāvīra also introduced the practice of nudity among the monks. His predecessor, Pārśva, is said to have allowed an under and an upper garment to his followers.[4]

DOCTRINE OF THE NINE CATEGORIES OR TRUTHS (NAVA TATTVA)

It was in opposing to Gośāla's deterministic theory based on his biological researches that Mahāvīra is said to have gradually formulated his theory of the nine categories as well as his theory of *Karma*. His doctrine of the nine categories was meant to explain how the bondage of the soul arises by way

1. SBE, XLV, p. 122, f.n. 3.
2. *Sūtra*, II, 7. 39; *Uttarā*, XXIII, 12.
3. *Majjh*, II, 35-36; *Saṁ*, 1. 66.
4. *Uttarā*, XXIII, 13.

of karmic effects upon it and how these effects are got rid off and the liberation of the soul is obtained. The categories are as follows : (1) *Jiva* (soul), (2) *Ajīva* (inanimate things), (3) *Bandha* (the binding of the soul by *Karma*), (4) *Puṇya* (merit), (5) *Pāpa* (demerit), (6) *Āśrava* (that which causes the soul to be affected by sins), (7) *Saṁvara* (the prevention of *Āśrava* by watchfulness), (8) *Nirjarā* (the annihilation of *Karma*), and (9) *Moksha* (final deliverance). He who verily believes in the true teaching of the above nine fundamental truths possesses righteousness.[1]

As corollaries to these terms, the theory of the categories came to include two other groups of terms.[2] The *Pañcāstikāyas* (five substances) comprehending and characterizing the world of existence are : (1) *Dharma* (medium of motion), *Adharma* (medium of rest), *Ākāśa* (space), *Jīva*(soul) and *Pudgala* (matter). The three terms of substance (*Dravya*), qualities (*Guṇa*) and *Paryāya* (Development) comprehend and characterize the five *Astikāyas*.

The first pair of terms, *Jiva* and *Ajīva*, comprehends the world of existence as known and experienced. The *Jiva* signifies all that has life while *Ajīva* indicates those that are without life. The world of life is represented by six classes of living things and beings, three of which are immovable and three movable. Earth-lives, water-lives, and plants are immovable beings, while movable beings include all fire-lives, wind-lives, and those with an organic body. Living things are either subtle or gross, and living beings are either those still belonging to *Saṁsāra* or those whose souls are perfected. Through the gradation of living things and beings, one can trace the evolution of the senses. The lowest form of being is provided with only one sense, the sense of touch.[3]

It is only in relation to the six classes of beings that the process of *Karma* sets in and the nature of man's conduct is determined. "Know and understand," taught Mahāvīra, "that they all desire happiness; by hurting these beings, men do harm

1. *Uttarā*, XXVIII, 14 & 15.
2. Ibid, 5 & 7.
3. *Ibid.*, XXXVI, *Sūtra*, I, 7, 1.

to their own souls, and will again and again be born as one of them. Every being born high or low in the scale of the living creation, among movable and immovable beings, will meet with its death. Whatever sins the evil-doer commits in every birth, for them he must die."[1]

Things without life are either formed or formless. The formed are compound things and atoms constituting the world of matter. The world of the formless is represented by four *Astikāyas*, *viz.*, *Dharma*, *Adharma*, *Ākāśa* (space) and time. *Dharma* and *Adharma* explain motion and absence of motion respectively; *Ākāśa* (space) provides habitation for all living and non-living beings, and time explains their duration of existence. *Dharma*, *Adharma*, and space are each one substance only ; but time, matter and souls are in infinite number of substances. Thus the category of *Ajīva* helps us complete the study of the world of life and existence.[2]

The third term or category is *Bandha* or bondage of the soul. *Bandha* is the subjection of the soul to the laws of the birth and death, of youth and age, of pleasure and pain, and other vicissitudes of life brought about by the effect of *Karma*.

The soul, which is one of the *Astikāyas*, represents the principle of intelligence. The characteristic of the soul is knowledge, faith, conduct, austerities, energy, and realization of its developments.[3] Buddhaghosha in his commentary on the *Brahmajāla Sutta*, *Digha Nikāya* I, 2, 381, mentions the Niganthas as holding the opinion that the soul has no colour, and it continues to exist after death and is free from ailments. This description is consonant with the opinions of the Jainas about the nature of the soul.[4]

The categories of Merit (*Puṇya*) and Demerit (*Pāpa*) comprehend all acts or deeds, pious and sinful, which keep the soul bound to the circle of the births and deaths.

1. *Sūtra*, I, 7, 2-3.
2. *Uttarā*, XXXVI.
3. Ibid, XXVIII, 11.
4. SBE, XLV, p. xix.

Āśrava is that which causes the soul to be affected by sins, and *Saṁvara* is the principle of self-control by which the influx of sins is checked or stopped. The category of *Saṁvara* comprehends the whole sphere of right conduct.

Nirjarā or *Karmakshaya* consists in the wearing out of the accumulated effects of *Karma* on the soul by the practice of austerities, and *Moksha*, which logically follows from *Nirjarā*, signifies the final deliverance of the soul from the bondage of *Karma*. *Siddhi* or perfection is just another aspect of liberation.

THEORY OF KARMA

Mahāvīra's theory of *Karma* is known as Dynamistic philosophy or notion of the freedom of the will.[1] According to it, pleasure and pain, and happiness and misery of the individual depend upon his free will, exertion and manly strength. *Karma* is the deed of the soul. It is a material forming a subtle bond of extremely refined Karmic matter which keeps the soul confined to its place of origin or the natural abode of full knowledge and everlasting peace.

Mahāvīra's great message to mankind is that birth is nothing, caste is nothing, *Karma* is everything, and that on the destruction of *Karma*, all future happiness depends. The theory of *Karma* represents the most ancient and original feature of Jaina thought. According to H. JACOBI, "This *Karma* theory, if not in all details, certainly in the main outlines, is acknowledged in the oldest parts of the canon and presupposed by expressions and technical terms occurring in them. Some of the passages concerning the theory of *Karma* found in the old texts of Jainism are as follows :

"The painful condition of the self is brought about by one's own action, it is not brought about by any other cause (fate, creator, chance or the like)."[2]

"Individually a man is born, individually he dies, individually he falls (from this state of existence), individually he rises (to another). His passions, consciousness, intellect, perceptions, and impressions belong to the individual exclusi-

1. BHPIP, p. 385.
2. *Sūtra* I, 12. 11.

vely. Here, indeed, the bonds of relationship are not able to help nor save one."[1]

"All living beings owe their present form of existence to their own *Karma* ; timid, wicked, suffering latent misery, they err about (in the circle of births), subject to birth, old age, and death."[2]

"The sinners cannot annihilate works by new works ; the pious annihilate their works by abstention from works ; the wise and happy men, who got rid of the effects of greed, do not commit sins."

"Pleasant things are not produced from pleasant things."[3]

"He who intends (to kill) a living being but does not do it by his body, and he who unknowingly kills one, both are affected by that through a slight contact (with it) only, but the demerit (in their case) is not fully developed."[4]

"He who knows himself and the world ; who knows where (the creatures) go, and whence they will not return ; who knows what is eternal and what is transient ; birth and death, and the future existences of men."[5]

"He who knows the tortures of beings below (in hell); who knows the influx of sin and its stoppage ; who knows misery and its annihilation,—he is entitled to expound the *Kriyāvāda*".[6]

"A perfect saint believes in the soul, believes in the world, believes in reward and believes in action. I did it, I shall cause another to do it ; I shall allow another to do it."[7]

The passages cited above are sufficient to prove that *Kriyāvāda* expounded by Mahāvīra is in its essential feature only a theory of soul and *Karma*. According to this theory, there are as many souls as living individuals, and *Karma* consists of acts, intentional and unintentional, that produce effects

1. *Sūtra*, II, 1. 41.
2. Ibid, 1, 2, 18.
3. Ibid, I, 3, 4, 6.
4. Ibid, I, I, 2, 25.
5. Ibid, I, 12. 20.
6. Ibid, I, 12, 21.
7. *Āchā*, I, 1. 1. 4.

on the nature of the soul. Thus the soul is not passive in the sense that it remains untouched or unaffected by what a person does, but is susceptible to the influences of *Karma*.

Even in some early Buddhist texts, we find the traces of *Kriyāvāda* as expounded in Jainism. In *Aṅguttara Nikāya*, III, 74, for instance, a learned Lichchhavī prince of Vaiśālī, Abhaya, gives the following account of some Nigaṇṭha doctrines : "The Nigaṇṭhas Nātaputta teaches the annihilation by austerities of the old *Karma*, and the prevention by inactivity of new *Karma*. When *Karma* ceases, misery ceases ; when misery ceases, perception ceases ; when perception ceases, every misery will come to an end. In this way, a man is saved by pure annihilation of sin (nijjarā) which is really effective."

Another piece of information about Nigaṇṭha doctrines may be gathered from the *Mahāvagga*.[1] There a story is told of Sīha who wanted to pay the Buddha a visit, but Nātaputta tried to dissuade him from it simply because the Nigaṇṭhas held to *Kriyāvāda* while the Buddha's beliefs were grounded in *Akriyāvāda*.

These passages throw light on the doctrine of *Karma* expounded by Mahāvīra. The theory of *Karma* has special significance if we consider it along with the views of Mahāvīra's contemporary religious thinkers. The Vedic thinkers thought that the world has been created and is governed by the gods. Pūraṇa Kassapa maintained that when a man acts or causes others to act, it is not his soul which acts or causes to act.[2] Kātyāyana advocated that whether a man buys or causes to buy, kills or causes to kill, he does not thereby commit any sin.[3] Keśakambain explained that life ends here, and there is no world beyond. Denying the hereafter and the efficacy of all social institutions founded upon beliefs in the future existence of man, he cannot inform us whether an action is good or bad, virtuous or vicious, well done or otherwise, whether it is in man's power to reach perfection or not, or whether there is a heaven and a hell.[4] Gośāla denies that

1. Mv, VI, 31.
2. Sūtra, I, 1.1 13.
3. Ibid, I, 1.1.15 ; II. 1.22-24.
4. Ibid, I, 1.11-12 ; II, I, 16-17.

our happiness and misery, weal and ill, are caused by us individually or determined by any other cause than what we term fate or necessity.[1]

Karma is believed, according to Mahāvīra, to be the result of actions arising out of four sources : (1) the first source of *Karma* is attachment to worldly things such as food, raiment, dwelling place, women, etc. ; (2) it is produced by uniting one's body, mind, and speech to worldly things ; (3) it is also engendered by giving the reins to anger, pride, deceit or greed ; and, (4) lastly by false belief which is a fruitful source of it. *Karma* accumulates energy and automatically works it off without any outside intervention.

Karma is divided according to its nature, duration, essence, and content. It is intimately bound up with the soul. There are eight kinds of *Karmans*: (1) *Jñānāvaraṇiya* acts as an obstruction to right knowledge ; (2) *Darśanāvaraṇīya* prevents one from beholding the true faith ; (3) *Vedaniya* leads to the experience of pain or pleasure ; (4) *Mohanīya* leads to delusion; (5) *Āyukarma* determines the length of life ; (6) *Nāma* determines the name or individuality of the embodied soul ; (7) *Gotra* determines his *Gotra*, and (8) *Antarāya* prevents one's entrance into the path that leads to eternal bliss.[2]

While it is on the first step (*Mithyāttvaguṇasthānaka*) the soul is completely under the influence of *Karma* and knows nothing of the truth. Whirling round and round in the cycle of rebirth, it loses some of its crudeness and attains to a state which enables it to distinguish between what is false and what is true. A soul remains in an uncertain condition, one moment knowing the truth and the next doubting it. Either through the influence of his past good deeds or through the teachings of his *Guru*, man comes to acquire what is true faith. He then realises the great importance of conduct and finds himself quite capable of taking the twelve vows. As soon as he reaches the state of an *Āyogikevalīguṇasthānaka*, all his *Karma* is purged away, and he proceeds at once to *Mokṣa* as a *Siddha*.

1. *Sūtra*, I 1.2.1-5; I, 1.4 8-9; II 1. 32; *Uva*, VI. 166.
2. *Uttarā*, XXXIII, 2-3.

There are four kinds of destructive *Karma* (*Khātiyakarma*) which keep the soul tethered to mundane existence. They are as follows : (1) knowledge-obscuring *Karma*, (2) faith-obscuring *Karma*, (3) *Karma* which obstructs the progress of the soul, and (4) *Karma* which deludes the soul. Indeed *Karma* plays an important part in Jaina metaphysics. Jainism as a practical religion teaches us to purge ourselves of impurities arising from *Karma*.

SIX LEŚYĀS

The *Leśyās* are different conditions produced in the soul by the influence of different *Karmans*. They are, therefore, not dependent on the nature of the soul, but on the *Karma* which accompanies the soul, and are, as it were, the reflection of the *Karmans* on the soul.[1] The *Leśyā* is, according to the *Sūtrakṛitāṅga*, a term signifying, 'colour'.[2]

The *Ājīvika* expression *Chalābhijātiyo* as explained by Buddhaghosha implies the same method of classification of men in terms of six colours.[3] According to H. Jacobi,[4] Mahāvīra borrowed the idea of the six *Leśyās* from the Ājīvikas and altered it to bring it into harmony with the rest of his own doctrines. This view is not correct because the idea of the six *Leśyās* was prevalent in Jainism earlier than Mahāvīra. The classification of living beings in terms of six colours may be traced back to Pārśva's doctrine of six *Jivanikāyas*.[5]

The *Mahābhārata* expression *Jīva-Shaṭvarṇāḥ* hardly leaves room for doubt that *Leśyā* is a term indicative of colour. The Buddhist idea of the contamination of mind by the influx of impurities from outside, illustrated by the simile of a piece of cloth dyed blue, red, yellow, or the like[6] would seem to have some bearing on the Jaina doctrine of the *Leśyās*.

The Jaina religious efforts are directed towards the acqui-

1. SBE, XLV, p. 196, f n. 2.
2. Ibid, p. 289, f.n. 1; *Sūtra*, I, 6.13.
3. BHPIP, pp. 309, 318.
4. SBE, XLV, p. xxx.
5. *Āchā*, II, 15. 16.
6. B.M. Barua : *Chittaviśuddhiprakaraṇa* and its Pāli Basis, published in Indian Culture.

sition of pure *leśyā*. This doctrine of the six *Leśyās* is merely hinted at here and there in the *Sūtrakṛtāṅga*[1] and fully explained in the *Uttarādhyayana*.[2] They are named in the following order : black, blue, grey, red, yellow, and white. The black *Leśyā* has the colour of a rain-cloud, a buffalow's horn. The blue *Leśyā* has the colour of the blue Aśoka having red flowers. The grey *Leśyā* has the colour of *Atasī* having blue flowers. The red *Leśyā* has the colour of vermilion. The yellow *Leśyā* has the colour of orpiment. The white *Leśyā* has the colour of a conch-shell. The taste of the black *Leśyā* is more bitter than that of *Tumbaka*. The taste of the blue *Leśyā* is infinitely more pungent than that of *Trikaṭuka* (black pepper and dry ginger). The taste of the grey *Leśyā* is infinitely sourer than that of unripe mango. The taste of the yellow *Leśyā* is infinitely better than that of excellent wine and various liquors. The taste of the white *Leśyā* is infinitely better than that of dates, grapes, and milk.

The smell of the bad *Leśyās* (*viz.*, of the first three) is infinitely worse than that of a dead cow, dog or snake. The smell of the three good *Leśyas* is infinitely more pleasant than that of fragrant flowers and of perfumes when they are pounded. The touch of the bad *Leśyās* is infinitely worse than that of a saw, the tongue of a cow, or the leaf of the teak tree. The touch of the three good *Leśyās* is infinitely more pleasant than that of cotton, butter or *Śirīsha* flowers.

The degrees of the *Leśyās* are three, or nine, or twenty-seven, or eighty-one, or two hundred and forty-three. Each of these degrees is three-fold : low, middle, and high. He who acts on the impulse of the five sins, who commits cruel acts, and who is wicked and mischievous, is described as one fostering the black *Leśyā*. He who nourishes anger, ignorance, hatred, wickedness, deceit, greed, carelessness, love of enjoyment, etc., develops the blue *Leśyā*. He who is dishonest in words and acts, who is a heretic, a deceiver, a thief, etc., develops the grey *Leśyā*. He who is humble, well-disciplined, restrained, free from deceit, who loves the law, develops the

1. *Sūtra*, I, 4, 21, where a Jaina saint is described as a person whose soul is in a pure condition (*Leśyā*).
2. *Uttarā*, xxxiv.

red *Leśyā*. He who controls himself and is attentive to his study and duties, develops the yellow *Leśyā*. He who controls himself, who abstains from constant thinking about his misery, who is free from passion, who is calm and who subdues his senses, develops the white *Leśyā*. The black, blue, and grey *Leśyās* are the Lowest *Leśyās*; through them, the soul is dragged into certain miserable courses of life. The red, yellow, and white *Leśyās* are the good *Leśyās*, for through them the soul is brought into a state of happiness. In the first and last moment of all these Laśyās, when they are joined with the soul, the latter is not born into a new existence.

DOCTRINE OF NAYAS

Sañjaya is an important landmark in the development of Mahāvīra's philosophy. H. JACOBI assumes that in opposition to the agnosticism (*Ajñānavāda*) of Sañjaya, Mahāvīra propounded his doctrine of *Nayas*.[1] The canonical texts just mention *Nayas* without fixing up their number four or seven. It is true that the *Bhagavati* and the *Pannavaṇā* refer to the sevenfold *Naya*, but these texts contain a good deal of later material. In the post-canonical works, the doctrine of *Nayas* was called *Syādvāda* (*Saptabhaṅginyāya*), according to which there can be seven alternatives to a decisive conclusion. *Nayas* were actually the ways of expressing the nature of things from different points of view ; they were the ways of escaping from the tendencies of insensitivity and dogmatism which Mahāvīra disliked. They appealed to the masses because they encouraged a tolerant attitude towards different religions.

The questions with regard to which Sañjaya suspended judgment were in fact the questions to be excluded from the problems of knowledge. Is the world eternal, or is it non-eternal ? Is it both eternal and non-eternal, or is it neither eternal nor non-eternal ? Is the world finite or infinite ? Is there any individual existence of man after death, or is there not ? Is the absolute truth seen face to face by a seer, comprehended by a philosopher, part of real tangible existence, or not ? It was with regard to these and similar questions that Sañjaya refused to submit any affirmative answer. To avoid

1. SBE, XLV, p. xxvii.

error, he contented himself with the four famous negative propositions : A is not B; A is not not-B;[1] A is not both B and not-B, A is not neither B nor not-B.

It is with regard to these questions that Mahāvīra declared : "From these alternatives, you cannot arrive at truth; from these alternatives, you are certainly led to error."[2] The world is eternal as far as that part is concerned which is the substratum of the (*dravya*) "world"; it is not eternal as far as its ever-changing state is concerned. In regard to such questions, Mahāvīra's advice to his disciples was neither to support those who maintained that the world is eternal nor those who advocated that it is not eternal. He would have said the same thing regarding such propositions as the world exists and it does not exist ; the world is unchangeable ; the world is in constant flux; the world has a beginning ; the world has no beginning ; the world has an end ; the world has no end, etc. Those who are not well-instructed differ in their opinions and hold fast to their dogmas without reason.[3] And these were precisely the questions which Buddha regarded as unthinkable on the ground that those who will think about them are sure to go mad, without ever being able to find a final answer, or to reach apodeictic certainty.[4]

If one has to answer such questions, one should answer them by saying, contrary to both a dogmatist and a sceptic, "It may be that in one sense, looking from one point of view, A is B. It may be that in another sense, looking from another point of view, A is not-B. It may again be that looking from a third point of view, A is both B and not-B. It may equally be that when viewed from a fourth point of view, A is neither B nor not-B."

EXERTION OF RIGHTEOUSNESS

Mahāvīra has given instructions regarding exertion of righteousness. Those who believe in it, accept it, practise it,

1. *Dia*, II, pp. 39-40; 75.
2. *Sūtra*, II. 5.3.
3. *Āchā*. I. 7.3.
4. *Aṅgu*, II. p. 80.

comply with it, study it, and understand it, have obtained perfection, enlightenment, deliverance and final beatitude. He has dealt with the following subjects :[1]

1. *Longing for liberation (Saṁvega)*

By longing for liberation, the soul obtains an intense desire for the Law. Impelled by an intense desire for the Law, he quickly arrives at an increased longing for liberation. He destroys anger, pride, deceit and greed. He becomes possessed of right faith and by the purity of faith, he will reach perfection after one birth.

2. *Disregard of worldly objects (Nirveda)*

By disregarding worldly objects, the soul quickly feels disgust for pleasures enjoyed by men, gods and animals. He becomes indifferent to all objects and ceases thereby to engage himself in any undertaking, with the result that he enters the road to perfection.

3. *Desire for the Law (Dharmaśraddhā)*

Through his desire for the Law, the soul becomes indifferent to pleasures. He abandons the life of householders and as a houseless monk, he puts an end to all sufferings, mental and physical.

4. *Obedience to the Co-religionists (Guruṣādharmika-susrūshaṇā)*

Through obedience to them, the soul obtains discipline. Through discipline and avoidance of misconduct, he avoids being born as a denizen of hell ; through his devotion to the *Guru*, he obtains truth as a good man and gains perfection and beatitude.

5. *Confession of sins before Guru (Ālochanā)*

By this act, the soul gets rid of the thorns of deceit, wrong belief, etc. He obtains simplicity and annihilates *Karma*.

6. *Repenting of one's sins to oneself (Nindā)*

By this act, the soul obtains repentance, and becoming indifferent by repentance, he prepares for himself an ascending

1. *Uttarā*, XXIX.

scale of virtues, by which he destroys the *karmans* resulting from delusion.

7. *Repenting of one's sins, before the Guru* (*Garhā*)

By this act, the soul obtains humbleness. He will leave off all blamable occupations and apply himself only to the praiseworthy ones.

8. *Moral and intellectual purity of the soul* (*Sāmāyika*)

This purity enables the soul to refrain from all sinful occupations.

9. *Adoration, of the twenty-four Jinas* (*Caturviṁśatistava*)

Through this adoration the soul arrives at the purity of faith.

10. *Paying reverence to the Guru* (*Vandanā*)

It enables the soul to destroy such *Karma* as leads to birth in low families. He wins the affection of the people and brings about general good-will.

11. *Expiation of sins* (*Pratikramaṇa*)

Through expiation of sins the soul obviates transgressions of the vows and thus stops the *Āśravas* or sins.

12. *A particular position of the body* (*Kāyotsarga*)

Kāyotsarga helps the soul get rid of the past and present transgressions which require *prāyaśchitta* (expiatory rites).

13. *Self-denial* (*Pratyākhyāna*)

Self-denial enables the soul to close the door against *Āśravas* and to prevent desires from arising in him.

14. *Praises and hymns* (*Stavastutimaṅgala*)

Through praises and hymns he obtains wisdom consisting in knowledge, faith, and conduct.

15. *Keeping the right time* (*Kālasya pratyupekshaṇā*)

By keeping the right time, he destroys *Karma* which obstructs right knowledge.

16. *Practising penance* (*Prāyaścittakaraṇa*)

By practising penance, he gets rid of sins and commits no transgressions.

17. *Begging forgiveness* (*Kshamāpaṇa*)

By begging forgiveness, he obtains happiness of mind.

18. *Study* (*Svādhyāya*)

Study helps him destroy the *Karma* which obstructs right knowledge.

19. *Recital of the sacred texts* (*Vācanā*)

By the recital of the sacred texts, he obtains destruction of *Karma* and preserves the sacred lore.

20. *Questioning the teacher* (*Paripṛicchanā*)

By questioning the teacher, he arrives at a correct comprehension of the *Sūtra* and its meaning.

21. *Repetition* (*Parāvartanā*)

By repetition, he reproduces the sounds or syllables and commits them to memory.

22. *Pondering* (*Anupreksha*)

By pondering on what he has learnt, he loosens the firm hold which the seven kinds of *Karma* have upon the soul ; he shortens their duration and mitigates their power.

23. *Religious discourse* (*Dharmakathā*)

Through religious discourses he destroys his *Karma* and exalts the creed, and by exalting the creed, he acquires *Karma* for the future bliss.

24. *Acquisition of sacred knowledge* (*Śrutasyārādhanā*)

By the acquisition of sacred knowledge, he destroys ignorance.

25. *Concentration of thoughts* (*Ekāgramanaḥsanniveśanā*).

By concentration of his thoughts, he obtains stability of the mind.

26. *Control* (*Saṁyama*)

By control, he achieves freedom from sins.

27. *Austerities* (*Tapas*)

Austerities help him cut off *Karma*.

28. *Cutting off Karma* (*Vyavadāna*)

By cutting off *Karma*, he obtains freedom from action.

29. *Renouncing pleasure* (*Sukhāsāta*)

By renouncing pleasures, he obtains freedom from false longing.

30. *Mental independence* (*Apratibaddhatā*)

Through mental independence he gets rid of attachment.

31. *Using unfrequented lodging and beds* (*Vicitrasayanāsanasevanā*)

By using unfrequented lodgings and beds, he obtains *Gupti* or conduct. He will be steady in his conduct.

32. *Turning away the world* (*Vinivartanā*)

By turning away from the world, he will strive not to perform any bad action.

33. *Renouncing collection of alms in one district only* (*Sambhogapratyākhyāna*)

By doing so, he overcomes obstacles and unhindered by them, exerts himself to attain liberation ; he is content with the alms he gets, and does not hope for, care for, or covet those of a fellow-monk. Not envying other monks, he takes up a separate, agreeable lodging.

34. *Renouncing articles of use* (*Upadhipratyākhyāna*)

By renouncing the articles of use, he studies successfully ; in the absence of the articles of use he becomes exempt from desires, and does not suffer misery.

35. *Renouncing food* (*Āhārapratyākhyāna*)

By renouncing (forbidden) food, he ceases to act for the sustenance of his life ; ceasing to act for the sustenance of his life, he does not suffer misery when without food.

36. *Conquering the passions* (*Kashāyapratyākhyāna*)

By conquering his passions, he becomes free from passions ; thereby he becomes indifferent to both happiness and pain.

37. *Renouncing activity* (*Yogapratyākhyāna*)

By renouncing activity, he obtains inactivity ; by ceasing to act, he acquires no new *Karman*, and destroys the one he had acquired before.

38. *Renouncing the body* (*Śarīrapratyākhyāna*)

By renouncing his body, he acquires the pre-eminent virtues of the *Siddhas*, by the possession of which he goes to the highest region of the universe, and becomes absolutely happy.

39. *Renouncing Company*

By renouncing company, he obtains singleness and aviods disputes, quarrels, passions, etc.

40. *Renouncing all food* (*Bhaktapratyākhyāna*)

By renouncing all food, he prevents his birth many times.

41. *Perfect Renunciation* (*Sadbhāvapratyākhyāna*)

Through perfect renunciation, he enters the final stage of pure meditation where there is no return.

42. *Confirming to the Standard* (*Pratirūpatā*).

By conforming to the standard of monks, he obtains ease and will be careful. He will inspire all beings with confidence and practise austerities.

43. *Doing Service* (*Vaiyāvṛitya*)

By doing service, he acquires *Karma* which gets for him the name and family name of a Tīrthaṅkara.

44. *Fulfilling all virtues* (*Sarvaguṇasampūrṇatā*)

By fulfilling all virtues, the boon he receives is that he will not be born again ; he will thus be exempt from the pains of the body and mind.

45. *Freedom from passion* (*Vitarāgatā*)

Freedom from passion enables him to cut off the ties of attachment and desire, making him indifferent to all agreeable and disagreeable sensations of sound, touch, colour, and smell.

46. *Patience* (*Kshānti*)

Patience enables him to overcome troubles.

47. *Freedom from greed* (*Mukti*)

Freedom from greed helps him welcome voluntary poverty and frees him from the desire for material prosperity.

48. *Simplicity* (*Ārjava*)

Through simplicity, he will become upright in action, thought and speech, and will become veracious and a true practitioner of the law.

49. *Humility* (*Mārdava*)

Through humility he will acquire freedom from self-conceit ; he will become a man of kind and meek disposition, and avoid the eight kinds of pride.

50. *Sincerity of Mind* (*Bhāvasatya*)

Sincerity of mind will help him obtain the purity of mind, which will induce him to exert himself for the fulfilment of the Law ; and he will practise the Law in the next world too.

51. *Sincerity of Religious Practice* (*Karaṇasatya*)

Through sincerity in religious practice, he obtains proficiency in it ; being proficient in it he will act up to his words.

52. *Sincerity in Acting* (*Yogasatya*)

Through sincerity in acting, he will become pure in his actions.

53. *Watchfulness of the Mind* (*Manoguptatā*)

Through the watchfulness of the mind, he concentrates his thoughts, thereby practising true control.

54. *Watchfulness of Speech* (*Vāg-guptatā*)

Watchfulness of speech ensures freedom from prevarication and enables one's mind to act properly.

55. *Watchfulness of the Body* (*Kāyaguptatā*)

Through the watchfulness of the body, he obtains restraint (*Saṁvara*) and prevents sinful *Āśravas.*

56. *Discipline of the Mind* (*Manaḥsamādhāraṇā*)

By disciplining his mind, he obtains concentration of his thoughts and obtains development of knowledge, which produces righteousness and annihilates wrong belief.

57. *Discipline of the Speech* (*Vāksamādhāraṇā*)

By disciplining his speech, he obtains development of faith and acquires facility in becoming enlightened, destroying all preventing causes.

58. *Discipline of the body*, (*Kāyasamādhāraṇā*)

Through the discipline of the body he facilitates the development of his conduct. He may also obtain perfection, enlightenment, and deliverance.

59. *Possession of Knowledge* (*Jñānasampannatā*)

Through his possession of knowledge, he acquires an understanding of words and their meanings.

60. *Possession of Faith* (*Darśanasampannatā*)

Through his possession of faith, he destroys wrong belief, which is the cause of worldly existence, and he will not lose his inner light ; but he endues his self with the highest knowledge and faith, and purifies it.

61. *Possession of Conduct* (*Cāritrasampannatā*)

Possession of conduct helps him obtain stability, with which a houseless monk destroys the four remnants of *Karma* which even a *Kevalin* possesses; after that he obtains perfection, enlightenment, deliverance and final beatitude, and puts an end to all misery.

62. *Subduing the Ear* (*Śrotrendriyanigraha*)

By subduing the organ of hearing, he overcomes his delight in all pleasant or unpleasant sounds and acquires no new *Karma* while destroying the old one.

63-66. *Subduing the eye, the organ of smell, tongue and the organ of touch* (*Cakshurindriyanigraha, Ghrāṇendriyanigraha, Jihvendriyanigraha and Sparśanendriyanigraha*)

This applies also to his subduing the organs of sight, smell, taste and touch with regard to pleasant colours, smells, tastes, and touches.

67. *Conquering anger* (*Krodhavijaya*)

By conquering anger he obtains patience; he acquires no *Karma* productive of anger, and destroys the *Karma* he had acquired before.

68. *Conquering Pride* (*Mānavijaya*).

By conquering pride he obtains simplicity.

69. *Conquering Deceit* (*Māyāvijaya*)

By conquering deceit he obtains humility.

70. *Conquering greed* (*Lobhavijaya*)

By conquering greed he obtains contentment.

71. *Conquering Love, Hate and Wrong belief* (*Premadveshamithyādarśanavijaya*)

By conquering love, hatred and wrong belief, he exerts himself for right knowledge, faith and conduct. After destroying various kinds of *Karma*, he obtains absolute and complete knowledge and faith.

72. *Stability* (*Śaileshī*)

He first stops the functions of his mind, then the functions of his speech, then those of the body, and at last he ceases to breathe. During the short interval required for pronouncing five short syllables, he is engaged in the final pure meditation in which all the functions of his bodily organs cease and the four remnants of his *Karma* are at the same time destroyed.

73. *Freedom from Karma* (*Akarmatā*)

After getting rid of his *Audārika Kārmāṇa* (and *Taijasa*) bodies the soul takes the form of a straight line, goes in a moment, without touching anything and taking up no space, (upwards to the highest *Ākāśā*), and then develops into his natural form and obtains perfection.

THE FOUR REQUISITES

It is difficult for a living being to obtain these four things of great value : (1) Human birth, (2) Instructions in the Law, (3) Belief in it, and (4) Power of self-control.[1] The universe is filled with innumerable creatures born in the world in different families and castes for having done various actions. Sometimes they go to the world of gods and sometimes to hell and sometimes they become *Asuras* (demons) in accordance with their actions ; sometimes they become *Kshatriyas* or *Chaṇḍālas* or worms or ants. Living beings of sinful actions, who are born again and again, are not disgusted with this *Saṁsāra*. Through the destruction of their *Karma*, living beings will reach in time a pure state and will be born as men.[2] Though born as human beings, it would be difficult for them to hear the law ; having heard it, they will do penances, combat their passions, and abstain from killing living beings. It will be difficult for them to believe in the law though indeed they will hear it. Many who are shown the right way are led astray.

The pious obtain purity and the pure stand firmly in the law. Having enjoyed in due time the unrivalled pleasures of human life, they will obtain true knowledge through their pure religious merit acquired in a former birth ; knowing full well that the four requisites are difficult to obtain, they will apply themselves to self-control and will be eternal *Siddhas* (perfected

1. *Uttarā*, III, 1.
2. Ibid, III, 7.

ones) when they will be able to shake off the remnant of *Karma* by their penances.[1]

IMPURITY

Since one cannot prolong life,[2] one should not on that account be careless. Those who acquire wealth by evil deeds and by adhering to wrong principles, will lose it. People in this world and in the next cannot escape the effect of their own actions. Wealth will never protect a careless man in this world. Like a wise man, trust nobody but be always wary and on the alert.

One cannot quickly arrive at discernment ; therefore one should exert oneself, abstain from pleasures, understand the world, guard oneself, and be impartial like a sage. External things weaken the intellect and allure many ; therefore keep them out of mind. Remove pride, delusion, greed and deceit. Heretics, who are impure and proud, are always subject to love and hatred, and they are wholly under the influence of their passions. Despising them as unholy men, one should desire virtue till the end of one's life.[3]

DEATH AGAINST (AND WITH) ONE'S WILL

There can be two ways of dying[4] : (1) Death with one's will, and (2) death against one's will. Death against one's will is the death of an ignorant man, and it happens to him several times. Death with one's will is the death of a wise man, and it happens only once as, for instance, in the case of a *Kevalin.* A fool being attached to pleasure does cruel actions. He who is attached to pleasures and amusements will be caught in the trap of deceit. The pleasures of this life are within the reach of your hand but the future pleasures are uncertain. It is doubted whether there is any world other than our own. An ignorant man kills, lies, deceives, drinks wine and eats meat, thinking that there is nothing wrong in doing what he does. A man desirous of possessing wealth and woman accumulates sins by his act and thought. Fools, who do cruel deeds, will

1. *Uttarā*, III.
2. Ibid, IV. 1., *Sūtra*, I. 2, 2, 21.
3. *Uttarā*, IV, 10-13.
4. Ibid, V, 1-32.

suffer violently. When death really comes, the fool trembles in fear. He dies against his will. Some householders are indeed superior to some monks of self-control. But the saints are verily superior to all householders in self-control. A faithful man should practise the rules of conduct meant for householders. He should never neglect the fast. Those who are trained in self-control and penance, whether monks or householders, and those who have obtained liberation by the absence of passions, go straight to the highest regions. The virtuous and the learned do not tremble in the hour of death. A wise man will become calm through patience and will have an undisturbed mind at the time of death. When the right time for death has come, a faithful monk should in the presence of his teacher suppress all emotions of fear or joy, and wait for his end. When the time for quitting the body comes the sage dies willingly.[1]

ON DISCIPLINE

A wise man should not be angry if reprimanded. He should rather, be a man of forbearing temperament. Nor should he associate with mean persons and be guilty of doing anything mean (*chaṇḍāliya*) or evil. He should meditate by himself after having learnt his lessons. He should never refuse to confess if he does anything mean. He should not speak unasked for. He should not tell a lie when asked. If the self is subdued, a person will be happy. It is better to subdue one's own self by self-control and penance than be subdued by others with fetters and corporal punishment.[2] He should never do anything disagreeable to his superiors either in words or deeds, openly or secretly. He should never remain silent if spoken to by his superiors. He should always approach his teacher politely. An intelligent pupil will rise from his seat and answer the teacher's call modestly and attentively.[3] A good pupil has the best opinion of his teacher, for he thinks that his teacher treats him like his own son or brother. He should not provoke his teacher's anger, nor should he himself lose his

1. *Āchā*, I, 7, 8.
2. *Uttarā*, I, 16.
3. Ibid, I, 21.

temper. If the teacher is angry, he should pacify him by kindness and appease him with folded hands. An intelligent man, who has learnt the sacred texts, takes his duties upon himself. When a worthy teacher is satisfied with a pupil, he will transmit to him his vast knowledge of the sacred texts, and the pupil will gladden the heart of his teacher by his good deeds.[1]

Egoism, delusion, carelessness, illness, and idleness are the five causes which render good discipline impossible. Discipline calls upon the practitioner : (1) not to be fond of mirth, (2) to control himself, (3) not to speak evil of others, (4) not to be without discipline, (5) not to be of wrong discipline, (6) not to be covetous, (7) not to be choleric, and (8) to love truth.[2]

ACTIONS OF IGNORANT AND WISE MEN

All men, who are ignorant of truth, are subject to pain. A wise man who considers well the way that lead to bondage and birth should search for the truth. A man of pure faith should realize the truth that he will have to suffer for his own deeds.[3]

Clever talking will not bring salvation. Even while sinking lower and lower through their sins, fools believe themselves to be wise men. One should move about carefully in the endless *Saṁsāra*. One should never desire worldly objects but sustain one's body only to be able to annihilate one's *Karma*. Recognising the cause of *Karma*, one should move about waiting for one's death.[4]

It is an ignorant man who kills, tells lies, robs on the highway, steals goods, and deceives others.[5] He will go to the world of the *Asuras* (demons) against his will. Those men who, through the exercise of various virtues, become pious householders, will surely reap the fruit of their actions. A virtuous man cheerfully ascends to the state of gods. He who

1. *Uttarā*, I, 47.
2. Ibid, XI. 4-5.
3. Ibid. VI, 3 ; *Sūtra*, I, 9, 5.
4. Ibid, VI, 10-14.
5. Ibid, VII, 5.

has not given up pleasures will not be able to reach the true end of his soul. He will go astray again and again though he has been taught the right way. A sinner will be born in hell and a virtuous man will be born in heaven.

The best of the sages who are free from delusion and possess perfect knowledge and faith, speaks for the benefit, eternal welfare, and the final liberation of all beings.

It is difficult to satisfy anybody. The more one gets the more one wants. Man's desire increases with his means. One should not desire women who continually change their minds, who entice men, and then make a sport of them as of slaves.[1]

VANITY OF WORLDLY PLEASURES

Karma is produced by sinful thoughts, and it is by the influence of his *Karma* that Chitra and Sambhūta were separated.[2] All singing is but prattle, all dancing is but mocking, all ornaments are but a burden, all pleasures produce but pain.[3] Pleasures, which are liked by the ignorant and which produce pain, do not delight pious monks who do not care for pleasures but are intent on the virtue of right conduct.[4] He who has not done good deeds in this life and who has not practised the Law, repents of it in the next world or even when he has become a prey to death which leads off a man in his last hour. He alone will have to endure his sufferings, neither his kinsmen, nor his friends, nor his sons, nor his relations, for *Karma* follows the doer.[5] Life drags on towards death continuously, and old age carries off the vigour of man.[6] Time runs out and the days quickly pass. Pleasures which men enjoy are not permanent. They leave them as soon as they come just as a bird leaves a tree devoid of fruits. If one is unable to give up pleasures, then one must do noble

1. *Uttarā*, VIII. 17-18.
2. Ibid, XIII, 8.
3. Ibid, XIII, 16.
4. Ibid, 17.
5. Ibid, 21-23.
6. Ibid, 26.

deeds, follow the Law and have compassion on all creatures.[1]

Man's life is transitory and precarious. He finds no delight in domestic life. Pleasures bring him only a moment's happiness. But suffering for a long time brings intense suffering and no happiness. Pleasures are an obstacle to the liberation from existence, and are a mine of evils.[2] The soul cannot be apprehended by the senses because it possesses no corporeal form ; and, since it has no corporeal form, it is eternal. The fetter of the soul born of our evil deeds is called the cause of worldly existence. Being ignorant of the law, human beings formerly did sinful actions, and through their wrong-mindedness, they could not enter the order. Mankind is harassed by death. He who has acquired righteousness may look upon death as his friend.[3] Faith will enable him to put aside attachment.[4] The pleasures he enjoys cause the continuance of his worldly existence.[5] One should be cautious in this matter. He should learn the law thoroughly, practise severe penance, and never dissipate his energy.[6]

THE CAUSES OF CARELESSNESS

Through the possession of true knowledge, through the avoidance of ignorance and delusion, and through the destruction of love and hatred, one arrives at deliverance which is nothing but bliss.[7] One should serve the *Guru* and the old teachers, avoid foolish people, apply oneself earnestly to study, and to ponder over the meaning of the *Sūtras*.[8] A *śramaṇa* who engaged in austerities longs for righteousness should eat only the quantity of food allowed, should select a companion of right understanding and should live in a solitary place.[9] If he does not meet with a suitable companion, he should live by himself, abstaining from sins and not devoted to pleasures.[10] Love and hatred are caused by *Karma* which has

1. *Uttarā*, XIII, 31-32.
2. Ibid, XIV, 13.
3. Ibid, 19, 20, 21, 23, 24, 25, 27.
4. Ibid, 28.
5. Ibid, 47.
6. Ibid, 49-50.
7. Ibid. XXXII, 2.
8. Ibid, 3.
9. Ibid, 4.
10. Ibid. 5.

its origin in delusion. *Karma* is the root of birth and death.[1] Misery ceases with the absence of delusion, delusion with the absence of desire, desire with the absence of greed, and greed with the absence of property.[2] Rich and delicious food should not particularly be preferred, for it generally makes men overstrong, and desires rush upon the strong.[3] The mind of those who always live in unfrequented lodgings, who eat poor food, and who subdue their senses, will not be attached by passions which are vanquished as disease is by medicine.[4]

A monk engaged in penance should not allow himself to watch the shape, beauty, coquetry, laughter, prattle, gestures, and glances of women nor retain a recollection of them in his mind.[5] Not to look at women, nor to long for praise, and think of them, is the high ideal of all noble souls and is always wholesome to those who delight in chastity.[6] Those who possess the three *Guptis* cannot be disturbed by the well-adorned goddesses.[7] To a man who longs for liberation, who is afraid of *Saṁsāra* and lives according to the law, nothing in the world offers so many difficulties as women who delight the mind of the ignorant.[8] To those who have overcome the attachment of women all other attachments will offer no difficulties.[9] From the desire for pleasure arises the misery of the whole world. The dispassionate will put an end to whatever misery of the mind and body there is.[10] A monk who is engaged in austerities and who longs for righteousness should not fix his thoughts on the pleasant objects of the senses.[11]

He who is passionately fond of colours will come to

1. *Uttarā*, XXXII, 7.
2. Ibid, 8.
3. Ibid, 10.
4. Ibid, 12.
5. Ibid, 14.
6. Ibid, 15.
7. Ibid, 16.
8. Ibid, 17.
9. Ibid, 18.
10. Ibid, 19.
11. Ibid, 21.

untimely ruin.[1] He who passionately hates a colour will, at the same moment, suffer pain.[2] He who is very fond of a lovely colour hates all others, hence a fool suffers misery.[3] He who has a passion for colour will kill many movable and immovable beings. A passionate fool intent on serving his own personal end torments those beings in many ways.[4] When he is not satisfied with these colours and when his craving for them grows stronger and stronger, he will become discontented. Misled by greed, he will grab another man's property.[5] When overcome by a violent desire, he grabs another man's property and when he is not satisfied with those colours, then his deceit and falsehood increase in proportion to his greed ; yet he will not get rid of his misery.[6] He who is indifferent to true colours is free from sorrows.[7] All such passions as anger, pride, deceit, disgust, aversion to self-control, delight in sexual things, mirth, fear, sorrow, carnal desire for women, arise in him who is attached to pleasures.[8] When he ceases to desire the objects of his senses his desire for pleasure also becomes extinct. A dispassionate man, who performs all duties, will quickly remove the obstacles to right knowledge and right faith.[9] Then he knows and sees all things. He is free from delusions, hindrances, and sins. He is proficient in meditation and being pure attains beatitude.[10] He gets rid of all misery which afflicts mankind. He becomes infinitely happy and obtains the final aim.[11]

SINFUL AND WICKED DEEDS

There are three ways of committing sins : by one's own action, by commission, and by approval of the deed.[12] A learned

1. *Uttarā*, XXXII, 24.
2. Ibid, 25.
3. Ibid, 26.
4. Ibid, 27.
5. Ibid, 29.
6. Ibid, 30.
7. Ibid, 34.
8. Ibid, 102, 103.
9. Ibid, XXII, 108.
10. Ibid, 109.
11. Ibid, 110.
12. *Sūtra*, 1, 1. 3, 26.

or a virtuous man will generally be punished for his deed when he is given to actions of deceit.[1] Men who are drowned in lust and addicted to pleasures will be deluded for want of self-control.[2] Heroes of faith, who do not commit sins, and who exert themselves as they should, who subdue anger and fear, will never kill living beings.[3] The wicked suffering latent misery wander about in the circle of births, subject to old age and death. One should not kill living beings in the threefold way (in thought, act and speech) if one is intent on spiritual welfare and abstention from sins.[4] A sinner does not confess himself to be wrong; instead he boasts of his sin when reprimanded. The adulterers are severely punished. The feet bound together with the fetters of sensuality, will be subject to delusion again and again.

Those who kill others for the sake of their own pleasure are wicked. Reckless men who cut down the sprouts for their own sport destroy many living beings.[5] Sprouts are beings capable of natural development. People who destroy seeds for their own pleasure are wicked.[6] All creatures who have committed sins will suffer. A miserable man who becomes a monk in order to get food from others and a flatterer in order to fill his belly will come to grief.[7] Wrong beliefs and bad conduct are worthless. A servile man should not desire pleasant sounds and colours; he should rather conquer his longing for all kinds of pleasures.[8]

Sinners, subject to love and hatred and wrong-doing, acquire *Karma* arising from passions and commit many sins. The careless commit sins in their thought, act and speech.[9] A cruel man does cruel things and is thereby involved in other cruelties.[10] Sinful undertakings will in the end entail suffering.

1. *Sūtra*, 2, 1, 7.
2. Ibid, 2, 1, 10.
3. Ibid, 2, 1, 12.
4. Ibid, 21.
5. Ibid, 1, 7, 8.
6. Ibid, 7, 9.
7. Ibid, 7, 25.
8. Ibid, 7, 26.
9. Ibid, 8, 6.
10. *Ibid*, 8, 7.

A pious monk, free from bonds and fetters, annihilates his bad *Karma* and removes the thorn of sin.[1] Following the rules of right conduct, he exerts himself.[2]

Sentient beings engage themselves in the following kinds of activities : sinning for one's own interest, sinning without a personal interest, sinning by staying, through accident, by error or sight, by lying, by taking what is not freely given, by mere conceit, through pride, through greed, through deceit, through bad treatment of one's friends, and actions concerning a religious life.[3]

HELLS

In hell, there is suffering from heat and cold.[4] The sinners are cut, pierced, and hacked to pieces with swords and daggers, with darts and javelins. They undergo sharp, horrible, and acute pain. The imprudent sinners, who injure many beings without relenting, will go to hell[5] and cross the river Vaitaraṇī, the waves of which cut like sharp razors.[6] They are pierced with long pikes and tridents.[7] They roll about and are roasted in the Kadamba Bāhula river.[8] They come to the great impassable hell called Asūrya,[9] where the Sun does not shine. Here also they are roasted.[10] The sinners are hewn with axes like pieces of timber. They are stewed in iron caldrons filled with their own blood.[11] They are not reduced to ashes. They undergo this kind of punishment for their misdeeds.[12] In hells sinners suffer on account of their sinful deeds done by them while on earth. The noses, ears, and lips of the sinners are cut off with razors and their tongues are pulled out

1. *Sūtra*, 1, 8, 10.
2. Ibid, 1, 8, 11.
3. Ibid, 2, 2, 4.
4. *Uttarā*, XIX, 47-48.
5. *Sūtra*, I, 5, 1, 5.
6. Ibid, 5, 1, 8.
7. Ibid, 5. 1, 9.
8. Ibid, I, 5, 1, 10.
9. Ibid, 5, 1, 11.
10. Ibid, 5, 1, 12.
11. Ibid, 5, 1, 15.
12. Ibid, 5. 1, 16.

with sharp pikes.[1] They are thrown into large caldrons and boiled there. They are compelled to drink molten lead and copper when they are thirsty.[2] In hell there is a terrible towering mountain called the Vaitālika where evil-doers are long tortured.[3] Thus the sinners are tortured day and night. They cry at the top of their voices in a dreadful hell which contains various implements of torture.

Hells are round inside, square outside, their floor thickly set with razor-like arrows. They are filled with perpetual darkness. Their floor is slippery with a coat of marrow fat, flesh, blood, and matter, and besmeared with grease. They are very rugged, difficult to pass and horrid. Those who are condemned to live in these hells do not sleep, nor do they get any consolation or comfort or recreation. The denizens of hell suffer intolerable agonies.

A GLOOMY VIEW OF THE WORLD

Mahāvīra presents a gloomy picture of the world. According to him, the soul has to undergo births and deaths, and all their concomitant experiences. The senses and mental faculties become manifest in varying degrees in the varying forms of beings. Because of affection, passion, and attachment, man finds himself in an awful situation. The world presents a constant scene of quarrel and strife, death and carnage, and of all mad pursuits of life, the ultimate end of which is disappointment. For the sake of food and drink, lodging and comfort, woman and wealth, man is involved in various difficulties that lead the soul from sin to sin. Because of their attachment to seductive pleasures of the senses like sounds and colours, tastes and smells, and touches and perceptions, living beings suffer and find no escape from pain. The path to these pleasures is the path to birth, disease, decay, and death. Looking at the miserable condition of the world, man craves for liberation, deliverance and perfection.

REAL BRĀHMAṆA

He who has no worldly attachment after entering the order, who does not repent of having become a monk, and who

1. *Sūtra*, 5, 1, 22. 2. Ibid. 5, 1, 25.
3. Ibid. 5, 2, 17.

takes delight in noble words is called a Brāhmaṇa.[1] He who is free from love, hatred, and fear is called a Brāhmaṇa.[2] A lean, self-subduing ascetic, who reduces his flesh and blood, who is pious, and who has reached *Nirvāṇa*, is a Brāhmaṇa.[3] He who thoroughly knows living beings and does not injure them in any of the three ways (by his thought, word, and deed), is a Brāhmaṇa.[4] He who does not speak untruth from anger, or from greed, or from fear is a Brāhmaṇa.[5] He who does not take anything which is not given to him is a Brāhmaṇa.[6] He who does not carnally love divine, human, and animal beings in thoughts, words, and deeds is a Brāhmaṇa.[7] He who is not defied by pleasures is a Brāhmaṇa.[8] He who is not greedy, who lives unknown, who has no house, and who has no friendship with householders, is a Brāhmaṇa.[9] He who has given up his former connections with his relations and parents and who is not given to pleasures is a Brāhmaṇa.[10] One does not become a *Śramaṇa* by the tonsure, nor a Brāhmaṇa by pronouncing the sacred syllable *Om*, nor a *Muni* by living in the forest, nor a *Tāpasa* by wearing clothes of *Kuśa*-grass.[11] One becomes a *Śramaṇa* by equanimity, a Brāhmaṇa by chastity, a *Muni* by knowledge, and a *Tāpasa* by penance.[12] One becomes a *Brāhmaṇa* or a *Kshatriya* or a *Vaiśya* or a *Śūdra* by one's actions.[13] He is a Brāhmaṇa who is exempt from all *Karma*.[14] The most excellent Brāhmaṇas, who possess good qualities, are able to save themselves and others.[15]

1. *Uttarā*, XXV, 20.
2. Ibid, 21.
3. Ibid, 22.
4. Ibid, 23.
5. Ibid, 24.
6. Ibid, 25.
7. Ibid, 26.
8. Ibid, 27.
9. Ibid, 28.
10. Ibid, 29.
11. Ibid, 31.
12. Ibid, 32.
13. Ibid, 33.
14. Ibid, 34.
15. Ibid, 35.

CODE OF CONDUCT FOR ASCETICS

Mahāvīra also prescribed certain rules of conduct for ascetics. These rules are classified under such general heads as begging, walking, modes of speech, entry into other's possessions, postures, place of study, and attending to the calls of nature. Here begging includes begging food and drink, begging a bowl, begging clothes, and begging a residence or a couch. Under these subheads are to be found the rules governing the modes of eating, drinking, and lying down. Walking includes travelling, crossing, swimming and other forms of movement. The postures are those that are involved in religious exercises.

The reasons why these rules have been laid down are grounded in such general principles as the avoidance of situations in which the monk or nun may be guilty of hurting or killing all forms of life, or of inconveniencing others, or of wounding the social, moral, or religious scruples of others, the avoidance of situations in which the monk or nun may run the risk of endangering his own position or of receiving bodily injuries, or of feeling discomfort, or of being found guilty of theft or trespass, or of moral degradation, or of mental perturbation, and the avoidance of all situations in which the monk or nun may be found acting under the slightest influence of greed, ill-will, evil intention, discontent, delusion, inconsideration, haughtiness, and the like.

DISCIPLINE

A monk on receiving an order from his superior goes to him, watching the movement of his head and motions. He is well-behaved.[1] He who desires his own welfare should adhere to the rules of good conduct.[2] He who desires liberation will be received everywhere.[3] He should acquire valuable knowledge and avoid what is worthless. He should rather be meek than talkative in the presence of the wise.[4] A monk should avoid untruth and never tell anything sinful or meaningless or

1. *Uttarā*, I, 2.
2. Ibid, 6.
3. Ibid, 7.
4. Ibid, 8.

hurtful.[1] On the highway or in a barber's shop, a monk, who is all alone, should not stand with a single woman, nor should he talk to her.[2] A monk should sally forth at the right time and return at the right time.[3] He should not approach dining people sitting in a row; he should collect alms that are freely given.[4] He should eat moderately at the right time. He should wait for his alms alone, not too far from other monks, nor too near them.[5]

ON TROUBLES

There are twenty-two troubles which a monk must learn and know, bear, and conquer in order not to be vanquished by them. They are as follows : hunger, thirst, cold, heat, gad-flies and gnats (all biting or stinging insects like lice), nakedness, women, to be discontented with the objects of control, erratic life, place for study, lodging abuse, corporal punishment, asking for something, to be refused, illness, the pricking of grass, dirt, kind and respectful treatment, understanding, ignorance, and righteousness. A monk, who is strong in self-control and does penance, should not cut or cause another to cut anything to be eaten, nor cook it or cause another to cook it, even though his body is weakened by hunger. He should know the measure of food and drink permitted and wander about with a cheerful mind. Though troubled by thirst, he should drink distilled, not cold, water. Wandering about in deserts and feeling thirsty, he should bear the suffering caused by thirst. If a restrained monk occasionally suffers from cold on his wanderings, he should not walk beyond the prescribed time, remembering the teachings of the Master. A monk should not entertain such a thought : 'I have no shelter and nothing to cover my skin, therefore I shall kindle a fire to warm myself.' If a monk suffers from the heat of things hot or from the heat of the body, he should not lament the loss of comfort.

1. *Uttarā*, 24.
2. Ibid, I, 26.
3. Ibid, 31.
4. Ibid, 32.
5. Ibid, 33.

A monk should remain undisturbed even if bitten by insects. He should not scare them away nor keep them off. He should not kill living beings. Nor should he entertain such thoughts : "My clothes are torn, I shall go naked or else I shall get a new suit." A houseless and poor monk, who wanders from village to village, should endure the hardships of an ascetic life. He should wander about free from sins and perfectly passionless. He knows that worldly men have a natural liking for women. Knowing this, he renounces women and easily performs his duties as a perfect monk.

A monk should acquire no property. He should sit down above in a burial place, or in a deserted town, or under a tree. Sitting there, he should brave all dangers. A monk, who does penances and is strong in self-control, will not be effected beyond measure by good or bad lodgings. If a layman abuses a monk, he should not be angry with him. If a monk hears bad words, he should silently overlook them and should not take them to heart. He should not be angry if beaten. He should not entertain sinful thoughts. He should meditate on the law. He should beg food from a householder when his dinner is ready. A monk who thinks thus, "I get nothing today, perhaps I shall get something tomorrow", will not be grieved by his want of success.

If a monk suffers pain or falls sick, he should cheerfully make his mind steady and bear the evils that attack him. He will be a true monk if he continues to search for the welfare of his soul. If a naked ascetic lies on the grass, his body will be hurt. Even then he will not use clothes. A wise monk should not lament the loss of comfort. He should overcome all difficulties while waiting for the destruction of his *Karma*. By practising the noble and excellent Law, he should carry the filth on his body till he expires. He should not evince any predilection for one who salutes him or rises from his seat on his approach or invites him to accept alms in his house. He should not think thus : "There is no life to come nor an exalted state to be acquired by penances."[1]

A monk should know what alms may be accepted and

1. *Uttarā.* II, 1-44.

beg food only for the sustenance of life. Those who explain the marks of the body and who know its imminent changes are not to be called novices.

THE LEAF OF THE TREE

Just as the yellow leaf of a tree falls to the ground when its days are done, so does the life of man come to its close.[1] As life is so fleeting and existence so precarious, one should wipe off the sins ever committed. A rare chance is human birth for living beings and hard are the consequences of actions. The soul, which suffers from its carelessness, is driven about in the *Saṁsāra* by its good and bad *Karmans*. It is a chance rare enough to become an elect. If one believes in the law, one will surely practise it when the human body grows old and the hair turns white, when the power of the ears, eyes and the tactile nerves diminishes—when, in short, all human power begins to decline. One should cast aside all attachments and give up wealth. The enlightened and liberated monk should control himself and should show all the road to peace.

THE TRUE MONK

If a monk is dogmatic in his assertions, if he is malicious, egotistical, greedy, and without self-discipline, if he is always unkind, if he does not share what he has with others, then he is ill-behaved. If he is always humble, steady, free from deceit, if he is not proud of his learning, if he listens to friendly advice, if he does not speak ill of his friend behind his back, if he is enlightened, polite, decent and quiet, then he is well-behaved.[2] Monks will go to the highest place only after their *Karma* has been annihilated.

He who adopts the law with a view to living as a monk should live in company of other monks, upright and free from desires. Free from love, he should live as a model of righteousness, abstaining from sins and versed in the sacred law.

1. *Uttarā*, X. This sermon was preached by Mahāvīra to Gautama to help him attain *Kevala-jñāna*. It contains much of Mahāvīra's doctrine. The sermon was meant to enable Gautama to cut off love and reach perfection.
2. Ibid, XI, 10-13.

Ignorant of abuse and iniquity a steadfast monk should be a model of righteousness, always protecting his soul from sins; neither rash nor passionate, he should endure everything. He controls himself, keeps the vows, practises austerities and meditates on his soul. A true monk does not care for his life, abandons every delusion, avoids men and women, and does not betray any curiosity. He does not progress and live on divinations. He also abstains himself from spells, roots, every kind of medical treatment, purgatives, emetics, fumigation, anointing of the eye, etc. A Jaina monk is forbidden to take beds, lodgings, drinks, food, dainties and spices from the householders. He who understands all religious disputations, who practises self-discipline, who meditates on his soul, who is wise, hardy, and observes everything, who is calm, and does not hurt anybody—he who does all this is a true monk. He who does not live by any art, who is without house and without friend, who subdues his senses, who is free from all bondages and sins and who eats little and lives single—he, too, is a true monk.[1]

THE TEN CONDITIONS OF PERFECT CHASTITY

There are ten conditions for the realization of celibacy. By hearing and knowing them, the monk will reach the highest degree of self-discipline, of contemplation, of stopping sins by means of *Samitis* and *Guptis*, will be well protected, will guard his senses and chastity. The ten conditions are the following :—

(i) A monk may occupy various places for sleep or rest, but he should not occupy such places frequented by women, cattle, or eunuchs. If he occupies such places for sleep or rest as are frequented by women, cattle, or eunuchs his chastity will be suspect or he will acquire a dangerous illness of long duration or he will become a slave to passion.

(ii) He should not talk about women.

(iii) He should not sit together with women on the same seat.

1. *Uttarā*, XV.

(iv) He should not look at or think of the charms or beauties of women.

(v) He should not eavesdrop behind a screen or wall and listen to the singing or laughing or crying of women.

(iv) He should not remember the pleasures and amusements which he enjoyed in the past in the company of women.

(vii) He should not eat well-dressed food.

(viii) He should not eat or drink to excess.

(ix) He should not wear ornaments.

(x) He should avoid sounds, colours, tastes, smells and sensations of touch.[1]

BAD MONKS

A bad monk is one who despises learning and discipline which his preceptors and teachers have taught him. He is disrespectful to his teachers and preceptors. He does not control himself though he believes himself to be well controlled. He hurts living beings and walks with great haste and without care. He is fierce and overbearing. It is the duty of a monk to examine very closely everything which he uses in order to avoid hurting living beings. He always slights his teachers and is deceitful, talkative, arrogant, greedy and rough. He delights in quarrels and perverts truth. He is not careful in sitting down. He is careless about his bed. He does not practise austerities. He eats after sunset, and when admonished, he makes an angry reply. Leaving his own teacher, he follows a heretical one. He is a man of bad disposition and frequently changes his school (*Gaṇa*). He lives by fortune-telling, not by alms, and eats the food given by his relations. A pious monk is one who avoids sins, who is welcomed in this world, and who is the conqueror of the world.[2]

DUTIES OF A MONK

One should adopt the Law of the monks as well as their vows, virtues, and their endurance of the calamities, an endurance which enables him to abandon the great distress and the

1. *Uttarā*, XVI.
2. Ibid, XVII,

great delusion.[1] He should keep the five great vows, *viz.* not to kill, to speak the truth, not to steal, to be chaste, and to have no property at all. A wise man should follow the law taught by the Jinas.[2] A monk should be of a forbearing nature, restrained, and chaste. He should live with his senses under control.[3] He should walk about in utter indifference and bear everything, pleasant and unpleasant. He should not approve of everything everywhere nor care for respectful treatment or blame.[4] A monk, who encounters dangerous and dreadful calamities, is not afraid of them.[5] He should endure with equal equanimity both cold and heat, unpleasant feelings and physical disorders which attack the human body.[6] An ascetic will by means of his simplicity enter the path of *Nirvāṇa.*[7] He is neither grieved nor pleased. He is intent on the benefit of his soul and strives for the highest good.[8] A merciful monk should use beds far from those which have not been prepared for him.[9]

THE SAMITIS AND THE GUPTIS

There are five *Samitis* and three *Guptis* which constitute eight articles of the Jaina creed. The *Samitis* are the following : (1) going by paths trodden by men, beasts, carts, etc., and looking carefully so as not to cause the death of any living being ; (2) gentle, sweet, and religious speech; (3) receiving alms in so nice a manner that the forty-two faults are avoided; (4) receiving and keeping things necessary for religious exercises; and (5) answering the call of nature in an unfrequented place. The three *Guptis* are the following : (1) preventing the mind from sensual pleasures by engaging it in contemplation, study, etc., (2) preventing the tongue from saying bad

1. *Uttarā,* XXI, 11.
2. Ibid, 12.
3. Ibid, 13.
4. Ibid, 15.
5. Ibid, 16-17.
6. Ibid, 18.
7. Ibid, 20.
8. Ibid, 21.
9. Ibid, 22.

things through a vow of silence, and (3) putting the body in an immovable posture.

A well-disciplined monk should have only such walks as are pure with regard to their cause, time, road, and effort. Knowledge, faith, and right conduct are included in the 'cause', the 'time' is daytime, the 'road' excludes bad ways, and the 'effort' is fourfold as regards substance, place, time, and condition of the mind. He should work diligently and avoid anger, pride, deceit, greed, laughter, fear, loquacity, and slander. He should use blameless and concise words at the appropriate time and avoid while begging faults in the search, in the receiving, and in the use of food, lodging, and the articles of daily consumption. There are sixteen *Udgama doshas* by which food becomes unfit for a Jaina monk : the undesirability for instance inherent in the food prepared by a layman for religious mendicants, the undesirability of the food which a layman has prepared for a particular monk, which has been prepared for festivities or which has been reserved for a monk when he has to open locks before he gets the food or when a monk calls while the dinner is being cooked, and for his sake more food is put in the pot which is on the fire, etc.

There are ten faults of receiving, e.g. when a monk accepts alms from a frightened layman (*Śaṅkita*), when the food is soiled by animate or inanimate matter (*Mrakshita*), when a layman mixes up pure with impure food (*Unmiśṛita*), etc. A zealous monk should wipe the thing after having inspected it with his eyes; then he should take it up or put it down. Excrements, urine, saliva, mucus, and uncleanliness of the body should be disposed of in the way prescribed. In a place neither frequented nor seen by others, which offers no obstacles to self-control, which is not covered with grass or leaves, which is spacious, in such a place he should leave his excrements, etc.

There are (1) truth, (2) untruth, (3) mixture of truth and untruth, and (4) a mixture of what is not true and what is not untrue. A zealous monk should not harbour any desire for the misfortune of others, nor should he think of causing misery to living beings or their destruction. In standing, sitting, lying down, jumping, going and in the use of his organs, a zealous monk should prevent his mind cherishing evil desires, etc. These are the *Samitis* for the practice of the religious life and *Guptis* for the prevention of everything sinful.[1]

THE CORRECT BEHAVIOUR OF MONKS DURING THE SEVERAL PARTS OF DAY AND NIGHT

'The correct behaviour of monks consists of the following: *Āvaśyikā* is required when a monk leaves a room; *Naishedhiki* on entering a place; *Āpṛichchhanā* or asking the Superior's permission for what he is to do himself; *Pratipṛichchhanā*, for what somebody else is to do; *Chhandanā* or placing at the disposal of other monks the things one has got; *Ichchhākāra* in the execution of one's intention by oneself or somebody else; *Mithyākāra* in blaming oneself for sins committed; *Tathākāra* in assenting to make a promise; *Abhyutthāna* in serving those who deserve respect, and *Upasampad* in placing oneself under another teacher.

After sunrise during the first quarter of the first *Paurushi* (the fourth part of a day or a night), a monk should inspect and clean his things and pay his respects to his superior. He should ask him with folded hands : what shall I do now ? If he is ordered to do some work, he should do it ungrudgingly. A clever monk should divide a day into four equal parts, and fulfil his duties in all the four parts. In the first *Paurushī*, he should study; in the second he should meditate; in the third, he should go on his begging-tour; and in the fourth, he should study again. The *Paurushī* increases or decreases a digit (equal to five minutes) every week, two digits every fortnight, and four digits every month. A clever monk should divide the night into four parts and do his duties in all the four parts. In the first *Paurushi*, he should study; in the second, he should meditate; in the third, he should sleep and in the fourth, he should study again. When a small part of the quarter is left in which the leading star is seen, a monk should watch.

In the first quarter of the first *Paurushi*, he should inspect his things, pay his respect to his superior, then begin his study not allowing himself to be affected by any pain. In the last

1. *Uttarā*, XXIV.

quarter of the first *Paurushī*, after paying his respect to the *Guru* a monk should inspect his alms-bowl without performing the expiation of sins concerning time. He should inspect his mouth cloth, then his broom; and, taking the broom in his hand, he should inspect his cloth. Standing upright, he should hold his cloth firmly and inspect it leisurely. Then he should spread it and at last wipe it. He should spread the cloth without shaking or crushing it in such a way as to make the folds disappear; he should fold it up six times in length and nine times in breadth, and then he should remove whatever living organisms that are there with his hands. He must avoid inattentiveness in commanding his work, in taking up the corners of the cloth, in folding it up, in removing the dust, in putting it down on some other piece of cloth, and in sitting upon the hunches (*Vedikā*). One must not hold the cloth loosely or at one corner. If he who is engaged in inspecting a thing talks with anybody, renounces something, receives his lessons from another, he obviously neglects his inspection. One who is careful in his inspection, protects the six kinds of living beings, e.g. the earth bodies, the water bodies, the fire bodies, the wind bodies, plants, and animals.

In the third *Paurushī*, he should beg food and drink for any of the following six reasons : (1) to prevent illness. (2) to serve the *Guru*, (3) to comply with the rules of walking, (4) to comply with the rules of self-control (5) to save one's life, and (6) to meditate on the Law. A zealous Jaina monk should not beg food for the following reasons : (1) in the case of illness, (2) in the case of disaster, (3) to preserve one's chastity, and the *Guptis*, (4) out of compassion for living beings, (5) in the interest of penance, and (6) to put an end to one's life.

In the fourth *Paurushī*, a monk should put away his alms-bowl, and then he should begin to study. In the last quarter of the fourth *Paurushī*, he should pay his respects to the *Guru*, and having performed *Kālapratikramaṇa*, he should inspect his lodging. A true monk should find a suitable place where to discharge his excrements and urine. He should reflect on the transgressions he has committed during the day with regard to knowledge, faith, and conduct. Having finished *Kāyotsarga* and paid his respect to the *Guru*, he should confess the sins committed during the day. Then, having recited the *Pratikramaṇa Sūtra* and having destroyed his sins, he should pay his respect to the *Guru*. Having finished *Kāyotsarga*, he should pronounce the customary prayers. A monk should do the same thing in the first *Paurushī* during the night, in the fourth *Paurushi*, and in the last quarter of the fourth *Paurushī*. Then he should reflect on all the sins committed during the night with regard to knowledge, faith, and conduct. Then he should confess the sins committed during the night. Having finished *Kāyotsarga* and paid his respect to the *Guru*, he should practise those austerities which he has undertaken, and praise the saints whc have attained perfection.[1]

MODE OF LIFE

A monk will not be subject to transmigration if he practises self-control in the different spheres of life. Love and hate are two evils which produce bad *Karma*. A monk should always keep away from hurtful, conceited and delusive acts. Hurtful acts (*daṇḍa*) are threefold since they refer to thoughts, words, and acts. Conceited acts are pride in riches, in taste and in pleasure or fashion. Delusive acts are *Māyā*, *Nidāna* and false belief (*Mithyādarśana*). A monk endures calamities and does his best to escape from the four different kinds of praises, passions, expressions of the emotions, and of the four meditations. He always exerts himself with regard to the five vows, the five objects of the senses, the five *Samitis*, and the five actions. He also exerts himself with regard to the six *Leśyās*, the six kinds of bodies, and the six regular functions as eating. He always exerts himself with regard to the seven rules of accepting alms and the seven causes of danger to others.

A monk guards himself against the eight objects of pride while following the ten-fold Law of the monks. The eight objects of pride are : caste, family, beauty, etc. The monk devotes himself to the eleven duties of the *Upāsaka* (lay-disciples) and to the twelve duties of the *Bhikkhus*. He always exerts

1. *Uttarā*, XXVI.

himself with regard to the thirteen actions productive of *Karma*, fourteen kinds of living beings, and the fifteen places of punishment of the wicked. He is always aware of the sixteen *gāthās*, eighteen kinds of continence, and nineteen *Jñātādhyayanas* (Nāyā), twenty-one fobidden actions, and twenty-two troubles. He always exerts himself with regard to the twenty-three lectures of the *Sūtrakṛtāṅga*, the twenty-five clauses, and the twenty-six chapters of the *daśās*. He always exerts himself with regard to the twenty-seven virtues of the laity and the twenty-eight lectures of the *Prakalpa*, the twenty-nine causes of wrong knowledge, the thirty causes of delusion, the thirtyone qualifications of the perfected ones, the thiry-two pure operations of the mind, speech, and body, and the thirty-three articles regulating the intercourse between monks, especially pupils and teachers.[1]

THE HOUSELESS MONK

Renouncing his wife, a sage should know and give up those attachments which enslave men. A monk possessing self-restraint should abstain from killing, stealing, dying, physical intercourse, and greed. He should not long for a pleasant dwelling house. He should happily live in a burial place, in a deserted-house, beneath a tree, in solitude, etc. A well-controlled monk should live in a place which is not much too crowded and where no women live. He should abstain from building a house. Full of compassion for living beings he should neither cook nor cause others to cook. He should cause nobody to cook because beings, living in water, corn, wood, etc., are destroyed in the process. A monk should not light a fire. He should not in his thoughts long for gold and silver. He is not to engage in buying and selling. He who is to live on alms should beg, not buy. He should collect his alms in parts and contentedly go at his begging hour, whether he gets alms or not. A sage should not eat for the sake of the delicious taste of the food but for the sustenance of his life. He should meditate on true things only, committing no sins and owning no property. He should walk about careless about his body till

1. *Uttarā*, XXXI

his end comes. Only such a sage obtains absolute knowledge and reaches eternal beatitude, free from passions and sins, and without property and without egoism.[1]

BEGGING FOOD

A monk or a nun on a begging tour should not accept as alms whatever herbs he or she recognizes. Only such things should be accepted as are pure and acceptable.[2] None should accept food which has been prepared for Brāhmaṇas, guests, beggars, etc.[3] Nor should one accept food which does not belong to the giver.[4] The monk and nun may accept food from noble families, distinguished families, and royal families.[5] They should not, however, attend any festive entertainment.[6] Nor should they accept food about which they have some doubts in their mind. A monk or a nun desirous of entering the abode of a householder should not do so when it is found 'that the milch cows are being milched, or the food is being cooked, and that it is not yet distributed.'[7]

A monk or a nun on a begging tour should not accept flattened grains, grains containing much chaff.[8] He or she should not accept fossil salt or sea salt which is impure and unacceptable.[9] He or she should not accept food which has been prepared over the fire, for such food is impure and unacceptable.[10] He or she should not accept food which has been placed on a post or on a roof or on a platform or some such elevated place.[11] He or she should not accept food which is kept in an earthen ware.[12] He or she should not accept food placed on the earth body, wind body or fire body, for such

1. *Uttarā*, XXXV.
2. *Āchā*, II, 1, I, 3, 4,
3. Ibid, II, I, I, 12.
4. Ibid, 13.
5. Ibid. II, I. II, 2.
6. Ibid, 5.
7. Ibid, II, I, 4. 3.
8. Ibid, II, I. 6, 8.
9. Ibid, 9.
10. Ibid, 10.
11. Ibid, II, I, 7, 1.
12. Ibid, II, I, 7, 3.

food is impure and unacceptable.[1] He or she should not accept food which is placed on vegetable or animal matter.[2] He or she should not accept such water as has been taken from the bare ground.[3] He or she should not accept juice of mangoes, pomegranates, cocoanuts, tamarinds, etc[4]. He or she should not accept raw things, such as mustard seeds, raw powdered fruits, unripe wild rice, honey, liquor, etc. He or she should not accept raw plants, vegetables, raw substances, etc. He or she should not accept any part of a sugarcane, as it is impure and unacceptable, meat or fish containing many bones; but food which is offered on a plate or in a copper cup may be accepted if the moisture on the hands of the giver is dried up. A monk or a nun should not use for religious postures a lodging used by a householder, in which there are workmen, children, cattle, food, and drink.[5]

A mendicant should not stay in halting places, garden houses, family houses, monasteries much frequented by fellow-ascetics. It is difficult to obtain pure and acceptable alms. A monk or a nun should not use for religious postures a lodging where the householder and his wife go about naked or hide themselves, or talk about sexual pleasures. He or she should not use for religious postures a lodging which is a common playground.

A monk shall not beg pointing at the householder with a finger or goading, the threatening, or scratching him with a finger, praising or cursing him.[6]

MODES OF SPEECH

He or she should speak with precision, employing his language with moderation and restraint, a language which is grammatically correct and whose true import, he fully understands. A monk or a nun should not use speech if it be sinful, blamable, rough, coarse and hard. Seeing a diseased person, he or she should not talk thus : "He has got boils or leprosy. His

1. Āchā, II, I. 7, 4.
2. Ibid, 6.
3. Ibid, 9.
4. Ibid, II, I, 8. 1,
5. II, I, 8, 4-15.
6. *Ibid*, II, 1, 6, 3.

hand, foot, nose, ear, or lip is affected." A monk or a nun seeing a man should speak about him thus : 'His body is well grown, well compacted, his flesh and blood are abundant.'[1]

WALKING

When a monk or a nun knows that in a village or a town, there is no large place for religious practices or for study, he or she should not remain there during the cold season. He or she may circumspectly wander from village to village. When on a pilgrimage, he or she should not choose a road passing through a forest. If there is some water-way on the way which must be crossed in a boat, he or she should not get into a boat which plies up or down or across the river. A monk or a nun entering a boat should not choose the stern or the prow or the middle of the boat. If a monk or a nun finds water entering through a leak in the boat which becomes dirty all over, he or she should not approach the boatman and inform him about it. While swimming in the water, he or she should not touch another person's foot, hand, or body with his or her own hand; he or she should not dive up and down, lest water should enter into his or her eyes, ears, nose, or mouth. If while swimming in the water he or she is overcome by weakness, he or she should throw off his or her clothes, either all or a part of them. A monk or a nun should not wipe or rub or brush or dry or warm or heat his or her body. If while going on a pilgrimage he or she comes across shallow water, he or she should first wipe his or her body from head to feet. He or she should wade through the shallow water in a straight line. A monk or a nun wading through the shallow water must not plunge into deeper water for the sake of pleasure.

If a monk or a nun perceives wagons, carts, a friendly or hostile army, he or she should not walk straight on. A monk or a nun, wandering from village to village together with a master or a teacher, should not touch the hand of the master or the teacher with his or her own.[2]

1. *Āchā*, II, 3, 1-3.
2. Ibid, II, 4, 1-2.

BEGGING CLOTHES

A monk or a nun wanting clothes may beg for clothes made of wool, silk, hemp, palm leaves, cotton, etc. He or she should not accept clothes which a layman has bought, washed, dyed, rubbed, cleaned, or perfumed. A monk or a nun should not accept clothes made of fur or clothes that are fine or beautiful, etc. He or she should not accept plaids of fur or other materials. He or she may ask a householder or his wife for clothes which have been well inspected. He or she should not accept clothes which are full of eggs or living organisms, for they are impure. He or she may accept clothes which are strong, lasting, and are fit for a mendicant.

If a mendicant borrows for a short time a robe from another mendicant, the owner of it should not take back such a robe for himself nor should he give it to somebody else. A monk or a nun should not make coloured clothes colourless, he or she should not, that is, colour colourless clothes. If a monk sees thieves on his way, he should not leave the robe out of fear to save his clothes.[1]

BEGGING FOR A BOWL

Monks, and nuns should not accept a bowl bought by a layman. They should not accept expensive bowls or bowls containing precious materials. They may accept a bowl from a householder or his wife after having it thoroughly inspected. They may beg for a bowl used by a former owner or by many people. Entering into the abode of a householder for the sake of alms, they should circumspectly leave it after examining their alms-bowl and removing all living beings from it if there be any. They should not wipe or rub a wet or moist alms-bowl.[2]

SPOT WHERE ONE CAN EASE ONESELF

They should not empty their bowls of excrement on the bare ground or on wet ground or on dusty ground or on a rock or clay containing life or a timber inhabited by worms. They

1. *Āchā*, II, 5, 1-2.
2. Ibid, II, 6, 1-2.

should not ease themselves at a place where the householders or their sons have sown or will sow rice, beans, pulse, or barley. They should not ease themselves at a place where there are heaps of refuse, mud, etc. They should not sit in fireplaces or at a place where suicide is committed, or in gardens, parks, woods, temples, or wells. They should not sit on cross-roads or on town-gates or on pathways or at a place where charcoal is produced or the dead are burnt. They should not empty their bowls at sacred places near rivers, marshes or ponds. They should not ease themselves in fresh clay-pits, fresh pasture-grounds for cattle or in a field of vegetables. Monks and nuns should take their own chamber-pot and ease themselves in a secluded place where no people pass or see them, and leave the excrement on a heap of ashes.[1]

OTHER MISCELLANEOUS ACTS

A monk is holy through his innocence. He allows no trouble to influence his words, thoughts and acts. He should take no notice of seductive pleasures and endeavour to shake off delusion. Knowing the highest Law, he should perform his religious duties. He should be free from attachment and earnest in the performance of austerities.

Begging is a hard task. It is painful never to take anything but what is freely given. Some weak men, who are unable to preserve their chastity, will become disheartened. Some fools take a pious monk for spy, bind him and insult him. Some low people, who lead a life of iniquity and who are subject to love and hatred, injure a monk.

There are some tender affections which monks cannot easily overcome. A monk should renounce attachment, for every attachment is a cause of sin. A holy monk may find many inducements and seductions in this world, but he should not break down like weak bullocks carrying a heavy burden uphill. A monk should snap off the ties that bind him to his house; he should wander about for the welfare of his soul. A wise and thoroughly restrained monk should bear all hardships

1. *Āchā*, II, 10.

and wander about till he attains his final liberation. The Buddhists hold that pleasant things are produced from pleasant things. Those who exert themselves at the proper time feel no remorse afterwards. The heroes, who get rid of their fetters, do not long for their life. A monk should strive for the attainment of *Nirvāṇa* which consists in peace.

Considering the consequences, a worthy monk should have no intercourse with women. He should avoid them. Those who have intercourse with women have ceased to practise meditation. When a monk breaks the Law, dotes on women and is absorbed by that passion, they afterwards scold him, lift their foot up, and trample down his head. One should not mind the entreaties of women, but abstain from their friendship and company. The pleasures which are derived therefrom are causes of blamable actions. A monk should abstain from women and commit no unnatural crime. A wise and learned monk, whose soul is uncontaminated, will abstain from doing work for others; he will endure all hardships with all his might.

A virtuous monk should never keep company with the wicked. He should not stay in the house of a householder except under compulsion. He should obey and serve a wise and pious teacher. If beaten, he should not be angry. With a placid mind he should bear everything.

A true monk should not say that this is meritorious and that is not meritorious. He should guard his soul, bring his senses under his control, and put a stop to the current of the *Saṁsāra*. Free from sins, he is entitled to expound the pure, complete, and unparalleled Law. He should try to attain beatitude.

If a poor monk, subsisting on the meanest food, clings to vanities and makes his monkhood a means of sustenance, he will suffer again and again. An eloquent monk gifted with bright ideas and possessed of a high intellect and pure soul, should combat pride of genius, pride of sanctity, pride of birth, and pride of good living. A monk having conquered aversion to self-control and delight in sensual objects, should silently repeat to himself, "A man must come and go according to his *Karma* alone." The pious are not given to blamable sinful practices. Avoiding all evils, monks should without embarrassment and passion preach the Law.

Making manifest the conduct of the virtuous, an intelligent monk should not leave the company of his teacher. A monk who complies with the rules for the *Yatis* regarding postures, lying down, sitting and exertion, who is thoroughly acquainted with the *Samitis* and *Guptis*, should explain each single point of conduct. He should not allow himself to be influenced by pleasant sounds. He should perserve in self-control. A novice, who has not mastered the law, does not know the law, but he will know it afterwards through the words of the Jainas. A monk possessed of a sound conduct will explain the moral nature of the virtuous. A monk, by hearing the desired truth, gets bright ideas and becomes a clever teacher; by desiring the highest good and practising austerity, he obtains his final liberation. Such virtuous men do not conceal the truth or falsify it. Nor do they cherish any desire for fame. Indeed, a monk should be honest and fearless in his exposition of the *Syādvāda*. He should use words appropriate to a monk and should be impartial and wise. He should utter pure speech in accordance with the creed of the Jinas and should learn the sacred text thoroughly. While his endeavour should be to teach the creed and not to speak unduly long, he should also do his utmost to deliver faithfully what he has learnt. He should not prevent the truth from coming to light nor render it obscure.

A monk, who does not act nor kill, who is free from anger, pride, deceit and greed, who is calm and happy, will never entertain the wish that after his departure from the world he will become a god or a perfected saint. He does nothing that arises from a sinful cause, nor does he get such things done by another person. A monk should not take food or drink when he knows that a householder, to satisfy him or a co-religionist, has brought it. One should eat when it is time for eating, seek cover when it is time for seeking cover, and sleep when it is time for sleeping. When a monk preaches the law, he should preach it not for the sake of food or drink, but he should preach it indefatigably for no other motive than the annihilation of *Karma*. Such a monk searches the law, knows the law, and endeavours to gain liberation. He renounces action and worldly occupation, he is free from passions, possesses the *Samitis*, is wise, virtuous and liberated, lives on simple food, desires to get across the shore of the *Saṁsāra* and never departs from general and particular virtues.

A monk abstains from the five cardinal sins, from the slaughter of living beings, etc. He does not clean his teeth with a tooth brush; he does not accept perfumes, emetics, and collyrium. Such a monk does not act nor kill; he is free from anger, pride, deceit, and greed; he is calm and happy. He is well controlled and restrained, avoids and renounces sins, is not active but careful and thoroughly wise.

The wrongly instructed *Śramaṇas* do not comprehend the soul's bondage through *Karma* (*Karmabandha*). A wise monk should improve his chances for final liberation. He should conform himself to the rules laid down by the Jinas and wander patiently about till he attains final liberation.

A monk, who has achieved his religious perfection through the instruction of the Awakened one and stands firm in it, who guards himself in the threefold way with regard to thoughts, words and acts, and who possesses the things requisite for crossing the immense Ocean of existence, may preach the law.

If a mendicant thinks that on account of his illness, he has become weak and is unable to wander from house to house, on his thus complaining the householder may bring food and give it to him. By practising monastic rules, one becomes tranquil, free from sin, and guards himself against the allurements of the senses. Entering a village or a town, a monk should beg for straw. After getting the straw, he should retire with it to a secluded spot. After having examined and cleaned the ground, he should spread the straw on it. A naked monk thinks thus: 'I can bear the pricking of the grass, the influence of cold and heat, the stinging of flies and mosquitoes. I can sustain all those painful feelings but cannot abandon the covering of the privities'. Knowing the two obstacles relating to the body and mind, a wise man who has thoroughly learnt the law, can get rid of his *Karma*. Subduing the passions and living on little food, he should endure hardships. If a mendicant becomes unattached internally and externally, he should strive after absolute purity. If crawling animals feed on his flesh and blood, he should neither kill them nor rub the wounds; even if these animals destroy the body, he should not stir from his position. A well-controlled monk should give up all motives except his own in thrice threefold way (of body, speech, and mind). He should not lie on sprouts or grass, but inspecting the bare ground, he could lie on it. Without any food or comfort, he should bear pain. If a sage becomes weak, he should strive after calmness, that is to say, he should not give way to melancholy thoughts. He should move about on the ground, and stretch his limbs for the benefit of the whole body. He should walk about when tired of lying and sit down when tired of standing.

CHAPTER V

LORD MAHĀVĪRA'S RELIGIOUS CONTEMPORARIES AND CONTEMPORARY SECTS

The age of Lord Mahāvīra (6th century B.C.) was of far-reaching religious reformist activities not only in India but also throughout the ancient world. It was an age of enlightenment for the human race. The materialistic interpretation of history would attribute this change in human consciousness to a change in social milieu. The idealist historiography would see here an unfoldment of the spirit or the progress of thought through its autonomous dialectic. Suddenly and almost simultaneously and almost certainly independently, there started religious movements at separate centres of civilization. Zoroaster gave a new creed to Iran; Confucius and Loa-tse taught in China; the Jews in their Babylonian captivity developed their tenacious faith in Jehova, and the Sophists in Greece began tackling the problems of life.

Even in India, this was an age of freedom of thought which gave rise to new religious movements and brought about radical changes for the better in the old ones. The *Sāmañña-phala Sutta* and the *Brahmajāla Sutta* in the *Dīgha Nikāya* of the Buddhists mention about sixty-three different philosophical schools—probably all of them non-Brāhmaṇa existing at the time of Buddha. In the *Sūtrakṛitāṅga*, *Bhagavatī*, etc., of the Jainas, we find a far larger number of such heretical schools. These statements about the number of sects may have been influenced by the tendency to exaggerate which was widespread in ancient India. We should not assume that they were independent religious sects or schools because these are distinguished only by very subtle and minor differences in matters of doctrine and practice. It is not possible today to prove once for all that all these sects originated at the same time. Some of them may have owed their origin to a time far more remote than that of Mahāvīra.

ORIGIN OF THESE SECTS

There are divergent views among the scholars about the origin of these ascetic intellectual movements. According to T.W. Rhys Davids[1], the growth of the wandering bodies of religieux, the *Paribbājakas*, was the result of an intellectual movement before the rise of Buddhism which was, in a large measure, a lay-movement, not a priestly movement. It is difficult to understand this movement as a lay-movement. It was in fact neither priestly nor lay. It originated neither in Brahmanical reform nor in Kshatriya revolt; nor was it a middle class effort. It was a classless and casteless movement, and it had no special affinity with the attitude and interest of any particular social classes.

Max Muller,[2] G. Buhler,[3] H. Kern,[4] and H. Jacobi[5] —all contend that the Brahmanical 'ascetic' was the model of the Buddhist, the Jaina, and the other heretical sects of this age. It has also been suggested that these arose out of the anti-ritualistic tendency gaining ground within the religion of the Brāhmaṇas. G. C. Pandey[6] has tried to show that the anti-ritualistic tendency within the Vedic fold is itself due to the impact of an asceticism which antedates the *Vedas*. Some of the sects, such as Jainism and the Ājīvikīsm, may represent a continuation of this pre-Vedic stream.

There was not one but several factors which gave rise to these religious movements. It was an age of frequent and bloody wars, which made people long for peace. The great economic prosperity also filled some of them with despair of material life. There was considerable social distress because of the rigid caste system. The clash of rival schools and sects also led the people to spiritual quest.

ŚRAMAṆA AND BRAHMANICAL SECTS

The sects of this age were divided into many classes, but

1. Rbi, p. 111.
2. Hibbert Lectures, p. 351.
3. Sbe, II, pp. 191, 192.
4. Manual of Indian Buddhism.
5. Sbe, XXII, p. xxiv.
6. Psob. p. 317.

the main division was between the two *Śramaṇa* or Non-Brahmanical sects and Brahmanical sects. The main differences between the two were as follows.

1. The attitude of the Brahmanical sects towards secular life was not so uncompromising, for they emphasized renunciation only after the proper fulfilment of social duties. On the other hand, in the Śramaṇa Sects, their followers practised a detached life with a view to liberating themselves from all worldly attachments. They could take to a life of renunciation (*pravrajyā*) any time after ceasing to be under age.

2. In Brahmanical sects, only a Brāhmaṇa or *Dvija* could become a *Parivrājaka*, while in the Śramaṇa sects, all members of the community, irrespective of their social rank and religious career (*Varṇa and Āśrama*), could be admitted to their church.

3. The difference in scriptures and in the attitude towards them was another dividing line between the two sects. The Śramaṇas challenged the authority of the *Vedas*.

4. The orthodox sects did not permit renunciation for women, who however, could and did join some of the heterodox ascetic Orders.

5. The Brahmanical sects emphasised the rituals, while the followers of the Śramaṇa Sects observed a set of ethical principles.

Some of Mahāvīra's chief contemporary religious teachers belonging to the Śramaṇa sects were : Pūraṇa Kassapa Pakudha Kachchāyana, Makkhali Gośāla, Ajita Keśakambalin, Sañjaya Belaṭṭhiputta, and Buddha. The following account of their views based on the Jaina and Buddhist texts is both brief and lop-sided and, therefore, it may not give us a correct picture.

PŪRAṆA KASSAPA

From the Jaina[1] and Buddhist[2] records, it is clear that Pūraṇa Kassapa (Pūrṇa Kāśyapa) was an old, experienced, and respectable teacher. Though his date is not definite, it is

1. *Sūtra.*
2. *Sāmañña*; *Dīgha.* I. 47; *Milinda*, p. 4; W. ROCKHILL's Life of the Buddha, pp. 80. 96 foll.

presumed that he might have lived in the sixth century B.C. as is evident from references to him as a contemporary of king Ajātaśatru of Magadha. He was the head of a religious order and the founder of a school (*tittha-karo*). He was followed by a large body of disciples and honoured throughout the country. It seems from his name that he was born in a Brāhmaṇa family. The name *Pūraṇa* (*Pūrṇa*) indicates that he was believed to have been fully enlightened and perfect in wisdom.

NO-ACTION THEORY (AKRIYĀVĀDA)

Pūraṇa Kassapa is known to be the exponent of the 'no-action' theory (*Akriyāvāda*). It is said that Ajātaśatru once visited Pūraṇa Kassapa, who expounded his views thus : "To him who acts or causes another to act, mutilates or causes another to mutilate, punishes, or causes another to punish, causes grief or torment, trembles or causes another to tremble, kills other creatures, takes what is not given, breaks into houses, commits dacoity or robbery or tells lies, to him, thus acting, there is no guilt.... no increase of guilt would ensure.... In giving alms, in offering sacrifices, in self mastery, in control of senses, and in speaking truth, there is neither merit nor increase of merit."[1] This is called an exposition of the 'no-action' theory (*Akriyāvāda*). According to it, man is an irresponsible agent, because his action brings neither any merit nor any demerit. In other words, this doctrine was amoral because one might do whatever one wanted to do without becoming sinful or virtuous.

The *Sūtrakṛitāṅga*[2] furnishes a parallel passage where the doctrine is expressly called *Akriyāvāda*. Śīlāṅka calls it *Akārakavāda* and implicitly identifies it with the Sāṅkhya view. The identity between the view of Pūraṇa Kassapa and this *Akārakavāda* is probable, not certain.

THE DOCTRINE OF THE PASSIVITY OF THE SOUL

Most probably, Kassapa was, as B.M. Barua[3] states, an advocate of the theory that the Soul was passive (*nishkriya*), that no action could affect it, and that it was beyond good and

1. Rbi. pp. 69-70.
2. *Sūtra*, I. 1. 1. 13.
3. Bhpip. p. 279.

bad, a view which many previous Vedic thinkers had enunciated. When we act or cause others to act, it is not the soul that acts or causes others to act. Whether we do good or bad, the result does not affect the soul in the least.

NO-CAUSE THEORY (AHETUVĀDA)

Kassapa is said to be an upholder of the 'No-cause theory' (*Ahetuvāda*). It is reported in the words of the Buddha that no *hetu* (cause) and no *pachchaya* (condition) are accepted by Pūraṇa Kassapa as instrumental in either defiling a person or purifying him.[1] Abhaya says that Kassapa accepts no cause for *ñāṇa* (knowledge) and *dassana* (insight).[2] B.M. BARUA[3] tries to bring his view under *Adhichcha-samuppāda* (fortuitous in origin) referred to in the *Brahmajāla Sutta*, i.e. *Ahetuvāda*. G.C. PANDEY[4] does not subscribe to the view that Pūraṇa Kassapa held to the doctrine of *Adhichcha-samuppāda*. Events may "have nothing to do with the soul," and yet may not be fortuitous in origin.

THEORY OF INTROSPECTIVE KNOWLEDGE

In the passage of the *Aṅguttara Nikāya*,[5] two Lokāyatika Brāhmaṇas are said to have stated that according to Pūraṇa Kassapa's theory only an infinite mind can comprehend the finite world, whereas according to Nigaṇṭha Nātaputta's theory the finite world can only be a context of finite knowledge. Pūraṇa Kassapa has been described as one always in possession of *ñāṇadassana* (introspective knowledge), while walking or staying etc., and that he perceived the finite world through infinite knowledge.[6] In another passage, Buddha is said to have represented Kassapa, along with other heretical teachers, as possessing the power of divining where a particular dead person was reborn.[7]

1. *Sam*, III, p. 69.
2. Ibid, V, P. 69.
3. BGPIP, pp. 278-279.
4. PSOB, p. 345,
5. *Aṅgu*, IV, p. 428.
6. Ibid,
7. *Sam*, IV, p. 398.

THE DOCTRINE OF THE SIX CLASSES OF BEINGS (CHHALĀBHIJĀTIYO)

In a passage of the *Aṅguttara-nikāya*,[1] Ānanda expounds to Pūraṇa Kassapa Makkhali Gośāla's doctrine of the six classes of human beings (*Chhalābhijātiyo*), such as *Kaṇhābhijāti* (black class of being), *nilābhijāti* (blue class of being) etc. A.L. Basham[2] has tried to prove that Pūraṇa, a heretical leader of long standing who maintained a fatalistic doctrine with tendencies to antinomianism, came in contact with Makkhali Gośāla, a younger teacher with doctrines much the same as his own, but with a more successful appeal to the public. Recognizing his eclipse, he admitted the superiority of the new teacher, and accepted the sixfold classification of men, which placed Makkhali Gośāla and his forerunners, Nanda Vachcha, and Kisa Saṅkichcha, in the highest category.

PAKUDHA KACHCHĀYANA (KAKUDA KĀTYĀYANA)

Pakudha Kachchāyana was an elder contemporary of the Buddha. He was a leader of some religious body and was held in great esteem by the people of the time. Buddhaghosha says that Pakudha is his personal name and Kachchāyana his family (*gotra*) name. The term 'Pakudha' has been traditionally interpreted as *prakrudha*, furious. Its alternative form is *Kakudha* or *Kakuddha* which means the same thing. Assuming 'Kakuda' to be the original and correct form meaning 'a man having a hump on his back, B.M. Barua connects this Kātyāyana with Kabandhī Kātyāyana, one of the pupils of the sage Pippalāda of the *Praśna* Upanishad.[3] The suggestion, though ingenious, lacks a convincing proof.

As Pakudha Kachchāyana has left us no records of his own, we have to depend for a knowledge of his doctrine on the *Praśnopanishad*, the *Sāmañña-phala-sutta*, and the *Sūtrakṛitāṅga*. In the *Praśnopanishad*, in answer to Kātyāyana's question to Pippalāda as to the roots of things, he was told that the roots were Matter (*Rayi*) and Spirit (*Prāṇa*). Buddhaghosha records

1. *Aṅgu*, III, pp. 383-84.
2. History and Doctrines of the Ājīvikas, p. 90.
3. Bhpip, p. 227.

that Kachchāyana never used to touch cold water.[1] He never even crossed a river or a marshy pathway, lest he should transgress his vow.

THE DOCTRINE OF SEVEN CATEGORIES

In the Buddhist *Sāmañña-phala-sutta*,[2] Kachchāyana's philosophy is described as the doctrine of seven categories (*Satta-kāya-vāda*). He has been represented as saying : "The following seven things are neither made nor commanded to be made, neither created nor caused to be created; they are barren (so that nothing is produced out of them), steadfast as a mountain peak, as a pillar firmly fixed. They move not, neither do they vary; they trench not one upon another, nor avail aught as to ease (pleasure) or pain or both. And what are the seven ? The four elements—earth, water, fire and air—, and ease (pleasure) and pain, and the soul as a seventh. So there is neither slayer nor causer of slaying, hearer or speaker, knower or explainer, when one with sharp sword cleaves a head in twain, no one thereby deprives any one of life, a sword has only penetrated into the interval between seven elementary substances."[3] Kāchchāyana accepted seven elementary substances as permanent and eternal, neither created nor caused to be created. This *Sattakāyavāda* furnishes an instance of what the Buddhists called *Sassatavāda*. Its plurality of substances recalls Vaiśeshika; its denial of interaction between soul and matter as well as the aloofness of the soul from *Sukha* and *Dukha* recalls Sāṅkhya.

THE DOCTRINE OF SOUL AS A SIXTH CATEGORY (ĀTMA-SHASHṬHAVĀDA)

The *Sūtrakṛitāṅga*[4] presents the system of six categories omitting pleasure and pain, adding ether or space in their place. Śīlāṅka named it 'the doctrine of soul as a sixth category (*ātma-shashṭha-vāda*) which somehow resembles the doct-

1. *Sumaṅgala-Vilāsinī*, I, p. 144.
2. *Dīgha*, I, p. 57.
3. Dia, I, p. 74.
4. *Sūtra*, I, 1. 1. 15-16.

rines of Pakudha. It is also somewhat different because the existence of *Ākāśa* (ether or space) is distinctly recognised, and it omits *sukha* and *dukha*. Śīlāṅka identifies the doctrine of soul as a sixth category with the doctrine of the *Bhagavad Gītā*, as well as with the *Sāṅkhya* and some of the Śaiva systems. There is no doubt about some sort of historical relationship existing between them.

VIEWS ABOUT ACTION AND THE SOUL

Like Kassapa, Kachchāyana denied not the appearance, but the reality of action and also asserted that the soul was really untouched by change and was therefore superior to good and evil. It is perhaps not too much to imagine that this doctrine was formulated in opposition to the doctrine of *Saṁsāra* according to which the soul suffered and was itself responsible for its sufferings. Gośāla accepted the process of *Saṁsāra* but gave of it a new explanation. Being apparently Brāhmaṇas, Kassapa and Kachchāyana were probably acquainted with the Upanishadic speculation and were still more radical in their denial of the real existence of the problem itself.

THEORIES OF ETERNALISM AND NON-ACTION

The fragment of the *Sūtra-kṛitāṅga* clearly shows that Kachchāyana adopted the Gotamaka or Eleatic postulate of being that nothing comes out of nothing.[1] It appears from the fragments of both the *Sūtrakṛitāṅga* and the *Sāmañña-phala-sutta* that the term Eternalism[2] was strictly applied by Mahāvīra and Buddha to the doctrine of Kachchāyana. It also comes under the definition of what Mahāvīra calls Pluralism (Aṇikka vāda).[3]

Mahāvīra and Buddha considered Kachchāyana's doctrine to be a doctrine of non-action (*akriyā-vāda*). If the elements are eternally existent and unchangeable by their very nature, if they mechanically unite or separate by Pleasure and Pain inherent in each of them, if there is no volitional activity of consciousness, there is no ground for the conception of or dis-

1. *Sūtra*, 11-2.
2. *Sthānāṅga*, IV; *Dīgha*, 1.13-17.
3. Ibid. IV, 4.

tiction between good and bad, between knowledge and ignorance, and so forth. From this it follows that in reality, there is no act of killing or hearing or instructing. The act of killing, if it is possible at all in the world, means nothing but the act of separating from one another the elements of being in their organic unity.

KACHCHĀYANA AND EMPEDOCLES COMPARED

B.M. Barua[1] compares Kachchāyana and Empedocles, looking upon the former as the Empedocles of India. Both of them maintained that the elements of being are so distinct qualitatively from one another that there is no transition from the one to the other. Just as Empedocles is called, justly or unjustly, an Eleatic, so is Kachchāyana called an Eternalist, an Eternalist being but an Indian Eleatic. In the view of both becoming is impossible. Both conceive Being as a plurality of unchangeable elements. According to both, the four roots of all things are the four elements, which are in their nature permanent, that is, they know no qualitative change. Just as Empedocles conceives some ground or cause of change, similarly Kachchāyana regards Pleasure and Pain (*Sukha*, *dukha*) as the two principles of change. Finally, they resemble each other in admitting that there are pores (*vivara*) in organic bodies, and they also deny the void. The only point of difference between the two thinkers is that while in the case of Empedocles, it is not known whether he left any room for the conception of soul in his scheme of existence, in the case of Kachchāyana, it is positive that he did.

AJITA KEŚAKAMBALIN

Ajita Keśakambalin is known to be the historical founder of Indian Materialism. He was held in great esteem by the people of his time. He was called *Keśakambalin* because he put on a blanket of human hair. The philosophical and religious ideas of Ajita Keśakambalin are known from the *Sāmaññaphala Sutta*.[2] There are two aspects of his philosophy, negative and positive.

1. BHPIP, pp. 284-287.
2. *Sāmañña*, (*Digha*, I No. 2), 23.

NEGATIVE AND POSITIVE ASPECTS

Ajita was antinomian in ethics. It is remarkable that his categorical assertions are all negative in form. According to him, there is no merit in sacrifice or offering, no resultant fruit from good and evil deeds. No one passes from this world to the next. No benefit results from the service rendered to mother and father. There is no afterlife. There are no ascetics or Brāhmaṇas who have attained perfection by following the right path, and who, as a result of knowledge, have experienced this world as well as the next and can proclaim the same.

There is no existence of individuality after death. The four elements of existence constitute a living body. When a man dies, earth returns to earth, water to water, heat to fire, air to air, and the sense faculties pass into space. It is a doctrine of fools, this talk of existence after death, for all alike, the foolish and the wise are cut off, annihilated, and cease to be after death.[1] Ajita in the negative aspect of his doctrine resembles Epicurus, while on the positive side of his speculations he seems to be more a Stoic than an Epicurean, his fundamental point being that nothing but the corporeal is real.[2]

DOCTRINE OF TAṀ-JĪVA-TAṀ-SARĪRA-VĀDA

Ajita's doctrine was described by Mahāvīra and Buddha as *Taṁ-jiva-taṁ-sarīra-vāda*, in contradistinction to the doctrine of the soul being distinct from the body (*Aññaṁ-jīva-aññaṁ-sarīra-vāda*). Ajita was not so much against the dogmas of the Brahmanic faith as against the doctrine of Kachchāyana and others who made a hard and fast distinction between the body and the soul, between matter and spirit, in short, who conceived the soul as an entity existing independently of anything corporeal or material. Thus in one sense like a Stoic, he identified the corporeal with the mental, and in another sense he did not. His intention was not to identify the body with the soul, judged as concepts, for what he sought to establish was that the real fact of experience is always a living whole, a whole which the appre-

1. *Dial*, B, II, 73-74.
2. BHPIP, p. 293,

hending mind can conceive in its various aspects.[1] Hence the distinction which Kachchāyana made between the elements of being is in the view of Ajita untenable, the distinction being only an act of our mind. No such distinction exists in the living concrete individual taken as a whole.

Ajita's view was followed by Pāyāsi, and it was made more intelligible. The soul is not an entity distinct from the body. We cannot separate the soul from the body like him who draws a sword from the scabbard and says, "This is the sword and that the scabbard."[2] We cannot say this is the soul and that's the body. Ajita and Pāyāsi viewed the corporeal from the point of view of the self on the ground that form cannot exist apart from matter.

THE MORAL DEDUCTIONS OF AJITA'S THEORY OF SELF

According to Mahāvīra, by denying future life, Ajita taught men to kill, burn, destroy[3] and enjoy all the pleasures of life. The truth seems to be quite the contrary. He taught us to believe rather in life than in death and to show proper regard to persons when they are alive rather than honour them when they are dead. In another Jaina passage, we are told that Ajita was an Akriyā-vādin, as he upheld the doctrine of non-Being. The study of the views of Śīlāṅka and Sāyaṇa Mādhava leads us to believe that the foundation of Ajita's doctrine was laid in a statement of Yājñavalkya which is : the intelligible essence emerging from the five elements vanishes into them at death.[4]

SAÑJAYA BELAṬṬHIPUTTA

Sañjaya Belaṭṭhiputta was one of the religious teachers of the sixth century B.C. As is obvious from the *Sāmaññaphala Sutta*, he was a wanderer and the founder of a religious Order as well as of a school of thought in Rājagṛha. He is believed to be identical with *Parivrājaka* Sañjaya, teacher of Sāriputta

1. *Vedānta-sāra* (Ed. by Cowell), p. 32.
2. SBE, XLV, pp. 340-341; Dia. B, III, 358-361.
3. Ibid, p. 341.
4. BHPIP, p. 296.

and Mogallāna described in the *Vinaya Mahāvagga*, and the *Dhammapada*. Such an identification is possible, because *Parivrājaka* Sañjaya is known to be a sceptic. Still, we are not definite as the name *Parivrājaka* Sañjaya is not found along with Sañjaya Belaṭṭhiputta in the early Buddhist work named *Sāmaññaphala Sutta*.

Sañjaya Belaṭṭhiputta was celebrated for an opinion which was a blend of scepticism on the one hand and a primitive stage of criticism of knowledge on the other, like that of the Sophists in Greek philosophy. From the point of view of their philosophical doctrine his disciples were known as Agnostics, Sceptics, or Eel-wrigglers, and from the point of view of their moral conduct, as friends or Good-natured ones.

JAINA ACCOUNT

The Jainas mention the theory of *Ajñanavāda* or Agnosticism of which Sañjaya Belaṭṭhiputta seems to be the chief advocate. Śīlāñka says : "Literally, the 'Agnostics' are those in whom there is 'ignorance' or 'who walk about in ignorance'. They think : even if we avowedly maintain a view—"That this is good" (Kuśala), we are conscious that we are not acquainted with truth, the matter is not familiar to our knowledge. Indeed, we have not as yet got beyond 'perplexity'—perplexity which is blindness and delusion of the mind.

"Some conceive the existence of an all-seeing soul, while others controvert it. Some speak of an all-pervading self ; others contend that the body being such an entity, it cannot be all-pervading. Some estimate that soul is equal to a digit in size, while others say that it is equal to a grain of rice. Some posit a soul that has a material form while others maintain that it is formless. Some point out that the heart is the seat of soul, while others oppose them by saying that the forehead would be the right place....

"How can there be an agreement of views among these philosophers ? Many moral injuries may result from the issues of such antagonistic blunders. For us, ignorance is far better than these follies."[1]

1. *Sūtrā, Tī*, pp. 451-452.

BUDDHIST ACCOUNT

According to the Sāmaññaphala Sutta[1], Sañjaya's doctrine was neither a doctrine of acceptance nor a doctrine of denial. He neither denied the existence of the next world nor accepted it. Whether the beings are produced by chance, or whether there is any fruit of good or bad action, or whether a man who won the truth continues after death—to all these questions he gave the same answer.

A follower of this sect has been described in the *Brahmajāla Sutta*[2] as *Amarāvikkhepika*, who, when asked a question, would equivocate and wriggle out like an eel. B.M. BARUA[3] thinks that the *Aviruddhakas* mentioned in the *Aṅguttara Nikāya* were also followers of Sañjaya, that they were called *Amarāvikkhepikas* for their philosophical doctrines and *Aviruddhakas* for their moral conduct.

SAÑJAYA'S PLACE IN THE HISTORY OF INDIAN PHILOSOPHY

The very fact that Sañjaya's opponents were compelled to put his views to the hardest test demonstrates that these could not be so easily dismissed. He had a large following, a fact which goes at once to prove that there was some truth in his teaching that could appeal to so many thoughtful men. He suspended his judgments only with regard to those great questions of which a decisive answer will ever remain a matter of speculation. He called away the attention of the philosopher from fruitless inquiries and directed it towards the *Summum bonum*, which is the attainment and preservation of mental equanimity.

Sañjaya may be considered to be a true precursor of Mahāvīra who propounded a doctrine of antinomies (*Syādvāda*) and of the Buddha who advocated a critical method of investigation (*vibhājyavāda*). Both Mahāvīra and the Buddha agree that there are some important questions of cosmology, ontology, theology and eschatology on which no finality is possible.

1. *Sāmañña*, 31.
2. *Brahma*, 37.
3. BHPIP, p. 327.

MAṄKHALI GOŚĀLA

Mahāvīra's contemporary leader of the Ājīvaka sect was Maṅkhali Gośāla who seems to have been preceded by Nanda Vachchha and Kisa Saṁkichchha.[1] He was born at Saravaṇa near Sāvatthi. His father was Maṅkhali and his mother's name was Bhaddā. His father was Maṅkha, that is, a dealer in pictures. Gośāla himself followed his father's profession in the beginning and hence he was so named.[2] As he is said to have been born in the cow-shed, he was called Gośāla. In the Buddhist records, the name is also spelt : 'Makkhali', which means one who stumbled in the mud. The true name seems to be Maskarin, the Jaina-prakrit form of which is Maṅkhali, and the Pali form Makkhali. This name indicates a school of Wanderers or Sophists who were so named not because they carried a bamboo staff about them but because they denied the freedom of the Will.

RELATIONSHIP OF GOŚĀLA AND MAHĀVĪRA

When Gośāla grew up, he left home for some unknown reason and became a homeless wanderer, spending twenty-four years as an ascetic. After his meeting with Mahāvīra at Paṇiyabhūmi, he spent six years with him. Probably because of this association we find some points of similarity in Jaina and Ājīvika doctrine and practice. From the account of the *Bhagavati Sūtra,* it is known that Gośāla became a disciple of Mahāvīra. Contrary to Jaina account, H. JACOBI[3] and B.M. BARUA[4] are of opinion that Mahāvīra remained a disciple of Gośāla for some time. Gośāla was much senior to Mahāvīra in age, and was recognised as a teacher some time before the latter. Afterwards, Gośāla parted company with Mahāvīra on account of doctrinal differences and went to Śrāvastī where he spent sixteen years as a religious leader of the Ājīvika sect. The two years intervening between these two periods were no doubt filled with a journey to Kumāragāma, six months'

1. A.F.R. HOERNLE suggests that Kisa and Nanda were probably Makkhali's contemporaries.
2. *Bhag,* XV.1; *Uvā,* p. 1.
3. SBE, XLV, p. xxx.
4. BHPIP, p. 300.

penance, and preliminary wanderings before making Śrāvastī his headquarters.

HIS EFFORTS FOR PROPAGATION

It is not likely that Gośāla resided for sixteen years continually at Sāvatthi; probably like his great rivals Mahāvīra and the Buddha, he travelled from place to place among the towns and villages of the Gaṅga valley, preaching and gathering converts. There is evidence that the Ājīvikas, both ascetics and laymen, existed in a fairly large number at this time. His mission consisted largely in knitting together local Ājīvika holymen and their followers, regularising their doctrines and gaining converts by the display of pseudo-supernatural powers. He obtained the strongest support for this sect at Sāvatthi. The Kośalan king Pasenadi was more favourably disposed towards this sect than was his contemporary Bimbisāra of Magadha.

ĀJĪVIKA SCRIPTURES AND THE DEATH OF GOŚĀLA

When Gośāla made his headquarters at Sāvatthi in the workshop of the potter woman Hālahalā, he was surrounded by many disciples. At this time, he was visited by six *disācharas*, in consultation with whom he codified the Ājīvika scriptures. The scriptures of the Ājīvikas consisted of ten *Puvvas*, i.e., eight *Mahāṇimittas* and two Maggas, like the fourteen *Pūrvas* of the Jainas. The dialect adopted for their scriptures was closely allied to *Ardha Māgadhi*, a few stereotyped fragments of which have survived in the Jaina and Buddhist literatures.

Soon after the visit of the six *diśācharas*, Mahāvīra exposed Gośāla openly with the result that the relations between the two sects became very hostile. Afterwards Gośāla suffered from delirium and died. His death took place sixteen years before that of Mahāvīra.

The comparison of the Buddhist references with those found in Jaina sources enables us to form a tolerable picture of the doctrines of Gośāla. While discussing these doctrines, we must also keep in mind that both Gośāla and Mahāvīra lived together for some time and that the scriptures of the Ājīvikas and the Jainas are said to have some common sources of origin.

DOCTRINE OF TRANSFORMATION (PAUṬṬAPARIHĀRA-VĀDA)

Gośāla was the propounder of a 'doctrine of change through re-animation' (*pauṭṭaparihāravāda*), or, better still, of a theory of natural transformation (*pariṇāmavāda*) which he came to formulate from the generalisation based on the periodical re-animations of plant life.[1] He came to the conclusion that just as the sesame seeds after having completely perished come to life from their inherent force or will-to-be, so are all living beings capable of re-animation.

THEORY OF PURIFICATION THROUGH TRANSMIGRATION (SAṀSĀRA-ŚUDDHI)

The basic idea underlying the above doctrine implies a process of purification through transmigration.[2] In the Buddhist phraseology, purification is the equivalent of 'the end of pain' (*dukkhassanta*), and the word transmigration signifies the passing of soul from one state of experience to another. According to this theory of purification through transmigration, one will put an end to pain after wandering through various births for the allotted term. There are eighty-four hundred thousand periods during which both fools and wise, wandering in transmigration, shall at last make an end of pain. Neither the wise nor the fool can get rid of the *Karma*—there can be no increase or decrease thereof. Everything is predestined. Just as a ball of string when unrolled, spreads out as far as and no farther than it can unwind, so shall both fools and wise alike, wandering in transmigration exactly for the allotted term, make an end of pain.

FATE, SPECIES AND NATURE (NIYATI-SAṄGATI-BHĀVA PARIṆATĀ)

Gośāla offers for his theory of perfection through transformation no less than three explanations : Fate or Necessity, Class or Species, and Nature.[3]

As a rigid determinist, Gośāla exalted fate (*Niyati*) to the status of the motive factor of the universe and the sole agent of

1. *Bhag*, XV. 1.
2. *Dīgha*, I, p. 54 ; *Majjh*, 1, p. 31; *Jā*, V, p. 228.
3. *Dīgha*, I, 53.

all phenomenal change.[1] Man's destiny is pre-ordained, human effort could effect no change in it, and emancipation was to be obtained only through a long series of transmigrations. Pleasure and pain are not caused by the souls themselves nor by others, but by destiny. There is no such thing as exertion or labour or power or vigour or manly strength, but that all things are caused by destiny which is unalterably fixed. The *Sāmāññaphala Sutta* also gives an account of Gośāla's teachings from where we get the same denial of the usefulness of effort or manly vigour.

The attainment of a certain peculiar condition, and of a certain peculiar character on the part of all things, all lives, all beings, depends in part on the class or type to which they belong. It is partly according to their position in this class or that that they possess certain special properties, that they have certain physical characteristics, that they inherit certain peculiar habits, develop certain faculties, and so on. Thus fire, for example, is hot, ice is cold, water is liquid, stone is hard, a thorn is sharp, a peacock is painted, the sandal tree possesses fragrance, the elephant's cub, if it does not find leafless and thorny creepers in the green wood, becomes thin ; the crow avoids the ripe mango, etc.[2]

Buddhaghosha explains Gośāla's term 'nature' as 'the peculiar nature of each being'.[3] The world originates and develops from its inherent force or immanent energy. It is also probable that he sought for an explanation of the diversity of appearances, characteristics, habits and behaviour of things in nature. He conceived Nature as a self-evolving activity. Nature has two modes of operation : by one made things come to pass and by the other they cease to be (*pravṛtti* and *nivṛtti*). More accurately, he seems to have understood by Nature the specific faculties or characteristics of a living substance other than those which it possesses in common with the race or species.[4]

1. *Uvā*, vi-vii.
2. *Buddhacharita*, IX. 47, 48, 52; *Śīlāṅka's Sūtra. Ṭīkā*, p. 30; *Sarvadarśanasaṅgraha*, p. 7.
3 *Sumaṅgala Vilāsinī*, I. 161.
4. BHPIP, p. 312.

VIEWS OF KAMMA

Gośāla's views on *Kamma* appear to have been peculiar. The classifications found in *Sāmaññaphala* passages are obscure, and Buddhaghosha sheds little light. From this it appears that once earned, the inheritance of *Kamma* was held to be independent of individual will and supposed to work its way out along its own logic. From the statement just made, it appears that *Kamma* was considered to be in some way casually connected with *Sukha-dukkha*. How, then, was it supposed to be related to the triad of *Niyatisaṅgatibhāva*? Since individual initiative is denied, *Niyati*, probably, was considered to be the cause of *Kamma* prior to the attainment of liberation. Gośāla, in short, considered man bound to the cycle of rebirth by a force—*Kamma* or *Niyati* over which he had no voluntary control.

SIXFOLD CLASSIFICATION OF HUMANITY

Gośāla's classification of human beings into six abhijātis[1] (groups) according to their psychic colour is as follows: black (*Kaṇha*) includes all who live by slaughter and cruelty, such as hunters, thieves, fishermen and others; blue (*nīla*) contains 'monks who live as thieves'; red (*lohita*) probably applies to all monks of Jaina type; (4) green (*halidda*) seems to refer to Ājīvika laymen; (5) white (*sukka*) is related so Ājīvika ascetics of both sexes; and (6) Supremely white (*Parama-sukka*) contains only three names, that is, those of Nandi Vachcha, Kisa Sankichcha, and Makkhali Gośāla. The *Abhijātis* have much is common with the Jaina *leśyās*, and it is possible that both Gośāla and Mahāvīra might have *derived* from some common source. By urging this doctrine, Gośāla wants to emphasize that the supreme spiritual effort of man consists in restoring the mind to its original purity, i.e., rendering it colourless or supremely white by purging it of all impurities that have stained it.

1. *Dīgha*, 1, 53; *Aṅgu*, III, pp. 383-84.
Sumaṅgala-Vilāsinī, I, p. 162
Majjh, I, p. 36.

THEORY OF EIGHT STAGES OF DEVELOPMENT (AṬṬHAPURISA-BHŪMIYO)

Gośāla advocated that there are eight stages of development through which every man must pass for the attainment of perfection in order to become a Jina.[1] The first stage is babyhood which begins with the birth of a person. Babyhood is followed by the play-time, and that again by the third stage when the child attempts to walk. This period of trial is duly succeeded by the period when the child is able to walk. When he becomes older, he is sent to learn under a teacher. In course of time, he renounces the world and equips himself, sooner or later, with all that his teacher knows. Then comes a time when he realizes that what his teacher taught him was not all, that in fact it was nothing. The *Āśrama* theory of the *Dharmaśāstras* was based on the notion of the gradual development of the self but it was formulated as a biological principle of evolution in its application to education.

PENANCES

We also know about the penances of the Ājīvikas. The *Bhagavatī Sūtra* says that they abstained from eating *umbara* (ficus glomerata), *vaṭa* (ficus Indica), *bora* (jujube), *satara* (?) and *pilaṅkhu* (ficus infectoria), all fruits, and also from eating roots, etc. The *Sthānāṅga Sūtra*[2] says that the Ājīvikas practised four kinds of austerities, *viz*., severe austerities, fierce austerities, abstention from ghee and other delicacies, and indifference to pleasant and unpleasant food. They observed the fourfold *brahmacharya* consisting of (1) *tapassitā*, asceticism; (9) *lūkhachariyā*, austerity; (3) *jeguchchita*, comfort-loathing; and (4) *pavivittatā*, solitude. The *Aupapātika Sūtra*[3] describes the system of collecting alms as adopted by the Ājivika ascetics. Some of them begged in every second or third or fourth or fifth or sixth or even in every seventh house; there were *seven* who accepted lotus stalks only as alms under certain conditions; some begged in every house, but did not accept alms if there was a flash of lightning. There were some ascetics who practised penances by entering into big earthen vessels.

1. *Dial*, II, p. 72; *Uvā*, II, p. 24; *Jā*, IV, pp. 496-97.
2. *Sthānā*, 4. 2. 310.
3. *Aup*, 41.

ETHICS

Both the Buddhists and the Jainas regarded the Ājīvikas as amoralists and proceeded to condemn them as immoral in practice. On the evidence of Jaina scriptures, A.F.R. HOERNLE[1] accuses Gośāla of hypocrisy and incontinence.

B.M. BARUA[2] on the other hand considers these strictures merely sectarian. According to him, Gośāla's theory of *Pariṇāmavāda* seeks to establish even with the help of its fatalistic creed a moral government of law in the universe where nothing is dead, where nothing happens by chance, and where all that is and all that happens and is experienced are unalterably fixed as it were by a pre-determined law of nature.

It teaches that as man is pre-destined in certain ways and as he stands highest in the gradations of existence, his freedom, to be worth the name, must be one within the operation of law, and that the duty of man as the highest of beings is to conduct himself according to law, and to act and behave in a manner that does not induce him to trespass upon the rights of others, to make the fullest use of one's liberties, to be considerate and discreet, to be pure in life, to abstain from killing living beings, to be free from earthly possessions, to reduce the necessaries of life to a minimum, and to strive for the best and highest, i.e., Jinahood, which is within human powers.

This fatalistic creed, which is a logical outcome of *Pariṇāmavāda,* confirms popular Indian belief that action has its reward and retribution and that heaven and hell are the inevitable consequences hereafter of merits and demerits of this life.[3]

ĀJĪVIKA DOCTRINE VIS-A-VIS THE NIGAṆṬHAS

Apart from those relating to practice, the chief differences between the Ājīvikas and the Nigaṇṭhas concerned the nature of will and of the soul. As to the latter, Buddhaghosha

1. ERE, I, pp. 263-265.
2. BHPIP JDL, II, pp. 12-13.
3. Ibid, pp. 317-318.

informs us that while Gośāla held the soul to be *Rūpī*, Mahāvīra considered it *Arūpī*. Among the striking similarities between the two doctrines ; one may mention the common expression *Sabbe Sattā Sabbe pāṇā...bhūtā...Jīvā*, the division of animals into *Ekendriya, Dvindriya*, etc. Belief in the omniscience of the released was also common. Gośāla and Mahāvīra both enjoined the practice of nudity on saints.

THE BUDDHA

Gautama Buddha, the founder of Buddhism, was the junior contemporary of Mahāvīra. We possess no authentic accounts of his life and teachings. Two poems in the *Sutta Nipāta* and a few early *Suttas* supply us with some data but for details, we have to depend upon comparatively later works, which appear to have preserved older traditions.

EARLY LIFE

Gautama alias Siddhārtha was born in 563 B.C. at Lumbinivana, now identified with Rumminidei on the border of Nepal. His father Śuddhodana of the Sākya clan was the ruler of Kapilavastu. His mother Māyā died seven days after his birth, and he was brought up by his mother's sister Mahāprajāpati Gotamī. When he grew up, he married Yaśodharā, and had a son, Rāhula.

The idea of renunciation, according to the later text, came into his mind from seeing four persons in four different stages—an old man, a cripple, an ascetic, and a corpse. In the early texts like the *Sutta Nipāta*, it is simply stated that looking at the miseries of the world, he embraced the life of a wandering hermit at the age of twentynine.

Passing through a number of villages, Gautama at last reached Vaiśālī where he stayed at a hermitage of the teacher Ārāḍa Kālāma. There he became his disciple and learnt the Sāṅkhya doctrine from him. Since evidently he was not satisfied, he left the hermitage of Ārāḍa to become a disciple of another teacher Rudraka Rāmaputra, who was then living in the outskirts of Rājagṛha. Not satisfied with Rudraka either, he left him and began to observe severe penances along with five other Brāhmaṇa ascetics. He was deserted by the Brāhmaṇa companions when they noticed slackness on his part in observing penances, and he decided to take food just sufficient to sustain his body.

After leaving Rudraka's hermitage, Gautama went to Uruvilva where he took his seat under a *pīpal* tree. After spending seven weeks in meditation under this tree, he finally realized the Truth. He thus became the Buddha (the Enlightened One). With his attainment of both insight and knowledge, he became emancipated from birth and rebirth. He then turned his attention to his five Brāhmaṇa companions who were then residing at Ṛishipattana (Sārnāth) near Banaras. He proceeded there and delivered before them his first sermon, which is metaphorically represented in Buddhist literature as "turning the wheel of the Law".

MISSIONARY LIFE

Along with these five Brāhmaṇa companions, Buddha went to Banaras where he converted Yaśa, a rich Seṭṭhi's son. and other followers. From Banaras, he proceeded to Rājagṛiha where he spent the second, third, and fourth *Vassās* (retreats). In Magadha, at this time, there were many Brahmanical and non-Brahmanical teachers and wandering monks. The Buddha spent much of his time and energy in refuting their doctrines and convincing them of the excellence of his teaching. He succeeded in making a large number of converts, the most notable among them being Sāriputra and Maudgalyāyana, who were formerly disciples of Sañjaya Belaṭṭhiputta, the Brahmanical ascetics, the Jaṭilas, Upāli Grahapati, and Abhayarājakumāra, all staunch followers of Nigaṇṭha Nātaputta ; Anāthapiṇḍika a merchant possessing fabulous wealth ; kings Bimbisāra and Ajātaśatru, and later, king Muṇḍa. Besides Rājagṛiha, Buddha visited Gayā, Uruvilva, Nālandā, and Pāṭaliputra.

Buddhism gained a footing even at Kośalā (Sāvatthi) where the Buddha spent the last twentyone *vassās*. His favourite resort was the famous Jetavaṇa monastery, which was purchased for him by Anāthapiṇḍika at a fabulous price. King Prasenajit (Pasenadi) became interested in his discourses, while his queen Mallikā and his two sisters, Somā and Sakulā, became lay-devotees. Another influential supporter was Visākhā, who built the Pubbārāma monastery for him.

The Buddha visited Kapilvastu and converted the members of his family including his son Rāhula and foster-mother Mahāprajāpati Gomatī. Buddha also spent the fifth *Vassā* at Vaiśālī, where Ambapālī, the famous courtesan became his devotee and offered her mango grove to the Saṁgha. The Buddha passed the ninth *Vassā* at Kauśāmbī where queen Sāmavatī of Udayana became his follower. He visited a distant place Verañjā (near Mathurā) to spend his twelfth *Vassā* there and deputed his disciple Mahākachchāyana for the propagation of Buddhism in Avanti. He converted king Pradyota and others to Buddhism. He made his last journey to Malla's capital Kusinārā where he gave up his body after a fatal illness and attained *parinirvāṇa* at the age of eighty.

TEACHINGS

The earliest available source of our knowledge of the Buddha's teachings is the Pāli *Piṭaka* which consists of the five *Nikāyas*, *viz.*, *Dīgha*, *Majjhima*, *Saṁyutta*, *Aṅguttara* and *Khuddaka*. As many alterations and additions were made in it from time to time by the succeeding generations, it cannot be called homogeneous, nor is it possible to state definitely what actually were the original teachings of the Buddha.

Buddhism, like Jainism, was originally a moral code rather than a metaphysical or religious system. The Buddha instructed his followers to pursue practical methods in order to arrive at the Truth. For the removal of ignorance, thirst, attachment, etc., for instance, he advocated the four *Aryasatyas* (Noble Truths), *viz.*, (1) that worldly existence is full of misery (*dukkha*) ; (2) that thirst, attachment, etc., are the causes of worldly existence (*samudaya*) ; (3) that worldly existence can be ended (*nirodha*) by the destruction of thirst, etc. The Path is the well-known Eightfold Way, *viz.*, right speech, right action, right means of livelihood, right exertion, right mindedness, right meditation, right resolution, and right point of view. The first three practices lead to physical control (*Śīla*), the second three to mental control (*chitta*), and the last two to intellectual development (*prajñā*).

The exposition of the Eightfold Path is said to be the Buddha's first discourse. It is also widely known as the Middle Path (*madhyama pratipat*) as it keeps clear of the two extreme ways of life, one being that of ease and luxury and the other of rigorous asceticism. This path allowed a monk to live a life of moderate comfort, with the bare requirements of food, clothing and residence, but with the wind intent on achieving the goal.

The second discourse, which is said to have been delivered by the Buddha, strikes the keynote of his teachings, *viz.*, that the five constituents which make a being are without a self (*anātma*), impermanent (*anitya*), and are not desirable (*dukkha*). He who realizes the absence of soul or substance in the constituents knows that he does not exist as an individual and as such there can be no relationship between himself and the objects around him. There is nothing in this world to make him happy or sad and so he is free (*vimukta*), he is an *arhat*—perfect.

ASCETICS OF THE BRAHMANICAL SECTS

The Brahmanical ascetics were probably divided into two classes, *i.e.*, the one retiring to the forests *Vānaprasthins* and then passing to the stage of *Sannyāsa*, and the other consisting of the *Tāvasa*, the *Geruya* or *Parivrājaka* etc. The *Jātakas* most probably depict the life of the *Vānaprasthins* and the S*annyāsins*, but there is no line of demarcation drawn between the two. It is only in the *Dharmasūtra* literature of a later period that a clear distinction is made between the two stages of life. Now the question is : how far does the account of the *Jātakas* correspond with that of the *Dharmasūtra*. According to the *Baudhāyana-Dharmasūtra,* to cite one example, one could renounce the world after the student life, or after being a householder, or from the forest.[1] Āpastamba and Vasishṭha allow one to have the option of becoming an ascetic after the completion of the *Brahmcharya* stage or after becoming a householder.[2] Thus we find the Brahmanical sources supporting the Buddhist account.

1. *Bau*, *Dh. S*, II, 10. 2-6; SBE, XIV, 273.
2. SBE, II, 153; XIV, 40, 46.

TĀVASAS

The *Tāvasas* lived in forest where they occupied themselves with meditation, sacrificial rites, self-torture, and in reading the scriptures. They gathered fruits and roots for their sustenance and visited the villages for alms. On one of the journeys he made during his ascetic life, Mahāvīra put up in a hermitage (*āsamapada*) in Sannivesa.[1] He came across another hermitage named Kanakakhala in Uttaravāchāla where five hundred hermits were staying;[2] still another hermitage is referred to in Poyaṇapura where Vakkalachīri was born.[3]

The *Ovāiya Sūtra*[4] mentions the following classes of *Vānapattha Tāvasas* residing on the bank of the Gaṅga. It is possible that some of the classes might have belonged to the later period than that of Mahāvīra but we are not in a position to distinguish them positively.

Hottiya : they offered sacrifices.

Kottiya : They slept on the bare ground.

Pottiya : They put on a special kind of clothes.

Jaṇṇaī : They performed sacrifices.

Saḍḍhai : They belonged to the devotional class of ascetics.

Thālaī : They carried all their belongings with them.

Humbauṭṭha : They carried a water vessel with them.

Dantukkhaliva : They lived on fruits and used their teeth as mortar.

Ummajjaka : They bathed taking only a dip.

Sammajjaka : They bathed without taking a dip in water.

Nimajjaka : They remained in water only for a short time.

Sampakkhāla : They rubbed and cleansed their limbs with mud.

Dakkhiṇakūlaga : They dwelt on the south bank of the Ganga.

1. *Āva*, *Nir*, 463.
2. *Āva. chū*, p. 278.
3. Ibid, p. 457 ; *Bāhiya Dāruchīriya* in the *Dhammapada* A. II, pp. 209 f.
4. *Ovā*, p. 170 ; *Niryā*, 3, p. 39.

Uttarakūlaga : They dwelt on the north bank of the Ganga.

Saṁkhadhamaga : They blew a conch-shell to keep people away.

Kūladhamaga : They blew a conch-shell on the river bank to keep people away while they took their meal.

Miyaluddhaya : They killed animals.

Hatthitāvasa : They used to kill an elephant every year with arrows and lived many months on its flesh. The motive was to spare the lives of other animals for as long as the flesh of the elephant would last. They claimed that they committed but one sin in a year, the killing of the elephant, which was counterbalanced by the merit earned by not killing other lives during this time.[1]

Uḍḍaṇḍaya : They moved about raising their staff and are referred to along with Boḍiya and Sasarakkha mendicants who went about naked and used the hollow of their hands as alms-bowl.[2]

Disāpokkhī : They sanctified all sides by sprinkling water and then collected flowers and fruits. The *Bhagavatī*[3] refers to the royal sage Śiva of Hattināpura, who joined the order of the *Disāpokkhiyas* on the bank of the Ganga. He practised *chaṭṭhama* (a fast, broken at sixth meal), and on the day on which he broke his fast, he sprinkled the eastern quarter, propitiated Soma, the lord of the east, and collected bulbous roots, leaves, flowers, fruits, seeds and green vegetables. Then he returned to his hut, cleaned the sacrificial altar (*Vedikā*) and went to bathe in the Ganga. He made another altar with grass and sand, kindled a fire by the friction of pieces of wood, and keeping ritualistic paraphernalia by his side, offered honey, ghee, and rice to the fire. Then he prepared *Charu* (oblation), worshipped *Vaissadeva* and the guests, and then took his meal. Then Śiva observed the *Chaṭṭhama* fast again and proceeded to the south to propitiate Yama, then to the west to propitiate Varuṇa, and finally to the north to propitiate *Vesa-*

1. *Bhag.* 11. 9. 418; *Aup*, 38; *Sūtra*, II, Vi, 52.
2. *Ach. chū*, p. 169.
3. *Bhag*, 11.9.

maṇa. Somila was another hermit of Vārāṇasī who belonged to the same order and was a worshipper of the four *diśās.*[1] King Pasannachand also belonged to the same order which he joined along with his queen and the nurse.[2]

Vakavāsī : They put on a dress of bark.
Ambuvāsī : They lived in water.
Bilavāsī : They lived in caves.
Jalavāsi : They remained submerged in water.
Velavāsī : They lived on the sea-coast.
Rukkhamūlia : They lived under trees.
Ambubhakkhī : They lived by drinking water only.
Vāubhakkhī[3] : They lived by inhaling air only.
Sevālabhakkhī[4] : They lived by eating moss.

The *Tāvasas* followed the rules of the *Vānaprastha Āśrama.* Like other ascetics, they also moved in a body. We hear of three hermits, Koḍinna, Dinna and Sevāli, who were followed by a body of five hundred disciples each. They lived on roots, bulbs, decayed leaves, and moss; they set out to pay a visit to Aṭṭhāvaya.[5]

THE PARIVRĀJAKA OR GERUYA SAMANAS

Though they formed a distinct and separate group, the *Parivrājakas* belonged to the class of ascetics. According to T.W. RHYS DAVIDS,[6] "the *Paribbājakas* or the wandering mendicants were teachers or sophists who spent eight or nine months of every year wandering about, and they were often lodged in the public halls where conversational discussions were held on philosophical and religious questions. Besides, they lived on alms collected from door to door." B.M. BARUA[7] mentions that these Brāhman wanderers were in a position to learn the

1. *Niryā*, 3, pp. 39ff.
2. *Āva. chū*, p. 457.
3. The *Rāmāyaṇa* III, 11-13 mentions Māṇḍakarṇī, a hermit who lived on air.
4. *Lalitavistara*, p. 248.
5. *Uttarā. Ṭī*, 10, 154.
6. RBI, p. 161.
7. BHPIP, p. 350.

languages, customs, and usages of the people living in different parts of the world in which they themselves lived. In those early ages of civilization, when there was neither any printing press nor any easy means of communication between one country and another, elements of knowledge could be gathered, disseminated or utilised for scientific purpose by no better means than such travelling.

The *Parivrājakas* or the wanderers were the great teachers of the Brahmanic lore and were highly respected. In the *Vasishṭha Dharmasūtra*, it is stated that a *Parivrājaka* should shave his head, clothe himself with one piece of cloth or skin, cover his body with grass pulled off by cows, and he should sleep on bare ground.[1] The *Parivrājakas* maintained their regular monasteries (*Avasaha*) and wandered from place to place in order to propagate their teachings. From the *Ovāiya*, we know that they were versed in the four *Vedas*, *Itihāsa*, *Nigghaṇṭu*, six *Vedāṅgas*, and six *Upāṅgas*. They preached the doctrine of charity (*Dānadhamma*), purity (*soadhamma*), and that of bathing at holy places. According to them whatever was impure became pure by applying mud to it and by being washed with water. They believed that they were pure themselves and that by taking bath they would attain heaven. They never travelled in a cart or a litter, never entered a lake or a river for bathing, never rode a horse or an elephant, never visited the performance of a dancer or a bard, never trampled upon or rubbed green vegetables, never indulged in talks regarding women, food, country, king, and thieves, never kept any costly pots except a bottle gourd, wooden, or an earthen pot, never put on garments of various colours except one pair dyed with red-clay, never wore any ornaments except one copper ring, never wore any garland except a pair of flower earings, never besmeared their body with any fragrant substance except the clay of the Ganga, and they took only one *Magadha prastha* (a measure used in Magadha) filtered (*Paripūya*) water for drinking purposes.

From the *Bhagavatisūtra*,[2] we know about one wandering

1. *Vas. Dh. S*, 11-6. 11.
2. *Bhag*, 2. 1.

mendicant, Ajjakhanda of Kachchāyana *gotra*, a disciple of Gaddabhāli, who was putting up in Sāvatthi. Once he took his ritualistic objects, *viz.*, triple staves, water pot (*Kuṇḍī*), rosary (*Kañchaṇiyā*), earthen bowl (*Karoḍiyā*), seat (*bhisiyā*), sweeping duster (*Kesariyā*), teapoy (*chaṇṇāliyā*), hook (*aṅkusaya*), ring (*pavittaya*), and the forearm ornament (*kalāchikā*), and taking an umbrella and wearing shoes and dyed robes, proceeded to pay a visit to Mahāvīra. He was well-versed in Vedic literature.

In the early Buddhist records,[1] we have frequent mention of a number of such *Parivrājakas* (wanderers), all of whom were the contemporaries of the Buddha, e.g. Poṭṭhapāda, Dīgha-nakha, Sakula Udāyi, Anna-bhara, Varadhara, Poṭāliya or Poṭali-putta, Uggahamāna, Vekhanassa Kachchāna, Māgaṇḍiya, Sandaka, Uttiya, three Vachchhagottas, Sabhiya, and Pilotika Vachchhāyana. Besides these wanderers, we have to take into account many celebrated Brāhmaṇa teachers of the Buddha's time, such as Pokkharasāti (*Pushkarasādi*), Sonadaṇḍa (*Śaunadanta or Śaunaka*), Kuṭadanta, Lohichcha, Kaṅki (*Chaṅki*), Tarukkha (*Tārukshya*), Jānussoni (*Jātaśruti*), Todeyyas, Todeyya-putta or Subha, Kāpaṭhika Bhāradvāja, Aggika Bhāradvāja, Piṇḍola Bhāradvāja, Kāsi Bhāradvāja, Vāseṭṭha, Assalāyana, Moggallāna, Pārāsariya, Vassakāra, and others.[2]

Most of these religious teachers belonged to Magadha, and Rājagṛiha was the centre of their activities. The famous Parivrājaka Sañjaya lived at this place with two hundred and fifty disciples among whom Sāriputta and Moggallāna were the foremost. Sāriputta was the first to resolve to embrace the faith and was followed by Moggallāna.[3] These two friends tried to persuade their teacher, Sañjaya, to see the Buddha, but failing to convince him, abandoned him and went over to the Buddha, followed by all the disciples of Sañjaya.[4] Sakula-Udai was also residing at Rājagṛiha. Poṭaliputta and

1. *Dīgha*, I, 178; *Majjh*, I. 359, 481, 483, 489. 491, 501, 513; II. 1, 22, 29, 40; III. 207. *Aṅgu*, II. 30. 1; II. 185. 1; etc.
2. *Dīgha*, I. 87, 111, 127, 224, 234; *Majjh*, I. 16, 164. 175 etc.
3. *Mv*, I, 23. 1.
4. Ibid, 23, 2-10.

Dīghanakha also established their headquarters at this place. Moliyasīvaka and Sabhiya are said to have met the Buddha here. The *Aṅguttara Nikāya*[1] refers to Annabhāra Sarabha and others as staying in the Parivrājakārāma on the bank of the Sappiniyā river. Anugāra and Varadhara are mentioned as staying at Moranivāpa Parivrājakārāma in Rājagṛiha which had several delightful spots like Veluvana, Ghijjhakūṭa mountain, Moranivāpa, the Parivrājakārāma on the bank of the Sappiniyā river, Tapodārāma, Jīvaka's Āmravana, Sītavana, Maddakuchchi, and so on which were resorted to by a large number of *Parivrājakas*. These had made Rajagṛiha famous as a halting place for the wandering monks.

There was another pleasant and delightful *Āśrama* at Uruvela on the bank of the river Nerañjara. Pavārika's mango grove at Nālandā, Ghaggara Pokkharaṇī at Champā, Mahāvana near Vaiśālī, Mallikārāma in Śrāvastī, and others were important places meant for the *Parivrājakas* during this period. Vachchhagotta stayed at Vaiśālī in the Puṇḍarīka Parivrājakārāma. Jambukhādaka is known to have met Sāriputta at Nālakagāma (in Magadha) and Ukkavela (in Vajji). Ugghamāṇa had seven hundred *Parivrājakas* under him.[2] The leaders of the Brāhmaṇa ascetics were known as the *Gaṇasatthās*.[3]

Besides these, other *parivrājakas* too have been mentioned.[4]

Charaka : It is said that they begged alms while moving in company and kept on moving even while eating. They accepted cleansed alms and put on a lion-cloth. It is said that these mendicants were the direct descendants of Kapilamuni.[5]

Chirika : They picked up rags from the road side.[6]

Chammakhaṇḍia : They either wore a dress of hide or else their religious requisites were made of hide.

1. *Aṅgu*, II, 29, 176.
2. *Majjh*, II, 22-29.
3. *Jā*, II, 72.
4. *Anu*, 20; *Nāyā Ṭī*. 15.
5. *Paṇṇa*, *Ṭī*, II, 20 p. 405; also *Āchā*, p. 265.
6. The *Dīgha*, I, p. 166 also mentions such ascetics.

Bhikkahuṇḍa : They would eat nothing except what had been obtained by alms and would not take cow-milk etc. They are considered identical with Buddhist monks.

Paṇḍuraṅga or Paṇḍaraga : These were Śaiva mendicants who besmeared their body with ashes. According to the *Niśītha chūrṇi*, however, the disciples of Gośāla were called *Paṇḍarabhikkhu*. The *Anuyogadvārachūrṇi* identifies them with the *Sasarakkha* (*Sarajaska*) *Bhikkhus*.

Then there were other *Parivvāyagas*.

Saṅkha : They followed the Sāṁkhya system.

Joi : They followed the Yoga system.

Kavila : They followed the atheistic *Sāṁkhya* system and regarded Kapila as their master.

Bhiuchcha : They were the disciples of Bhṛigu.

Haṁsa : They lived in mountain caves, roads, hermitages, shrines, and gardens and entered a village only to beg.

Paramahaṁsa : They lived on river banks, the confluence of streams and discarded clothes before they died.

Bahūdaga : They lived one night in a village and five nights in a town.

Kuḍivvaya : They lived in their own house and considered getting victory over greed, illusion, and egotism as their goal.

Kaṇhaparivvāyaga : They worshipped the Nārāyaṇa.

JAṬILAS

Some Brahmanical hermits were called the Jaṭilas on account of their matted hairs.[1] These ascetics lived in large groups in forests, had group leaders, engaged in austerities, tended fire, and performed sacrifices. They were also called *Aggikā Jaṭilakā*.

Uruvelā, the place of the Buddha's *Sambodhi*, was then a great centre of Vedic religion. There were three settlements or colonies of the Jaṭilas on the banks of the river Nerañjara under three Kassapa brothers, Uruvela Kassapa, Nādi Kassapa, and Gaya Kassapa, each at the head of 500, 300 and 200 Jaṭilas respectively.[2] They were born in a Brāhmaṇa family of Magadha and were highly respected by the inhabitants of

1. DPPN, I, 931; *Udāna Aṭṭhakathā*, 74.
2. SBE, XIII, 118; *Jā*, VI, 219-20.

Aṅga and Magadha.[1] Most probably they were *Naishṭhika Brahmachārins.* It is said that Uruvela Kassapa used to perform annually a great sacrifice which was attended by the neighbouring people with abundant food.[2] On the occasion of the *Ashṭakas*, in the snowy-cold winter nights, they are described as plunging into the river Nerañjara and emerging out of it repeatedly on account of their belief in purification by bathing.[3]

That these three brothers had gathered quite a large number of followers and had made three colonies of them, shows that they had developed a congregational life. In the opinion of B.M. BARUA, there was no corporate life, and among the Jaṭilas forming three distinct groups, the tie in each group was rather domestic than congregational.[4] To convert these Brāhmaṇa ascetics who performed Vedic rites and enjoyed the respect of their people, was the principle aim of the Buddha, for that would, he thought, produce a magical effect on popular monks. According to *Mahāvagga*, he was successful in changing the heart of 1000 Jaṭilas along with their leaders who entered the Order.[5]

LOKĀYATAS

There is a reference to the *Lokāyatas* in the *Dighanikāya.* A Brahmaṇa well-versed in the Lokāyata doctrine asking the Buddha a series of questions has been mentioned.[6] A *Jātaka* passage refers to Lokāyatika doctrine.[7] The teacher and the student of this doctrine were both known as *Lokāyatika.* The name of this school was identical with the theory of elements as the prime cause (*Bhūtavāda* and *Uchchhedavāda*).

OTHER SCHOOLS AND SECTS

THE FOUR GREAT SCHOOLS

The *Sūtrakṛitāṅga*[8] describes the four heretical creeds of

1. *Mv*, I, 15.
2. SBE, XIII, p. 124.
3. Ibid, p. 130.
4. Gayā and Bodha-Gayā, Vol. I, p. 99.
5. *Mv*, I, 20, 17-24
6. *Saṁ*; DPPN, II, 787
7. *Jā*, VI. 286.
8. *Sūtra*, I. 12-1.

the time of Mahāvīra, creeds called *Kriyāvāda*, *Akriyāvāda*, *Ajñānavāda*, and *Vinayavāda*. These four great schools comprise three hundred and sixty-three schools : *Kriyāvāda* consists of one hundred and eighty schools; *Akriyāvāda* of eighty four schools, *Ajñānavāda* of sixty-seven schools, and *Vinayavāda* of thirty-two schools.

KRIYĀVĀDA

Kriyā denotes the existence of the soul (*jiva*), and those who believe in the existence of the soul are called *Kriyāvādins*. It is stated that one who knows the tortures of beings below in hell, one who knows the influx of sin and its stoppage one who knows misery and its annihilation, is entitled to expound *Kriyāvāda*.

AKRIYĀVĀDA

The *Akriyāvādins* deny the existence of the soul, etc., for according to them everything is of a momentary existence, and a state comes to an end the moment it comes into existence, and, therefore, it cannot have any *kriyā*. Without continuity of existence, no *kriyā* is possible; the existence itself is the cause and effect of it. They are identified with the Buddhists, who hold the doctrine of *Kshaṇikavāda*. *Akriyāvādins* were also called *Viruddhas*, since they held to doctrines opposed to those of other heretics.

AJÑĀNAVĀDA

The *Ajñānavādins* deny the necessity or importance of knowledge to attain salvation, since there is assertion of contradictory statements in it.

VINAYAVĀDA

The *Vinayavādins* or *Vainayikas* are mentioned as *Aviruddhakas* in the *Aṅguttara*.[1] They do not accept signs, external rules of ceremony, and the scriptures, but uphold the supremacy of reverence as the cardinal virtue leading to perfection. The upholders of this faith paid equal reverence to eight classes of beings, viz. god and master, ascetics, men, aged persons, inferiors, mother and father, and they maintained that to each of these eight classes of persons reverence may be shown in

1. *Aṅgu*, III, p. 276.

four ways, *i.e.*, physically, mentally, verbally and with gifts. Vasāyaṇa was a *Vinayavādī* ascetic who was practising *pāṇāmā pavajjā* with his arms uplifted when Mahāvīra and Gośāla arrived in Kummagāma.[1]

Besides these, the names of some other sects too have been mentioned in Jaina literature.

Attukkosiya : They belonged to the class of ascetics who were proud of themselves.

Bhūikammiya : They administered ashes to the people suffering from fever, etc.

Bhujjo bhujjo Kouyakāraka : They administered auspicious baths for procuring good luck. They are also known as Ābhiogias.

Chaṇḍidevaga : They had hangers (*sikkaka*) as their ritualistic paraphernalia.

Dagasoyariya : An adherent of the *Dagasoyariyas*, also known as *Suivādi*, who took bath after cleaning his body sixty four times if touched by anybody, has also been mentioned. A *Dagasoyariya* ascetic, it is said, was putting up in the Nārāyaṇa Koṭṭha in Mathura. After breaking his three-day fast he pretended to have taken cow-dung; he never uttered the word *itthi* (woman) and observed silence. People were so much attracted by his practice that they offered him robes, food, and drink. According to Malayagiri, however, these ascetics were the followers of the Sāṁkhya religion.

Dhammachintaka : They studied religious books, and contemplated on the *Dharmasaṁhitās* composed by Yājñavalkya and other sages, and acted accordingly.

Giyarai : They devoted themselves to songs and pleasures of love.

Goama : They earned their living by painting and decorating a young bull with cowries in his neck and performing tricks of touching feet etc., and created amusement for the people. These ascetics lived on rice.

Govvaia : They behaved like a cow, and in order to support their bovine character, followed a cow wherever it went.

1. *Āva. Nir*, 494.

grazed, drank water, returned home, and slept. They lived only on grass and leaves.

Kammārabhikkhu : They led a procession with idols.

Kuchchiya : They grew beard and moustaches.

Paraparivāiya : They spoke ill of other ascetics.

Piṇḍolaga : They remained very dirty, and their body which was an abode of lice emitted a foul smell. A *Piṇḍolaga* is said to have crushed himself under a rock on the mountain Vebhāra.

Sasarakkha : They were adepts in casting spells, etc., and stored dust for the rainy season. They moved about naked, and used the hollow of their hands as alms bowl.

Vaṇimago : They were greedy of food and begged alms by exhibiting themselves to the devotees of Śākya, etc. They put themselves in a pitiable state, and in order to divert the attention of the donors spoke pleasing words.

Vāribhadraka : They lived on water or moss and engaged themselves in bathing and washing their feet.

Vārikhala : They washed their pot with mud twelve times.

CONTEMPORARY SCHOOLS OF PHILOSOPHICAL THOUGHT (FROM BUDDHIST SOURCES)

The *Brahmajāla Sutta* in the *Digha Nikāya* classifies the contemporary philosophical thought into sixty-two schools which were in existence in the sixth century B.C. The four schools of Eternalists or *Sassaṭavādas* held that the soul and the world are both eternal. The first three schools held this view as a result of their having perceived through a recollection of the memories of past lives that the soul and the body have always been in existence, and the fourth school held this view not as a result of memory but on logical grounds.

The four schools of Semi-Eternalists or *Ekachcha-Sassatikas* were also well-known. The first school believed that while Brahmā was eternal, individual souls were not. The second school believed that debauched souls are not eternal but that undebauched souls are. The third school believed exactly the same thing as the second school except that in the case of the former the debauchery of the gods is mental unlike the debauchery of the gods of the latter school which is physical. The fourth school held that the soul was eternal but not the body.

The first of the four schools of Extentionists or *Antānantikas* held that the world was finite, the second that it was infinite, the third that it was infinite sidewise but finite upward and downward, and the fourth that it was neither finite nor infinite.

The four schools of Eel-wrigglers or *Amarāvikkhepikas* did not give categorical replies to any question but avoided them by ambiguous and equivocating replies, and differed only in respect of the motives for giving such replies.

The two schools of Fortuitous-Originists or *Adhichchasamuppannikas* held that the soul and the world came into being without a cause. The first came to this conclusion as a result of the remembrance of past lives and the second as a result of logical reasoning.

The thirty-two schools of consciousness-maintainers or *Uddhamāghatanikas* believed that the soul after death passed into various states of existence, *viz.*, conscious or unconscious, subject to decay or not subject to decay, neither conscious nor unconscious, and all in respect of the form, finitude, different modes of consciousness, and happiness of the soul.

The seven schools of *Annihilationists* or *Uchchedavādis* maintained that the soul is annihilated after death and identified it with the body, essence of the body, mind, infinite space, infinite consciousness, or with the boundless and with that which is beyond ideas.

The five schools of *Nirvāṇists* or *Diṭṭhadhammanibbānavādas* believed that a soul was capable of obtaining complete emancipation in this visible world through full enjoyment of the pleasures of the senses or through each of the four stages of *dhyāna*.

VEDIC PANTHEON AND RELIGIOUS PRACTICES

People had not forgotten the Vedic pantheon and religious practices because of the rise of different religious sects and schools during the time of Mahāvīra. The Vedic rituals were scrupulously performed by a large section of people. Though their number grew smaller and smaller, they never died out altogether.

The Jaina and Buddhist literary sources throw some light on Brahmanical religion and practices. The *Sotthiyas* and the Brāhmaṇa *Mahāsālas* of the age were custodians of the Vedic religion which was mostly sacrificial. The Brāhmaṇa *Mahāsālas* sometimes performed sacrifices for themselves, and sometimes officiated as priests in the *Yájñas* performed for kings. Descriptions of the preparations for the *Mahāyajñas* of the Brāhmaṇa Kūṭadanta of Magadha[1], of the Brāhmaṇa Uggatasarīra of Sāvatthi[2] and of king Pasenadi of Kośala[3] throw considerale light on the method of performing these *Yajñas*. Animals sacrificed included cows, bulls, steers, goats, sheep, etc. The number of animals used for sacrificial purposes sometimes rose to 500 or 700.

There are references to the performance of the *Assamedha*, the *Parisamedha*, the *Sammapasa* and the *Vājapeya* sacrifices.[4] *Yajñas* were performed with pomp and grandeur, and people flocked from neighbouring places to witness it. They were attended by big feasts, offerings, gifts of cows, beds, garments, women, chariots, carpets, and even places filled with corn. The picture of the *Yajñās* thus revealed by the Buddhist sources is similar to that painted by the Brahmanical sources leaving aside a few exaggerations.

The Brāhmaṇas appear as teachers representing various Vedic schools, such as the *Addhariyas* (*Aitareyas*), *Tittiriyas* (*Taittiriyas*), *Chhandokas* (*Chhāndogyas*), *Chhandāvas*, and so on.[5] They worshipped Indra, Soma, Varuṇa, Īśāna, Prajāpati, Brahmā, Mahiddhi, Yama, etc. They invoked them and offered prayer.[6]

POPULAR DEITIES

Because of the new notions regarding religion current during the time of Lord Mahāvīra, the functions of the

1. *Dīgha*, I, 127.
2. *Aṅgu*, IV, 41.
3. *Saṁ*, I. 76.
4. Ibid.
5. *Dīgha*, I,p. 237.
6. Ibid, p. 244.

old gods underwent modification and alteration, and new gods were created. Contact with indigenous cults at this time was responsible not only for the importation of new objects of worship, but also for the incorporation of new mythologies of the older cult. Not only from Brahmanical literature, but from Buddhist and Jaina literature also, we know about the popular deities worshipped during the sixth century B.C.

INDRA

Indra, the chief of all other gods, is the Vedic god of great antiquity, and it appears that he was one of the most popular deities. In the *Kalpasūtra*,[1] Indra has been described as enjoying divine pleasure in heaven in the company of various gods, eight chief queens, three assemblies, seven armies, seven commanders-in-chief, and body-guards. *Indramaha* was most prominent among all other *mahas* in ancient days. The festival of Indra was celebrated with great pomp and show. In Buddhist literature, he is mentioned by various names such as *Sakka*, *Vāsava*, *Maghavā*, and so on. He is also described as descending to this world for helping the virtuous punishing the evil-doers.[2] He resides in the place known as Sudhammā, Vejayanta, and Missakasāra in the beautiful Tāvatinsa heaven.[3]

BRAHMĀ

During the period of the Brāhmaṇas, Prajāpati occupied the supreme position and was looked upon as the creator. In the sixth century B.C., he was called Brahmā. In the Buddhist *Nikāyas*, it is this personal Brahmā of the popular religion that is pictured, attacked, and ridiculed. In fact, his unity is not recognized, and many Brahmās with different appellations, such as Sanatkumāra, Sahampati, and so on were conceived for worshipping.[4]

1. *Kalpa*, 1. 13.
2. *Jā*, No. 540.
3. KS. I, 284-307; *Jā*. II, 312.
4. *Mv*, I. 5.4; *Digha*, I. 244; *Saṁ*, I, 219; KS, I, 281. 191-2, 298; *Aṅgu*, II, 21.

AGNI

Agni (Fire-god) occupied an important place in Brahmanism on account of the importance of *Agnihotra.* The *Gṛihya-sūtras* and the *Dharmasūtras* prescribe a number of domestic sacrifices for which Agni is needed. Agni was given a high position due to his use in *yajña.* The Buddhist writers[1] ridicule Agni-worship probably due to the association of fire with *yajña* which involves slaughter of living beings.

SŪRYA

In the Vedic period, the Sun occupied an important position but the moon was insignificant. From Buddhist literature, it appears that both were popular deities as they were worshipped by a fairly large number of people.[2]

FEMALE DEITIES

Siri and *Sirimā* the goddesses of Fortune and Luck, were the popular deities of this period. They are referred to also in the *Kalpasūtra.*[3] In Buddhist literature, *Siri* has been regarded as the daughter of *Śakra* while *Sirimā* as the daughter of Dhṛitarāshṭra.[4] Of the abstract deities that were worshipped,[5] some were Vedic and others new additions. Saddhā (Śraddhā) is a Vedic deity, but Āsā and Hiri are non-Vedic.

Ajjā and *Koṭṭakiriyā* were two different forms of the goddess Durgā who is also called *Chaṇḍiyā*. The *Āchārāṅga* refers to the worship of Chaṇḍiyā with the sacrifice of goats, buffaloes, and human beings to please an inferior type of god.[6] The peaceful goddess Durgā is called *Ajjā*, and when she rides on a buffalo she is called Koṭṭakiriyā.

LOKAPĀLAS

There are four Lokapālas (*Chātumahārājika Devas*)[7] in the four quarters. Dhataraṭṭha Mahārāja, Virulhaka Mahārāja, Virupakkha Mahārāja, and Vessavaṇa Mahārāja are the lords of the East, the South, the West and the North res-

1. *Su. Ni*, III, 7.21.
2. *Therīgathā*, 87; *Jā*, I, 474; *Vi*, 1, 263.
3. SBE, XXII, 232.
4. *Jā*, III. 262.
5. *Jā*, V, 392.
6. *Āchā.* p. 61.
7. *Mv*, I, 6. 30; *Majjh.* II, 194.

pectively.[1]

YAKSHA WORSHIP

From the Brahmanical, the Jaina, and the Buddhist sources, it appears that Yakshas were objects of worship. In Vedic literature, the word 'Yaksha' signifies a supernatural being, or a ghost-like appearance. In the sixth century B.C., the worship of the Yakshas or Jakkhas became very popular, and so every important city had its own shrine dedicated to the Yaksha. The Yakshas sometimes granted worldy desires, especially progeny and wealth while some of the Yakshas have been associated with cosmological functions, others are looked upon as malevolent beings who take possession of men's persons inducing in them symptoms of frenzy.

Yaksha Gaṇḍitinduga of Vārāṇasī guarded the great sage Mātaṅga in the Tinduga garden.[2] Bihelaga was another Yaksha who paid reverence to Lord Mahāvīra when the latter was engrossed in meditation.[3] Gaṇgadatta,[4] Subhadda,[5] and Bhaddā[6] were blessed with a child by the worship of the Yakshas. The Yakshas are also said to have cured diseases, Pūrṇabhadra and Maṇibhadra, both Yakshas, seem to be more popular, for to them offerings of food were made.[7] Some of the Yakshas caused trouble to the people and often were satisfied only after killing them. We hear of Sūlapāṇi Jakkha who used to kill persons who happened to stay in his shrine.[8] Another strange belief regarding the Jakkhas was that they enjoyed sexual intercourse with human maidens. The Gaṇḍitindurga Jakkha is said to have had sexual intercourse with the princess Bhaddā.[9]

Like Yakshas, the *Vāṇamantarīs* or the Jakkhiṇīs also played an important part in ancient Indian life. The Vāṇa-

1. *Dīgha*, II, 220-21.
2. *Uttarā*, 12 and the com. p. 173 (a).
3. *Āva, Nir*, 487.
4. Vivāgasuya. 7, p. 42 f; also of Hatthipāla Jā, (IV. No. 509), p. 474.
5. *Āva, chū*, II, p. 193.
6. *Nāyā*, 2, p. 49 f.
7. *Nisī. chū*, II, p. 709.
8. *Āva, chū*, pp. 272-4.
9. *Gaṇḍatindu Jā*, (No. 520).

mantrī Salejjā is said to have paid reverence to Mahāvīra[1] whereas Kaṭapūtanā gave him trouble.[2] Various feasts and festivals were celebrated in honour of the Jakkhas. Bhaṇḍīravaṇa, the abode of Bhaṇḍīra Jakkha, a popular deity of Mathurā,[3] drew a large number of pilgrims.

The abode of a Yaksha is often referred to as *cheiya*, a term which was applied to the whole sacred enclosure containing a garden grove or park and a shrine. Mahāvīra, the Buddha, and many other religious ascetics are represented as halting or resting in these shrines. From the *Uvāsaga-dasāo*, we learn that Mahāvīra visited the shrine of Pūrṇabhadra at *Champā*, the shrine called Dvipalāsa of Vaṇijagrāma, the Koshṭhaka shrine of Vārāṇasī, the garden called Saṅkhavana of Ālabhī, the garden called Sahasrāmravana of Kampilyapura, Sahasrāmravana of Polāsapura and the shrines called Gunasila and Kushṭhaka of Rājagṛiha.

Buddhist literature refers to the cities and haunts of the *yakkhas*. Their cities were known as *Yakkhanagaras*, which were usually situated in islands, deep forests, and deserts. A *Jātaka* story mentions a *Yakkhanagara* called Sirisavatthu in Tambapaṇṇidīpa[4] and another in a forest.[5] But some had individual haunts.[6] More than thirty individual Yakshas are known by name.[7] Yakkha Sūchiloma had his haunt near Gayā.[8] The *Saṁyutta-Nikāya* and the *Sutta-Nipāta* describe him as discoursing with the Buddha.[9] Yakkha Indrakūṭa made the Indrakūṭa hill at Rājagṛiha his abode.[10] For yakkha Maṇimāla, there was the Maṇimāla *chetiya*.[11] Ajakalāpaka resided at Pāṭaliputra in the Ajakalāpaka *chetiya*.[12]

1. *Āva. chū*, p. 294.
2. Ibid, 490; the *Ayoghara Jā*, (V. No. 510), p. 491.
3. *Āva chū*, p. 281.
4. *Jā*, II. 127. There are references to other *Yakkhanagaras*. *Jā*, I, 240.
5. *Jā*, I, 399.
6. *Saṁ*, I, 207.
7. DPPN.
8. *Saṁ*, I, 207; KS, I. 264; *Su. Ni*, II. 5.
9. *Saṁ*, I, 207; KS, I. 264; *Su. Ni*, II. 5.
10. *Saṁ*, I, 206; KS, I. 262.
11. SN, I. 208; KS, 1,266.
12. *Udāna* I,7.

NĀGA WORSHIP

Nāga worship seems to have a non-Aryan origin. Its emergence as a cult may be traced to the time of the civilization of Mohenjodāro as it is clear from the two seals where it appears in an attitude of devotion to a figure in Yogic posture. It appears that this cult was adopted by the Aryans partly as a consequence of the absorption of non-Aryan deities into the Brahmanical fold, and partly as a protection against snake-bites.

References to Nāga-worship, like those to the worship of Yakshas, are abundant in the Jaina[1] and the Buddhist[2] sources. Jainism and Buddhism had to admit the serpent in a subordinate capacity in their own religious systems. Pārśvanātha has a serpent as his special symbol. It is said that the Buddha received the homage of Muchilinda and Elāpattra. The Buddha advised the *Bhikshus* to honour the royal families of the Nāgas, so that they could be protected from snake-bites, and the regions which were covered with dense forests may have given impetus to snake worship. As Magadha was originally a non-Aryan land, it remained a centre of *Nāga* worship from the earliest times. The *Mahābhārata* refers to the images and temples of the *Nāgas* at Rājagṛiha. The Buddhist sources tell us that the *Nāgas* were worshipped by the offerings of milk, rice, fish, mẹat, strong drink, and the like.[3] According to the Gṛihya-sūtras, they were offered fried grain, flour of fried barley, and flour over which ghee had been poured.[4]

TREE WORSHIP

That the tree was a non-Aryan object of worship is clear from some of the seals of the Indus-Valley Civilization. These seals show that the *Pippal* tree was worshipped by the people in two forms, i.e., in its natural form and in the form of the spirit of the tree which was shown emerging from the tree. Because of the absorption of the non-Aryan tribes in the Aryan fold, many non-Aryan objects of worship were also gradually incorporated in Brahmanism.

1. *Nāyā*
2. *Jā*, I. 498; II, 149.
3. Ibid, 498.
4. SBE, XXIX, pp. 128-29; 201-2; 328-30.

During the time of Mahāvīra, tree-worship seems to have been well known. Trees were considered to be the residences of some divine spirits who were worshipped by people for the fulfilment of their desires for sons, daughters, honour, wealth, and so on. Sometimes they were regarded as abodes of evil spirits like *Pretas*, and people worshipped them out of fear so that these malignant spirits may not harm them. The tree cult became further popular when the custom of using trees as symbols of saints and worshipping them as such became fashionable. The Bodhi tree, for instance, was one such tree for the Buddhists.

MISCELLANEOUS DEITIES

Besides the celestial gods worshipped by their devotees, people seem to have worshipped various animals and birds too, such as elephants, horses, bulls, cows, dogs, and crows.[1] The Buddhist sources[2] speak of the honour shown to the bull, sometimes in normal course and sometimes on occasions like his death. The custom of showing reverence to the bull was probably on account of his indispensability to agriculture.

Rivers and sacred streams began to be venerated, and *tirthas* or sacred spots on their banks came into existence and began to be thronged with worshipful pilgrims. People made pilgrimages to these holy places because facilities for travel were available.

The dread of demons must have driven people to take recourse to rites in order to keep them in good humour. Magical formulae and incantations must have been largely used to placate the invisible spirits and to control their vagaries. There are numerous allusions to persons versed in demonology (*bhūyavāiya*). There were dealers in antidotes as well as charmers who knew the science of spirits, and by means of various ceremonies, enchantments, and preservatives cured those possessed.[3] The *Bṛihatkalpabhāshya* refers to a shop called *Kuttiyāvaṇa*[4]

1. India as described in Early Texts of Buddhism and Jainism, pp. 195, 197-198.
2. *Jā*, II. 225; *Jā*, IV 326.
3. *Uttarā. Ṭī*, I, p. 5 ; *Āva, Ṭī*, p. 399.
4. *Bṛih. Bhā*, 3. 4214; *Āva. Ṭī*, p. 413.

where everything living or non-living was available. It is said that there were nine such shops in Ujjeṇī during the reign of Chaṇḍapajjoya.

From about the sixth century B.C., the old Vedic religion and practices gradually underwent transformation, and formed some sort of a new religion. Although the final form of this new religion is not clearly perceptible, its beginnings were marked in this age by the adoption of theistic Vaishṇavism and Śaivism within the fold of the Brahmanical religion. These two theistic religions centred round two deities, Vishṇu and Śiva, and they both emphasized devotion.

The first step in the evolution of Vaishṇavism was the identification of Vāsudeva-Kṛishṇa with the Vedic deity Vishṇu, standing originally for the 'Sun'. This reference in the *Chhāndogya Upanishad* seems to point to a date in the seventh or sixth century B.C. Next, that Vāsudeva-Kṛishṇa-Vishṇu was identified with a sage Nārāyaṇa, is clear from the *Baudhāyana Dharmasūtra*. This *Bhāgavata* or Vaishṇava religion seems to have originated first with the Yādava-Sātvata-Vṛishṇi people of the Mathura area.

The cult of Śiva probably goes back to a very early period. That it was current among the non-Aryans of the pre-Vedic period is obvious from the fact that some scholars have identified the figures on seals with Śiva who is also identified with the Vedic god Rudra. In the *Śvetāśvatara Upanishad*, Śiva figures as the Great God (Mahādeva) superior to the Vedic pantheon.

Belief in heaven and hell was widespread at this date and it was said that those who perform various noble acts attain heaven, while those who indulge in evil acts go to hell.

CHAPTER VI

POLITICAL CONDITIONS AND INSTITUTIONS

Since at the time of Lord Mahāvīra, there was no paramount power in North India, the region was divided into many independent states. The period, however, was politically very important in ancient Indian history and marked the end of the tribal stage of society, while it also gave rise for the first time to those organized states which were known as sixteen great countries *Solasamahājanapada.* These states formed some definite territorial units and included both monarchies and republics. A trial of strength was taking place amongst the monarchies, and, what is more, between the monarchical and the non-monarchical forms of government. It led to the decline of the republics, the rise of absolutism, and the growing success of Magadhan imperialism.

The Jaina, Buddhist, and Purāṇic texts furnish catalogues of these states. In spite of the striking resemblances between one list and another, there are also important differences, a fact which leads to the assumption that the lists were originally drawn up at different times, and they reflect the difference in their author's knowledge of or interest in or even his intimacy with the different parts of the country.

The Jaina *Bhagavatī Sūtra,*[1] (otherwise called *Vyākhyā-Prajñapti*), provides a list of sixteen *Mahājanapadas* at the time of Lord Mahāvīra as follows :

(1) Aṅga, (2) Baṅga (Vaṅga), (3) Magaha (Magadha), (4) Malaya (5) Mālava (ka), (6) Achchha (7) Vachchha (Vatsa) (8) Kochchha (Kachchha), (9) Pāḍha (Pāṇḍya or Pauṇḍra) (10) Lāḍha (Lāṭa or Rāḍha), (11) Bajji (Vajji), (12) Molī (Malla), (13) Kāsi (Kāśī), (14) Kosala (15) Avāha and (16) Sambhuttara (Suṁhottara).

1. *Saya* XV, *Uddessa* I (Hoerule-the *Uvā*, II, Appendix).

The Buddhist texts,[1] which testify to their existence in the sixth century B.C., only incidentally refer to them. Among them, the *Aṅguttara Nikāya* is the most important as it is the earliest. The sixteen states enlisted in it are as follows :

(1) Kāsi (Kāśī), (2) Kosala (Kośala), (3) Aṅga, (4) Magadha, (5) Vajji (Vṛiji), (6) Malla, (7) Chetiya (Chedi), (8) Vaṁsa (Vatsa), (9) Kuru, (10) Pañchāla, (11) Machchha (Matsya), (12) Sūrasena, (13) Assaka (Aśmaka), (14) Avanti (15) Gandhāra and (16) Kamboja.

The *Janavasabha Suttanta* (Dīgha Nikāya, II) refers to some of them in pairs, viz., Kāsī-Kosala, Vṛiji (Vajji)-Malla, Chedi-Vaṁsa, Kuru-Pañchāla, and Matsya-Śūrasena. The *Chullaniddesa* and Kaliṅga to the list aud substitutes Yona for Gandhāra. The *Mahāvastu* list agrees with that in the *Aṅguttara Nikāya* save that it omits Gandhāra and Kamboja and mentions Śivi and Daśārṇa instead.

Aṅga, Magadha, Vatsa, Vajji, Kāsi, and Kosala are common to both the *Bhagavatisūtra* and the *Aṅguttara Nikāya* lists. Mālava of the *Bhagavatī* is probably identical with Avanti of the *Aṅguttara*. Molī is probably a corruption of Malla. The other states mentioned in the *Bhagavati* are new, and indicate a knowledge of the far east and the far south of India. E. J. Thomas[2] suggests that the author of this work lived in South India, and that the more extended horizon clearly proves that its list belongs to a later period than the one given in the Buddhist *Aṅguttara*. Along with the monarchies, both the Jaina and Buddhist texts mention the existence of republics which formed the distinctive feature of Indian politics in the sixth century B.C. Pāṇini, in his *Ashṭādhyāyi* (500 B.C.), mentions both classes of states, viz., the Republics, to which he applies the term *Saṁgha* or *Gaṇa*, and the kingdoms called *Janapadas*. Baudhāyana in his *Dharmasūtra* mentions states like Surāshṭra Avanti, Magadha, Aṅga, Puṇḍra, and Vaṅga.

AÑGA

The Jaina *Prajñāpanā* ranks Aṅga and Vaṅga in the first

1. Aṅgu, I, 213; IV, 252, 256, 260; *Mahāvastu*, I, 34, II, 3; *Vinaya* Texts. II, 146 fn; *Niddesa*, II. 37.
2. History of Buddhist Thought. p. 6,

group of Aryan peoples. Aṅga seems to have comprised the districts of Bhagalpur and Monghyr. Dadhivāhana is known to Jaina tradition[1] as having ruled over this region in the time of Lord Mahāvīra. His daughter Chandanā or Chandrabālā was the first female who embraced Jainism shortly after Mahāvīra had attained the Kevaliship. There is another tradition[2] that when Śreṇika (Bimbisāra) conquered Aṅga, he posted his son Kūṇika (Ajātaśatru) as its Governor.

The capital of Aṅga was Champā which stood at the confluence of the river of the same name. A. CUNNINGHAM[3] points out that there still exist near Bhāgalpur two villages Champānagara and Champāpura, which most probably represent the actual site of the ancient capital. At the time of Mahāvīra, the capital was a beautiful and prosperous city, a detailed description of which is given in the *Ovāiya*.[4] It was one of the ten important capitals, a big centre of trade, from where merchants travelled as far as Mithilā, Ahichchhatrā, Pihuṇḍa, and other places with their merchandise.

The *Dīgha Nikāya* also refers to Champā as one of the six principal cities of India. It was noted for its wealth and commerce, and traders sailed from it to Suvarṇa-bhūmi in the Trans-Gangetic region for trading purposes.[5] Other important cities in Aṅga were Assapura (Aśvapura) and Bhaddiya (Bhadrika).[6]

KĀŚI

That Kāśī was more powerful than most of the contemporary *Janapadas*, including Kosala, is clear from the combined testimony of many *Jātakas* and the *Mahāvagga*. The kingdom of Kāśī, whose extent is given in the *Jātakas* as three hundred leagues, was wealthy and prosperous. The twenty-third Jaina Tīrthaṅkara Pārśvanātha, who died 250 years before Mahāvīra, i.e. in or about 777 B.C., was the son of

1. *Āva. chū*, p. 205 ff; *Uttarā Ṭī*, 9, p. 132.
2. *Bhag*, 300; *Dīgha*, 1, 111.
3. B. C. LAW, Geography of Early Buddhism, p. 6.
4. *Ovā*, 1, 2, 10.
5. *Jā*, No 539, VI, p. 34
6. DPPN, p- 16.

King Aśvasena of Banaras. Kāśī was conquered by Kosala some time before Mahāvīra. Kāśī and Kosala were known for their eighteen confederate kings (*Gaṇarājā*), who fought against Kūṇiya on the side of Cheṭaka. Several *Jātakas* bear witness to the superiority of its capital Banaras over the other cities. It was also a commercial centre of repute.

KOSALA

Kosala was one of the most important kingdoms in Northern India during the life-time of Lord Mahāvīra. It exactly corresponds to modern Oudh. It was probably bounded by the Sadānīra (Gandak) river on the east, Pañchāla on the west, the Sarpikā or Syandikā (Sai) river on the south, and the Nepal hills on the north. Kosala contained three great cities, namely Ayodhyā, Sāketa, and Sāvatthi or Śrāvastī, besides a number of minor towns like Setavyā and Ukkaṭṭhā.

The only kings or princes in the Purāṇic list, who are known from the Vedic and early Buddhist texts to have reigned in Kosala or over some outlying part of it, are Hiraṇyanābha, Prasenajit, and Śuddhodana. Though the Purāṇic chroniclers make Hiraṇyanābha an ancestor of Prasenajit, they are not sure of his position in the dynastic list.[1]

Prasenajit of Kosala, a contemporary of Mahāvīra, figures as one of the most important rulers of the time. Under him, Kosala became a powerful kingdom. First of all, he annexed Kāśī to his kingdom. That he soon extended his supremacy over the Śākyas of Kapilavastu, probably also over the Kālāmas of Kesaputta, and other neighbouring states, is clear from the evidence of the *Aggañña Suttanta*[2] and the introductory portion of the *Bhaddasāla Jātaka*.[3] His relations with Śreṇika (Bimbisāra) of Magadha were cordial. He married Śreṇika's sister and gave him the dowry of a village in Kāśī with a revenue of 100,000. But after the death of Śreṇika, he carried on a protracted struggle with Kūṇika (Ajātaśatru). The Jaina texts present Ajātaśatru as the conqueror of the

1. AIHT, 173.
2. *Dīgha*, III (P.T.S.), 83; *Dia*, III. 80.
3. *Jā*, No, IV. 145.

powerful political confederacy which included the *Gaṇa-Rājyas* of Kāśī and Kosala.[1] Viḍūḍabha, who succeeded him, seems to be the last ruler. The rivalry with Magadha ended in the absorption of the kingdom into the Magadhan empire.

VṚIJI

The Vṛijji (*Vajji*) territory lay north of the Ganges and extended as far as the Nepal hills. At the time of Lord Mahāvīra, it was ruled by the Vajjian republic, about the constituent clans of which we are in the dark. On the basis of the name of a Judicial committee of the Republic—*Aṭṭhakulaka* (*Ashṭakulakā*) some scholars[2] assumed that the confederacy consisted of eight *Kulas* (clans). Of these, the old Videhas, the Lichchhavīs, the *Jñātrikas,* and the Vṛijis were the most important. The remaining seem to be the Ugras, the Bhogas, the Aikshvākavas, and the Kauravas because these are associated with the Jñātṛis and the Lichchhavīs as subjects of the same ruler and members of the same Assembly.[3] The *Aṅguttara Nikāya*[4] too refers to the close connection of the Ugras with Vaiśālī, the capital of the Vṛijian confederation.

There is no reason to believe that the eight members of the judicial court represented the eight clans of the republic. Yogendra Mishra[5] has tried to prove that Videhas of Mithilā did not form part of the Vajjian Republic. Vṛiji was only the name of the confederacy but not of the constituent clan. Only the six clans may be treated as inhabiting the Vajjian territory. The Lichchhavī capital was definitely at Vaiśālī, which is represented by modern Besarh (to the east of the Gaṇḍak) in the Muzaffarpur district of Bihar. The Jñātṛikas were the clan of Siddhārtha and his son Mahāvīra, the Jina. They had their seats at Kuṇḍapura or Kuṇḍagrāma and Kollāga, suburbs of Vaiśālī. Though dwelling in suburban areas, Mahāvīra and his fellow clansmen were known as

1. *Bhag*, 300.
2. CAG, pp. 512 ff. RBI, p. 25; B.C. Law, Geography of Early Buddhism, p. 12.
3. SBE, XLV, 339; *Uvā*, II, p. 138 fn. 304.
4. *Aṅgu*, I. 26; III, 49; IV, 208.
5. An Early History of Vaiśālī, p. 122.

Vesālie, i.e. inhabitants of Vaiśālī.[1] The remaining people of the confederacy, *viz.*, the Ugras, Bhogas, Kauravas, and Aikshvākavas, resided in the suburbs, andin villages or towns like Hatthigāma and Bhoganagara.[2]

The Lichchhavīs were on friendly terms with king Prasenajit of Kosala. Their relation with the neighbouring Mallas was on the whole friendly. The Jaina *Kalpasūtra*[3] refers to the nine Lichchhavīs as having formed a league with the nine Mallakīs and eighteen clan-lords of Kāśī-Kosala. We learn from the *Nirayāvalī Sūtra* that an important leader of this alliance was Cheṭaka whose sister Triśalā or Videha-dattā was the mother of Mahāvīra, and whose daughter Chellanā or Vaidehī was, according to Jaina writers, the mother of Kūṇika-Ajātaśatru. The great rival of Vaiśālī was Magadha. According to tradition, the Vaiśālians sent an army to attack Magadha at the time of Bimbisāra.[4] The matrimoninl alliance was, according to D.R. BHANDARKAR, the result of the peace concluded after the war between Bimbisāra and the Lichchhavīs. In the reign of Ajātaśatru, this great confederacy Vṛiji was utterly destroyed.

MALLA

Originally, the Mallas had a monarchical form of Government, but at the time of Mahāvīra, they were a Saṁgha or corporation, of which the members were called *Rājās*. The Jaina Kalpasūtra[5] refers to the nine clans of the Mallas, and each of them ruled over a separate territory. Among these, two were prominent : one with its headquarters at Kuśīnārā and the other with Pāvā as its chief town. The river Kakutsthā (Kakutthā) formed the boundary between the two territories. Kuśīnārā is identified with Kāsiā on the smaller Gandak about 56 km. to the east of Gorakhpur, and Pāvā with Padaraona 19 km. to the north-east of Kasiā.[6] In the *Saṅgīti Suttanta*, we

1. HOERNLE. *Uvā*, II, p. 4 n.
2. PHAI, p. 121.
3. SBE, XXII, p. 266.
4. HTB, II, 166.
5. SBE. XXII, p. 266.
6. CAG, p. 498. CARLLEYLE, however, proposes to identify it with Fazilpur, 10 miles S.E. of Kasiā.

have a reference to the Mote Hall of the Pāvā Mallas named Ubbhaṭaka.[1] There were some other Malla towns, namely, Bhoganagara lying between Jambugrāma and Pāvā, Anupiyā between Kuśınārā and the river Anomā and Uruvelakappa.

The relations between the Mallas and the Lichchhavīs were sometimes hostile and sometimes friendly. They became allies for self-defence at the time of Kūṇika-Ajātaśatru's invasion, though the *Bhadasāla Jātaka*[2] offers us an account of a conflict between them.

Jainism and Buddhism found many followers among the Mallas. From the Jaina *Kalpasūtra*, we learn that the nine Mallakis or Malla Chiefs were among those that instituted an illumination on the day of the new moon, saying, "Since the light of intelligence is gone, let us make an illumination of material matter."[3] At the time of the Buddha's death, we find both the main sections of the Mallas claiming a share of his bodily remains. This also proves that these two main clans retained their distinctive independence.

Soon after the Buddha's death, the Mallas appear to have lost their independencc with their dominions annexed to the Magadhan empire.[4]

CHEDI (*Cheti*)

The Chedis were one of the most ancient tribes of India. They had two distinct settlements, of which one was in the mountains of Nepal and the other in Bundelkhand. D. R. BHANDARKAR[5] maintains that Cheta or Chetiya corresponds roughly to modern Bundelkhand. Sotthivatīnagara, probably identical with Śukti or Śuktimatı of the *Mahābhārata*, was its capital. Other important towns of the Chedis were Sahajāti and Tripurī. Sahajāti lay on the trade route along the river Ganga.[6] We learn from the *Vedabbha Jātaka*[7] that the road from

1. DPPN, II, 194.
2. *Jā*, No. 465.
3. SBE, XXII, p. 266.
4. CL, 1. 79.
5. Ibid, 1. 52.
6. RBI, p. 103.
7. *Jā*, No. 48.

Kāśī to Chedi was unsafe on account of its being infested with roving bands of marauders.

The *Mahābhārata* and some of the *Jātakas* mention the names of the early kings of Chedi, but their accounts are legendary and cannot be relied upon for genuine historical purposes.

VATSA

Vatsa or Vaṁśa was the country south of the Ganga of which Kauśāmbī, modern Kosam, on the Yamuna, near Allahabad, was the capital. The king of Vatsa in the time of Mahāvīra was Udayana.

According to the Purāṇic evidence, Udayana was a scion of the Bhārata *Kula*. There is no unanimity in regard to the names of even the immediate predecessors of Udayana. His father's name is said to be Śatānīka II[1]. He married a princess of Videha on account of which his son is called Vaidehīputra.[2] He is said to have attacked Champā, the capital of Aṅga, during the reign of Dadhivāhana.[3]

There are legendary traditions about Udayana Vatsarāja of Kauśāmbī and his contemporary Pradyota of Avanti. A critical examination of these legends will yield a number of historical facts of considerable importance. Udayana and Pradyota, both rulers of two adjoining kingdoms, appear to have been connected by marriage and to have engaged in war. It seems that later on cordial relations were established between them. According to the *Priyadarśikā* he conquered Kaliṅga and restored his father-in-law, Dṛiḍhavarman, to the throne of Aṅga. The latter is probably the same as Dadhivāhana who, according to another legend, was defeated by Udayana's father.

Udayana had a son named Bodhi, but we do not know anything definite about Vatsa after Udayana, not even whether Bodhi ever succeeded his father to the throne.

1. In the Buddhist texts, his father's name is given Parantapa. See *Vinaya* II, 127; IV, 198; Majjh, II, 97; *Jā*, III, 157. In the Jaina Texts his name has been mentioned *Sayāṇīya*.
2. *Svapna-vāsavadatta*, Act VI, p. 129.
3. JASB, 1914, p. 321.

MAGADHA

In the time of Lord Mahāvīra, Magadha corresponded roughly to the present Patna and Gaya districts of South Bihar. The boundaries were probably the Ganga to the north, the Son to the West, a dense forest reaching to the plateau of Chotā Nagpur to the south, and Aṅga to the East. The river Champā formed a boundary between Magadha and Aṅga : but in Mahāvīra's time Aṅga was subject to Magadha. Its earliest capital was Girivraja or Rājagṛiha.

Mahāvīra's contemporary rulers of Magadha were Bimbisāra and Ajātaśatru. In their reign, Magadha was the first among the states of the sixth century B.C. to make a successful bid for the establishment of its supremacy over them. By his conquests and matrimonial alliances, Bimbisāra enlarged his influence and power. Afterwards, his son crushed the great republic of the Lichchhavīs after sixteen years of struggle, vanquished Kosala, and annexed Kāśī. The kingdom of Bimbisāra is stated to have been 300 leagues in extent, to which an addition of 200 leagues was made by Ajātaśatru's conquests.

Jaina writers mention two early kings of Rājagṛiha, Samudravijaya and his son Gaya.[1] Little reliance can be placed on them in this regard because what they say is not corroborated by any other evidence. Bimbisāra, who belonged to the *Haryaṅka-Kula*, occupied the throne of Magadha immediately after the fall of Bṛihadratha dynasty in the sixth century B.C. According to the *Mahāvaṁśa*, he was fifteen years old when he was anointed king by his father. This would show that he was not the founder of the royal family. D.R. BHANDARKAR has inferred that Bimbisāra, who was originally a *Senāpati* probably of the Vajjis, made himself the king.

Bimbisāra was helped in his political career by his matrimonial alliances. His first wife was a sister of Prasenajit, the king of Kosala, who gave him the dowry of a village of Kāśī with a revenue of 100,000. His second wife was Chellanā, daughter of the Lichchhavī Chief, Cheṭaka. His

1. SBE, XLV, p. 86.

third wife was Vaidehī Vāsavī. His fourth wife was Khemā, daughter of the king of Madra (Central Punjab).

Not content with these matrimonial alliances, Bimbisāra embarked upon his career of conquest and aggrandisement. His father was defeated by Brahmadatta, king of Aṅga. It was probably to avenge this defeat that Bimbisāra led a compaign against Aṅga. He was completely successful and enlarged Magadha by conquering and annexing this powerful and prosperous kingdom. He appointed his son Kūṇika as the Governor at Champā. According to Jaina legend, Pradyota of Avanti set out to attack Rājagṛiha even during the lifetime of Bimbisāra but he was foiled in his attempt by the cunning art of Prince Abhaya.[1] Bimbisāra is known to have friendly relations with Pradyota and with Pushkarasārin, king of Gandhāra. When the king of Avanti was suffering from jaundice, he sent his own physician Jīvaka.

According to Buddhist traditions, Bimbisāra lost his life at the hands of his son Ajātaśatru who was incited to the crime by Devadatta. But Jaina tradition is more charitable to Ajātaśatru. It does not represent him as a parricide. It relates that in his eagerness for the throne, he put his father in prison, but Bimbisāra took poison and killed himself.

Ajātaśatru added largely to the extent of the kingdom by his conquests. He started with a war against Kosala because Prasenajit revoked his gift of the Kāśī village after the death of the Kosalan princess. Ajātaśatru was defeated and had to surrender himself to Prasenjit along with his army. In the end, peace was concluded between the two by Prasenjit restoring to Ajātaśatru his liberty, army, and the disputed village of Kāśī and even giving his daughter Vajīrā in marriage to him.

The Jaina texts present Ajātaśatru as the conqueror of the powerful political confederacy which dominated Eastern India at that time and comprised thirtysix republican states—nine Mallakī, nine Lichhhavīs, and eighteen *Gaṇarājyas* of Kāśī and Kosala.[2] The overthrow of this confederacy resulted from

1. ABORI. 1920-21. 3.
2. *Bhag*, 300.

Ajātaśatru's conquest of its most powerful member, the Lichchhavī republic, although the cause of the conflict between the two is differently stated in different texts.

(1) According to the Buddhists, a jewel mine was discovered at the foot of a hill at a port in the Gaṅgā and it was agreed that Ajātaśatru and the Lichchhavīs would have an equal share of the gems. The Lichchhavīs violated this agreement and so brought on the conflict.

(2) According to the Jaina version[1], the bone of contention was the Magadha state elephant Śreyanāka and a huge necklace of eighteen strings of pearls which were given by Bimbisāra to his sons Halla and Vehalla. They carried off the elephant and the necklace to Vaiśālī and sought the protection of their grandfather, king Cheṭaka, against Ajātaśatru. Having failed to obtain them peacefully, Kūṇika-Ajātaśatru declared war on Cheṭaka.[2]

(3) It is also stated that Pamāvatī incited her husband Ajātaśatru to this conflict.

It was not easy to conquer the Lichchhavīs who were then at the zenith of their power as the head of a vast confederacy. Their leader Cheṭaka actually mustered up the confederate powers, including the *Gaṇa-rājās* (republican chiefs) of Kāśī and Kosala and inspired them to fight.[3] They all maintained their high traditions and were ready to stake everything for the success of the republic. Ajātaśatru proved equal to his difficult task and took recourse to three means for the subjugation of the hostile state—machination, military strength, and strategy. He deputed his minister Vassakāra on the mission of sowing seeds of disunion among the Lichchavīs at Vaiśālī. Infected with jealousies and quarrels between the different classes, between the rich and the poor and the strong and the weak, the Lichchhavīs became a changed people, lacking the social unity of former days.

But Ajātaśatru had to plan his military preparations for the conquest on a large scale. Rājagṛiha was too far inland

1. *Uvā,* II, App. p. 7; B.C. Law : Some Jaina Canonical *Sūtras,* (*Nirayā*) p. 87.
2. *Āvaśyaka*, p. 684.
3. B. C. Law : Some Jaina Canonical *Sūtras,* (*Nirayā*), p. 87.

to serve as a base of operations against the distant Lichchhavīs on the other side of the Ganga. Therefore he selected a convenient site directly on the Ganga for the construction of a fort and laid the foundation of Pāṭaliputra, his new capital. He also made secret weapons of war which may be compared to modern tanks.

The construction of the fort was followed by his expedition against Vaiśālī. The war between Ajātaśatru on the one hand and these various republics under the leadership of Cheṭana of Vaiśālī on the other was a long-drawn-out and arduous affair. It must have lasted for at least sixteen years. Ajātaśatru came out successful on account of his manifold and well-designed preparations.

These conquests of Ajātaśatru by which he became the paramount power of Eastern India provoked feelings of hostility in his equally ambitious rival king Chaṇḍa Pradyota of Avanti. He was planning an attack upon his capital at Rājagṛiha. Ajātaśatru applied himself to the task of strengthening its fortifications. But the king of Avanti could do nothing against him. He thus extended the boundaries of his kingdom and laid the foundations of the Magadhan empire on solid grounds.

KURU

Kuru is identified with modern Kurukshetra or Thaneshwar. As is apparent from the *Mahā-sutasoma Jātaka*,[1] it was three hundred leagues in extent. The capital of the Kurus was Indraprastha near modern Delhi, which extended over seven leagues. Another important town was Hastināpura. Besides other small towns and villages known to us, were Thullakoṭṭhita, Kammāssadamma, Kaṇḍi, and Vāraṇāvata.

The *Jātakas*[2] mention the names of some Kuru kings and princes such as Dhanañjaya, Koravya, and Sutasoma, but we are not sure of their historicity in the absence of further evidence. The Jaina *Uttarādhyayana Sūtra* mentions a king named Ishukāra ruling at a town, Ishukāra, in the Kuru country.[3] It seems that the Kuru realm was divided into small

1. *Jā*, No. 537.
2. *Jā*, Nos. 276, 413, 515 and 545.
3. SBE, XLV, 62.

states of which Indraprastha and Ishukāra were apparently the most important. "Kings" are mentioned as late as the time of the Buddha when one of them paid a visit to Raṭṭhapāla, son of a Kuru magnate, who had become a disciple of the Śākya Sage.

PAÑCHĀLA

Pañchāla roughly corresponds to the modern Badaun, Farrukhabad, and the adjoining districts of the Uttar Pradesh. In very early times, this country was divided into northern or Uttara-Pañchāla and southern or Dakshiṇa-Pañchāla. The Northern Pañchāla had its capital at Ahichchhatra (identified with modern Rāmnagar in the Bareilly district) while Southern Pañchāla had its capital at Kāmpilya. i.e. Kampil in the Farrukhābad District.

The history of Pañchāla from the death of Pravāhaṇa Jaivali to the time of Bimbisāra of Magadha is obscure. A great Pañchāla king named Chulani Brahmadatta is mentioned in the *Mahā-Ummagga Jātaka*[1], the *Uttarādhyayana Sūtra*,[2] the *Svapnavāsavadatta*,[3] and the *Rāmāyaṇa*.[4] In the *Uttarādhyayanasūtra*, Brahmadatta is styled a universal monarch. The story of this king is, however, essentially legendary, and little reliance can therefore be placed on it.

The *Uttarādhyayana Sūtra* mentions a king of Kāmpilya named Sañjaya who gave up his kingly power and adopted the faith of the Jinas.[5] It is difficult to assign any definite date to this ruler. It seems that in the sixth century B.C., the Pañchālas like others established a *Saṁgha* form of Government of the *Rāja-śabd-opajīvin* type and its leaders assumed the title of *Rājās*. One of these *Rājās* was apparently the maternal grandfather of Viśākha Pañchālīputra, a disciple of the Buddha.[6]

1. *Jā*, No. 546
2. SBE, XLV, 57-61.
3. Act V,
4. *Rāmāyaṇa*, I. 32.
5. SBE, XLV, 80-82.
6. DPPN, II, 108.

MATSYA

The Matsya or Machchha country corresponds to the modern territories of Jaipur and Alwar. Its capital was Virāṭanagara (modern Bairāṭ) named after its founder king Virāṭa. Upaplavya was another city of Matsya kingdom where the Pāṇḍavas transferred themselves from Virāṭa on the completion of the period of their exile. The *Mahābhārata*[1] refers to a king named Sahaja who reigned over the Chedis as well as Matsyas. The Matsyas had no political importance of their own during the time of Mahāvīra. In Pāli literature, the Matsyas as a people are usually associated with the Śūrasenas.

ŚŪRASENA

Mathurā was the capital of Śūrasena which is identified with the region round Mathurā. In the *Mahābhārata* and the *Purāṇas*, the ruling family of Mathurā is labelled as the Yadu or Yādava family. The Yādavas were divided into various branches, namely, the Vītihotras, Sātvatas, etc.

At the time of Lord Mahāvīra, Avantiputra was the ruling chief of Śūrasena country. It may be inferred from the epithet 'Avantiputra' that Avanti and Śūrasena were bound to each other by a matrimonial alliance. Avantiputra, king of the Śūrasenas, was the first among the chief disciples of the Buddha through whose help Buddhism gained ground in the Mathurā region. Mathurā was also a centre of considerable importance for the Jainas. It is said to have been visited by Mahāvīra, Ajja Maṅgu, and Ajja Rakkhiya.

SINDHU SAUVĪRA

Sindhu Sauvīra is the Lower Indus Valley, Sindhu being the name of 'the inland portion lying to the west of the Indus' while Sauvīra includes the littoral as well as the inland portion lying to the east of the Indus as far as Multan. Vītabhaya was the capital of this province.[2] Udayana was a very powerful monarch of Sindhu Sauvīra. He was converted after he heard Mahāvīra's sermon at Vītabhaya. In course of time,

1. Mbh, V. 74. 16; VI. 47, 67; 52. 9.
2. PHAI, pp. 507 and 619.

he anointed Keśīkumāra, his sister's son, king over Sindhu Sauvīra and joined the order under Mahāvīra.[1] On the other hand, according to the Buddhists, Udrāyaṇa, king of Roruka, accepted Buddhism and was ordained by the Buddha.

AŚVAKA

The early Buddhist texts refer to Aśvaka as *Mahājanapada* the capital of which was Potana or Potali corresponding to Paudanya of the *Mahābhārata*. This Aśvaka of Buddhist literature was a south Indian country and it was located either on the Godāvarī or comprised the region of Mahārāshṭra.

The Kingdom of Aśvaka is believed to have been founded by Ikshvāku chiefs. The *Mahāgovinda Suttanta* mentions Brahmadatta, king of the Assakas, as a contemporary of Sattabhu, king of Kaliṅga, Vessabhu, king of Avanti, Bharata, king of Sauvīra, Renu, king of Videha, Dhataraṭṭha, king of Aṅga, and Dhataraṭṭha, king of Kāśī.[2] The *Chulla Kāliṅga Jātaka* mentions Aruṇa, a king of Assaka, and his Minister Nandisena, and refers to a victory which they won over the king of Kaliṅga. We are not definite about the historicity of these early rulers. In the sixth century B.C. at the time of Lord Mahāvīra, the ruler of Assaka was a king whose son was prince Sujāta.

AVANTI

The kingdom of Avanti seems to have comprised roughly modern Malwa, Nimar, and the adjoining parts of Madhya Pradesh. It was named after Avantis, one of the branches of Haihayas. It seems that when the Vītihotras and Avantis passed away, the country of Avanti was divided into two kingdoms, one placed in the Dakshiṇāpatha having Māhishmatī for its capital, and the other, i.e. the northern kingdom, having its capital at Ujjayinī. The southern kingdom, with its capital Māhishmatī, was ruled by Viśvabhū, one of the seven contemporary kings of the line of Bharata.[3] At Ujjain,

1. *Bhag*, 13. 6.
2. *Dia*, Part II, p. 270.
3. *Dīgha*. II, 236. The *Mahāgovinda Suttanta* also refers to this ruler. See, PHAI, p. 145.

a Minister named Pulika (Puṇika) is said to have killed his master and appointed his own son, Pradyota, the ruler in the very sight of the Kshatriyas.[1] Pradyota was thus Puṇika's son, and with him commenced the Pradyota dynasty.

Pradyota was one of the most powerful monarchs of North India in the days of Lord Mahāvīra, and during that period Avanti rose to a high position. It was no less than Magadha in strength and position. According to the Buddhist text *Mahāvagga*,[2] Pradyota was a great soldier; and, according to the *Purāṇas*, he reduced many of his contemporary rulers to subjection. The *Purāṇas* do not give us a detailed list, but those subjugated may have been among the rulers of *Shoḍaśa-Mahājanapadas*.

The relations of Pradyota with Bimbisāra of Magadha were cordial. Bimbisāra sent his famous physician Jīvaka to cure Pradyota when he fell ill. On the other hand, the Jaina legends mention that Pradyota went forth to attack Rājagṛiha, even during the lifetime of Bimbisāra, but the attempt was foiled by the cunning prince Abhaya.[3] It is however definite that Pradyota's relations with Bimbisāra's son, Ajātaśatru became strained. Ajātaśatru adopted an aggressive policy of attacking and conqueringVaiśālī. Being an ambitious ruler himself, Pradyota could not tolerate the aggression launched upon him by Ajātaśatru. Both of them wanted to establish their supremacy in northern India. Pradyota was planning an attack upon his rival's capital at Rājagṛiha.[4] Apprehending this invasion by Pradyota, Ajātaśatru fortified his capital.

Pradyota wanted to consolidate and extend his kingdom. In his neighbourhood, there was the powerful kingdom of Kauśāmbī ruled by his rival Udayana Vatsarāja of the celebrated Bharata family. Pradyota seems to have engaged in war with Udayana[5] but later on amity between them was

1. *Matsya*, p. 272, I, V. 37. 303.
2. SBE, XVII, p. 187.
3. ABORI, 1920-21; DPPN, I, 128.
4. CHI, I, p. 311.
5. RBI, pp. 4-7.

restored. Pradyota gave his daughter Vāsavadattā in marriage to Udayana.

Pradyota engaged in hostilities with Pushkarasārin of Taxila but he was unsuccessful in his war.[1] Pradyota seems to have established close relations with the Śūrasenas of Mathura. The king at this time was known as *Avantiputra*, a name signifying the existence of some relationship between Pradyota and the ruler of Śūrasenas. The *Lalitavistāra*[2] gives the personal name of the king of Mathura as Subāhu.

Pradyota is said to have ruled for twenty-three years. That he was cruel is evident from the sobriquet *Chaṇḍa* and from the fact that he hardly ever followed a good policy. His younger brother, Kumārasena, was killed when he tried to put a stop to the practice of selling human flesh in the Mahākāla temple.[3]

GANDHĀRA

Gandhāra comprised the region of the modern districts of Peshawar and Rawalpindi. Its capital was Takshaśilā. It was an ancient seat of learning where people from different provinces came for learning. It was also a great centre of trade and its distance from Banaras was 2,000 leagues.[4]

The *Purāṇas* represent the Gandhāra princes as descendants of Druhyu.[5] Jaina writers inform us that one of the early kings, Nagnajit, who is reported to have been a contemporary of Nimi, king of Videha, and other rulers, adopted the faith of the Jainas.[6] As Pārśva (777 B.C.) was probably the first historical Jain, Nagnajit, if he really became a convert to his doctrines, must be placed between 777 B.C. and 544 B.C., the date of Pushkarasārin, the Gandharian contemporary of Bimbisāra.

In the time of Lord Mahāvīra, the throne of Gandhāra was occupied by Pushkarasārin. He is said to have sent an

1. RBI, p. 15.
2. Ed. by RAJENDRA LAL MITRA, p. 24.
3. PRADHAN : Chronology of Ancient India, pp. 72, 335,
4. *Jā*, No. 406; *Telepaṭṭa Jā*, No. 96; *Susīma Jā*, No. 163.
5. *Matsya*, 48.6; *Vāyu*, 99. 9
6. SBE, XLV; 87.

embassy and a letter to king Bimbisāra of Magadha, and waged war on Pradyota of Avanti who was defeated.[1] He is also said to have been threatened in his own kingdom by the Pāṇḍavas who occupied a part of the Punjab. In the latter half of the sixth century B.C., Gandhāra was conquered by the king of Persia. In the Bahistan inscription of Darius, Cir. 520-518. B.C., the Gandhārians (Gadara) appear among the subject people of the Achamenidan or Achaemenian Empire.

KĀMBOJA

Kāmboja, which is included in the *Uttarāpatha*, is generally associated with Gandhāra in ancient literature. The Kāmbojas occupied roughly the province surrounding Rajaori or ancient Rājapura, including the Hazara district of the North-West Frontier Province and probably extending as far. as Kafiristan. Dvārakā, mentioned by T.W. Rhys Davids as the capital in the early Buddhist period, was not really situated in this country, though it was connected with it by a road.[2] Their capital seems to have been Rājapura, while Nandi Magura was another important city.

Though the Vedic texts do not mention any king of Kāmboja, they do refer to a teacher named Aupamanyava who was probably connected with this territory.[3] The *Mahābhārata*[4] mentions their kings Chandravarman and Sudakshiṇa, but we are not definite about them. In latter times, the monarchy gave place to the *Saṁgha* form of government,

SMALL REPUBLICS IN THE AGE OF LORD MAHĀVĪRA

Besides these sixteen big states in the time of Lord Mahāvīra, there were also small republics ruled by autonomous or semi-independent clans such as the Śākyas of Kapilavastu, the Koliyas of Devadaha and Rāmagāma, the Bhaggas (Bhargas) of Suṁsumāra Hill, the Bulis of Allakappa, the Kālamas of Kesaputta and the Moriyas of Pipphalivana.

The *Śākya state* was bounded on the north by the Himalayas, on the east by the river Rohiṇī, and on the west and on the

1. RBI, p. 28; DPPN, II, 215; Essay on Guṇāḍhya, p. 176.
2. DPPN, I. 536.
3. Vedic Index, I. 127, 138.
4. *Mbh*, 1. 67. 32; II 4. 22; V, 165, 1-3; VII. 90-95, etc.

south by the Rāpti. Their capital was Kapilavastu, represented most probably by the ruins of Tilaura Koṭ near Lumbinī-vana now identified with Rummindei in Nepal Tarai. Another town was Devadaha which they appear to have shared with their eastern neighbours, the Koliyas. They acknowledged the suzerainty of the king of Kośala.

The Koliyas of Rāmagrāma were the eastern neighbours of the Śākyas on the side of the river Rohiṇī which helped to irrigate the fields of both the clans. A. CUNNINGHAM places the Koliya country between the Kohāna and Aumi (Anomā) rivers. The Anomā seems to have formed the dividing line between the Koliyas on the one hand and the Mallas and Moriyas on the other.

The Bhaggas (Bhargas) are known to the *Aitareya Brāhmaṇa*[1] and the *Ashṭādhyāyī* of Pāṇini[2]. In the latter half of the sixth century B.C., the Bhagga state was dependent on the Vatsa kingdom—a fact evident from the preface to the *Dhonasākha Jātaka* in which we are told that prince Bodhi, the son of Udayana, king of the Vatsas, dwelt in Suṁsumāragiri of Bhagga State and built a palace called Kokanada.

About the Bulis and the Kālāmas, we possess little information. The *Dhammapada* commentary refers to the Buli territory as the kingdom of Allakappa and says that it was only ten leagues in extent. Allakappa was perhaps not far away from Veṭhadīpa, the home of a famous Brāhmaṇa in the early days of Buddhism who set up a cairn over the remains of the Buddha in his native land.

The Kālāmas were the clan of the philosopher Ālāra, a teacher of Gautama, before he attained *Sambodhi*. They seem to have acknowledged the suzerainty of the king of Kośala because their town, Kesaputta, was annexed by this state in the sixth century B.C.

The Moriyas (Mauryas) were the same clan which gave Magadha its greatest dynasty. They are sometimes spoken of as Śākyan in origin, but the evidence is late. The name is derived, according to one tradition, from *Mora* (Mayūra)

1. *Ait. Br*, VIII. 28.
2. *Pā*, iv, i, iii, 177.

or peacock. Pippahalivana, the Moriya capital is identical with the Nyagrodhavana or Banyan Grove mentioned by Hiuen Tsang.

POLITICAL INSTITUTIONS

The age of Lord Mahāvīra witnessed a number of important changes in the political sphere. The tribal stage of society gradually disappeared, giving place to organized states. Magadha, Vatsa, Kośala and Avanti became very powerful. The position and functions of the king gained in importance. The *Samiti* of the Vedic period was replaced by the Council of Ministers. The income of the states considerably increased on account of the induction of new resources. The government machinery became complicated and new officers were appointed to meet the new requirements.

We may divide the states of this period into two groups, monarchical and non-monarchical. We shall first discuss the government machinery of the monarchical states.

MONARCHICAL GOVERNMENT

King and Kingship

In ancient India, a king was absolutely necessary and was considered an essential factor for the well-being of the people. He was regarded as the head of men.[1] Generally, the rulers of these monarchical states belonged to the Kshatriya caste. Though an absolute despot, the king was to follow the ten prescribed traditional duties of the king (*dasarājadhamme*) : giving alms, a moral course of life, sacrifice, truthfulness, mildness, self-denial, forgiveness, not to cause any pain to anybody, patience, and a yielding disposition.[2] These are but prescriptions of the general Buddhistic morality applicable to all lay disciples.

According to the *Ovaiyā*, king Kūṇika-Ajātaśatru had all the qualifications of the royalty; he was honoured by the people, he belonged to a pure Kshatriya family, was duly consecrated on the throne, and was compassionate. He was a warden of the marchers, an upholder of peace, and a protector of the *janapada*. He was the master of palaces, bed-

1. *Rājā mukhaṁ manussānaṁ, Su. Ni*, p. 107; *Mv*, VI, 35. 8.
2. FSONB, p. 100.

rooms, seats, carriages and vehicles in large quantity. His treasury was full of gold and silver, and his people had ample food. He was the master of the slaves of both sexes, of cows, buffaloes, oxen, and sheep. His treasury, granaries, and armouries were brimming to the full.[1]

Very often we see in kings an unrestrained tyrant guided by his own whims and caprices, who oppresses and puts down his subjects by punishments, taxes, torture, and robbery. He suffers from many vices such as drunkenness, cruelty,[2] corruptibility,[3] untruthfulness, and unrighteousness.[4]

There are instances of tyrannical rulers being removed from the throne or killed by the people. In the *Padakusalamāṇava Jātaka*,[5] there is probably a trace of authentic history; in spite of its legendary garb, it may have preserved the memory of actual facts. It is narrated how a young Brāhmaṇa, after discovering by magic the treasures stolen and concealed by the king and his *purohita*, calls the king a thief in the presence of the assembled people who resolve to kill the bad king so that he may not plunder them any more. Another example of such a violent removal of the unrighteous king is found in the *Sachchaṁkira Jātaka*.[6] Here also the king is driven out of the town by the enraged Khattiyas, Brāhmaṇas, and other citizens, and in his place, a Brāhmaṇa is installed king.

Pālaka, the ruler of Avanti, was reputed to have been a tyrant. The populace headed by the President of the guild merchants of the capital deposed him, and, having brought out Gopāla from the prison, put him on the throne.[7]

Those were the times when wars and quarrels among these states were very frequent as were internal rebellions too. Under such circumstances, the first and foremost duty of the king was the protection of the subjects against internal and

1. *Ovā*, 6.
2. *Khantivādi Jā*, II, 3919
3. *Bharu Jā*, II, 169.
4. *Chetiya Jā*, III, 454
5. *Jā*, III, 501.
6. *Jā*, I, 326.
7. JBORS, Vol I Pt. I, 915.

external enemies. The people on their part bore the cost of administration of the state, the army, and the court by paying taxes. Gradually, with the growth of civilization, there came other interests as well into the foreground like the king's own cares : the land was made fertile, cities were built, and trade and commerce were encouraged.

According to the *Jātakas*, kingship was generally hereditary and when there were several sons, it was the eldest who succeeded his father to the throne, while the second son became the viceroy (*Uparājan*). As a rule, only the sons of the eldest queen (*aggamahisi*) who must be of the same caste as the king himself and thus a Khattiya, were deemed legitimate. If the king was without a male heir and if he had a daughter, his son in-law became heir to the throne. If there was neither a male heir nor a kinsman who could succeed to the throne, the successor was chosen by the ministers. The Jaina texts mention two types of kings, *viz.*, *Sāvekkha* and *niravekkha*. The former established the crown-prince on the throne within his life-time thus avoiding civil wars and other calamities. In the latter type, however, the crown-prince succeeded after the death of the king.[1] The question of succession to the throne was sometimes complicated by the ambitions and jealousies of the princes. The prince Kūṇiya-Ajātaśatru of Rājagṛiha succeeded to the throne after putting his father Śreṇika-Bimbisāra into prison.

The ceremony, which accompanied the accession to the throne was, according to the *Jātakas*, the same as that which we know from the *Vedas* and the epics. The priest or the *Purohita* consecrated the king and sprinkled water upon him. Originally its significance may have been only a religious one, as symbolizing an act by which the blessings of the gods were showered or, more correctly expressed, invoked by magic, upon the king. It signified a certain dependence of the king upon the priest consecrating him.

The king lived with his court in a fortified town. The *Pañchaguru Jātaka*[2] describes the royal entry of a prince how

1. *Vya. Bhā*, 2, 327,
2. *Jā*, I, 470.

he went to the spacious hall of the palace and took his seat in godly pomp upon a throne studded with precious stones, over which a white umbrella was spread; surrounding him, there stood, bejewelled with all their ornaments, the ministers, the *Bāhamanas*, the *Gahapatis* etc., and the princesses, while sixteen thousand dancing girls skilled in dancing, singing, and music, sang and played.

The Jaina canons[1] give exaggerated account of the royal palaces. They are described as seven-storeyed, adorned with towers and pinnacles and supported by many columns. They are described as lofty, touching the sky and decorated with flags, banners, umbrellas, and garlands. They had domes and their floors were richly studded with various gems and jewels. The harem, (*anteura*), which was a part of the royal pomp,[2] played an important role in the inner and outer politics of the country. The kings were fond of enriching their harem with beautiful women and girls without any distinction of caste. The harem was a great source of danger to the king and was, therefore, carefully guarded by eunuchs and old men: Besides, the Jaina texts mention the type of guards who should keep watch over the inmates of harem.

OTHER MEMBERS OF THE ROYAL FAMILY

The handing over the Viceroyalty (*Uparāja*) to the king's eldest son generally took place after the completion of his studies.[3] If he was still minor, the eldest among the younger brothers of the king would go to *Uparāja*.[4] On ceremonial occasions, the *Uparāja* sat behind the king on the back of an elephant,[5] a seat which was otherwise occupied by the *Purohita*. In the evening, the Viceroy would do the king's work. We read repeatedly of the king's fears that the *Uparājan* might one day become very powerful and dominate him and of disciplinary measures taken by him to guard against such an eventuality. When Śreṇika annexed Aṅga to his kingdom of Magadha, he posted his son Kūṇika as Viceroy. The heir apparent thus

1. *Nāyā*, I. p 22; *Uttarā. Ṭī*, 13, p. 189.
2. *Nāyā*, 16, p. 185.
3. *Jā*, I, 259, III, 123-407.
4. *Jā*, I, 133; II. 367.
5. *Jā*, II, 374.

got an opportunity of having considerable administrative experience before succeeding to the throne.

In addition to the *Uparājan* (Viceroy) there was the *Senāpati*, a kinsman of the king. From the *Devadhamma Jātaka*, we learn that the king gave his younger brother the office of *Uparāja* and his step-brother that of *Senāpati*.[1]

MINISTRY

The Council of the *Ratnins* disappeared and its place was taken by the council of Ministers variously described as *Mantrins*, *Sachivas* and *Amātyas*. The number of Ministers usually depended upon the size of the state but the Ministry usually consisted of five members only. Among the Ministers of the king, *Rajjugāhaka amāchha* (Surveyor) occupied an important position. The *Atthadhammānusāsaka amāchchha* guided the king in worldly and spiritual matters. Thc *Senāpati* was the Minister of War. The *vinichchāyamachchha* (Minister of Justice) not only gave judicial decisions but also advised on matters of law and morality.

The influence of Ministers upon the course of internal and external politics depended upon the ability of the ruler. When there was a weak ruler, these Ministers had a dominating voice. The decision regarding the successor was often left to the Ministers. Indeed, allusions to the actual exercise of sovereign powers by the Ministers are also found. In the *Ghaṭa Jātaka*, for instance, the king sick of worldly life hands over the reins of government to his Ministers.[2]

When there was a powerful and self-willed ruler like Bimbisāra upon the throne of Magadha, some Ministers were dismissed for giving bad advice, others were degraded for inefficiency, while a few were promoted for the wise counsel they gave.[3] Vassakāra and Sunīdha were the Ministers of Ajātaśatru ;[4] his contemporary in Kośala, king Prasenajit, relied upon the advice of his Ministers, Mṛigadhara and Śrīvṛidha, in carrying out important schemes.[5]

1. FSONB, p. 135.
2. *Jā*, III. 170.
3. *Chu*, V. 1.
4. *Dia*, II, p. 78.
5. *Uvā*, II, Appendix, p. 56.

OFFICERS OF THE CENTRAL GOVERNMENT

The Secretariat might have gradually evolved in the post-Vedic period. The art of writing was coming into more extensive use ; kingdoms were developing into empires, and functions of government were becoming more numerous. It may safely be presumed that some kind of Central Secretariat must have existed in the courts of historical emperors like Bimbisāra and Ajātaśatru.

The important officials at headquarters were called *Mahāmātras* and were divided into three classes, *viz.*, (1) the Executive (*Sabbātthaka*), administering all affairs and interests ; (2) the Judicial (*Vohārika*) ; and (3) the Military (*Senānāyaka*). In addition to these, there were other officers too as is evident from the *Jātakas*.

Purohita : The family priest of the king, the *Purohita*, occupied an extremely peculiar position in the court. For the performance of sacrifices and magical chantings, the king needed a *Purohita*. The sacrifice was meant to protect the king from imminent misfortune and to help him in acquiring a city which was difficult to conquer. He not only guarded the king's treasures—this was part of his duties but also acted as a judicial officer.

There were officers who increased the wealth of the king. *Rajjugāhaka*[1] was the officer of survey. *Doṇamāpaka*[2] was one who measured with a dry measure. *Balipaṭiggāhakas*, *Niggāhakas*, and *Balisādhakas* were the tax-collectors who sometimes plundered and oppressed the people by levying heavy taxes.[3] *Rājabhoggas*[4] were Royal officers appointed and paid by the king whose orders they had all to obey.

Sārathi[5] was the king's charioteer. The Keeper of the king's purse was known as *Heraññika*[6] and the superintendent

1. *Jā*, IV, 179.
2. Ibid. II, 378.
3. FSONB, p. 120.
4. *Rājabhogga* is explained in the *Suttavibhaṅga*, *Nissaggiya* 10 2.1 (*Vinaya Piṭaka* ed. Oldenberg, Vol. 3, p. 222.)
5. *Jā*, II. 377.
6. Ibid, III. 193.

of the king's storehouse as *Bhaṇḍāgārika*.[1] *Dovārika*[2] had for his duty the closing of the gate of the city at night, while *Nagaraguttika*[3] was charged with the duty of arresting and executing the robbers of the city. *Choraghāṭaka*[4] occupied the public office of the executioner of thieves.

PROVINCIAL AND VILLAGE ADMINISTRATION

In provincial administration, a considerable degree of autonomy was allowed. We hear not only of a sub-king at Champā, but of *Maṇḍalika rājās*[5] corresponding perhaps to the Earls and Counts of medieval European polity. In the small towns and villages, the king's power must have been represented by his officers.

The superintendent of the village, the *Gāmabhojaka*,[6] held a position of power and honour. He collected the taxes of the village and exercised judicial powers in the village, insofar as he settled quarrels and made the guilty to pay a fine. He issued prohibitory orders against the slaughter of animals and against the sale of intoxicating liquors.

While according to the *Jātakas* the villages transacted their business themselves[7] evidence corroborating the existence of any regular Council or Standing Commitee is not found in these works. Initiative was usually left with the headman, but if he acted unreasonably or against the established customs of the locality or realm, the village elders could set the matter right by pointing out his mistake.[8]

With the growth of the royal power, self-government was increasingly and proportionately reduced. In the Magadha kingdom, the *Gāmabhojaka* (village Superintendent) remained under the personal supervision of the king, as it is clear from a passage of the *Vinaya Piṭaka*.[9] To the king Bimbisāra, the

1. *Jā*, IV. 43.
2. Ibid, II. 379.
3. Ibid, III. 59.
4. Ibid, IV. 41; III. 179.
5. DPPN, II, 898.
6. *Jā*, I. 354; I. 483; and IV. 115.
7. *Kuṇāla Jā*.
8. *Pāniya Jā*.
9. *Mv*, V, I.

overlordship of 80,000 villages was apportioned ; he collected together the chiefs (*Gāmikas*) of these villages and gave them instructions in worldly things.

JUDICIAL ADMINISTRATION

In times of peace, the principal work of the king was to attend to the administration of justice. In the *Rājovāda Jātaka*, it is said of the king that he gave decisions in law-suits. The final decision in law-courts as well as the final word regarding the punishment for breaking the law remained with him.[1] The legal life of the smaller towns and villages passed very much out of the direct sphere of action of the king and remained a matter for his representatives as long as no appeal was made against the judgments of these to the king as a higher authority.

The Ministers, especially the *Vinichchayāmachcha*, and also the *Purohita* and the *Senāpati*, both took part in the administration of justice, advised the king and, in some cases, had some influence upon his judgments. *Vinichchayāmachcha* was the Minister of justice. His judgment was final in the case of aquittal ; in other cases, the matter was referred to the *Vohārikas*.[2] He not only gave judicial decisions, but also advised on matters of law and morality. The *Grāmabhojaka* also exercised judicial powers in the village. The penal code in the reign of Bimbisāra included as punishments imprisonment in jails (*Kārā*), mutilation of limbs, and the like.[3]

MILITARY ORGANIZATION

As wars and frontier troubles were very common in those days, the state had necessarily to keep and maintain a well-equipped and organized military force always at its command. The army consisted of four branches, namely, chariots (*raha*) elephants (*gaya*), cavalry (*haya*), and infantry (*pāyatta*).

1. *Jā*, II. 2.
2. *Vohārikas*—Sk. *Vyāvahārikas* are not found in the *Jātakas*. In Mv, 1.40.3 and in the Chv, VI, 4.9, they have been mentioned. They were judicial officers.
3. *Vinaya*, VII, 3, 5.

A chariot was a very important means of conveyance in olden days. Excellent horses were yoked to it and it was provided with an accomplished charioteer. The king's chariots bore special names. For instance, the chariot of Pajjoya (Pradyota) was called *Aggibhiru* (fire proof) and was considered to be one of the four jewels.[1]

The elephant played an important part in the army as well as on certain royal occasions. The kings were very fond of elephants, and the state-elephants bore special names. We hear of the elephant Sechanāga over which a great battle was fought between Kūṇika-Ajātaśatru and Halla and Vehalla.[2] The *Bhagavati*[3] refers to two other elephants of Kūṇika, *viz.*, Udāyin and Bhūtānanda. Nalagiri, another elephant which belonged to Pajjoya, was considered one of his four precious possessions.[4] Bhadravatī belonged to Udayana who successfully carried off Vāsavadattā on its back from Ujjayinī to Kośāmbī.[5] King Udayana was an adept in the art of winning over elephants by music.[6]

While the third constituent of the army was the cavalry, the foot-soldier formed its main portion. The whole army was under the control of the *Senāpati* whose duty was to enforce discipline among the soldiers.

Realizing the terrible loss of both men and money, people tried to avoid wars in general. They first tried the four diplomatic means, *viz.*, *Sāma*, *dāna*, *daṇḍa*, and *bheda*, failing which they had to declare war. Before the two parties actually entered into war, a *Dūta* or a courtier, who conveyed the royal proclamation to the opposite party, was deputed with the message. We learn that before entering into war with Cheḍaga, Kūṇiya sent his *Dūta* to his opponent thrice, finally giving him orders to place his left foot on the foot-stool of the enemy (in a spirit of defiance) and deliver him the letter keeping it on

1. *Āva. chū*, II, p. 160.
2. *Āva chū*, II, p. 170f.
3. *Bhag*, 7. 9.
4. *Āva. chū.* II, p. 160.
5. Āva. chū, II, pp. 161 f.
6. Ibid, II, p. 161.

the edge of the spear.[1]

The art of warfare together with its various tactics, stratagems, and practices, was well known in those days. Jaina texts give some interesting details of the military operations of the Magadhan forces. The *sagaḍavūha* (waggon array) and *garuḍavūha* (eagle array) are mentioned in *Niryāvaliyāo*.[2] The army of Cheḍaga formed the former while that of Kūṇika the latter. Kūṇika for the first time made use of two secret weapons of war. The first, the *Mahāśilākaṇṭaka*, was a kind of catapult hurling heavy pieces of stone. The other was the *Rathamussala*, a chariot which created havoc by wheeling about and hurling destruction by its attached rods.[3]

Siege-warfare, which was the usual mode of fighting, sometimes continued for a considerable time. Kūṇika is said to have besieged the city of Vaiśālī for a long period.[4] It was for this reason that the cities of those days were strongly fortified. Since Rājagṛiha was too far inland and remote to serve as an efficient base of operations, Kūṇika had to construct a new base, a fort at a convenient site on the river Gaṅgā, and thus was laid the foundation of the new capital, Pāṭaliputra. It was constructed under the supervision of his chief ministers, Sunīdha and Vassakāra.

Strategy and diplomacy played an important part in this type of warfare. Manoeuvres and novel tactics were adopted to compel the other party to surrender. We are told as to how Abhayakumāra, by a clever subterfuge which consisted in burying counterfeit coins in the enemy's camp, created suspicion in the mind of Pajjoya about the fidelity of his soldiers and thus foiled his attack on Rāyagiha.[5] A regular system of espionage was another feature of siege-warfare. Spies were regularly employed to watch, over the activities of the enemy. Kūṇika deputed his Minister Vassakāra on the nefarious mission of sowing seeds of disunion among the Lichchhavīs at Vaiśālī.

1. Niryā, I.
2. Ibid, I, p. 28.
3. *Uvā*, II, App. pp. 59, 60; *Bhag*, 299 ff.
4. *Āva. chā*, II, p. 173.
5. Ibid, p. 159.

TAXATION

About the system of taxation during this period, we possess little information. *Jātakas* may be presumed to give us a glimpse of this age, but the information they give is meagre. They tell us how good kings levied only legal taxes and how the bad ones so oppressed the subjects by illegal impositions that they would often flee to forests to escape from tax-collectors.[1]

Besides the taxes, there were certain privileges of the king which he could use for filling up his treasury. The unclaimed property belonged to the king.[2] If anybody died without heirs, his succession would devolve upon the king. Sometimes the entire worldly possession of a person who renounced the world went to the ruling chief.[3]

CONSTITUTION AND ADMINISTRATIVE MACHINERY OF THE REPUBLICS

Along with the monarchical states, there existed some republican states too in the time of Lord Mahāvīra. The terms *Gaṇa* and *Saṁgha* have been used for these republican states as distinguished from the monarchical ones. A Jaina work warns a monk that he should avoid visiting a country which has no king, or has a crown prince as its ruler or two kings fighting with each other or is governed by the *Gaṇa* form of government.[4] This passage denotes a definite form of government in which the power was vested not in one person but in a *Gaṇa* or group of people. These ancient republican states do not satisfy the modern definition of 'republic' in which the power is vested in the whole body of citizens. There were republican states like Sparta, Athens, Rome, and Medieval Venice where sovereignty was not vested in one individual, but sometimes either in a small number of persons or in a fairly numerous class.

There is paucity of evidence regarding the constitution and administrative machinery of these ancient Indian repub-

1. See Jā, IV. p. 399; V, pp. 98-9; 101; II, p. 17.
2. Jā, III, 299.
3. Ibid, IV, 485.
4. Āchā, I, 3. 160.

lics. The early authentic literary works make only general statements about these republics, while the detailed information given by the *Jātakas* is also undependable unless confirmed by some other evidence. These ancient Indian republics possessed certain common features, though they reveal at the same time certain significant differences which were due to their needs and temperaments.

DIRECTIVE PRINCIPLES OF STATE POLICY

When Varshākāra, the chancellor of the king of Magadha, wanted to know the opinion of the Buddha on behalf of his master, as to the advisability of invading the Vajjis—the Lichchhavīs and the Videhas—the Buddha indicated to Ānanda their seven points of excellence. These may be regarded as the directive principles of state policy. It is not improbable that similar directive principles might have been followed by other contemporary republic states. These principles are as follows:[1]

1. The Vajjians hold full and frequent public Assemblies;
2. They meet together in concord and rise in concord and carry out Vajjian business in concord;
3. They enact nothing not already established, abrogate nothing that has been already enacted, and act in accordance with ancient institutions of the Vajjians as established in former days;
4. They honour and esteem and revere and support the Vajjian elders, and regard it as a point of duty to hearken to their words;
5. No women or girls belonging to their clans were detained among them by force or abduction;
6. They honour and esteem and revere and support the Vajjian shrines (*chaityas*) in town or country, and do not allow the proper offerings and rites, as formerly given and performed, to fall into desuetude; and

1. *Mahāparinibbāṇa-Sutta*, For Eng. tr. See SBE, 11, pp. 3-4 and Dia, 11, pp. 79-80,

7. Rightful protection, defence, and support is fully provided for the *Arhants* among them, so that they may enter the realm from distant lands, and may live therein at ease.

CITIZENSHIP

It seems that the right of citizenship was not granted to the whole population but was confined to the aristocratic Kshatriyas who had a voice in the administration of their respective countries. The artisans, farmers, servants and serfs had no such privileged position. When a quarrel arose beween the farmers and servants of the Koliyas and the Śākyas about the distribution of the water of Rohiṇī, they reported it to the officer of their own state, who in turn apprised their *Rājās* of it. It is the latter who decided to go on war with the enemy state. This incident therefore shows that the commoners did not have much influence on the momentous decisions taken by the central government on important topics, such as peace and war, that affected the whole population.

Although there was a privileged system of citizenship, outsiders were eligible to it if they settled in the realm permanently. Khaṇḍa, who was a refugee of Videha country, settled in Vaiśālī and rose to the post of *Senāpati* and *Gaṇapramukha*.[1] Thus, once a person acquired citizenship, he was offered all opportunities to show his abilities in the political life of the country.

THE GENERAL ASSEMBLY

There were separate Supreme Assemblies in each republic state. The Assembly of the Śākyas seems to have been composed of 500 members. A few details of the Supreme Assembly of the Lichchhavīs of Vaiśālī are preserved in the *Jātaka* stories. The *Ekapanna Jātaka*[2] speaks about the number of members of this Assembly. The *Chullakāliṅga Jātaka*[3] informs us that these members were given the right of argument and disputation. Further, the *Bhadasāla Jātaka*[4] refers to the tank

1. IHQ, XXIII, p. 59.
2. *Jā*. No 149.
3. Ibid, III, No. 301, p. 1.
4. Ibid. IV, p. 148.

in the Vaiśālī city from where the families of the kings drew water for ceremonial sprinkling.

K. P. JAYASWAL[1] interprets the passage of *Ekapanna Jātaka* in this way : "The rule vested in the inhabitants, 7707 in number, all of whom were entitled to rule. They became Presidents, Vice-Presidents, Commanders-in-chief and Chancellors of Exchequer." What the *Jātaka* means to say is that 7707 of the inhabitants, probably the foundation families, were the ruling class, that it is they who became the executive office holders. The natural meaning and interpretation of the *Jātaka* text would make it mean that 7707 *Rājans* lived at Vaiśālī and that the number of *Uparājans*, *Senāpatis*, and *Bhaṇḍāgārikas* was the same in each case. As regards K.P. JAYASWAL's view that the *Rājan*, the *Uparājan*, the *Senāpati* and the *Bhaṇḍāgārika* constituted the Cabinet of the executive authority, it seems to be a mere hypothesis unsupported by facts. So far as the monarchical state is concerned, the *Jātaka* evidence conclusively proves that the *Rājan*, the *Uparājan*, etc. formed successive grades in the official hierarchy instead of forming a co-ordinate body.

R.C. MAJUMDAR[2] thinks that while the number 7707 may be dismissed as a purely conventional one, it may be accepted that the Supreme Assembly of the state consisted of a pretty number of members and must as such be held to be a popular one. Again, he says that the reference to the like number of Viceroys, Generals, and Treasurers would imply that each member of the Supreme Assembly possessed a full suite of officers requisite for the administration of a state. In other words, the whole state consisted of a number of administrative units, each of which was a state in miniature by itself and possessed a complete administrative machinery. The business of the state as a whole was carried on by an Assembly consisting of the heads of these states who were in their turn attended by their principal officers. R. C. MAJUMDAR concludes with the observation that those who are familiar with the Cleisthenian Constitution of the city state of Athens cannot fail to find its prototype in the city of Vaiśālī.

1. Hindu Polity, p. 48.
2. *Corporate Life in Ancient India*, pp. 92-94.

D.R. BHANDARKAR[1] makes the Lichchhavī state a federation of small principalities. He writes, "The number of the kings constituting the Lichchhavi *Gaṇa* was pretty large. It again seems that each Lichchhavī king had his separate principality where he exercised supreme power in certain respects. Nevertheless, the *Gaṇa* as a whole had power to kill, burn or exile a man from their kingdom which meant to aggregate of principalities of the different kings." Again he says, "The Lichchhavī *Gaṇa* was a Federation of the chiefs of the different clans of a tribe who were also each the ruler of a small principality. Each confederate principality maintained its separate autonomy in regard to certain matters and allowed the *Saṁgha* to exercise supreme and independent control in respect of others affecting the kingdom." D.R. BHANDARKAR concludes by suggesting some points of resemblance between the constitution of the Lichchhavi *Saṁgha* and the confederation of the German States called the German empire.

A.S. ALTEKAR[2] has tried to justify the famous *Jātaka* statement that there were 7707 kings and an equal number of *Upa-rājās*, *Senāpatis* and *Bhaṇḍāgārikas* in the Vaiśāli State. When the Aryans came and occupied this territory, it seems to have been divided into about 7707 Kshatriya families, who were something like so many *Zamindār* families of the state. They were all *Kshatriyas* and were known as *Rājans*. The heads of these families lived in the capital while their managers stayed in the countryside and were known as their treasurers. If the *Kshatriya* householders were known as *Rājans*, their sons were naturally called *Uparājans* or *Yuvarājas*. When they were unable to lead their army themselves, they used to nominate a *Senāpati* or General to act for them.

U.N. GHOSHAL[3] points out that the statements in the *Jātaka* text belong to a late chronological stratum, while all references in older and more authentic canonical tradition describe the Lichchhavī constitution in very general terms simply as *Saṁgha* or *Gaṇa*. There are therefore grave reasons for doubting the genuineness of the later account.

1. C L, 1918, pp. 155-156.
2. State and Government in Ancient India, p. 115; Homage, p. 69.
3. IHQ. XX, 334 ff; XXI, 1 ff.

The number of Vaiśālī nobles exercising sovereign power is 7707, not a round number. It means that there were nobles enjoying privileges who lived outside Vaiśālī. There is no mention of priests, traders and farmers. How, then, could they form a popular body ?

The reference to as many *Rājans*, *Uparājans*, etc. is not corroborated by any other text. To base a definite conclusion on the authority of a single belated and uncorroborated text seems to be opposed to all canons of history. It is, however, hard to understand how a cumbrous constitution of the kind sought to be found in the *Jātaka* text which puts a premium upon disruptive tendencies, could work in actual practice.

The analogy of the Cleisthenian constitution seems to be hardly convincing. The ten Cleisthenian tribes consisting of the inhabitants of different demes were groups of citizens scattered over the whole of Attica, and their function was to elect five hundred members. On the other hand, according to the interpretation suggested above, the Lichchhavī *Rājans* with their staff of *Uparājans*, etc. would also be resident at the capital, each forming a state in miniature.

Equally unwarranted is the analogy of the constitution of the late German empire. In this constitution, the emperor was the head of the army and controlled a considerable portion of the imperial finance. Among the Lichchhavīs on the other hand, the constituent provinces had their separate armies and treasuries while there was no single ruler in charge of the federal army and finance. Again, the German princes, unlike the Lichchhavī princes, ruled their states from their respective capitals.

R. C. MAJUMDAR[1] has published an article in support of his earlier views and has thrown some new light on the constitution of the Lichchhavīs. His observations are as follows :

The analogy of the Lichchhavī Constitution with the Cleisthenian constitution of Athens is not unfounded. The main object of the Cleisthenian constitution was the substitution of the deme for the clan. The transition from the principle of kinship to that of locality was also achieved by Athens.

1. IHQ, XXVII, p. 327 ff.

The recently discovered *Vinaya* text of the *Mūlasarvāstivādas* sheds some interesting light on the constitution of the Lichchhavīs which we do not find in Pali texts. According to it, Vaiśālī was divided at this time into three quarters inhabited by the high, the middle, and the low classes. The *Vinaya* text does not favour the view that the Supreme Assembly of the state consisted merely of the Lichchhavī nobles. For we find even new comers to Vaiśālī not only admitted into the assembly but also elected to the highest post. It also demonstrates the popular character of the Assembly. It contains strong sentiments against hereditary privileges and enunciates the principle of free election by the *Gaṇa* to all important posts, including that of the Commander-in-chief which seems to have been the highest in the state.

Membership of the Assemblies depended upon whether the aspirant belonged to the privileged order or he did not. There was no electoral roll giving a list of qualified voters; nor were there any periodical elections. Had any such existed, they would have been referred to in the literature bearing upon the science of polity.

The place where the General Assembly met was called *Santhāgāra*. In the Assembly, there were different groups known as *vargya*, *gṛihya*, and *pakshya* who clashed from time to time for power, a phenomenon so common that it has been referred to even by the grammarians. The term *dvandva* was used to denote the rival parties and the term *Vyutkramaṇa* to their rivalry.

The rules of procedure and debates in these Assemblies seem to be the same as those of the Buddhist *Saṁghas* which were modelled on *Saṁgha* or *Gaṇa* states. Transaction of the Assembly business strictly required a quorum without which it was considered to be invalid.[1] Pāṇini refers to *gaṇa-titha* as the person whose attendance completed the quorum in a *Gaṇa* and to *Saṁgha-titha* as one who completed the quorum of the *Saṁgha*. The person who acted as a 'whip' to secure the quorum was known as *Gaṇapūraka*.[2] There was an officer

1. *Mv*, IX. 4. 1; V. 13. 12; I.31.2; VIII. 24. 7; IX. 3·2.
2. Ibid, III. 3. 6.

known as *Āsanapaññāpaka* (seat regulator) who was in charge of the allotment of seats. Probably the executive officers had their seats on a dais and other members were grouped partywise in their front. A person who acted as a Polling Officer in the Assembly was known as *Śalākāgrahāpaka,*[1] or he who collected votes. The technical term for vote was *Chhanda,* which meant free choice. The *Saṁghamukhya* or the President of the state presided over the Assembly and regulated its debates. He was expected to observe strict impartiality; if he failed, he was furiously criticised.

Definite rules were laid down regarding the method of moving resolutions in the Assembly. Generally, a proposal was repeated thrice, and if no objections to it were raised, it was taken as passed. In case of objection, it was determined by votes of the majority. When the ultimatum was received by the Śākyas from the Kośala king, who was besieging their capital, their Assembly sat to deliberate whether they should open the gates or not. Some favoured the proposal, others opposed it. Eventually, therefore, votes were taken to ascertain the majority view, which, it was discovered, favoured capitulation.[2] Accordingly action was taken. This practice must have been followed by other assemblies also.

Voting was sometimes done by the secret method (*gūṭhaka*), sometimes by whispering method (*Sakarṇajapakam*), and sometimes by the open method (*vivatakam*)[3]. Generally, complicated questions were referred for settlement to different Committees.[4] It seems that there were clerks in the Assembly who kept records of its proceedings. Matters, when once properly and finally decided, were not allowed to be reopened.[5]

The evidence of Buddhist literature shows that the General Assemblies of the republics controlled foreign affairs, entertained ambassadors and foreign princes, considered their

1. *Chv,* 14. 26; *Vinayapiṭaka.* II, 315; JASB—1838. p. 993 f. n.
2. W. ROCKHILL: Life of Buddha, pp. 118-9.
3. *Chv,* IV. 14. 24.
4. Ibid. XII, 2, 8.
5. *Dīgha,* II. p. 220.

proposals and decided the momentous issues of war and peace.[1] Generally, this Assembly controlled the Executive. Though there is no specific evidence, it is almost certain that the appointments to the state services were made by this Assembly. That must have been one of the reasons for the keen contest for power that was often witnessed in that body.

The Assembly Hall also served the purpose of a social club, where social and religious topics were discussed at times. The Mallas of Kusinagara discussed the problems of the funeral of the Buddha and the disposal of his ashes in their Assembly Hall. They, as well as the Lichchhavīs, are known to have requested the Blessed One to perform the opening ceremonies of their new Assembly Halls by first using them for delivering a sermon to a congregation assembled therein. The matters concerning commerce and agriculture were also deliberated there.

EXECUTIVE

The membership of the Executive varied with the size and traditions of each state. The Malla state, which was small, had an Executive of four members only, all of whom are known to have taken a prominent part in the funeral of the Buddha. The Jaina *Kalpasūtra* refers to a passage *Navagaṇa Rāyāṇo*[2], the exact sense of which is uncertain. It may stand for the nine kings or Executive officers of the Lichchhavī *Gaṇa*. The confederation of the Lichchhavīs and the Videhas had an Executive of eighteen members.[3] It appears that normally speaking the Executive of a Republic consisted of four to twenty members. The General Assembly must have elected the members of the Executive council, because it is inconceivable that the affairs of a state could have been managed by it.

The President (*Rājā*), the Vice-President (*Upa-Rājā*), General (*Senāpati*), and *Bhaṇḍāgārika* seem to be the designations of the four Executive members. The President of the

1. Jā. IV, p. 145 (No. 465); W. Rockhill: Life of the Buddha, pp. 118-9.
2. SBE, XXII, p. 266.
3. Ibid.

Executive was probably the President of the Assembly also, a person whose main function was the general supervision of the administration. Besides, he was to ensure internal harmony by promoting concord and preventing quarrels. The general looked after the army. The treasury was in charge of the Chancellor of the Exchequer. There must have been also the portfolios of foreign affairs and of justice. In the course of time, the posts of Executive Members became more or less hereditary, and they assumed the title of *Rājā*.

The members of the Executives of the Republic States must have been normally capable captains and dauntless leaders, competent to guide the State on occasions of emergency. In addition, they were men of tact and experience, energetic in action, firm in resolution and well grounded in the laws, customs, and traditions of the country. Cheṭaka, the Head of the Lichchhavī republic, was an influential leader of eighteen confederate kings (*Gaṇarājā*) of Kāśī and Kośala who were his vassals.[1] His sister, Tisalā, was, as pointed out earlier, the mother of Mahāvīra, the son of Siddhārtha, a petty chief of Kuṇḍiyapura near Vaiśālī. Khaṇḍa and his son Siṁha, who were competent enough, were elected to be Generals (*Senāpati*) in succession.[2] The President of the Śākya republic bore the title of *Rājā* which in this connection does not mean king, but rather something akin to the Roman Consul or the Greek Archon. At one time, Bhaddiya, a young cousin of the Buddha, was *Rājā*, at another the Buddha's father, Śuddhodana, held that rank.[3]

FEDERATION

The Lichchhavīs, according to Buddhist documents, formed a league with the Videhas and were together called the Vajjis. We also know from a *Jaina Sūtra* that the Lichchhavīs had once formed a federation with their neighbour, the Mallas.[4] The Federal Council was composed of eighteen members, nine Lichchhavīs and nine Mallakīs.[5] The members of

1. *Niryā*; Some Jaina Canonical *Sūtras*, p. 87.
2. IHQ, XXIII, p. 60.
3. *Dīgha*, II, 52.
4. SBE, XXII, p. 166.
5. Ibid.

the Federal Council are designated *Gaṇa Rājās*. The composition of the Federal Council shows that the Federal states had equal votes and that the federation was based on terms of equality. Though the Mallas were not so great a political power as the Lichchhavīs, yet in Federal Council, both had an equal number of members, *i.e.*, equal voice. Leagues were naturally formed to oppose the great powers amidst whom they were situated, namely, Magadha and Kośala.

JUDICIARY

It seems that the Judicial administration of the republic states was remarkable, and the liberty of the citizens was efficiently guarded. A person was not declared guilty unless his crimes were proved by all the courts.

The *Aṭṭhakathā*[1] throws light especially on the judiciary of the Lichchhavīs of Vaiśālī. A criminal was at first sent for trial to the officer called *Vinichchaya Mahāmatta*. If he found the accused innocent, he acquitted him but if in his opinion, he was guilty he could not punish him but had to send him to the next higher tribunal *viz.*, that of the *Suttādhara*. If he considered him guilty, there were three other tribunals with similar functions *viz.*, those of *Aṭṭhakulaka*, *Senāpati*, and *Uparājā*, each of which could acquit the accused, if innocent, but had to send him to the next higher tribunal if found guilty. The last tribunal, *viz.*, that of the *Rājā*, had alone the right to convict the accused, and in awarding the punishment, the *Rājā* was to be guided by the book of precedents. Thus a person could be punished only if seven successive tribunals had unanimously found him guilty, and he was quite safe if but one of them found him innocent.

U.N. Ghoshal[2] expresses doubt in the Judicial system of the Lichchhavīs described above. The first difficulty in accepting the above interpretation lies in the lateness of the Sinhalese tradition which has come down to us only as prescribed by Buddhaghosha who flourished some eight centuries after the fall of the Vajji republic. Again, the very elaborate procedure described above for which there seems to be no

1. JASB, VII (1938), pp. 993 ff.
2. IHQ, XX, p. 334 ff; XXI, 1 ff,

parallel elsewhere, is enough to raise suspicion about the genuineness of the whole account. But to suppose that no one in the Vajji state could be convicted unless unanimously found guilty by seven successive courts is to imply that the supreme authority in the state had little or no confidence in the judicial capacity or honesty of its own officers. In any case, a cumbrous procedure of the kind suggested above providing ample loopholes for the escape of criminals from the hands of justice would be attended with grave risk of abuse of liberty by the subjects.

CHAPTER VII

SOCIAL CONDITIONS

The age of Lord Mahāvīra is remarkable for many social changes. The religious reformers of this period opposed the caste system based on birth and even challenged the superiority of the Brāhmaṇas. The *Sannyāsa Āśrama* became quite distinct from *Vānaprastha* during this period because of the influence of Jainism and Buddhism. Marriage was made gradually compulsory both for men and women. While society was based upon the joint-family system, the idea of proprietary rights had also begun to grow. The *Gotra* and *Pravara* came into existence. The old system of *Niyoga* gradually disappeared because of the growth of ascetic ideas in the society. Women enjoyed a high position. Because of the propagation of the doctrine of *Ahiṁsā*, people began to prefer a vegetarian diet.

SOCIAL ORGANIZATION

The four *Varṇas*, Brāhmaṇas, Kshatriyas, Vaiśyas and Śūdras, which were formed more or less on birth during the later Vedic period, became gradually rigid and fixed. The influence of the Brāhmaṇas greatly diminished both in the intellectual and political field and their place was taken by the Kshatriyas who began to consider themselves superior to other classes on account of the great importance they attached to their purity of blood. Consequently, they occupied the first position in the caste hierarchy. This period also witnessed the deterioration in the position of the Śūdras, with the result that a number of religious leaders raised their voice for their uplift. Mixed castes resulted from organizations like guilds of people following different arts and crafts. Inter-caste marriages also led to the origin of such castes.

The feeling of caste superiority was intense during this period. Both the Kshatriyas and the Brāhmaṇas considered themselves to be superior to other castes. This feeling of superiority was wide-spread even in certain groups of the same caste because they considered themselves higher than others. The Udichchha Brāhmaṇas who were proud of their origin, regarded themselves as higher than other Brāhmaṇas. The Śākya Kshatriyas regarded themselves as higher than other Kshatriya clans.

Both Mahāvīra and the Buddha opposed the idea of a hereditary caste system, emphasising all the time that one's caste should be determined by what one did rather than by the caste of the family to which one belonged. It is a mistake, however, to suppose that caste distinctions were abolished once for all during this period. No doubt, both succeeded in removing caste distinctions in their monastic order, but they failed in their attempts to abolish it permanently from society.

KSHATRIYAS

During the time of Lord Mahāvīra, the Kshatriyas of the Eastern countries consisted of kings, nobles, ministers, military commanders, and other officers. In Jaina *Suttas* and Buddhist Pali texts, they are mentioned as occupying the foremost position in the caste order. It is believed that no Tīrthaṅkara was born in a family other than that of a Kshatriya. A legend tells us that before his birth, Mahāvīra was removed from the womb of Brāhmaṇī Devānandā to that of Kshatriyāṇī Triśalā.

The Kshatriyas took keen interest in the intellectual activity of the time. It is clear from the *Jātakas* that they used to devote considerable time to the study of the *Vedas* and other branches of knowledge. Several princes used to go to Taxila at the age of sixteen for higher studies. Even in the spiritual field, the Kshatriyas of this time were not behind any caste. The doctrine of salvation was advocated by Mahāvīra and the Buddha, who were Kshatriyas. The superiority of the Kshatriyas is clear from the legend in which the Buddha decided to be reborn as a Kshatriya and not as a Brāhmaṇa. In one of the Buddha's discourses, there is a dialogue between the Buddha and Ambaṭṭha, a dialogue in which the latter recognised the Buddha's superiority.

There were certain factors which led to the feeling of superiority among the Kshatriyas. They enjoyed the highest privilege, the right to rule, that is, which could not be claimed by others. It is natural that the ruling class should enjoy power, prestige, and dignity. The head of the state was known to be the best among men. In was in the Kshatriya caste that the leaders of the two new schools of thought, Buddhism and Jainism, were born. In was but natural that the members of the caste from which emerged Mahāvīra and the Buddha should have developed a sense of superiority. As both the Kshatriyas and the Brāhmaṇas received similar education under the same teacher, there was no valid reason for feeling inferior among the Kshatṛiyas in the intellectual sphere.

Certain Buddhist texts also show that instead of following their own professions strictly, the Kshatriyas worked as potters, basket-makers, reed-workers, garland-makers, and cooks.[1] We find Kshatriyas of the Śākya and Koliya clans cultivating their fields.

BRĀHMAṆAS

The Brāhmaṇas of this period may be divided into two broad categories : (1) true Brāhmaṇas and (2) worldly Brāhmaṇas. The true Brāhmaṇas included ascetics, Vedic teachers, and priests. In fact, the true Brāhmaṇa was one who attached value only to virtuous conduct. In a dispute between two youths as to whether a person is a Brāhmaṇa by birth or by his action, the Buddha is said to have given his decision in favour of the latter alternative. Mahāvīra himself was styled 'Māhaṇa'[2] or 'Mahāmāhaṇa'[3]

The general duties of the true Brāhmaṇas were the study of the *Vedas*, teaching, performance of sacrifice for themselves as well as for others, making and accepting gifts, etc. From the *Jātakas* we know of the Brāhmaṇas as renouncing the world and going to the forest either at an early stage[4] or after passing

1. *Jā*, V. 290.
2. *Sūtra*, 9. 1.
3. *Uvā*, 7.
4. *Jā*, 1. 333, 361, 373, 450; II. 131. 232, 262, 145 etc.

through the successive stages of Brahmacharya and *Gārhasthya*.[1] Brāhmaṇas have been described as well-grounded in the *Vedas* and versed in the different branches of learning such as *Nīghaṇṭu*, *Vyākaraṇa*, and *Lokāyata*.[2] Brāhmaṇas like Suṇetta[3], Sela,[4] and others[5] possessed vast knowledge and imparted education to a large number of students, some of whom came to be known as the teachers of world-wide repute.

The practice of offering sacrifices was very common among the Brāhmaṇas. During his tour, Mahāvīra is stated to have spent the rainy season in a sacrificial house of a Brāhmaṇa of Champā.[6] The Brāhmaṇas made sacrifices and assumed that the gods were willing to accept their offerings. On the occasion of these sacrifices, they used to receive *dāna*. In the *Somadatta Jātaka*, it is narrated that the king gave a Brāhmaṇa 16 cows, ornaments and a village. With the spread of Jaina and Buddhist doctrines, the cult of sacrifice gradually declined. It is said that while Vijayaghosha was engaged in performing Brahmanical sacrifice, Jayaghosha, a monk approached him for alms and converted him to his faith after telling him what true sacrifice really meant.[7]

The second category of the Brāhmaṇas, known as worldly Brāhmaṇas could not stick to their hereditary professions of teaching and priesthood but followed other professions under the pressure of social and economic necessities. According to Āpastamba and Gautama, trade and agriculture were to be taken up by them in times of distress. From the Buddhist sources, it is gathered that the Brāhmaṇas in the ordinary walk of life appeared as farmers, craftsmen, businessmen, soldiers, administrators, and so on. The *Daśa-Brāhmaṇa-Jātaka*[8] states how Brāhmaṇas in those days pursued ten

1. *Jā*, II. 85. 394, 411; III. 147, 352.
2. *Dīgha*, I. ii, 120; *Aṅgu*, III. 223; GS. I 146; *Su. Ni.* III. 5; *Majjh*, II. 133.
3. *Aṅgu*, III, 371.
4. *Su.Ni*, III, 7.
5. *Jā*,; VI. 32.
6. *Āva-Chū*, p. 320.
7. *Uttarā*. 25.
8. *Jā*, No. 495.

occupations against rules. They acted as : (1) physicians, carrying sacks filled with medicinal roots and herbs; (2) servants and wagon-drivers; (3) tax-collectors who would not leave a household without collecting alms; (4) diggers of the soil in the garb of ascetics with their long hairs and nails, and covered with dust and dirt; (5) traders selling fruits, sweets, and the like; (6) farmers; (7) priests interpreting omens; (8) policemen with arms to guard caravans and shops, like *Gopas* and *Nishādas*; (9) hunters in the garb of hermits killing hares, cats, fish, tortoises, etc.; and (10) menials of kings who helped them in their baths in the garb of *Yājñikas*. This may appear as over-exaggerated but in other *Jātakas* too, there are references to Brāhmaṇas practising as physicians,[1] ploughing the land,[2] trading[3] and hawking goods,[4] working as carpenters,[5] as shepherds,[6] as archers[7] and as hunters.[8]

There were others who expounded dreams[9] and went about telling fortune (*Lakkhaṇa-Pāṭhaka*),[10] reading the past, future, and the character of an individual from the signs on his body (*Aṅga-Vijjā-Pāṭhaka*),[11] and reading the luck of swords (*Asikkhaṇa Pāṭhaka*).[12] Some of them worshipped demons and practised magic. They possessed *Mantras* like the *Vedabbhamanta*,[13] the *Paṭhavijayamanta*[14] and *Chintāmaṇivijjā*.[15] The art of exorcism was also practised by a few.[16] It appears from these references and from the account of the *Brahmajāla Sutta* that

1. *Jā*. II. 213; VI. 181.
2. Ibid, II. 165; III. 162-63; *Jā*, V. 68.
3. Ibid IV. 15-21; V. 22, 471.
4. Ibid, II. 15.
5. *KS*, I. 2-27; *Jā*, IV. 207.
6. *Jā*, III. 401.
7. Ibid, III. 219; V. 127.
8. Ibid, II. 200; VI. 182. 170,
9. Ibid. I. 343; IV. 334-35; VI. 330.
10. Ibid, I. 272; IV. 79, 335; V. 211.
11. Ibid, 21, 250; V. 458.
12. Ibid, I. 455.
13. Ibid, I. 253.
14. Ibid, II, 243,
15. Ibid, III, 504.
16. Ibid, III, 511.

the Brāhmaṇas could be found in all walks of life, and that some of them took up objectionable practices such as hunting, carpentary, and chariot-driving.

The picture of the Brāhmaṇas in *Jātaka* literature is quite different from the one given in Brāhmanical literature. It is gloomy, especially in *Jātaka* literature. The Brāhmaṇas are pictured as greedy, shameless, and immoral. While the shamelessness of the Brāhmaṇas is clear from *Junha Jātaka*,[1] the *Sigāla Jātaka*[2] shows that they were greedy. That their moral standards were not quite high is clear from the *Sambhava Jātaka*.[3]

Brahmanical literature on the other hand makes it abundantly clear that the Brāhmaṇas enjoyed certain special privileges. For certain offences, for instance, they received milder punishment than those belonging to other classes. They were exempt from taxes. In the matter of treasure-troves, they were more favourably treated than the members of other classes. As a matter of fact, these privileges were granted only to learned Brāhmaṇas, not to all of them. Moreover the Brāhmaṇas did not occupy a privileged position in the eye of law. A criminal, whosoever he was, was executed, as is evident from a number of passages in the *Jātakas*, one of which also speaks of the execution of a Brāhmaṇa.

VAIŚYAS

The Vaiśyas were not homogeneous in their occupation but followed different professions. They were known as *Gahapati* or *Gāhāvai*, *Kuṭumbika* and *Seṭhīs*. *Gahapati* or *Gāhāvai* means, literally, a householder, but it seems to have constituted the high and rich middle-class families owning land and cattle. Jaina texts mention a number of *Gāhāvais* who were adherents of the Jaina faith. One such *Gāhāvai* was Ānanda, a rich landowner of Vāṇiyagāma, who possessed a large number of cattle, ploughs, and carts.[4] Pārāsara was another *Gāhāvai*, prosperous in agriculture (*kisi*) and hence known as *Kisipārāsara*; he

1. *Jā*, III. No. 456, p. 61.
2. Ibid, I. No. 113, p. 255.
3. Ibid, V. No. 515, p. 31.
4. *Uvā*.

had six hundred ploughs.[1] Kuiyaṇṇa is described as another *Gāhāvai* who is said to have owned a pretty large number of cows.[2]

The expression *Kuṭumbika* is used to denote the head of a family,[3] but during this period, he belonged exclusively to the Vaiśya community. We find him both in cities and in villages; in the former mostly as a businessman, dealing in corn,[4] practising trade[5] and money-lending[6] and in the latter as a well-to-do cultivator.[7] Some of the *Kuṭumbikas* figure as very rich citizens.[8]

The *Seṭhīs* were the richest aristocratic section of the Vaiśya caste. They are represented as respectable tradesmen, enjoying a high position of honour among the members of their caste. They rendered various services to the kings and tradesmen. It appears from the *Jātakas* that some of them occupied an official position in the royal court. Nanda is mentioned as an influential Seṭhī of Rājagṛiha.[9] Anāthapiṇḍika had spent considerable wealth for providing residence for Buddhist *Bhikshus*. They were usually charitable, and spent a good portion of their wealth in charities. Their sons received education along with the Kshatriyas and the Brāhmaṇa youths, and offered the teacher a handsome honorarium.[10]

THE ŚŪDRAS

The word 'Śūdra' denotes a number of castes. In the contemporary Jaina and Buddhist literatures, we do not find a specific mention of a caste called 'Śūdra'. But the occupation and status of a class of people living in those days make it clear that they were none other than the Śūdras. Both Mahāvīra and the Buddha tried their best to improve the general condition of these down-trodden people.

1. *Uttarā. Ṭī*, 2, p. 45.
2. *Āva. Chū*, p. 44.
3. *Jā*, II. 267.
4. Ibid.
5. Ibid, IV. 370.
6. Ibid, II. 388.
7. Ibid. II. 267.
8. Ibid, IV. 370.
9. *Nāyā*, 13, p. 141.
10. *Jā*, IV, 38.

The artisans were developing into different castes all engaged in their hereditary professions. The potters (*Kumbhakāra*)[1], smiths (*Kammāra*),[2] ivory-workers (*Dantakāra*)[3], carpenters (*Vaḍḍaki*),[4] etc., belonged to hereditary families and had their own settlements.

There were a number of unorganised, unsettled, and wandering castes, who earned their livelihood by entertaining the people. There were the dancers and singers (*Nāṭa*)[5], acrobats (*Laṅghanaṭaka*),[6] tumblers,[7] jugglers (*Māyākāra*),[8] snake-charmers (*Āhituṇḍika*),[9] mongoosetamers (*Koṇḍadamaka*),[10] musicians (*Gandhabba*),[11] drummers (*Bheri Vādaka*),[12] conch-blowers (*Saṅkhadhamaka*)[13] and so on. Expressions such as *Bherivādakakula*,[14] *Saṅkhavādakakula*,[15] *Naṭakakula*,[16] *Gandhabbakula*[17], and the like suggest that they formed separate castes of their own.

Similar in status to these people but leading a more settled life were the cowherds (*Gopālaka*), cattlemen *Paśupālaka*) grass-cutters (*Tiṇṇahāraka*), stick-gatherers (*Kaṭṭhahāraka*), and foresters (*Vanakammika*) as they are described in the *Majjhima-Nikāya*[18] and *Kuṇāla Jātakas*.[19] They probably lived an exclusive life, collecting together into villages of their own, away from the towns and cities which they visited for selling their produce to earn their livelihood.

1. *Majjh*, II. 18, 46; III. 118; Jā, II. 79; III. 376.
2. *Su. Ni*, 1.5; *Dīgha*, 33.
3. *Dīgha*, I. 78; *Majjh*, II. 18; *Jā*, 1. 320.
4. *Jā*, II. 18, 405; IV. 344.
5. Ibid, II. 167; III. 61, 507.
6. Ibid, I. 430.
7. Ibid, II. 142.
8. Ibid. IV. 495.
9. Ibid, I. 370; II. 267, 429; III. 198, 348.
10. Ibid, IV. 389.
11. Ibid, II. 249.
12. Ibid, I. 283.
13. Ibid, I. 284.
14. Ibid, I. 283.
15. Ibid, I. 284.
16. Ibid, II. 167.
17. Ibid, II. 248.
18. *Majjh*, I. 79.
19. *Jā*, V. 417.

THE DESPISED CASTES

There were certain castes which were looked down upon by the higher sections of society either due to their ethnic origin or on account of their following low professions. The *Chaṇḍālas*, the *Veṇas*, the *Nishādas*, the *Rathakāras*, and the *Pukkusas* appear as low castes.

Among the despised castes, the *Chaṇḍālas* were the most unfortunate. 'Contemptible like a *Chaṇḍāla*' became a proverbial expression. He was the lowest and the meanest on the earth[1], and the *Sigāla Jātaka* compares a jackal, low and wretched among animals, with a *Chaṇḍāla*.[2] The *Chaṇḍālas* were not only untouchable but also unseeable. The daughter of the *Seṭhī* and wealthy merchant washed her eyes when she saw the *Chaṇḍāla* at the city gate. Food was polluted at the sight of a *Chaṇḍāla*. Sixteen thousand Brāhmaṇas were once ostracized because they committed the sin of eating the food served by a *Chaṇḍāla*. One Brāhmaṇa was starved to death because of the same sin. The wind, that had touched the body of a *Chaṇḍāla*, was considered impure. The *Chaṇḍālas* lived outside the city gates. Their dialect was different and showed their ethnic difference. They were often engaged as carriers of corpses and as slaughterers of criminals condemned to death by the king.

However, we also come across some *Chaṇḍālas* who were respected in the society. Harikeshabala, born in the family of *Chaṇḍālas*, became a monk possessing some of the highest virtues. He subdued his senses and observed the rules of walking, begging, speaking etc. He controlled himself and was always attentive to his duty. He protected his thoughts, speech and body from sins.[3]

Along with the *Chaṇḍālas*, there were *Nishādas*, *Pukkusas*, and others. The *Nishādas* were generally hunters and foresters. The *Pukkusas* used to pluck flowers and lived generally by hunting and only occasionally by dirty work like cleaning temples and palaces. There were carpenters, basket-makers,

1. *Jā*, IV. 397.
2. Ibid, II. 6.
3. *Uttarā*, XII.

flute-makers, weavers, and barbers whose professions were considered to be low.

MIXED CASTES

There must have been a steady increase in the mixed castes during this period, and these are found mentioned in the *Dharmasūtras*. These mixed castes arose not only as a result of the permitted *anuloma* marriages (a member of a higher caste marrying a woman or women of lower castes), but also as a result of the prohibited *pratiloma* marriages (where the husband's caste was lower than that of the wife). Difference in occupation must have resulted sooner or later in an increase in the number of such mixed castes.

From the four *Varṇas*, there came into existence several castes and sub-castes, such as *Ambaṣṭha*, *Āyogava*, *Sūta*, and *Karṇa*. A passage in the *Sūtrakṛitāṅga*[1] names the following classes in this order—Ugras, Bhogas, Aikshvākavas, Jñātrīs, Kauravas, Warriors, Brāhmaṇas, Lichchhavis, commanders, and generals. Other passages of the Jaina scriptures add princes, artists,[2] and Kshatriyas.[3] The Nāgas, too, formed a part of the country's population.[4] Many cities were named after castes or professions, e.g., Uttara-Kshatriya-Kuṇḍapura (after Kshatriyas), Dakshiṇa-Brāhmaṇa-Kuṇḍapura (after Brāhmaṇas), Nātika (after Jñātis or Jñātrikas), Bhoganagara (after the Bhogas), and Vāṇijyagrāma (the village of commerce.)

SLAVERY

During this period, slavery was quite common in the society, and both male and female slaves (*dāsas* and *dāsīs*) were employed for doing all sorts of household work. Not only kings and wealthy people, but even ordinary families could keep slaves. The practice was confined not only to cities but was in vogue also in the villages. It was not restricted to a particular *Varṇa*, but even Kshatriyas, Brāhmaṇas, and men belonging to the upper strata of society were reduced to

1. SBE, XLV. p. 339.
2. Ibid, XLV. p. 71.
3. Ibid, p. 321.
4. *Dia.* II, p. 288.

slavery.[1] It is said that Pūraṇa Kassapa and Ajita Keśakambalī had been slaves in their previous lives.[2]

There were different categories of slaves. Slaves born of slave mothers were known. That slaves were bought and sold is mentioned in the Jaina, Buddhist and *Dharmaśāstra* literatures. According to *Nanda Jātaka*,[3] seven hundred *paṇas* were enough for the purchase of a slave. The *Sattubhakta Jātaka*[4] reveals that one hundred *Kārshāpaṇas* were more than sufficient for having nine slaves.

The physical fitness of a male slave and the beauty of a female one might have been responsible for a higher price. Slaves were also given in gift. The *Dīgha* and *Aṅguttara Nikāyas* say that the Buddha had prohibited the *Bhikshus* from accepting the gifts of slaves, either male or female.[5] According to a *Jātaka*, a Brāhmaṇa demanded a hundred slave girls from a king along with other requisites as his gift, and his demands were fulfilled.[6]

War-captives, who were reduced to complete subjection, might have been either sold or given in gifts to others by their masters. Chandanā, the first female disciple of Mahāvīra, was a slave of this type.[7] Some people became slaves for paying off their debts. A widow who purchased two *palis* of oil from a grocer on credit, had, when unable to pay off the debt, to serve him as a slave girl.[8] Slaves were made during famine for want of food.[9] The *Vidhura-pandita-Jātaka* refers to those men who were driven to slavery mainly on account of fear.[10] Some were condemned to slavery as a punishment for their crimes.[11]

1. U. N. GHOSHAL: Studies in Indian History & Culture, pp. 461-467.
2. BANDOPADHYAYA, N. C : Economic Life and Progress in Ancient India, p 297.
3. *Jā*, IV. No. 39.
4. Ibid, No. 402.
5. *Dīgha*, I. 64; *Aṅgu*, II. 209.
6. *Jā*, IV. 99
7. *Āva. chū*, p. 318.
8. *Piṇḍa. Nir*, (319).
9. *Vya. Bhā*, 2. 207; also *Mahā. Ni*, p. 28,
10. *Jā*, No. 545.
11. Ibid, I. 200.

The nature of the work of a slave depended upon his own ability as well as the social and financial status of the master. In the case of rich masters, the qualified slaves could be kept as treasurers, store-keepers, and even private secretaries.[1] Thus, from the *Nanda-Jātaka,*[2] it is known that the master showed his full faith in his slave by giving the latter all sorts of information relating to his treasure. In the *Nānachchhanda Jātaka,*[3] the Brāhmaṇa master is found taking the advice of Pannā, a slave girl, about the boon he would ask of the king.

In spite of all the commendable jobs given to slaves, there is no doubt that most of them were employed to perform ordinary household duties. U. N. GHOSHAL rightly observes, "A slave was ordinarily engaged in cooking, fetching water, pounding and drying rice, carrying food to and watching the field, giving alms, ministering to the master when he retired, or handling the plates and dishes, bringing the spitoon and fetching the fans during meals, sweeping the yards and stables and other such duties."[4]

As regards the treatment meted out to the slaves, it depended upon the temperament of the master. There are conflicting statements on this subject. Generally masters harassed their slaves but in a few cases, they showed kindness towards them. Slaves were punished for their acts of commission and omission. Sometimes they were ill-treated by their masters when the latter chose, in a wanton mood, to do so. The *Aṅguttara-Nikāya*[5] states that the slaves toiled with tearful faces for fear of the rod. One *Jātaka*[6] informs that the wanton daughter of a high treasurer used to revile and beat her slaves and servants. According to the *Nāmasiddhi Jātaka,*[7] the master of the slave girl Dhanapālī used to beat her. She was also sent

1. FSONB, p. 311.
2. *Jā*, No. 39.
3. Ibid, No. 289.
4. *Studies in Ancient Indian History & Culture*, p. 463.
5. *Aṅgu*, II. 207-8.
6. *Jā*, I. 295.
7. Ibid, No. 97.

on hire to work for others. Slaves were given thrashing and kept in fetters by their masters.

No serious attempt was made to improve the lot of slaves. Even a great reformer like *Mahātmā* Buddha did not have courage enough to admit any slave into his Order. The Lichchhavīs were not prepared to recognize the sons born of their female slaves as free men. Vāsavakhattiyā was not recognized by them as a member of the Śākya family only because she was the daughter of Prince Mahānāma's slave girl Nāgamuṇḍā.[1]

There are some instances to prove that some slaves received good treatment from their masters. They were given opportunities to learn reading, writing, and handicrafts along with their masters' sons. Kaṭāhaka grew up in the company of his master's son, got his education along with him, learnt two or three handicrafts, and was appointed as the store-keeper of his master.[2] Sometimes, the daughters of the masters fell in love with their slaves. In the *Kaṭāhaka*[3] and *Kalaṇḍuka Jātakas*,[4] girls of some reputed families are found marrying their slaves and eloping with them.

Certain methods of liberating the slaves prevailed in the society. War-captives made slaves could get emancipation if the vanquished party subsequently regained its strength and conquered the enemy. Slaves could also be liberated either by accepting *Sannyāsa* (monkhood) or by the will of the masters or by paying them a ransom for their emancipation.

ORDERS OR STAGES OF LIFE

Even before the time of Mahāvīra and the Buddha, the existence of the three well-known *Āśramas* (stages), namely, *Brahmacharya*, *Gṛihasta*, and *Tapas*, is a fact evident from the *Chhāndogya Upanishad* and the *Bṛihadāraṇyaka Upanishad*. As a matter of fact, the number of *Āśramas* is four, not three, though there are slight differences in their nomenclature and in their sequence. All the four were known by their

1. Economic Life and Progress in Ancient India, p. 297.
2. *Jā*, I. 451.
3. Ibid, No. 125.
4. Ibid, No. 127.

specific names to the *Jābālopanishad*. From the time of the early *Dharmasūtras*, these four *Āśramas* with their successive stages became well known. The *Āpastamba Dharmasūtra*[1] says, "There are four *Āśramas*, *viz.*, the stage of a householder, that of one staying in the teacher's house, the stage of being a *Muni*, and the stage of being a forest-dweller. Āpastamba places the householder first among the *Āśramas* probably on account of the importance of that stage to all other *Āśramas*. To Gautama[2] the four *Āśramas* were *Brahmachāri*, *Gṛihastha*, *Bhikshu* and *Vaikhānasa*. *Vasishṭha Dharmasūtra*[3] names the four *Āśramas* as *Brahmachāri*, *Gṛihastha*, *Vānaprastha* and *Parivrājaka*. The Buddhist literature[4] knew all the four stages into which the life of the three upper classes was divided.

The first part of man's life is *Brahmacharya* in which he studies in his teacher's house ; in the second part he marries and becomes a householder, pays off his debts to his ancestors by begetting sons and to the gods by performing *Yajñas*. When he sees that his hair is growing grey and that there are wrinkles on his body, he resorts to the forest, *i.e.*, becomes a *Vānaprastha*. After spending the third part of his life in the forest for some time, he spends the rest part of his life as a *Sannyāsin*.

It is believed that the scheme of the *Āśrama* was so devised that the individual may attain the four goals of existence, namely, *Dharma*, *Artha*, *Kāma*, and *Moksha*. In the *Brahmacharya* stage, through the discipline of his will and emotion, he attains *dharma*. In the *Gṛihastha Āśrama*, he marries, becomes a householder, tastes the pleasures of the world, enjoys life, has sons, discharges his duties to his children, to his friends, relatives and neighbours and becomes a worthy citizen, the founder of a family. He is supposed to attain *Artha* and *Kāma* during this period. In *Vānaprastha*, he is called upon to resort to a forest life for pondering over the great problems of the life hereafter and to accustom himself to self-abnegation,

1. *Āp. Dh.S*, II. 9. 21-1,
2. *Gau. Dh. S*, III. 2.
3. *Vas. Dh. S.* VII, 1-2.
4. *Abhidhammapadipika*, 409; *Dhammapada*, 135.

austerities, and a harmless life. In *Sannyāsa*, he may succeed in realizing the supreme goal of *Moksha* in this very life or he may have to continue to rise in spiritual height until after several births and deaths the goal is in view.

This *Āśrama* system was related to the theory of the three debts—*Ṛishiṛiṇa*, *Pitṛiṛiṇa*, and *Devaṛiṇa*—and through this tripartite system, an attempt was made to pay them off. The debt to the *Ṛishis* was paid off by studying their works at the stage of *Brahmacharya*, the debt to parents by procreating sons and educating them at the stage of *Gṛihasta*, and the debt to gods by performing sacrifices at the stage of *Vānaprastha*.

It is difficult to accept the theory propounded by RHYS DAVIDS[1] to the effect that the four orders of life were of Post-Buddhistic origin and that the Brahmanical class unable to cope with the progress of new ideas formulated the theory of *Āśramas* according to which no one could become either a hermit or a wanderer without having first many years as a student in the Brahmanical school. The theory of *Āśrama* was formulated long before the advent of Buddhism. It is possible that the separation of the last two orders, and particularly the development of the last one, may be due to the development of ascetic ideas stemming from the rise of Jainism and Buddhism.

No attempt was ever made to make the four stages obligatory except the first stage. It was not compulsory for an individual to enter into other stages. This system was never imposed arbitrarily with state legislation, ex-communication, perpetual banishment, or execution. The hold of the *Āśrama dharma* on the life of the people was rather loose. Had it been strictly imposed on the whole population, the consequences would have been disastrous. It seems that it was confined only to the superior communities like the Brāhmaṇas without any binding obligation.

FAMILY LIFE

Throughout this period the system most in vogue was the joint-family system, and it included father, wife, children,

1. RBI. p. 113.

mother, minor brothers, and sisters. The relationship between the different members of the family was mostly cordial and affectionate. The father was the head of the family, and he was respected by all the members. His wife was the mistress who performed her household duties, looked after the members of the family, and was obedient to the master. The mother was highly respected by one and all. We hear of king Pūsanandi who was greatly devoted to his mother.[1] The mother on her part had great love for her children. When prince Meghakumāra decided to embrace the life of an ascetic, his mother became unconscious and fell to the ground like a log of wood. She was sprinkled over with water, fanned with a palm-leaf, and was consoled by her friends. Her eyes were filled with tears, and using some of the most pathetic words, she persuaded her son not to give up worldly pleasures.[2]

There are also instances which reveal that amity did not exist between one member of the family and the other. Daughters-in-law and mothers-in-law often sought refuge in nunneries to escape from the tyranny of one another. One daughter-in-law even conspired to kill her mother-in-law. In one case, four daughters-in-law drove their father-in-law out of the house. We have the case of a son who refused to marry on the ground that wives generally showed scant respect to their parents-in-law and even domineered over them.[3]

The conception of proprietary rights came into existence in the family circle. The reason was that trade and commerce prospered highly, and the number of professions increased. The members of the family began to earn their living independently. Some of the *Dharmasūtra* writers began to give due recognition to the self-acquired property of the son. Gautama says, "Among the brothers one who is *Vaidya*, need not give his own earning to those who are not *Vaidyas*." Vishṇu clarifies the point a little further, saying that if the *Vaidya* had acquired his knowledge with the help of the family property, he must share the property with others.

1. JLAIDJC, p. 147.
2. *Nāyā*, 1. p. 25 f; *Uttarā*, 19.
3. *The Position of Women in Hindu Civilization*, pp. 107-8.

Formerly, the father had extraordinary powers. There was a time when the gift or a sale of a son was not regarded as beyond the power of the father. These practices came to be disallowed during this period, no matter whether this was due to a Śāstric prohibition in the proper sense of the term or to an alteration in the conception about the extent of the father's right over the son. With the beginning of the *Vānaprastha* system, the joint-family system began to crumble. Before becoming a *Vānaprasthī*, the father had to divide his property among his sons. Sometimes he had to divide his property among his sons against his will. The son started demanding his legitimate share in the property even against the wishes of the father. Some of the *Dharmasūtras* declared that a son, who would force a partition upon his father should not be invited to perfoım the latter's *Śrāddha*. This shows that such a procedure was disapproved by the society, but the son had legal rights and could get them enforced through the court of law. Gautama says that sons have rights by birth. Āpastamba opines that the connection of the son with inheritance cannot be broken.

MARRIAGE

In the sixth century B.C., marriage was generally regarded as necessary and desirable for all. There are also exceptional cases where both males and females thought of leading an unmarried life by renouncing the world under the influence of religion. Sometimes such persons were unable to live up to their high ideals, and their lapses were furiously commented upon by the public. Hence it was the married who enjoyed real respect in society and felt elevated and dignified.

FORMS OF MARRIAGES

From the Jaina and Buddhist sources, it appears that *Brāhma*, *Prājāpatya*, *Āsura*, *Gāndharva*, and *Rākshasa* marriages were common during this period. Marriages referred to in the *Dharmasūtras* are of eight forms, *viz.*, *Brāhma*, *Daiva*, *Ārsha*, *Prājāpatya*, *Āsura*, *Gāndharva*, *Rākshasa* and *Paiśācha*. *Brāhma* and *Prājāpatya* marriages were the most popular. In these two forms, marriage was settled by parents. Auspicious days were fixed for the marriage ceremony[1] and the bridegroom's party reached the house of the bride on a fixed day. The bride was carried in a car to the bridegroom's place escorted by a number of people.[2]

The *Āsura* form of marriage, in which a wife was procured by paying a substantial amount to her father, was also prevalent. The minister Teyaliputta wanted to marry the daughter of a goldsmith.[3] A merchant, after leaving his negligent wife, married another girl by paying a large sum.[4] A robber, who had plenty of money, paid the desired amount, and married a girl.[5] From Buddhist literature we know that the father of Isidasi had received a bride as price for her in her marriage.[6]

The *Gāndharva* or love marriage was also popular among the nobles of the time. In this form of marriage, both the bride and bridegroom made their own choice by falling in love with each other without the knowledge of their guardians, and were married without rites or ceremonies. The marriage of Udayana with Vāsavadattā is well known. We hear of King Sīharaha of Puṇḍavaddhaṇa who married a girl in the *Gāndharva* way.[7] Some *Jātaka* stories[8] also refer to this type of marriage. The *Baudhāyana Dharmasūtra*[9] refers with approval to the view of some thinkers that love-unions ought to be commended as they presuppose reciprocal attachment.

People sometimes resorted to the *Rākshasa* form of marriage. The forcible carrying of the girl to be married was the essential feature of this kind of marriage. There are many instances of elopement and abduction. Suvarṇāṅgulikā, a maid servant of Udayana, was abducted by king Pajjoya, Ruppiṇi

1. *Dīgha*, I. 11; *Jā*, I. 258.
2. *Jā*, I. 258.
3. *Nāyā*, 14, p. 148.
4. *Uttarā*, *Ṭī*, 4. p. 97.
5. *Uttarā*, *Chū*, p. 110.
6. *Therī*, 5, 5/120 and 153.
7. *Uttarā*. *Ṭī*, 9, p. 141, also 13. p. 190.
8. *Jā*, VI, 364 f; I. 134-36; I. 300.
9. 1/11/13/7.

by Kaṇha, Kamalāmelā by Sāgarachanda[1], and Chellaṇā by king Seṇiya. The Jaina texts[2] also refer to the abduction of Dovaī by king Paumanāva of Amarakaṅka. This type of marriage figures frequently in the *Jātakas*,[3] and it remained quite popular among the warrior class from very early times.

The Jaina and Buddhist texts of this period do not refer to the *Paiśācha*, *Ārsha*, and *Daiva* marriages which are known from certain Brahmanical sources. In the *Paiśācha* marriage, the bride is either duped very often by making her overdrunk or physically overpowered by the bridegroom in order to make her yield to passion. Jainas and Buddhists do not regard it as marriage at all. When a daughter was offered in marriage to an officiating priest by the sacrificer, the marriage was designated as a *Daiva* one. This marriage was not practised among the Jainas and the Buddhists, who might have included it in the category of *Brāhma* and *Prājāpatya* forms of marriage. In *Ārsha* marriage, the bride's father received a bull and a cow at the time of his daughter's marriage. Since it was thought to be a variety of *Āsura* marriage, it was probably not mentioned.

The most interesting type of marriage known as *Svayaṁvara* (self-choice) was confined originally to the Kshatriya class, wherein a princess selected her husband of her own free will, from among the assembled suitors, or as a result of a tournament or contest in the use of warlike weapons. There are several instanccs of this type of marriage. The *Nāyādhammakahā* refers to the *Svayaṁvara* of Dovai which was attended by various prominent kings and princes.[4] The *Uttarādhyayana* commentary refers to another *Svayaṁvara* marriage of the princess Nivvui.[5]

CASTE AND GOTRA CONSIDERATION

During this period, caste and family (*jāti* and *kula*) became important factors in determining marriages in order to preserve the purity of blood. Brāhmaṇas, Seṭhīs, clans-

1. *Bṛih. Bhā, Ṭī*, p. 57.
2. *Nāyā*, 16, p. 186.
3. Jā, V. 425-6; Jā, I. 297.
4. *Nāyā*, 16, pp. 179-82.
5. *Uttarā. Com*, I, 3. p. 59,

men, treasurers, and others are mentioned as solemnising marriages with the members of their respective castes of equal family status. The Jaina and Buddhist accounts are supported by the *Dharmaśāstras* which prescribe that the bride should be of the same caste. Generally, endogamy was in practice, and restrictions were imposed on the intermixture of castes.

During the Vedic period, *Gotra* denoted a cow-pen, but it came to be used in the sense of lineage or ancestry at this time. When king Prasenajit asked the *Gotra* of Aṅgulimāla's parents, the latter replied that his father was of the *Gārgya Gotra*, and his mother of the *Maitrāyaṇi*.[1] Opinions are divided about the consideration of *Gotra* in settling marriages. Some of the law-givers (*e.g.*, Gautama and Baudhāyana) are silent on this point, but some of them prohibit *Sagotra* marriages. A verse in the *Kachchhapa Jātaka* suggests that generally, parties united in wedlock belonged to different *Gotras*.[2]

There are during this period a few examples of brothers marrying their own sisters. Buddhist literature speaks of the Śākyas marrying their sisters for the sake of continuing their family line.[3] Incestuous marriages were also prevalent among the Lichchhavīs.[4] Marriage with one's own cousin was also in vogue. Bambhadatta married his maternal uncle's daughter.[5] The *Jātaka* stories refer to the marriages of Kāśī and Śivi princes with their maternal uncle's daughters.[6] The sister of the Kośala king Prasenajit was married to Bimbisāra, and his daughter Vājirā was wedded to Ajātaśatru, the son of Bimbisāra.[7] The marriage of Jyeshṭhā to Nandivardhana, the elder brother of Mahāvīra, also belongs to this category. Such marriages were not confined to the royal families, but were prevalent also among the common folk as is evident from several popular stories. Some *Dharmasūtras* refer to the custom of marrying one's maternal uncle's daughter, but this practice was confined to the South.[8]

1. *Majjh*, 11. 102.
2. *Jā*, 11. 360.
3. *Dia*, 11-115; *Jā*, V. 413 (No. 536).
4. IHQ, II, p. 563.
5. *Uttara*, *Ṭi*, p. 189,
6. *Jā*, I. 457; *Jā*, II. 327 and *Jā*, VI. 486.
7. Ibid, II, 237, 403-4; IV. 342-43.
8. Bau. Dh.S I. I. 19-26.

Marriage was guided by two special laws among the Lichchhavīs of Vaiśālī. One of them prohibited the marriage of a Lichchhavi lady with any outsider.[1] This law was so strictly followed that the secret marriage of Siṁha's daughter[2] with the romantic king Bimbisāra of Magadha brought on the dreadful fight between the Lichchhavīs and the Magadha people, resulting in the discomfiture of the former and their resolve to make "a requital of enmity (*Vairaniryātana*) even to the sons of the king." They were so particular about it that this resolution was got recorded and kept in a box duly sealed.[3]

The second law was in connection with *Strīratna* 'the jewel of women' (the most excellent woman).[4] According to this law, the *Strīratna* was not allowed to be married for herself, but was to adorn and entertain the society in which she was brought up, for which she was called *Nagaraśobhini*. She was thought to be one of the greatest treasures of the nation, a treasure which was not to be under the possession of an individual, however great he might be in position or in wealth. She was to belong to the whole *Gaṇa*. At this time, Ambapālī, for example, was the most excellent girl, and was therefore made *Nagaraśobhinī*.

INTER-CASTE MARRIAGE

The system of inter-caste marriages was not a common practice. Only the people of higher classes practised it, but not quite often. The marriage of a bridegroom belonging to a higher caste with a bride of a lower caste was known as *Anuloma* marriage, and the marriage of a high-caste girl with a low-caste boy was named *Pratiloma* marriage. We find in a *Jātaka* that a king saw a beautiful girl named Sujātā, daughter of a greengrocer selling jujubes, fell in love with her and made her his queen consort.[5] A *Jātaka* describes *Senāpati* Ahipāraka as marrying Ummadantī, a merchant's daughter.[6]

1. W. W. Rockhill: *The Life of the Buddha*, p. 62; IHQ. XXIII, p. 58.
2. IHQ. XXIII, p. 59 f. n.
3. Ibid.
4. Ibid.
5. *Jā*, III. 81.
6. Ibid, V. 211.

MARRIAGEABLE AGE

There seems to be no doubt that the usual age of the bride at the time of her wedding was sixteen. The bridegroom used to be older than his partner and it can well be presumed that he used to be at least eighteen or twenty. The *Therigāthā* states that Isidāsī in her former birth was married at the age of sixteen.[1] Nuns like Viśākhā and Kuṇḍalakeśa were sixteen years old at the time of their entry into the nunnery when their marriages were being contemplated. The commentary on the *Dhammapada* describes the girls of sixteen years as eagerly pining for being united with husbands.[2] The *Jātakas* clearly state that girls of this age were regarded as ripe for marriage and were possessed of rare beauty and grace.[3]

The *Gṛihyasūtras* composed during this period lay down that the consummation of the marriage (*Chaturthikarma*) should take place on the fourth day after marriage. Some *Gṛihyasūtras* also provide for the contingency of the bride being in her monthly course during the marriage ceremony. All this proves that the girl was married at an advanced age.

REMARRIAGE AND DIVORCE

As far as the husband was concerned, he was allowed to remarry after the death of his wife. With regard to widow-remarriages, evidence is conflicting. There are cases of permission as well as prohibition. Some Brahmanical sources of this period taking an idealistic view disapprove of widow remarriage. Their rules were followed by the priestly class and the higher section of society, but the ordinary people generally followed local customs. It appears that only a few among the higher section of society took recourse to widow-remarriage. Widows having no issue might have found it easier to remarry than those who had the burden of looking after their sons and daughters. The term *Punarbhu* was used to denote a widow who remarried.[4] The Brahmanical authors are of opinion that generally the remarriage of the widow should be confined to a member of the family of her deceased husband.

1. *Therīgāthā*, 445.
2. Commentary on the *Dhammapada*, 120.
3. *Jā*, III. 93; *Jā*, I. 456.
4. *Vas. Dh.S* XVII. 20.

The reason was the popularity of *Niyoga* from the earlier period.

It appears from the Buddhist sources that there was no such restriction. Probably liberal rules were followed by people of the eastern part of the country where widows had more freedom in the selection of their new husbands than those of Madhyadeśa. According to the *Nanda Jātaka*,[1] a squire who had a young wife was apprehensive of her marrying after his death and transferring the movable family property to her new husband. The *Susima Jātaka*[2] describes a king's priest marrying the widowed queen. In the *Aṅguttara Nikāya*,[3] we find a lady assuring her husband on his death-bed that she would never remarry, but would look after her household and her children.

Besides widowhood, a lady had to face the problem of remarriage when her husband either became a recluse or went abroad and did not return. Because of the rise of the new religious ascetic orders like Jainism and Buddhism, a large number of young men renounced the world in their youthful age abandoning their young wives. We know from the *Jātakas* that some of them followed their husbands while others, whose desires and cravings for their youthful pleasures were still unsatisfied, remarried and restarted their conjugal lives. In some of the *Jātakas*, husbands are represented as expressing their views to the effect that their wives would take new husbands after they had renounced the world.[4] Some Brahmanical sources tell us that in case a husband became an ascetic or went abroad and did not return, the wife was free to marry within a limited time.[5]

Marriage after divorcing the husband or wife on certain grounds was also prevalent in society. According to Vasishṭha, one can seek a new husband if the first proves to be impotent or mean or insane. The Buddhist *Jātakas* also refer to such cases. It appears that marriage by divorce was common in the lower section of society, but in the higher classes, it was resorted to only in a few cases. The *Piyajātika Sutta* of the

1. *Nanda Jā*, (No. 39).
2. *Jā*. III. No. 411, p 237.
3. *Aṅgu*, III. 295.
4. *Chullasutasoma Jā*, (No. 525) and *Vessantara Jā*, (No. 547).
5. *Vas. Dh S.* XVII, 78-80.

Majjhima-Nikāya states that the relatives of a woman, who did not like her husband, intended to separate her from him and to unite her with another person.[1] A *Jātaka* relates the story of princess Phusati of Madra, who wanted to get rid of her ugly husband Kansa (the Bodhisattva) of Kuśāvatī and to marry another prince who was handsome, according to her wishes.[2]

Family and local traditions also played an important part in controlling this custom. A *Jātaka* story shows that in spite of the absence of any deep-rooted love for the husband the wife did not exercise her right of divorcing him, but preferred to remain in her uncomfortable condition.[3] It is said that a Brāhmaṇa who was asked, whether he would keep or abandon his wife found guilty of adultery, expressed his view against deserting her and remarrying.[4]

POLYGAMY AND MONOGAMY

Generally monogamy was followed by the vast majority of the people, but polygamy was a fashion among the rich and ruling sections of the society. The kings and princes considered it a privilege to have a crowded harem. In the *Jātakas*, most of the princes have been described as polygamous.[5] Kings like Bimbisāra, Prasenajit, Udayana, and Ajātaśatru were all polygamous. The rich house-holder of Rājagṛiha, Mahāsayaga, had thirteen wives.[6] The *Raṭṭhapāla-Sutta* describes Raṭṭhapāla, the son of a Brāhmaṇa, *Gṛihapati*, as having several wives.[7] In the *Aṅguttara-Nikāya*, a wealthy and happy householder is described as being waited upon by four wives with all their charms.[8] The *Therīgāthā* tells us that Isidāsī in her former birth was married to a merchant's son who had already another wife.[9] The *Pāraskara Gṛihyasūtra* states that a Brāhmaṇa should have three wives, a Kshatriya two and a Vaiśya one, besides one Śūdra wife to all.[10]

1. *Majjh*, II. 109.
2. *Jā*, No 531 (*Kusa Jā*).
3. Ibid, IV. 35.
4. Ibid III. 351.
5. *The Chullasutasoma Jātaka* (*Jā*, V. 178).
   Suruchi Jātaka (*Jā*, IV. 316).
6. *Uvā*, p. 152.
7. *Majjh*, II. 63.
9. *Aṅgu*.
8. *Therīgāthā*, 446.
10. *Pa. G.S*, I. 4. 8-11.

THE COURTESANS

Courtesans became a special feature of city life during this age, especially in cities like Rājagṛiha. Champā, Vaiśālī, Mithilā, Sāketa and Śrāvastī. People had become wealthy and begun to entertain themselves in different ways. As the courtesans were custodians of such fine arts as singing, dancing, and music, they occupied a respectable position in the society of the period. They were beautiful, graceful and pleasant. As their presence in a royal city was material to its citizens, they were especially installed with honour. They appeared even in royal palaces on festive occasions to give the finest exhibition of their artistic talent.

Sālavatī of Rājagriha and Ambapālī of Vaiśālī were two of the most well-known courtesans of this time. When Ambapālī was installed as a courtesan of Vaiśālī, her example was followed by installing Sālavatī as a courtesan of Rājagriha.[1] Both were not only superbly charming but also well versed in singing, dancing and music. The fact that the Buddha accepted an invitation extended to him by Ambapālī and went to her residence with the *Bhikshu Saṁgha*[2] and that she dedicated the Ambapāli grove to the Saṁgha[3], shows that a courtesan occupied no mean position. The way in which Ambapālī proceeded to see the Buddha at Koṭigāma with a number of magnificent vehicles[4] shows that her equipage was almost royal. She was supposed to be "the pride of the city" (*Nagaraśobhinī*). King Bimbisāra of Magadha was so much intoxicated by her beauty that he risked even his life to pay a visit to her at a time when a severe fighting was going on between Magadha and Vaiśālī. He is said to have stayed with her for some time. And it was Ambapālī who is said to have given birth to prince Abhaya, son of Bimbisāra. That the great physician Jīvaka was born of Sālavatī,[5] the courtesan of Rājagṛiha,[6] shows that some of the sons of the courtesans could

1. *Mv*, VIII. 1. 2.
2. *Mv*, vi. 30. 2.
3. Ibid, VI. 30. 5.
4. Ibid, VI. 30. 1.
5. W. W. ROCKHILL: The Life of the Buddha, p. 64.
6. *Mv*, VIII. 1. 4.

rise to eminence and occupy positions that had a prestige value in society.

The *Jātakas* inform us about Sāmā,[1] Sulasā[2], Kālī[3] and other courtesans.[4] Kālī is described in the *Takkāriya Jātaka* as one possessed of the qualities of social decency and self-respect. The *Sulasā Jātaka* represents Sulasā as a woman of rare wisdom and courage. About the income of these courtesans, the *Jātaka* stories give exaggerated accounts which are not reliable. On the other hand, the information given by the *Vinaya Piṭaka* appears to be authentic and we may accept fifty to one hundred silver punch-marked coins as their daily income. Ambapālī is described as earning 50 *Kahāpaṇas* per night, whereas Sālavatī is said to have been charging 100 Kahāpaṇas.[5]

The character of the courtesans has also its seamy side. Generally, they sold their flesh for money for which they were looked down upon by men and women alike. Their profession is described as a vile trade (nichakamma).[6] Expression like 'a house of ill fame' (*nichch-ghara* or *gaṇikāghara*)[7] and 'a low woman,[8] (*duratthi kumbhadāsī*) indicate that the profession of the prostitute was not considered respectable.

FOOD AND DRINK

Both literary and archeological sources reveal that rice, wheat, and pulses were the main cereals which people consumed. Rice, no doubt, was known in the preceding age too, but wheat and pulses were added to the dietary system of this period. Rice was very popular. The chief varieties[9] of rice were *Sāli*, *Taṇḍula*, *Hāyana*, *Shashṭika*, and *Nīvāra* which seem to have been cultivated in this region. Rice of superior quality

1. *Kaṇavera Jā*, (No. 318).
2. *Sulasā Jā*, (No. 419).
3. *Jā*, IV. 248 (No. 481, *Takkāriya Jā*).
4. *Aṭṭhāna Jā*. (No, 425).
5. *Mv*, VIII. 1. 1-1. 3.
6. *Jā* III. 60.
7. Ibid, III- 61; IV. 249.
8. Ibid, VI. 228.
9. *Majjh*, I. 57; III. 90; *Jā*, I. 429, 484; II. 110, 135, 378; IV. 276; VI. 367.
   Āśva. G S, I. 17. 2; *Śāṅ*. G. S, I. 24. 3; I 28 6;
   Pā, III 1.48; III. 3. 48; V. 1. 90; V. 2. 2.

was taken by the rich sections of society, whereas the inferior variety was the food of the people belonging to the lower strata.[1]

Cooked rice was called *Bhatta* or *Bhakta*[2], and by Pāṇini *Odana*.[3] It was ordinarily eaten with *sūpa* (pulses) and vegetables.[4] *Pāṇini* tells us that meat, sūpa, vegetables, *guḍa*, ghee, etc. were added to *Bhāta*.[5] Rice-milk was highly praised by Buddha, and he recommended it for the *Bhikshus* as a morning breakfast.[6] Honey was also mixed with it. *Yavāgū* (rice-barley gruel) was a common liquid food.

There were a few special preparations known to us. *Sattu*[7] was also eaten during this period. *Kummāsa* or Kulmāsha was a coarse food of the poor.[8] Sweet cake now known as *Puvā* was a favourite dish. According to the *Illisa Jātaka*, it was prepared from rice, milk, sugar, ghee, and honey. *Piṭṭhakhajjaka* (*Khāja*) was another sweetmeat liked by all. Sāriputta was fond of it but took a vow not to eat it, for it tended to make him greedy.[9] *Palala* (modern *tila-kuṭa*) was a delicious sweetmeat mentioned by Pāṇini.[10] It was made of powdered *Tila* and sugar or *Guḍa*. *Pishṭaka*, now known as *Pithā*, was prepared from the ground paste of rice.[11]

Milk and milk-products like curd, butter, and ghee were largely eaten.[12] Vegetables like pumpkins, gourds, and cucumbers and fruits like mango and jamboo were included in the diet of the people.[13]

That during this period a large number of people were nonvegetarian is proved by the discovery of bones at different archaeological sites. They seem to have been very fond of meat

1. *Jā*, I. 486; III
2. Ibid, IV. 43;
3. *Pā*, IV. p. 67.
4. *Jā*. VI. 372.
5. *Pā*, VI. 1. 128.
6. *Mv*, VI. 24-25.
7. *Sattubhasta Jā*, (No. 402).
8. *Kummāsapiṇḍa Jā*, (No. 415).
9. *Jā*, I. 31. (*Visavanta-Jā*,) (No. 69).
10. *Pā*, VI. 2, 128.
11. Ibid, IV. 3. 147.
12. *Aṅgu*, II. 95.
13 *Jā*, V. 37; *Pā*. IV. 1. 42; VIII. 4. 5; IV. 3. 165.

and fish. There were butchers[1] who earned their livelihood by killing various animals in the slaughter-houses and by supplying their meat to the people. The flesh of goat, pig, sheep, and deer was much used. In certain sections of society and on special occasions, cows and oxen were also slaughtered, but the tendency to revere the cow and to spare the useful bull was gaining ground. The *Jātaka* stories mention pigeons,[2] geese[3], herons,[4] peacocks[5], crows[6] and cocks[7] as eatables. A large number of people cherished fish diet. Meat and fish were carried in carts to the towns and cities where they were sold in the open market.[8]

Meat and fish were important items of diet in the royal kitchen.[9] On festival days and on occasions of marriage, meat was lavishly consumed. Even from the *Jātakas*, we know that the Brāhmaṇas relished meat and fish with great delight. They are nonvegetarian diet on sacrificial occasions[10] and on the occasion of the *Śrāddha* ceremony.[11] A guest was also served with meat so that the fruits of the merit of honouring him could be reaped.[12] It seems that the custom of meat-eating was so common that the Buddha did not prohibit it, except for the *Bhikshus*, who could accept it only in alms and could not procure it otherwise. In the *Mahāparinibbāna-suttanta*, the Buddha himself is described as eating pig-meat (*Sūkara-maddava*),[13] and in a *Jātaka* story, he is found cherishing cooked meat at the house of a householder.[14]

This widespread practice of meat eating during this period

1. Majjh, I. 364; II. 193; KS, II. 170-11; KS, II. 171; G.S, I. 229, KS, II. 171.
2. *Romaka Jā*, (No. 277).
3. *Puṇṇandi Jā*, (No. 214).
4. Ibid.
5. Ibid.
6. Ibid.
7. Jā, II. 412.
8. *Māṁsa Jā*, (No. 315).
9. Ibid, I 242.
10. Ibid, III. 429.
11. Ibid, I. 166 (No. 18).
12. *Āp Dh. S.* II. 3. 7. 4.
13. *Dīgha*, II. 127; *Udāna*, VIII. 5.
14. *Jā*, II. 262.

might have produced a natural reaction in the mind of Lord Mahāvīra which led to the propagation of the doctrine of non-injury to living beings. For the protection of animal life, he instructed both monks and laymen to abstain from meat-eating.

Drinking was fairly common during this period. There are references to *Surā* and *Meraya* (*Maireya*) as intoxicating drinks.[1] The kings, princes, nobles, warriors, and rich people called *Seṭhīs* drank liquor. The religious people and the *Brahmachārins* of all castes were to abstain from drinking. The *Jaina sūtras* prohibit the Jaina monks from visiting festive gatherings in which people drank:[2] According to the rules of the *Vinaya*, the novices were not to drink strong drinks and intoxicating liquors,[3] and the same rule applied to the elders. We learn from the D*harmasūtras* of Āpastamba,[4] Gautama,[5] and Vishṇu[6] that the Brāhmaṇas were not allowed to indulge in drinking.

The Jaina and Buddhist sources inform us that the festive occasions were marked by feasting, drinking, and merry-making.[7] There used to be a festival known as *Surā-Nakkhata* (drinking festival) which was marked by unrestricted drinking, feasting and dancing,[8] leading finally to brawls in which people broke their heads, feet, and hands.[9]

Liquor was manufactured or consumed on a large scale. Taverns (*Pāṇāgāra* : *Kappasālā*) where various kinds of wine were sold were common. From the *Jātaka* stories, we know that there were crowded taverns, where liquor was kept filled in jars and sold.[10] The owners of the taverns kept apprentices who helped them in their business.[11] Generally, these taverns

1. *Chu*, XII, 1 3; *Aṅgu*, II. 53, II. 54; IV. 5; 246; *Itivuttaka*, 74; *Pā*, II. 4.25; VI. 2.70.
2. SBE, XXII; pp. 94-95.
3. SBE, XIII. 211, 215.
4. *Āp. Dh. S*, I, 5 17. 21.
5. *Gau. Dh. S.* II. 26.
6. *Vas, Dh. S*, XXII. 84.
7. SBE, XXII, pp. 94-95.
8. *Jā*, I. 362, 489.
9. Ibid. IV. 115-16.
10. Ibid. I. 251-252 (Nos. 47, 78).
11. Ibid.

were managed by the *Seṭhīs* who were the aristocratic Vaiśyas owning considerable property. Some people used to go to these taverns for drinking with their wives.[1]

DRESS AND ORNAMENTS

Besides the usual *vastra* and *vasana* denoting clothing in older literature, *chīra*, *chela*, *and chīvara* began to be used during this period. There were different fabrics used for preparing clothes. The *Āchārāṅga*[2] mentions some of them as wool (*jaṅgiya* or *jāṅghika*), *bhaṅga* (bhag tree), hemp (*sāṇiva*), palm leaves (*pottaga*), linen (*khomiya*), and *tūla* (*tūlakada*). It is stated that a monk or a nun could beg for the garments mentioned above.[3] Although cotton (*kārpāsa*) was the material generally used, cloths made of Silk (*kauśeya*); linen (*kshauma*), and wool (*aurṇa*) were also in demand.

The dress of the people consisted of *antaravāsaka* (under garment), *uttarāsaṅga* (upper garment), and *Ushaṇisha* (turban or headgear). The *Vinaya* texts[4] refer to the variety of ways in which *dhotis* (undergarments) were arranged—*hastiśauṇḍika* (forming the trunk of an elephant), *tālavṛintaka* (in the shape of a fan), *matsyavālaka* (like a fish-tail), *chatushkarṇaka* (having four angles), and *Śatavallika* (having a hundred folds). The same texts refer to a complete weaving outfit. The cloth was fastened at the waist by a *Kāyabandha* (girdle), and a variety of girdles are mentioned in the *Vinaya* Texts,[5] such as *Kalābuha* (those made of many strings plaited together), *deḍḍubhaka* (those made like the head of a water-snake), *muraja* (those with tambourines or beads on them), or *maddavīna* (those with ornaments hanging from them). Both men and women wore *Kañchuka*, a robe probably like the modern shirt.[6] Women wore *sārīs* known as *saṭṭa-sāṭṭaka*.[7] Ladies of the upper strata of society wore coloured garments, while widows were dressed in white.

1. *Jā*, IV 114.
2. *Āchā*, II. 5. 1. 364, 368.
3. *Bṛh*, (2.24) and the *Sthānā*, (5.446) mention *tiridaṭa ṭa* in place of *tūlakaḍa* which was made from the bark of the *tiriḍa* tree.
4. *Chv*, V. 29. 4.
5. Ibid. 29. 2.
6. Ibid.
7. *Jā*. No. (431) Vol. 3. 196.

A Jaina monk was allowed to wear three robes, two linen (*Kshaumika*), undergarments (*omachela*) and one woollen (aurṇika) uppergarment.[1] The Buddha also allowed three robes : a double waist cloth (*saṁghāta*), an upper robe (*uttarā-saṅga*), and a single undergarment (*antaravāsaka*)[2].

Both from the Jaina[3] and Buddhist[4] sources, it is evident that sewing and stitching of clothes were coming into fashion. There are references[5] to the needle, thread, scissors, etc. The monks were allowed to sew their clothes.

People also put on shoes. A large variety of shoes is also referred to in the *Vinaya* Texts, such as shoes with one, two, three, or even more linings ; shoes adorned with skins of lion, tiger, panther, antelope, otter, cat, squirrel, and owl; boots pointed with horns of rams and goats, ornamented with scorpions' tails, sewn round with peacock feathers : boots, shoes, slippers of all hues, such as blue, red, yellow, brown, black, and orange. Sometimes, the shoes were ornamented with gold, silver, pearls, beryls, crystal, copper, glass, tin, lead or bronze. Poorer people used wooden shoes, shoes made of leaves of palmyra and date-palm, or of various kinds of grass. Shoes were also made of wool. The *Bṛihatkalpa Bhāshya*[6] prescribes the use of shoes for the Jaina monks, especially when they were on tours, and in the case of illness single-soled (*egapuḍa*) shoes, *puḍaga* or *Khallaka* shoes to cover the foot sore, *vāgurā* shoes to cover the toes and also the feet, *Kosaga* shoes to cover the toes, *Khapusa* shoes to cover the ankles, and *ardhajaṅghikā* and *jaṅghikā* shoes to cover the half and full thighs respectively.

The difference between the male and female dresses and ornaments was not much marked. The ornaments, which decorated the bodies of both men and women, were costly and of various types and designs. Every part of the body from head

1. *Āchā*. 7. 4 208.
2. *Mv*. VIII, 13. 4, 5.
3. *Sūtra*, 4. 2. 12; Āchā, II. 5. 1. 364.
4. *Chv*, V. 11-1, 2, 3, 5, 6, 7; Mv, VII. 1. 5, VII. 12. 2; viii. 21. 1. *Jā*, No. 387. Vol. 2, pp. 178-79.
5. *Vinaya*, II 14 ff.
6. *Bṛih*. 1. 2883; 3 3847.

to foot had its appropriate ornaments made of gold, silver, pearls, gems and precious stones. We know from the *Vinaya* Texts,[1] that at first even monks used to wear ear-rings, ear-drops, strings of beads for the neck, girdles of beads, bangles, necklaces, bracelets and rings. The only ornaments referred to as worn by women alone were waist-bands and anklets. The *Jātakas*[2] also mention earrings, frontlet pieces and torques round the neck. Among ornaments, Pāṇini refers to *aṅguliya* (finger-rings)[3] *Karṇika* (ear-rings),[4] *lalāṭika* (ornaments of the forehead),[5] and *graiveyaka*[6] (torques or necklaces). Some luxurious ornaments of this time like ear-lobes, torques of different shapes, necklaces, bangles, pendants, and rings made of different materials such as terracotta, precious stones, glass, ivory, bone and copper, have been discovered from North Indian sites.

There are elaborate references to toilet articles in the *Vinaya* Text. Hair was besmeared with pomade or hair-oil of bees-wax, and them smoothed with a comb. Scents, perfumes, garlands, and unguents were used, and faces were rubbed with ointment and painted. The body was also painted, and feet were rubbed with sandstone, gravel, and seafoam. To keep long hair seems to have been the fashion. Beards were also dyed blue, red, purple or green according to individual taste. Nails were polished or cut with nail-cutters, and tooth-sticks were used for cleaning the teeth. Some of the objects of toiletry discovered in the excavations included antimony rods of copper, hair-pins of bone, combs of ivory, terracotta flesh rubber, and nail parer.

When bathing, people used to rub their bodies-thighs, arms, breast and back—against wooden pillars or walls. *Chunam* (lime) was also rubbed over the body by means of a wooden instrument in the shape of a hand or a string of beads. Special bathing pools or tanks are also referred to.

1. *Chv*, V. 2. 1.
2. *Jā*, VI. 590.
3. *Pā*, IV. 2. 96.
4. Ibid, IV. 3. 65.
5. Ibid.
6. Ibid. IV. 2 96.

They were floored or faced with brick, stone, or wood, and had walls or steps of the same material. To prevent water becoming stale, pipes were laid to drain it off. There were also arrangements for hot-bath rooms with chimney and fire-place, and the roof covered with skins. The bathers put scented clay over their faces and took their bath seated on stools. There were cells to be used as cooling rooms after the steam bath.[1] The *Brahmajāla Sutta* contains a stock list of dress-and-toilet processes comprising no less than twenty items.[2] Of these items, Pāṇini[3] refers to mirror, collyrium, garlands, perfumes, shoes, and staff.

FURNITURE AND UTENSILS

The progress of civilization during this period brought with it certain amenities, such as furniture and utensils, to make life easy and the homes comfortable. The *Vinaya Texts*[4] give a long list of the articles of furniture and utensils. There was a pretty large variety of chairs rectangular, cushioned, cane-bottomed, straw-bottomed arm-chair and state chair, and sofas with or without arms. There were also different types of bedsteads with legs carved to represent animals' feet. Some bedsteads had lofty supports with arrangements for rocking backwards and forwards, and the bed, comprising mattresses stuffed with cotton and pillows half the size of man's body, was strewn over with flowers. Bolsters stuffed with wool, cotton cloth, bark, grass or talipot leaves, and chairs and bedsteads covered with upholstered cushions to fit them were in use. For poorer people, there were mats made of grass and bedsteads made of laths of split bamboo.

For reclining their bodies people used lofty and large things such as large cushions, divans, coverlets with long fleece counterpanes of many colours, woollen coverlets, white or marked with thick flowers, mattresses, cotton coverlets dyed with figures of animals, ruga with long hair on one or both sides, carpets inwrought with gold or with silk, large woollen

1. *Chv.* V. 14.
2. G. P. Majumdar, Toilet, Ind. Culture, Vol, I. p, 651.
3. Pā, V. 2.6; IV. 9-9; vi. 3. 65; IV. 4.53-54; V. 1. 110; V. 1. 14.
4. *Chv*, Sixth Khandhaka.

carpets with designs such as a nautch girl's dance, couches covered with canopies or with crimson cushions at both ends. There were also rich elephant housings and horse-rugs or carriage-rugs. Sheep-skins, goat-skins, and deer-skins were used as coverlets, and fine skins, such as those of lions, tigers, panthers or antelopes, were either used for reclining upon or cut into pieces and spread inside or outside the couches and chairs. We also hear of sun-shades, mosquito-curtains, filters for straining water, mosquito-fans, flower-stands, and fly-whisks (*chāmara*) made of tails of oxen and peacocks or of bark and grass.

Costly utensils were used such as bowls of various kinds made of beryl, crystal, gold, silver, copper, glass, tin, lead or bronze, and some of them were painted or set with jewels. Even circular supports of bowls were made of gold or silver, The increasingly large use of pottery vessels during this period is proved by archaeological excavations. The most remarkable is North Black Polished Ware which enjoyed the status of a de luxe ware of the period on account of its beauty and durability. Bowls and dishes of this ware have been found in a large number.

FESTIVALS AND GAMES

People amused themselves by participating in *Samājas* (festival gatherings) which formed a regular feature of social life during this period. The *Jātakas* inform us that the *Samājas* were special gatherings where crowds of men, women and children gathered together and witnessed various kinds of shows and performances, such as dancing and music, combats of elephants, horses and rams, bouts with quarter-staff and wrestling.[1] The *Jaina sūtras* inform us that festive entertainments were characterised by feasting, drinking and amorous acts.[2]

Though the festive assemblies at this time were mostly secular, some of them were no doubt religious in nature. The centres of these festivals were the cities and towns where people gathered from the neighbouring villages to enjoy them-

1. *Pre-Buddhist India*, p. 355.
2. SBE, XXII, pp. 91-95.

selves. On the occasion of a festival the cities were decorated, displaying great pump and show. Generally these were organized by the kings themselves who went on elephants round the city in solemn processions. The beauty of the festivals lay in the nocturnal decorations when people in their fine and colourful garments came out of their houses to enjoy and entertain themselves. On the occasion of some festivals, people were given holidays. Some festivals lasted for seven days while some continued even for a month.

The *Chāturmāsyas* were old seasonal festivals. The *Āpastamba-Gṛihya-Sūtra*[1] tells us that there were three *Chāturmāsya* festivals, each celebrated at an interval of four months, which indicated the advent of the three seasons, spring, rainy, and winter. They were celebrated on the full-moon days of *Phālguna*, of *Āshāḍha*, and of *Kārttika*.

Jaina and Buddhist texts mention various other festivities. The *Chāturmāsya* festival of the month of *Kārttika* was known as the *Kaumudi* or the *Kattikā*. On the day of *Kaumudīmahotsava*, men and women came out of their houses after sunset, and spent the whole night in wanton merriment.[2] In the *Sāmaññaphala Sutta* of the *Digha-Nikāya*,[3] king Ajātaśatru of Magadha is described on the *Kaumudī* night as sitting on the upper terrace of his palace, surrounded by his ministers. The *Sañjiva-Jātaka*[4] tells us that when Ajātaśatru was the king of Magadha, the city of Rājagṛiha was so lavishly decorated on the *Kattikā* festival days that it looked like a veritable city of gods.

The name of a festival *Surā-Nakkhata* dedicated only to drinking points out that drinking was so much in vogue that people thought it necessary to organise festivals in honour of a popular habit. A drinking festival at Rājagṛiha is mentioned in the *Sigāla Jātaka*.[5] Another *Jātaka* tells us of a drinking festival held at Vārāṇasī.[6] The occasion was characterized by

1. *Life* in North-*Eastern India* in *Pre-Mauryan Times*, p. 83,
2. JLAIDJC, p. 238.
3. *Digha*, I 47; SBE. II. 66.
4. Ja I, No. 150, 499.
5. Ibid. 489.
6. Ibid, 362.

unrestricted enjoyment of drinking and dancing. Even ascetics, for whom drinking is strictly prohibited, were for a while led astray. Women also drank hard, danced, and sang in a large number.

Saṅkhaḍī (*Saṇkhati* in Pali)[1] or *bhojja* was another special festival during this period. *Saṅkhaḍi* is so called because at this time animals were killed in large numbers[2] and their flesh was served to the guests. It is stated that monks and nuns should not participate in a festival when they know that they would be served chiefly with meat or fish or roasted slices of meat or fish.[3]

The *Hatthi-Maṅgala* (Elephant Festival) was celebrated with a view to exhibiting the feats of elephants in a spectacular manner. The *Susīma Jātaka*[4] describes this festival held annually in the royal courtyard. The chaplain of the king conducted the festival and was expected to know the three *Vedas* and the elephant-lore (*Hatthisuttam*). This festival was performed for the entertainment of the nobles and of those associated with royal dignity.

Śālabhañjikā festival was a popular festival during this period and a large number of people assembled on certain days in the *Sāla* groves, plucked *Sāla* flowers, sported, and spent the time in merry-making. The *Avadānaśataka*[5] gives a graphic account of this festival: "Once the Lord Buddha dwelt at Śrāvastī in the Jetavana, the garden of *Anāthapiṇḍika*. At that very time, the festival called *Śālabhañjikā* was being celebrated at Śrāvastī. Several hundred thousands of beings assembled there and, having gathered *Sāla* blossoms, they played, made merry and roamed about." The description of the *Śālabhañjikā* festival celebrated in the Lumbini garden situated between the two towns, Kapilavatthu and Devadaha, has been given in the *Nidānakathā*[6] : "The whole of Lumbinī Grove was like a wood of variegated

1. *Majjh*, I, p. 418.
2. *Bṛih*, I. 3140.
3. *Āchā*, II. I. 4, 245.
4. *Jā*, II. 46.
5. *Avadānaśataka*, p 21.
6. RHYS DAVIDS : Buddhist Birth Stories, London 1880, Vol. I, p. 66.

creepers, or the well-decorated banqueting hall of some mighty king. The queen beholding it was filled with the desire of disporting herself in the *Sāla* grove ; and the attendants entered the wood with the queen. When she came to the root of an auspicious *Sāla* tree, she wanted to take hold of a branch of it. The branch, bending down, like a reed heated by steam, approached within reach of hand. Stretching out her hand, she took hold of the branch, and then her pains came upon her." According to Pāṇini, this festival was peculiar to the eastern people.[1]

The people of Rājagṛiha were very fond of festivals. In the *Vinaya-Piṭaka*, a festival celebrated at an elevated place at Rājagṛiha is described as *Girajjasamajja*. That it took place at the top of a hill, probably a sacred place, points to the religious nature of the gathering. From the *Visuddhimagga*[2] we learn that there was a festival at Rājagṛiha in which five hundred virgins (*Kumāris*) offered Mahākassapa there a kind of cake which he accepted. There used to be held at Rājagṛiha a festival known as the *Nakkhattakilam* (the spot of the stars) in which the rich took part. This festival lasted for a week.[3] Chhaṇa and Sabbarttivāro were the most important festivals in which the Lichchhavīs of Vaiśālī spent the whole night in merry-making.[4]

There was a ploughing festival which has been described in the *Kāma-Jātaka*.[5] It is said that on that day the king held the plough. Most probably, the first ploughing at the beginning of the rains was observed as a sacred day and celebrated as a festival. In addition to these important festivals, there were other minor ones celebrated in honour of gods like Skanda, Rudra, and Mukunda ; there were festivals to propitiate Demons, Yakshas, and Nāgas : there were festivals to honour shrines and tombs, and there were festivals to worship trees, cows, wells, tanks, ponds, rivers, lakes, seas, and mines.[6]

1. *Kāśikā* on VI. 2. 74; III, 3. 109; II, 2.17.
2. P. T. S. p. 403.
3. *Vimānavatthu* Commentary, pp. 63.
4. W.W. Rockhill : The Life of the Buddha, p. 63.
5. *Jā*, No, 467.
6. SBE, XXII, p. 92.

Some household ceremonies too were celebrated with great rejoicings. *Avāha* was celebrated before wedding when betel leaves etc. were served ; *vivāha* was the wedding ceremony ;[1] *āhena* was held at the time of the bride entering the bridegroom's house ; *pahena* was celebrated when she returned to her father's house. Then *hiṅgola* was celebrated in honour of the deceased person or a yaksha ; in *piṇḍanigara*, food was offered to fathers. Then *sammela* or *goṭṭhī* was a social gathering in which the relatives and friends assembled.[2] According to the Jaina tradition, it was king Bimbisāra who first promulgated this feast.

Besides participating in festivals, people amused themselves in different ways. They took keen interest in singing and dancing. King Udayana of Kauśāmbī was a great musician who by his music could control elephants run amuck. He was asked by king Pradyota of Avantī to teach music to the princess Vāsavadattā.[3] A court-musician named Pañchaśikha of Sakka is known to have pleased the Buddha by his music.[4] It seems that singing and dancing played an important part in Ājīvika religious practices. The Ājīvika scriptures namely two *Maggas* (paths) are said by Abhayadeva to have been those of song and dance.[5] Possibly the Ājīvikas in their *Ājīviya-sabhā* gathered together for ecstatic religious singing and dancing. "Wandering dancers and musicians"[6] gave additional pleasure to the people by showing their skill. There were drummers and conch-blowers[7] to entertain them.

The gatherings of religious preachers and learned philosophers[8] certainly soothed their hearts and quenched their mental thirst. Besides, dramatic performances were also quite popular, and they might have been an important source of recreation. Painting[9] and embroidery,[10] apart from proving

1. *Jīva*, 3, p 280a; *Kusa Jātaka*, No. 531.
2. *Nisī. Chū* 8, p. 502; *Āchā* II. 1. 3. 245.; *Āva. chū*, II, p 172.
3. *Āva. Chū*, 11, p. 161,
4. *Dīgha*. II, 263.
5. *Bhag*, Fol. 659.
6. FSONB, p. 286.
7. Ibid, p. 297.
8. Economic Life and progress in Ancient India, p. 241.
9. *Aṅgu*, PTS, III, p. 76.
10. PBI, pp. 31, 41.

sources of income, must also have charmed the people. The manufacture of clay figurines of both human and animal forms was an object of amusement for children. The performance of jugglers[1] and snake-charmers (*ahiguṇṭhika*[2]) gave them special delight. As long as the festivities lasted, the youths had the pleasure of enjoying the company of the *nagaraśobhinīs*.[3]

Parks and gardens with diverse flowers and fruits were also the places where people used to visit for recreation. The existence of several beautiful tanks[4] and the nearness of rivers must have facilitated them in cultivating the habit of taking interest in swimming and sailing. There were forests where they took special delight in hunting animals and birds. Chariot-races, archery matches, wrestling, cock-and-peacock fights, and combats of buffaloes, bulls, horses and elephants[5] were the noteworthy pastimes of the people.

1. FSONB. pp. 294, 296
2. Ibid, p. 296.
3. JASB, XVII, p. 267.
4. Vaiśāli Excavations, 1950, p. 1.
5. *Āchā*, II, 11, p 392; *Dīgha*, I, p. 6.

CHAPTER VIII

ECONOMIC CONDITIONS

The period of Lord Mahāvīra was epoch-making in economic history because of the numerous important changes that occurred in it. States well organised came into existence for the first time, leading to the establishment of peace and order. As a result, this period witnessed an allround development of agriculture, industry and trade. The increased use of iron for different purposes resulted in the surplus of wealth and prosperity. Many new arts and crafts came into existence, and they became localised and hereditary. Both trade and industries were organized into guilds. The coined money was introduced, which facilitated trade and commerce. The merchants became very prosperous and a number of cities and towns came into existence. Population increased by leaps and bounds on account of better means of subsistence and living condition.

RURAL ECONOMY

(*i*) *Village*

Rural economy had its centre in the *grāma* or village, a collection of *gṛihas* (houses) and *kulas* (families) numbering from 30 to 1000. It was closed by a wall or stockade provided with gates.[1] Beyond this enclosure lay the arable land of the village, the *grāma-kshetra*, which was protected by fences[2] and field watchmen[3] against pests like birds and beasts. This land was divided into separate holdings cut off from one another by ditches dug for co-operative irrigation.[4] Usually these holdings were small enough to be cultivated by their owners and families with the help of hired labour, if necessary.[5]

1. Jā, 1, 239; II, 76, 135; III 9; IV, 370.
2. Ibid, I, 215.
3. Ibid, II, 110; IV, 277.
4. *Dhp*, Ver. 80—145=*Theragā*, 19; *Jā*, V, 167; I. 336; V. 412.
5. *Jā*, I, 277; III, 162; III, 167.

Large holdings were not unknown. We read of estates of 1000 *Karisas* (probably acres) and more, farmed by Brāhmaṇas.[1] In the *Suttas*, again, the Brāhmaṇa Kāśībhāradvāja employed 500 ploughs and hired men (*bhatikā*)[2] to drive his plough and oxen.[3]

The rural economy at this time was based chiefly on a system of village communities of landowners. There was no such proprietary right as against the community. We hear of no instance of a shareholder selling or mortgaging his share of the village-field to an outsider ; and it was impossible for him to do so at least without the consent of the village council. Nor had any individual the right of bequest, even to the extent of deciding the shares of his own family. No individual could acquire either by purchase or inheritance any exclusive right in any portion of the common grassland or woodland. The king granted not the land, but the *tithe* due, by custom to the government as yearly tax.

Adjoining the arable land of the village lay the grazing pastures[4] of herds of cattle[5] and goats,[6]—herds belonging to the king[7] or commoners.[8] Commoners customarily entrusted their flocks to a communal neatherd called *Gopālaka* whose duty was to pen up the flocks at night or to return them to their owners by counting heads. Besides pastures, villages had their suburban groves like the *Veluvana* of king Bimbisāra at Rājagṛiha, *Aṅjanavana* of Sāketa, or Jetavana of Śrāvastī.

(*ii*) *Different types of villages*

Gāma,[9] Gāmaka[10], Dvāragāma[11], and Pachchantagāma[12]

1. *Jā*, III, 293; IV, 276.
2. *Saṁ*. I, 4; *S*. I., 171; *Jā*, III, 293.
3. *Jā*. II, 165; 300.
4. Ibid, I, 388.
5. Ibid, III, 149; IV, 326.
6. Ibid, III, 401.
7. Ibid, I, 240.
8. Ibid; I, 194, 399.
9. *Dīgha*, I. 193; *Majjh*, 1, 189. II. 40; *Aṅgu*, IV. 365; Su. Ni, 1. 4.
10. Jā, I. 283, 378; II. 68.
11. Ibid, III. 33.
12. Ibid, I. 478; II. 76; IV. 326, 31.

mentioned in Pāli literature seem to be different types of villages. The *Gāma* and the *Gāmaka* were probably the ordinary village and the hamlet respectively, the difference being only in size. The *Nigama* was probably a busy market village, distinct from the quiet agricultural one. The *Dvāragāmas* were situated at the gates of cities, and probably were suburbs, most of them being industrial villages. The *Pachchantagāma* was located at the border of the kingdom. Owing to border invasions, the economic condition of such villages always remained unstable.

Several industrial villages, exclusively inhabited by men of the same craft, came into existence during this period. Such villages were those of carpenters,[1] smiths,[2] weavers,[3] and so on. Another feature of some of the villages was that they were peopled by the men of the same caste. Such caste villages were *Brāhmaṇagrāma* named after the Brāhmaṇas,[4] *Kshatriya-grāma*[5] after the Kshatriyas, *Baniyagrāma*[6] after the *Vaiśyas*, *Chaṇḍālagāma*[7] after the Chaṇḍālas, and *Nesādagāma*[8] after the *Nesādas*. There were also villages of park-keepers (*Ārāmika-gāma*)[9] and robbers (*Choragāmaka*).[10] Thus the economic factor of specialisation of labour was responsible for the localisation of various industries at separate villages and for the grouping of the people of the same profession and caste. The number of such villages, however, was small. Most of the villages had the mixed population of persons of different castes, occupations and trade, following their own professions.

These villages can be classified into two categories—the agricultural villages and the industrial ones. In the agricultural

1. *Jā*, II. 18, 405; IV. 159, 207.
2. Ibid; III, 281.
3. Psalms of Sisters, p. 88.
4. The Buddhist evidence tells us of several Brāhmana villages. See *Dīgha*, I, 127; *Dīgha*, II, 263-64; KS, I, 216; KS I. 143; *Jā*. II. 293. IV. 276; *Majjh*, I, 285, 400; GS, I, 162; *Aṅgu*. IV, 340-41.
5. *Vaiśālī Abhinandana-Grantha*, pp. 85-86.
6. Ibid.
7. *Jā*, IV. 200. 376, 390. The *Mahāvaṁśa* (V. 41) speaks of Chaṇḍāla village to the east of pāṭalīputra.
8. *Jā*, II. 36; IV. 413; VI. 71.
9. MV, vi. 15. 4.
10. *Jā*, IV. 430.

villages, the main occupation of the people was agriculture. With the growth and development of industries, there came into existence the industrial towns where the craftsmen migrated to pursue their crafts. It seems that the *Dvāragāmas*, which supplied the needs of the cities, were industrial towns. Such expressions as *Dvāragāmavāsi Vaḍḍhaki*,[1] *Dvāragāmavāsī Kumbhakāra*,[2] etc., probably refer to the inhabitants of such villages. The *Uvāsagadasāo* tells us of a village of 500 potters outside the city of Polāsapura.[3]

(*iii*) *Agriculture*

(*a*) *Methods* : Agriculture was the main source of people's livelihood. It made further progress during this period with the methods of cultivation becoming more perfect than those of the Vedic period. Vast areas were brought under cultivation. New devices were introduced for the irrigation of agricultural land. The literary sources of this period make references to the ploughing and fencing of the fields, irrigating them, sowing the seeds, getting the weeds pulled up, reaping the harvest, arranging the crops in bundles, getting them trodden, picking of the straw, removing the chaff, winnowing and garnering of the harvest as the various successive stages of the agricultural process.[4]

For the purpose of cultivation, big ploughs were also used.[5] At some places, the land was ploughed with hundreds and thousands of ploughshares. We read of the *gāhāvai* Ānanda who limited the cultivable land to five hundred ploughshares, each one ploughing one hundred acres (*niyattaṇa*) of land.[6] The ploughing of land and harvesting of crops became easy with iron sickles and hoes which began to be used.

(*b*) *Crops*: Some new crops seem to have been discovered during this period, crops which are conspicuously absent from Vedic literature. *Vihi* and *Taṇḍula* are the terms used for rice

1. *Jā*, IV. 344.
2. Ibid. III. 376.
3. Uvā, VII, 184.
4. *Chū*, VII. 1, 2; GS, I, 209, 221; *Aṅgu*, IV, 237-8; *Jā*, No. 36.
5. Saṁ, III, 155.
6. Uvā, I, p. 7.

in the Pāli *Nikāyas*[1] and the *Jātakas*[2] which probably denote its different varieties. In the Jaina canonical literature, *Kalamaśāli*,[3] *ral* [illegible] *mahāśāli* and *gandhaśāli*[4] have been mentioned as different varieties of rice. *Godhūma* (wheat), barley (*Yava*), and millet (*Kaṅgu*) were also produced. Among pulses cultivated were grams (*Kalāya*)[5], beans (*Mugga*)[6], pear (*Māsa*)[7], and *Kolatthi*[8]. Among oil seeds, castor oil seed (*Eraṇḍa*), sesame (*Tila*), and mustard oil seeds were well known. The discovery of the cereals, namely, rice, wheat, and pulses in the excavations at Ter and Nevasa in the N.B.P. level, testifies that they were cultivated.

Among fibre-yielding plants, cotton (*Kappāsa*) was the most important.[9] Among other kinds of fabrics, silk (*Kosseya*), wool (*uṇṇiya*), linen (*khoma*), and hemp (*saṇa*) may be mentioned. Probably indigo (*guliya*)[10] and other chemical dyes were produced, for the mention of a variety of colours leads us to believe in their existence.

Among the spices mention is made of fresh ginger (*siṅgavera*),[11] dry ginger (*suṇṭha*), cloves (*lavaṅga*), turmeric (*haridrā*), cumin (*vesaṇa*), pepper (*mariya*), *pippala* (long pepper), and mustard (*sarisavatthoga*)[12].

Sugarcane (*uchchhu*) seems to have been a common crop. A sugarcane store-house (*uchchhughara*) is mentioned in Daśapura.[13] The sugarcane press (*Mahajanta* : *Kolluka*)[14] is also mentioned, There were sheds for pressing sugarcane (*janta*-

1. *Majjh*, I. 57; III, 90.
2. *Jā*, I. 429. 484; II. 110. 135, 378; IV. 276; VI. 367.
3. *Uvā*, I, p. 8,
4. *Bṛih*, 2. 3301, 3397.
5. *Su. Ni*, III. 10; *Jā*, II. 74
6. *Majjh*, I. 57, 80; III 90; *Aṅgu*, IV. 108; *Su. Ni*. III. 10; *Jā*, I. 429.
7. Majjh, I. 57; III. 90; *Aṅgu*, IV. 108.
8. KS, I. 189.
9. *Uttarā*, *Ṭī*, 4. p. 78a.
10. *Nāyā* I, p. 47.
11. *Bhag*, 8. 3; *Paṇṇa*, 1. 23. 31, 43-4.
12. *Āchā*, II, 1.8. 268.
13. *Uttarā*. *Ṭī*, 2. p. 23.
14. Ibid, 19. 53; *Bṛih. Bhā*. *Ṭī*, *P*. 575.

sālā)[1]. *Jantapilaṇa* was an occupation specialising in crushing sugarcane, sesame, and other articles by machine[2]. Puṇḍravardhana was noted for sugarcane cultivation.[3] Three varieties of sugar are mentioned, *viz.*, *Machchaṇḍikā*, *puppottara*, and paumuttara.[4] Gourds were grown[5] and were used by the ascetics.[6]

Betel (*tāmbūla*)[7] and arecanut (*pūyaphali*)[8] were known. Vegetables called *śāka* and *mūla* were grown in addition to *brinjal*, cucumber, radish, pālaṅka (mod. pālak), *karella* (mod. *Kerelā*), tuber roots (*āluga*), water-nuts *śṛiṅgatala*, (mod. *siṅghāḍā*), onion, garlic, and gourd. Vegetable-gardens (*kachchha*) were known where radish, cucumber, etc., were grown[9]. Among flowers, most important are *navamālikā*, *koranṭaka*, *bandhujivaka*, *kaṇera*, *jāti*, *mogara*, *yūthikā*, *mallikā*, *vāsantī*, *mṛigadantikā*, *champaka*, *kunda*, and *others*.[10] Among fruits mention may be made of mango, fig, plantain, date, wood-apple, citron, bread-fruit, pomegranate, grapes, cocoanut, and others.[11] *Koṭṭaka* was a drying place for fruits ; people used to gather fruits from jungles and store them at this place ; they carried them in waggons, bundles etc. to cities for sale. Among the miscellaneous products of this period mention may be made of saffron (*kuṁkuma*), camphor (*kappūra*), lac, sandal,[12] honey (*mahu*), and others.

For protection of the standing crops from animals and birds, various steps were taken by the farmers. They dug pitfalls around the fields, fixed stakes, set stonetraps, and planted snares.[13] They also guarded the fields by fences and

1. *Uva. Bhā*, 10. 484.
2. *Uva.* I, p. 11; *Jambū. Ṭī*, 3. p. 193a.
3. *Taṇḍula* Ṭī, p. 2.
4. *Nāyā*, 17, p. 203.
5. *Uttarā*, *Ṭī*, p. 103,
6. *Bṛih*, *Bhā*, 1. 2886.
7. *Uva*, I, p. 9.
8. *Paṇṇa*, I. 23. 36.
9. Ibid. 1. 23. 18-9, 26 ff. 37-8, 43 ff. *Uttarā*, 36. 96 ff.
10. *Paṇṇa*, 1.23. 23-5.
11. *Ibid.* 1, 23, 12-7; Āchā, II, 1. 8. 266.
12. *Nāyā*, I, pp. 3. 10.
13. *Jā*. I. 143.

placards.[1] Wealthy cultivators kept watchmen who guarded their fields day and night.[2]

Crops were also damaged by natural calamities like drought and flood.[3] Their references are found in many a literary work. Famines are known to have broken out in the countries of Uttarāpatha[4], Kosala,[5] and Dakkhiṇāvaha.[6] Pāṭaliputra,[7] Kañchanapura,[8] and Srāvastī suffered considerable loss due to floods.

Arrangements were made for irrigating the fields by drawing water from tanks and wells, the remains of which have been discovered in the archaeological excavations conducted at Ujjain, Vaiśālī, etc. There were engineers who constructed canals for watering the fields.[9] The Śākyas and the Koliyas had made a dam on the river Rohiṇī,[10] an example which might have been followed by others elsewhere too.

Agriculture depended upon cattle comprising cows, buffaloes, goats, sheep, asses, camels, pigs, and dogs. The possession of these animals meant a sort of wealth for the people. In fact, cattle-rearing was one of their main occupations. The pasture grounds were known as *gochara*. During the day time, cattle were taken out to the grazing-land by the cowherds (*Gopālakas*) and returned by the evening to the people.

There were large cow-pens (*gomaṇḍava*) where the herds of cows, bulls, and calves were kept. Cattle-lifters (*kūḍaggāha*) often went to the cow-pen and robbed the cattle at night.[11]

1. *Jā*, I. 153; IV. 262-3.
2. Ibid, II. 110; III. 52; IV. 277.
3. A*ṅgu*, III. 104; *Jā*, II. 135, 149, 367; V. 401; VI. 487.
4. *Āva. chū*, p. 396.
5. *Vya. Bhā*, 10. 557-60.
6. *Āva. Chū*, p. 404.
7. *Kalyan Vijaya, Vīra Nirvāṇa*, p. 42 ff.
8. 10. 450.
9. Dhp, 80; *Theragā*, 19, 877.
10. *Kuṇāla Jā*, (No. 536).
11. *Viva*, 2, P. 14 f.

Quarrels among cowherds are frequently referred to. Cows were often attacked and devoured by lions and tigers in the jungle.[1]

Dairy farming was in an advanced state and the supply of milk, and its four products (*gorasa*), *viz.*, curds, buttermilk, butter, and ghee, were abundant. People, therefore, could get highly nutritious food. References to the milk of cow, buffalo, camel, goat, and sheep are often met with.[2] *Khīraghara* was known as a place where milk products were available in plenty.[3] Bullocks were used for pulling the plough. The cattle were also utilized for the production of hide, bones, ivory nails, and hair.[4] Slaughter-houses were known. A slaughter-house where five hundred buffaloes were slaughtered every day has been mentioned.[5]

Flocks of sheep and goats were confined in an enclosure (*vāḍaga*).[6] They were utilized for woolproduction. Brooms (*rayaharaṇa*) and blankets were made of sheep wool.[7] People used to kill sheep and eat their flesh seasoned with salt, oil, and pepper.[8] Mention is made of a young ram which was fed on rice and grass till it was fattened and killed on the arrival of the guest.[9] Veterinary science also flourished.[10]

FOREST TRACTS

Near the village and town, forest tracts were located. A forest (*aḍavī*) of eighteen *yojanas* is said to have existed near Rāyagiha.[11] Many species of trees covered with fruits and flowers have also been mentioned: *nimba*, *āmra*, *jambu*, *śāla*, *aṅkola*, *bakula*, *palāśa*, *putrañjana*, *bibhītaka*, *śiṁśapā*, *śriparṇi*, *aśoka* *tinduka* *kapittha*, *mātuliṅga*, *bilva*, *āmalaga*, *phaṇasa*, *dāḍima*,

1. *Āva. chū*, p. 44.
2. Ibid II, p. 319.
3. *Niśī. Chū*, 9. p. 511,
4. *Piṇḍa*, 50.
5. *Āva. chū*, II. p. 169.
6. *Vivā*, 4, p. 30.
7. *Bṛih*, 2, 25; *Bhā*, 3. 3914.
8. *Sūtra*, II, 6. 37.
9. *Uttarā*, 7. 1 ff-
10. *Niśī. chū*, 19. p. 1244.
11. *Uttarā*, *Ṭī*, 8, p. 125.

aśvattha, udumbara, vaṭa, nandi, tilaka, śirīsha, saptaparṇa, lodhra, chandana, arjuna, tālatamāla, and others.[1]

The trees provided people with wood for the supply of firewood and litter. Various kinds of bamboos, creepers, grass, medicinal herbs, and roots were found in plenty. *Vanakamma* is mentioned as the occupation of those who dealt in wood, an occupation which included the felling of trees. *Iṅgālakamma* was another profession the followers of which prepared charcoal from firewood.[2] There were wood-gatherers (*Kaṭṭhahāraga*), leaf-gatherers (*pattahāraga* and grass-cutters (*taṇahāraga*) whom we meet frequently roaming about in the forest.[3]

The forests also yielded other valuable animal products such as hides, skins, sinews, bones, teeth, horns, hoofs, and tails of such creatures as the leopard, tiger, lion, elephant, buffalo, yak, crocodile, tortoise, snake, and birds.

ARTS, CRAFTS, PROFESSIONS AND INDUSTRIES

Arts and crafts made considerable progress during this period. The earlier industries continued to make progress, but there was a tendency towards specialization in different branches of the same industry. With the growth and development of urban life, some new arts and crafts also began to meet the needs. With the establishment of big kingdoms, military needs also increased. Wide use of metal further increased the efficiency of several industries.

TEXTILES

Next to agriculture, spinning and weaving should be regarded as most important. References to the weaver (*tantuvāya*)[4], the loom (*tanta*)[5], weaving appliances (*tantabhaṇḍa*),[6] and weaving sheds[7] (*tantuvāyaśālā*) in literary works suggest that weaving was fairly common in society. There were various textile fabrics such as linen (*Khomaṁ*), cotton (*Kappāsi-*

1. *Paṇṇa*, 1. 23. 12 ff. 35. f. *Rāya*, 3, p. 12. *Ṭhā*, 10., 736.
2. *Uvā*, 1, p. 11; *Vya. Bhā*, 3. 89; *Āchā*, II. 2. 303.
3. SBE, XIII. 28; *Dīgha*, I. 51; *Jā*, IV. 475, *Paṇṇa*, I. 37.
4. *Jā*, I. 356.
5. *Vinaya* II. 135.
6. *Āva. chū*, p. 282.
7. Ibid.

kam) silk (*kosseyam*), *wool* (*Kambalam*), and hemp (sāṇam) out of which threads were spun and woven into cloth of various varieties and qualities.[1]

There are references to what is called the Kāśī clothes which are said to be very fine.[2] It is likely that other cities such are Śrāvastī, Kauśāmbī, Rājagriha, Champā, Vaiśālī, Kusinārā, and Mithilā manufactured plenty of textile goods of high quality both for domestic as well as foreign market.

Textile goods manufactured in those cities were of numerous varieties. Various kinds of garments, blankets, and curtains were among the finished goods. Costly and dainty fabrics of silk and gur are said to have been worked out into rugs, blankets, cushions, coverlets, and carpets.[3] The *Jātakas* tell us that embroidered clothes were also manufactured. Kings put on turbans worked with gold.[4] State elephants were adorned with golden clothes.[5] Various kinds of garments, blankets and curtains were among the finished goods of the period.

Then there was also the washing and dyeing industry. Washermen formed one of the eighteen corporations and soda (*Sajjiyākhāra*) was one of their washing materials. Mention must also be made of the existence of laundries (*rayagasālā*).[6] Clothes such as towels were dyed in saffron.[7] Clothes dyed in red colour (*kāsāi*) were worn in hot weather.[8]

CARPENTRY

Carpentry, which was one of the important occupations during this period, made great strides. Prior to the development of stone-architecture, wooden architecture was common. Carpenters were employed for building houses, palaces, halls and staircases. Next to house-building, they built ships, boats, vehicles of all sorts, carts and chariots of different kinds, and

1. *Mv.* VIII. 2. 1; *Peta,* II. 1. 17; India as known to Pāṇini, pp. 125-26.
2. GS, I. 128; 225-26; *Aṅgu,* III. 50; *Jā,* III, 11; VI, 49, 50, 144.
3. *Jā,* I. 149; II. 274; III. 184; VI. 280.
4. Ibid, V. 322,
5. Ibid, IV. 404; V. 258.
6. *Vya. Bhā,* 10; 484.
7. *Nāyā.* 1, p. 7.
8. *Bṛih. Bhā.* Pi, 613.

various machines. They made furniture for houses, such as seats, chairs, bed-steads, pegs, boxes, and toys. Wooden Sandals (*pādalehaṇiyā*) were made by clever artists from the wood of various trees,[1] were set with *vaiḍurya* and excellent *rishṭa* and *añjana* (granite) and then ornamented with glittering and precious stones.[2] Axe, hatchet, and other implements were known as the tools of a carpenter.[3]

HOUSE BUILDING

With the rise of cities and towns, the house-building activity greatly increased. For building a house the services of different artists were required. Among them, the architect was the foremost and indispensable. He was skilled in divining good sites[4] and was well grounded in the science of constructing houses. Masons who worked with bricks (*Iṭṭhakavaḍḍhaki*)[5] and clod-hoppers (*Gahapatisippakāra*)[6] were also required for the construction of buildings. Apart from wooden structures, houses were built of bricks and mud. Probably such houses were of durable nature. Most probably houses of bricks and mud had wooden ceilings and roofs.

In the *Jātakas*, the stone-cutter (*Pāshāṇakoṭṭaka*)[7] also figures as taking part in house-building. There is no direct evidence of stone architecture prior to the Mauryan age and the *Jātakas* in this respect may be regarded as referring to the Mauryan and post-Mauryan periods. Stone was used for laying the foundations of buildings in the pre-Mauryan age, but whether it was cut into specific sizes is doubtful.

The *Jātaka* description of the construction and decoration of a play-hall[8] suggests that the practice of decorating the walls of buildings with various paintings was in vogue. It was the painter *Chittakāra* who gave the finishing touch to the work of the architect, the carpenter, and the stonecutter. He pro-

1. *Bṛih. Bhā*, 3, 4097.
2. *Kalpa*, 1. 44.
3. *Uttarā*, 19. 66.
4. *Jā*, II. 297-98.
5. Ibid, VI. 333.
6. Ibid, 438.
7. Ibid, I. 478.
8. Ibid, VI. 332-33.

bably painted frescoes on the clay and wooden walls after they were plastered.

MINING

Mining was an important industry at this time. The principal kinds of ores obtained from the mines were iron, copper, tin, lead, silver, gold and diamond.[1] Iron and other metals were obtained by fusion.[2] Besides metals, there were also several substances, such as salt (*loṇa*), Soda (*ūsa*), yellow orpiment (*hariyāla*), vermilion (*hiṅgulaya*), arsenic (*maṇasila*), mercury (*sāsaga*) and *antimony* (*Añjana*).[3]

SMITHY

The economy of this period is marked by the wide-spread use of iron. The blacksmith (*Kammāra*) occupied an important position among the artisans. In literary works, we find mention of smith-shops (*Kammārasālā* : *aggikamma*).[4] Iron furnaces (*ayakoṭṭha*) are referred to and it is said that they were filled with ore, and a man handled it with tongs (*saṇḍasī*), then it was taken out and put on the anvil (*ahikaraṇī*).[5] The existence of the villages of blacksmiths consisting of a thousand families suggests that this craft was in a flourishing condition.[6]

The discovery of different types of iron objects from the post-chalcolithic and pre-N.P. levels in the excavations at Ujjain, Nagda, Eran etc. confirms the wide popularity of iron to which the literary works of this period testify. Ujjain has yielded evidence of the existence of a kind of furnace meant for melting iron.[7] Both from the literary and archaeological evidences, it is clear that iron was used for several purposes. Tools and implements of warfare, such as daggers, knives, swords, arrow-heads, spear-heads, spikes and caltrops, were manufactured. Looking at the military needs of the time, production of war material must have been a large-scale industry that absorbed a number of blacksmiths. Articles

1. *Nisī*, 5. p. 412; *Paṇṇa*, 1. 15; *Thā*, 4. 349.
2. *Bṛih. Bhā*, 1, 1090.
3. *Uttarā*, 36. 74; *Sūtra*, II. 3. 61; *Paṇṇa*, 1. 15.
4. *Vya. Bhā*, 10. 484.
5. *Bhag*, 16. 1.
6. *Jā*, III. 281.
7. *IP*, p. 197.

of domestic use comprised blades, hooks, nails, chisels, drills, axes, lamps, ladles, bowls and rings. Iron had also penetrated into the sphere of agriculture in the form of hoes, choppers, hooks and sickles. The limitless potentialities of this new metal led to the quickening and expansion of agriculture, the utilization of forest wealth and the exploitation of mineral resources. It resulted in a surplus of wealth and prosperity. In the wake of the popularity of iron, use of copper became restricted. It was now used in the production of punchmarked and cast coins and also for manufacturing antimony rods, toys, rings, and beads.

INDUSTRY OF PRECIOUS METALS

Because of great general prosperity, the industry of precious metals made its mark. The gold-smiths (*suvarṇakāras*) and *maṇikāras* had a flourishing trade. Kumāranandi is mentioned as a rich goldsmith of Champā.[1] Musiyadāraya was another goldsmith (Kalāya) of Teyalipura.[2] Gold was first collected in the form of an ore metal; it was then refined and afterwards used for making ornaments. Both men and women were fond of wearing ornaments. The Buddhist, Jaina and Brahmanical sources reveal that several types of ornaments for different parts of the body were made out of such metals as gold and silver. We find allusions to *Paṭṭikā*, *muddikā* (ring), *vallikā* or *kuṇḍala* (ear-ring), *Keyūra or Graiveyaka* (necklace), *Suvarṇamālā* or *Kāñchanamālā* (golden chain), *Pāmaṅga* (ear-drop), *ovattikā* (bangles) *Hattharana* (bracelet), *mekhalā* (waist-band), etc.[3].

Not only men and women but even elephants and horses were adorned with ornaments. The elephant wore neck-ornaments made of various gems and jewels and an upper garment. The horses were adorned with small mirrors (*thāsaga*) on their waists and chowries.[4] *Mayūrāṅgachū-*

1. *Āva. chū*, p. 397.
2. *Nāyā*. 14.
3. *Chv*, V. 2. 1; *Majjh*, III. 243; GS. I. 232, 236; *Aṅgu*, III. 16; *Jā*. I. 134, II. 122, 273, III. 153, 377; IV. 60, 493; V. 202. 215, 259, 297, 400, 438; VI. 144-45, 217, etc. *Āchā*, II. 2, 1, 11 (SBE, XXII, pp. 123-24); India as known to Pāṇini.
4. *Vtvā*, 2, p. 13.

likās are referred to as ornaments of cows.[1] The *Saṁyutta-Nikāya*[2] and the *Jātakas*[3] inform us that elephants, horses, chariots, etc., were decorated with golden ornaments (*Sovaṇṇālaṅkāra*), golden banners (*Suvaṇṇadhaja*), golden network (*Hemajālapatichihhādana*) and the like.

The kings and nobles used golden bowls in which they ate and drank. The chair, bed-steads, thrones, and royal cars used by kings were inlaid with gold.[4] Golden vases (*bhiṅgāra*) were not unknown. Silver (*rajata*) was used frequently for preparing household utensils.[5]

PEARLS, GEMS AND PRECIOUS STONES

In Jaina literature, we find references to many precious stones, jewels, pearls, conches, corals, rubies,[6] *gomedaya* (zircon), *ruchaka*, *aṅka*, *sphaṭika* (quartz), *lohitāksha*, *marakata* (emerald), *masāragalla*, *bhujagamochaka* (serpentine), *indranīla* (sapphire), *haṁsagarbha* (a variety of rock-crystal), *pulaka*, *saugandhika*, (*a* ruby), *chandraprabhā*, *vaiḍūrya* (cat's eye), *jalakānta* or *chandrakānta* (moon-stone) and *Sūryakānta*[7] (sun-stone). Buddhist literature refers to *muktā* (pearls), *maṇi* (crystal), *beluriya* (beryl), *bhaddaka* (luck-stone), *saṅkha*, *silā*, *pavāla* (coral), *lohitaṅka* (ruby), and *masāragala* which were obtained from the ocean.[8] Most of the jems and precious stones mentioned above were used for making ornaments[9] and inlaid work. The art of skilfully cutting precious stones and giving them various shapes was known. Nanda is mentioned as a rich jeweller of Rāyagiha.[10] *Bhaṇḍāgāra* was known as a treasure-house where no less than sixteen kinds of jewels were preserved.[11] We also hear of ten expert stringers (*muttis*).[12]

1. *Vyā*, 2. p. 13.
2. *Jā*, III. 145.
3. Ibid, 11, 48, 143, IV 404; V. 258-59; VI. 39; 487-8, 510.
4. *Nāyā Ṭī* I. p. 429.
5. Ibid.
6. *Kalpa*, 4. 89.
7. *Uttarā*, 36. 75 f.
8. *Aṅgu*, IV, 255, 258, 262; *Aṅgu*, IV, 199, 203; *Udāna*, V. 5.
9. We come across *maṇikuṇḍala* (Jā, III, 153; IV. 422; VI, 238) *Maṇivalaya* (Jā. III. 377), *Maṇipatimā* (Ja. IV. J).
10. *Nāyā*, 13, p. 141.
11. *Niśī*, *chū* 9. p. 511.
12. *Āva*. *Ṭī*, 947, p. 426a.

IVORY WORK

Ivory work (*dantavāṇijja*) was also a well-known industry, and ivory workers are mentioned among important artisans (*śilpa-ārya*). Some of the cities having separate quarters for the ivory-workers became the centres of this industry. These ivory-workers made bangles, trinkets, and articles of diverse forms.[1] Costly carvings, ornaments, handles for mirrors, and inlaying of royal chariots were made by them.[2] An instrument resembling a saw (*kakacha* or *kharakakacha*) is known to have been used for shaping the ivory pieces.[3] Ivory was obtained from the forests, either from dead elephants or from the living ones.[4] This industry had probably given rise to a class of people whose occupation was to collect elephant tusks from the forests.

GARLAND-MAKING AND PERFUMERY

Garland-making and perfumery were practised because flowers were grown in large quantities. The garland-makers made beautiful garlands and bouquets.[5] Apart from being objects of daily consumption, these garlands were in special demand on the occasion of marriages and festivals. There was a garland-maker named Ajjuṇaya who had a flower garden (*pupphārāma*) in Rāyagiha where flowers of different shades and colours were grown.[6]

The perfumer (*gandhaka*) used to manufacture several kinds of perfumes from various materials. His shop, known as *gandhiyaśālā*, was also common in those times.[7] The *Mahāvagga* refers to sandalwood, *Tagara*, black *Anusāri*, *Kāliya*, and *Bhadramuktaka* which were used for perfuming ointments.[8] The *Nikāyas* refer to scents produced from roots (*Mūlagandha*), *sāra*, flowers (*Papphagandha*), Phegu, Tacha, *Papaṭi*, fruits (*phalagandha*), leaves (*pattagandha*), and juice (*rasagandha*).[9]

1. *Jā*, II. 197
2. Ibid, V. 302; VI. 223.
3. Ibid, I. 321, VI. 261.
4. Ibid, I, 320-21; II. 197. V. 45, 49.
5. *Nāyā* 8. p. 95.
6. *Anta*, 3. p. 31 f.
7. *Vya. Bhā*, 9. 23.
8. *Mv*, VI. 11. 2.
9. *Majjh*, III. 6-7; *Saṁ*, III. 156, 251-2; GS I. 205-6.

Among flowers from which perfumes were produced were *Vassika*, *Mallikā*, lotus and *Piyaṅgu*,[1] *Agara*, *Tagara*, and other flowers were also used for perfuming.

POTTERY

Literary as well as archaeological sources reveal that pottery was in a flourishing condition. The most important ware of this period is North Black Polished Ware. Smoothness and lustre are the characteristics of this pottery. It originated in the Indo-gangetic plains where much has been found in the excavations.

The *Jātakas* tell us that there existed potters' villages where various types of bowls, jars, and vessels of all types were made.[2] Like weavers and blacksmiths, the potters also found favour with the Jaina *Śramaṇas* who frequently took shelter in their shops. Saddālaputta is mentioned as a well-known potter of Polāsapura who owned five hundred shops outside the city, shops where a number of servants were employed.[3] Hālāhalā was another rich potter woman of Śrāvastī in whose shop Gośāla stayed.[4]

The usual way of making wares was this : lumps of clay (*maṭṭiyā*) were kneaded with water and mixed with ashes (*chāra*) and dung (*karisa*); the mixture was placed on a wheel (*chakka*) which was rotated in order to mould the mixture into various vessels. The wet vessels were then dried and baked. Besides these vessels, various types of toys were also produced.[5] This is also confirmed from the finds of terracotta figures of various objects from the archaeological excavations at several sites.

DYEING

From the Jaina and Buddhist sources, it is known that dyeing was the profession of *Rajaka*, both washerman and dyer, who dyed clothes after properly washing them. The *Vinayapiṭaka* informs us that dyed clothes—blue, light yellow, crimson, brown, black, brownish yellow and dark yellow—were prohibited for the monks.[6] This suggests that clothes of these

1. *Majjh.* III. 6; *Saṁ*, III. 156; *Dhp*, 54; *Jā*, VI. 336.
2. *Jā*, III. 368, 376, 385, 508; V. 291.
3. *Uvā*. Ed. by H. F. Hoernle, p. 119.
4. *Bhag*, XV, 539, vol. 658.
5. *Jā*. VI, 6. 12.
6. *Mv*, VIII. 29. 1.

colours were used by the laity. The *Jātakas* mention garments, rugs, and curtains as dyed scarlet, orange, yellow, and red,[1] and umbrellas as red.[2] They also mention various colours such as white (*seta*), dark-blue (*Nīla*), brown (*Piṅgala*), yellow (*Halidda*), golden (*suvaṇṇa*), silvery (*rajatamaya*), red (*Ratta Indagopa*), black (*kāli*), madder-like (*Mañjeṭṭha*),[3] etc. It can be presumed that these colours were utilised for dyeing clothes.

The practice of dyeing clothes presupposes the existence of the industry of dye-making. Dyes were prepared from roots, trunks and barks of trees, leaves, flowers, and fruits.[4] Dyes were first boiled in order to give a fast colour to clothes.[5] Apart from dyeing clothes, dyes were needed for ladies who often painted their hands and feet.[6]

GUMS, DRUGS AND CHEMICALS

There were small industries of gums, drugs, and chemicals, all in a flourishing condition. The *Mahāvagga* mentions seven kinds of gums—*Hiṅgu, Hiṅgulaka, Sipātika, Taka, Takapatti, Takapaṇṇi*, and *Sajjulasa*.[7] Drugs and chemicals were made of various roots,[8] leaves,[9] and fruits.[10] For the mineral industry, acids were also produced.

HUNTERS, FISHERMEN AND FOWLERS

From Jaina and Buddhist literatures, it is known that people earned their livelihood as sheep-butchers, pork-butchers, fowlers, hunters, and fishermen. This indicates that eating flesh was common in those days. This is further confirmed by the discovery of a large number of bones from different archaeological sites.

Hunting (*miyavaha*) is referred to in the *Bhagavatī*;[11] there were regular hunters (*migaluddhaya*) whose occupation was to

1. *Jā*, IV. 258; V. 211.
2. Ibid, VI. 218.
3. Ibid, VI. 279.
4. *Mv*, VIII. 10. 1.
5. Ibid, VIII. 10. 2.
6. *Jā*, III. 183; VI. 218.
7. *Mv* VI. 7.
8. Ibid. VI. 3. 1.
9. Ibid, VI. 5. 1.
10. Ibid, VI. 6. 1.
11. Bhag, I. 8.

daggers, and slaves was disapproved for those who cared for morals.[1] The prices of goods were settled between the producer and merchant by haggling, competition, and custom.[2] There were hawkers[3] who earned their livelihood by retail trading. Local products were consumed in the villages and towns and the surplus, if any, was despatched to trade-centres in different parts of the country.

TRADE AND INDUSTRIAL CENTRES

Many trade and industrial centres of this period are known. Champā was an important industrial centre in those days. The *Nāyādhammakahā*[4] describes the sea-faring merchants of Champā, who loaded their waggons with various goods and proceeded to deep sea-harbours. Jiṇapāliya, Jiṇarakkhiya,[5] Pālita,[6] and Dhana[7] were famous merchants who dealt both in inland and foreign trade. Rājagṛha, Vaiśālī, and Banaras were rich, happy and thriving commercial centres where wealthy merchants resided.

Ujjeṇī was another great centre of trade. During the reign of king Pradyota, nine great stores or emporiums are mentioned in Ujjeṇī, where all sorts of goods, including diamonds, were available.[8] Dhanavasu, a merchant of this place who left for Champā with a caravan, was attacked by robbers.[9] Ayala of this place loaded his boats with goods and journeyed to Pārasaula ; he earned plenty of wealth there and anchored at Beṇṇāyaḍa.[10]

Mathurā was another business centre. People lived here on trade, and there was, curiously enough, no cultivation of land in this town.[11] The merchants from Mathura used to go

1. *Aṅgu*, III, 208.
2. *Jā*, III, 282 f.
3. Ibid, I, 111 f. 205, II. 424; III, 21. 282 f.
4. *Nāyā*, 8, p. 97 ff.
5. Ibid, 9, p. 121 f.
6. *Uttarā*, 21. 2.
7. *Nāyā*, 15. p. 159.
8. *Bṛih. Bhā*, 3, 4220 f.
9. *Āva. Nir*, 1276 f.
10. *Uttara*. Ṭī, 3, p. 64.
11. *Bṛih. Vṛ*, 1. 1239.

to the south on business.[1] Sopāraya is described as another emporium of trade, a centre which was inhabited by five hundred tradesmen.[2] Then there was Suraṭṭha[3] which was joined with Pāṇḍu Mahurā by sea.[4] We hear of horse merchants arriving in Bāravai for trade.[5] Vasantapura was another emporium whence traders used to journey to Champā.[6] We hear of a merchant going from Khilpaṭṭhiya to Vasantapura.[7] Hattisisa was a commercial centre where a number of merchants resided. From here they journeyed to Kāliyadīva where there were rich mines of gold, jewels, and diamonds and which was also noted for horses.[8] A merchant named Pālita of Champā went on business to the town of Pihuṇḍa or Pithuṇḍa a sea-coast town.[9]

COMMODITIES OF INLAND TRADE

With regard to inland trade, all we know is that there were several commodities that were exchanged. The sea-faring merchants of Champā loaded their carts with four kinds of goods, *viz*., that which could be counted (*gaṇima*) such as betelnuts etc., balanced (*dharima*) such as sugar etc., measured (*meya*) such as ghee, rice, etc., and scrutinized (*parichchhejja*) such as cloth, jewel, etc.[10] Gold and ivory were carried from Uttarāpatha to Dakshiṇāpatha for sale. Cloth seems to be an important exchangeable commodity. Mathurā and Vidiśā are mentioned as textile centres.[11] The country of Ganda was

1. *Āva. chū*. 472.
2. *Bṛih. Bhā*. 1. 2506.
3. *Das. chū*, p. 40.
4. *Āva. chū*, II, 197.
5. Ibid, p. 553.
6. *Āva. chū*, II, p. 531.
7. *Āva. Ṭī*, (Hari.), p. 114a.
8. *Nāyā*. 11, p. 201 f.
9. *Uttarā* XXI. See Indian Culture, XIII, p. 20.

   Pithuṇḍa is identified with Khāravela inscription's Pithuḍa and Ptolemy's Pitundrai, Levi locates Pitundra in the interior of Maisolia between the mouths of the two rivers, Maisolos and Manadas, *i.e.*, between the delta of the Godāvarī and Mahānadī nearly at an equal distance from both. It would therefore be convenient to search for its location in the interior of Chikakole and Kalingapatam towards the course of the river Nāgāvatī which also bears the name of Lāṅguliya.

10. *Nāyā*, 8, p. 98
11. *Āva. Ṭī*, (Hari.), p. 307.

famous for silken garments.[1] Textile fabrics coming from the east to the country of Lāṭa were sold at a higher price.[2] Tāmalitti,[3] Malaya,[4] Kāka,[5] Tosali,[6] Sindhu,[7] and Dakshiṇāpatha[8] were famous for various kinds of textile materials. Nepal was noted for fluffy blankets.[9] Woollen blankets were sold at a high price in Mahārāshṭra.[10]

The *Nāyādhammakahā* refers to various kinds of textile fabrics which were loaded in waggons and carried for sale.[11] There was another important commodity that was exchanged in those days. Kāliyapīva was known for beautiful horses, and it had mines of silver, gold, jewels, and diamonds [12] Another name celebrated for horses[13] is Kamboja. Uttarāpatha was famous for thorough-bred horses.[14] Dīlavāliyā was noted for mules.[15] Puṇḍra was known for black cows,[16] Bheraṇḍa for sugarcane,[17] and Mahāhimavanta for *gosīsa* sandal.

TRADE ROUTES AND TRANSPORT

There was a network of routes not only connecting the important cities and towns through roads and water-ways within the country but also leading to foreign lands. Rājagṛha, Vaiśālī, Śrāvastī, Vārāṇasī, and Champā were the important towns of Eastern India. From the account of the journeys made by Mahāvīra and the Buddha, we know about the routes connecting these towns. These cities had trade

1. *Āchā. Ṭī.* II, 5, p. 361a.
2. *Bṛih. Bhā.* Vṛ. 3, 3884.
3. *Uvā*, 7. 32.
4. *Anu*, 37, p. 30.
5. *Niśī. Chū*, 7, p. 461.
6. Ibid.
7. *Āchā. Chū*, p. 364; *Āchā.* Ṭī. II, 1, p. 361a.
8. *Āchā. Chū*; 363,
9. *Bṛih*; *Vṛ*. 3. 3824.
10. Ibid, 3. 3914.
11. *Nāyā*. 17, p. 203.
12. Ibid. p. 202 ff.
13. *Uttarā* 4, 11. 16.
14. *Das. chū*, 6. p. 213.
15. *Tanḍula Ṭī*, p. 269,
16. *Jīvā*, 3. p, 355.
17. *Uttarā*, *Ṭī*, 18, 2529.

transactions through land routes with distant lands like Gandhāra, Kamboja, Sind and Kashmir. Not only merchants but also warriors and saints traversed these routes.

There were several minor routes in Eastern India connecting towns and cities. As Rāagṛha was the capital of Magadha at this time, it was connected with Kapilavastu, Śrāvastī, Mithilā, Champā, and Kaliṅga by separate routes as is apparent from Buddhist literature. From the itinerary of Mahāvīra also, it seems that Rājagṛha was linked separately with Kuṇḍagrāma, Ālabhiyā, Śrāvastī, Vaiśālī, and Champā.[1] Besides, there were three distant routes which started from Rājagṛha to far off places.

RĀJGṚHA-PUSHKALĀVATĪ ROUTE OR THE UTTARĀPATHA

This route connected Rājagṛha with Takshaśilā and Pushkalāvatī which were great trade centres of North-west India. Takshaśilā became an international trade centre because it is through this place that India established trade relations with the West. This route has been referred to as *Uttarāpatha* by Pāṇini[2] and was known to the Greeks as 'Northern Route'. It seems to have passed through Pāṭaliputra, Vārāṇasī, Kauśāmbī, Mathurā, Indraprastha, and Sākala. From Pushkalāvatī, it probably branched off to Kashmir to the North-East and to Bactria to the North-West. It is only by this route that students from various parts of Eastern India, such as Rājagṛiha,[3] Vaiśālī, Mithila,[4] and Vārāṇasī, used to go to Takshaśilā, the famous seat of learning.

RĀJAGṚIHA-PRATISHṬHĀNA ROUTE

According to Pāṇini, this route was known as *Kāntārapatha*[5] because it passed through a forest region. It is the same as the above route (Kājagṛiha-Pushkalāvatī) upto Kauśāmbī, from where it passed through Vansahvaya, Vedisa, Gonaddha, Ujjeni, Mahissati, and then *Patiṭṭhāna*.[6] Caravans going to

1. Based on the authority of the Kalpa.
2. *Pā*. V. 1. 77.
3. *Darimukha Jā*, No. 378; *Nigrodha Jā*, No. 445.
4. *Suruchi Jā*, No. 489; *Vinīlaka Jā*. No. 160.
5. Agrawala : India as known to Pāṇini, p. 242.
6. *Su. Ni.* V 1. 36.

Bharukachchha passed through this route up to Māhishmatī from where they had to branch off to Bharukachchha.

RĀJAGṚIHA-SINDHU REGION ROUTE

This route led westward to Sind, the home of horses and asses, and to Sauvīra and its ports, with its capital called Roruka. Up to Mathurā, this western route was the same as the Rājagṛha-Pushkalāvatī route, but there it branched off to the Sindhu region. It passed through the desert of Rajasthan.

MEANS OF CONVEYANCE

For inland trade through roads, the chief modes of conveyance were carts drawn by oxen, horse· carriages, litters and sedan chairs. The merchant Ānanda had five hundred carts for distant traffic and the same number for local use. While the rich rode on elephants, the ordinary people employed camels, horses, and asses.

THE CARAVANS

Keeping in view the difficulties met with by the traveller on these land routes, merchants used to travel in a caravan. After loading their carts and animals with goods, these merchants started their long journey with their captain called *Satthavāha*, who gave them directions regarding halts, inns, routes, fords, and danger-spots. The *Jātakas*[1] inform us that the caravan had to face five major difficulties and dangers—robbers, wild beasts, draught, demons, and famine. The *Sattavāhas* had to have ample and proper equipment for a safe journey. The journey through the desert was hard as well as interesting. The guide, who led the caravan through the desert, was known as the *Thalaniyāmaka*[2] (desert pilot). Equipped with his knowledge of the stars, he led the caravan in the right direction. The *Āvaśyakachūrṇi*[3] gives an account of how a caravan suffered in passing through the desert due to scarcity

1. *Jā* I. 99.
2. Ibid, 107.
3. *Āva, Chū*, 553; II. 34.

of water. The *Vinaya* texts also refer to caravan going from Rājgṛiha to the west.[1]

RIVER TRANSPORT

Besides land routes, there were also river routes. The great rivers, such as Gaṅgā, Yamunā, Sarayū, Śoṇa, Gaṇḍakī, Kosi, and others, served the purpose of communication and transport. The famous riverports Champā, Pāṭaliputra, Vārāṇasī, and Kośāmbī were connected by waterways. These waterports were connected with trade centres on the land. Sometimes, the river routes were more convenient and less costly, and safer and quicker than roads. Because of these river routes, there must have been brisk inland trade. Ships, big boats, and small sailing boats were used for the purpose of navigation. Sometimes heavy objects such as pillars and logs were transported from one place to another.

OVERSEA TRADE

From the literary sources of this period, it is clear that Indians were carrying on brisk oversea trade. The *Theragāthā* speaks of merchants sailing on sea with the hope of earning wealth.[2] The *Jātaka* stories tell us of several shipwrecks,[3] specious ships[4] ship-building activities,[5] and of seafarers sailing to different countries for trade. The *Nāyādhmmakahā* gives a beautiful description of a sea voyage. Arhannaga and other merchants of Champā loaded their boats with merchandise and proceeded on their journey. There is a description of a shipwreck caused by a terrible cyclone.[6] The *Baudhāyana-Dharma-sūtra*[7] shows that navigation was peculiar to Brāhmaṇas of the North. The mention of various terms associated with navigation leaves no doubt about the practice of travelling far and wide during this period.[8]

1. *Sutta-Vibhaṅga*, SBE, XIII, 15.
2. *Theragā*, 530.
3. *Jā*, II. 111, 127-29; V. 75; *Jā*. No. 196.
4. Ibid, Nos. 446, 539.
5. Ibid, IV, 159; VI. 427.
6. *Nāyā*, 1. 8 p. 97 ff; 17, p. 201.
7. *Bau. Dh.* S, I. 1. 20.
8. AGARAWALA : India as known to Pāṇini, pp. 155- 156.

The *Jātakas* inform us that traders from the river-ports on the Gaṅgā went to the eastern lands across the sea. The *Saṅkha Jātaka* describes the journey of the Brāhamaṇa Sankha from Vārāṇasī to Suvarṇabhūmi (Burma and portions of Indo-Chinese Peninsula).[1] There are references to voyages from Champā to Suvarṇabhūmi. Prince Mahājanaka is said to have travelled in a ship with approximately 350 men and reached there.[2] Traders from Vaiśālī also seem to have been going to Suvarṇabhūmi and other places for trade. The *Vālahassa Jātaka* speaks of trade between Vārāṇasī and Tāmbapaṇṇidīpa.[3] It seems that these traders of Vārāṇasī, Champā, and Vaiśālī sailed to eastern lands with their ships carrying locally manufactured goods. Though only Suvarṇabhūmi and Tāmbapaṇṇidīpa are mentioned, it can be assumed that trade was carried on with many other islands of the East Indies. The *Mahāniddesa* tells us that India's trade to the East existed with Kālamukha, Suvaṇṇabhūmi, Vesuṅga, Verāpatha, Takkola, Tāmali, Tāmbapaṇṇi, and Jāvā. The first two of these places can be identified with Arakan coast and lower Burma. The next two correspond to Ptolemy's Besyngeitai, Barbai, and Takkala.[4] Tāmali has been identified by SYLVAIN LEVI with Tāmraliṅga in the Malaya Peninsula. The *Apadāna* states that traders from Malaya and China visited India.[5]

There is archaeological and literary evidence for a maritime trade between India and the western countries during this period. A beam of Indian cedar in the palace of Nebuchadnezzar (604-562 B.C.) at Birs Nimrud has been found. In the second storey of the temple of the Moon-god at Ur, rebuilt by Nebuchadnezzar and Nabonidus, TAYLOR found two rough logs of wood, apparently teak imported into Babylonia from India.[6] The *Baveru-Jātaka*[7] relates the adventures of certain Indian marchants who took the first peacock

1. *Jā.* IV, 15-17.
2. *Mahājanaka Jā*, (No. 539).
3. *Jā*, II. 127-29.
4. R.C. MAJUMDAR : Suvarṇadvīpa, p. 57.
5. *Apadāna*. I. p. 2.
6. A History of Indian Shipping.
7. *Jā*, III. 126.

by sea to Babylon. J. KENNEDY[1], who worked on this subject concluded that maritime commerce between India and Babylon flourished in the seventh and sixth centuries B.C., especially in the 6th century. B.C. Writing on India's ancient trade, Jackson has observed that the Buddhist *Jātakas* and some of the Sanskrit law-books too tell us that ships from Bhroach and Sopārā traded with Babylon from the eighth to the sixth century B.C.[2]

The *Suppāraka Jātaka*[3] says that a band of travellers sailed from the port of Bharukachchha and passed through six seas, under the leadership of a skilled mariner. The seas, thus mentioned, are Khuramāla, Aggimāla, Dadhimāla, Nīlakusamāla, Nalamāla, and Balabhāmukha. These seas have been identified with the Persian gulf, the Arabian coast, Nubia on the North-East corner of Africa, the canal joining the Red sea and the Mediterranean, the Mediterranean and some portion of the Mediterranean. If this identification is correct it can be established that Indians possessed the knowledge of a sea-route from the West coast to the Mediterranean.[4]

In the *Dīgha Nikāya*, there is an explicit reference to ships sailing out of sight of land. Certain Indian commodities, e.g., rice, peacocks and sandal-wood, were known to the Greeks and others with their Indian names in the fifth century B.C. It follows that they were imported from the west coast of India into Babylon directly by sea.[5]

India's trade relations with Persia during this period are known. Ayala is said to have loaded his boats (*Vāhaṇa*) with goods and journeyed from Ujjeṇī to Pārasaula (Persia); he earned plenty of wealth there and anchored at Beṇṇāyaḍa. Persia was used to export various commodities, such as *Śaṅkha*, *phopphala*, *chandana*, *agaru*, *mañjiṭṭha*, silver, gold, jems, pearls, and corals.[6] Trade relations between India and Persia were normal because Gandhāra (Northern Punjab) became a part

1. JRAS 1898.
2. A History or Indian Shipping, p. 90. Quoted by R.K. MOOKERJI.
3. *Jā*, IV. 138-143.
4. JBORS, VI, 195.
5. A History of Indian Shipping, p, 88.
6. *Uttarā*. Ṭī, 3, p. 64.

of the dominions of the Persian emperors in the sixth or fifth century B.C., and the Indians paid tribute in gold to them. Herodotus also refers to the Indian contingent of Xerxes' army clad in cotton garments and armed with cane bows and iron-tipped cane arrows.

The description in the Ceylonese chronicles[1] of prince Vijaya's voyage to Ceylon from Bengal with his 700 followers presupposes a regular sea trade and commercial intercourse. We read of traders coasting round India from Bharukachchha on the west to Suvarṇabhūmi and touching on the way at a port in Ceylon.[2] It is said that the sea-going merchants halted at Siṁhala dīva (Ceylon) in the middle of their journey.[3]

The head of the mariners (*Niyāmakas*) was known as *Niyāmakajeṭhaka*. He was probably the captain, the owner of the ship, and the leader of travellers voyaging with him. It was his great responsibility to pilot the ship efficiently and unerringly.

The merchants, who returned to their country with valuables, sometimes practised fraud in order to avoid payment of royal taxes. The *Rāyapaseṇiya* refers to those who traded in *aṅka* jewel, conch-shells or ivory, and to those who, instead of taking the regular highway, always chose the most difficult routes in order to evade taxes.[4] We hear of the king of Beṇṇāyaḍa who detected the trick of a deceitful merchant and had him arrested.[5]

The chief articles of export from India were spices, perfumes, medicinal herbs, pigments, pearls, precious stones like diamond, sapphire, turquoise, and lapis lazuli, iron, steel, copper, sandalwood, animal skins, cotton cloth, silk yarn, muslin, indigo, ivory, procelain, and tortoise-shell. The principal imports were cloth, linen, perfumes, medicinal herbs, glass, tin, lead, pigments, precious stones, and coral.

Progress in the sphere of trade and commerce is reflected in the general economic condition of the people. We have several references to very rich merchant-millionaires of those

1. *Dipavaṁsa*. IX, 10-28; *Mahāvaṁsa*, VI.
2. *The Age of Imperial Unity*, p. 602.
3. *Āchā*. Ṭī, 6. 3, p. 223a.
4. *Rāya*, 164.
5. *Uttarā*. Ṭī, op. cit.

days in literature. One of them, Anāthapiṇḍika, is said to have purchased the Jetavana park for the Buddha by covering the whole surface of it with gold coins. Ānanda from Vāṇijag-rāma, Kāmadeva from Champā, Sūradeva from Banaras, Sardalaputra from Polāsapura, and Mahasataka from Rāja-gṛiha were famous wealthy merchants who became followers of Mahāvīra. The wealth of the middle classes appears from their dress, ornaments, houses, and furniture. There is no reference to extreme poverty or to paupers as a class. On the whole, people lived happily in peace and prosperity.

ORGANIZATION OF TRADE AND INDUSTRIES

The most remarkable feature of the economic life during this period was that trade and industries were organized for the first time into guilds known as *Śreṇis*. These *Śreṇis* were the corporations of the people belonging to the same or different castes but following the same trade and industry. These guilds were autonomous bodies and their members managed their own affairs. There was little interference by the state in the affairs of the guild.

The Brahmanical, Buddhist, and Jaina sources make references to guilds. The *Gautama Dharma Sūtra*[1] mentions the guilds of cultivators, traders, herdsmen, and artisans. The *Jātakas*[2] refer to eighteen guilds which, though a conventional number, show the extensive character of the organisation. There are various branches of trade and industry which, together, considerably exceed the number eighteen. The guilds of woodworkers, the smiths, the leather-dressers, and the painters are specifically mentioned.[3] In Jaina literary works, the guilds of goldsmiths,[4] painters,[5] and washermen[6] are mentioned, and about the rest, we do not know much.

ORGANIZATION AND CONSTITUTION

The *Jātakas* throw some light on the organization and constitution of these guilds. These guilds were, to begin with,

1. *Gau. Dh.* S, XI,
2. *Jā*, VI. 22, 427; *Jā*, I. 267. 214; IV. 43, 411.
3. *Jā*, I., 314; III, 281; IV. 411; VI. 22.
4. *Nāyā*, p. 105.
5. Ibid, p. 107.
6. *Āva. chū*, II. p. 182.

well organized under their respective chiefs called *Pamukha* or *Jeṭṭhaka*, an officer who was something like an alderman or a president. Among such craft-guild chiefs, the names of *Baḍḍhakijeṭṭhaka*[1], *Mālākārajeṭṭhaka*[2], and *Kumārajeṭṭhaka*[3] are important. These chiefs might be important Ministers in attendance upon and in favour with the king. In the *Sūchi Jātaka*,[4] there is a description of *Kumārajeṭṭhaka*, a favourite of the king's.

There were also merchant-guilds under the chiefs called *Seṭṭhis*. Because of wealth, they got special status in society. They visited the royal court as representatives of the business community. One such chief was Anāthapiṇḍika, who was the *Mahāseṭṭhī*, the president of a commercial federation, with numerous *Anuseṭṭhīs* under him.[5] Different guilds also federated under a common president, called *Bhāṇḍāgārika*, to check their internal disunion. Such a *Bhāṇḍāgārika* was acting in the city of Banaras.[6] He was expected to be conversant with the affairs of trade and business and with the working of the guilds.

These guilds were gradually converted into hereditary castes on the basis of occupation. In ordinary times, the sons pursued their paternal occupation. Besides, these guilds became localized in particular areas. They gave impetus to specialization and efficiency of labour. Villages inhabited almost exclusively by one type of craftsmen came into existence. There are references to the villages of smiths, potters, carpenters, saltmakers, etc. Even in towns, there was provision for separate quarters and suburbs for the members of each guild.

The guilds were autonomous bodies having their own laws. The corporate existence of the guild was recognized by the state.[7] Guilds exercised considerable control over the

1. *Āva. Chū*, IV. 161; IV, 332.
2. Ibid, III. 405.
3. Ibid, III. 281.
4. Ibid.
5. Ibid, I. 93; *Jā*. V, 384.
6. Ibid, IV. 43; II. 12. 52.
7. *Jā*, III. 281.

members.[1] Probably the settlement of disputes among its members and the solution of the problems of trade and business fell under the jurisdiction of the guild. It could also settle the disputes between wives and husbands.[2] That guild organizations were well-disciplined and maintained solidarity is suggested by a *Jātaka* story which describes the shifting of 100 families of carpenters overnight.[3]

A guild worked for the welfare of its members, and it had a right to approach the king and demand justice. A painter was ordered to be executed by prince Malladinna; the guild of the painters visited the king, explained the matter, and requested him to quash the sentence passed against the member of its union. The king was pleased to commute the sentence into banishment.[4] Then we hear of a washermen's guild approching the king in order to demand justice.[5]

Some of the guilds probably carried on banking business too. In cities like Rājagṛiha, Śrāvastī, Vaiśālī and others, where brisk trade and business were carried on, the guilds of Śreshṭhins might have been functioning as banking institutions. They accepted money from others on interest and invested it in trade or lent it on interest to smaller tradesmen.

Some of these guilds might have issued coins. The earliest coins known as the punchmarked coins started in about the seventh or sixth century B.C. It is probable that some of them might have been issued by these guilds even in the sixth century B.C., because it seems, there was no state monopoly of manufacturing and of issuing coins. That Takshaśilā merchant guilds minted coins is almost certain in the light of the evidence yielded by Negama coins.[6]

The members of these guilds sometimes carried on their business in partnership. Some *Jātakas*, such as *Kūṭavaṇika Jātaka*[7], *Bāveru Jātaka*,[8] and *Mahāvaṇija Jātaka*,[9] describe

1 *Jā*, I. 267; IV. 411.
2. *Gau. Dh.* S, XI. 22-23.
3. *Majjh*, I. 286.
4. *Nāyā*, 8 p. 107.
5. *Āva. Chū*, II, p, 182.
6. A Cunningham; Coins of Ancient India.
7. *Jā*, I. p 404 also II, 181.
8. Ibid, III. p. 126.
9 Ibid IV. p. 350,

business partnership of merchants. This enabled the smaller traders to transact business on a fairly large scale. Such an undertaking was much useful for the land-trader (*Sātthavāhas*) transacting business under a *Jeṭṭhaka*.[1] Tho traders of Sāvatthi became partners and went to the west with a large caravan. Similar may have been the case with traders of Rājagṛha, Vaiśālī, Pāṭalīputra, and other centres of trade. The partners divided their earnings either equally or in proportion to their investments, or as agreed upon among themselves.

The exact nature of the relations between the guilds and the state is not known. The king used to recognise the guild laws and also consulted with the guilds on matters of mutual interest. There was probably a permanent representative of the guild at the royal court or in the Ministry. The *Uruga Jātaka*[2] tells as that two of the guild leaders were included among the Kosala *Mahāmātras*. A blacksmith is called *Rājaballabha* in one of the *Jātakas*, which suggests his close association with the royal court. In some of the stories, kings are described as summoning all the guilds (*Sabbaseṇiyo*) on certain occasions. Probably the Seṭṭhi visited the royal court as a representative of the business community, and the same may have been the case with the heads of the guilds.

COINAGE

The most remarkable feature of this period is the introduction of regular coins in business transaction. The ancient system of barter and of reckoning values by cows or by grains was gradually replaced by coinage. Before the beginning of the regular currency, there were ingots of gold and other metals of calculated weight. We find transition from this stage to that of the coin proper, *i.e.*, a piece of metal of recognized weight and fineness guaranteed by the stamp of authority.

The coins in use during this period are known as punchmarked coins and cast coins. The punchmarked coins were punched by a number of symbols successively by different punches. Sometimes the symbols overlapped one another and sometimes they were but partly accommodated on the flan.

1. *Jā*, II. 294.
2. Ibid, I, No. 154.

Insofar as the cast coins were concerned, the symbols were already carefully arranged and engraved on the die before they were struck on the bank.

Punchmarked coins were known at the time of their issue as *Kārshāpaṇas*—a term by which they are referred to in the *Tripiṭaka*, the *Jātaka*, and the *Ashṭādhyāyī* of Pāṇini, some of the *Dharmasūtras*[1] and Jaina canonical literature.[2]

Several hoards of punchmarked coins have been found throughout India, some of them containing even pre-Mauryan currency, The larger Bhir Mound[3] hoard of puchmarked coins at Taxila found in the second stratum contained two coins of Alexander the great and one of Philip Ariadeus which were in the mint condition, besides 1055 silver punch-marked coins. The stratification of this hoard and the mint condition of the coins of the two Greek rulers show that the hoard was buried not much later than 317 B.C. As some of these punchmarked coins of this hoard were old, blurred and indistinct, it may be assumed that they were used at least about two centuries earlier. The Paila hoard[4] contained about 1245 coins. These coins belong to very early times. They were probably the currency of Pañchāla before the rise of the Mauryan empire. The Golakhpur[5] hoard of 108 coins and the Ramna hoard[6] of 48 coins have been assigned to the pre-Mauryan age by G.H.C. WALSH. 709 out of 2873 coins of the Patraha hoard[7] and about one-third of the Machhuatoli hoard[8] fall under the category of pre-Mauryan currency. Early punchmarked coins have been found at Rājagṛiha.[9]

An analysis of the punchmarked coins found in different hoards helps us in postulating some rough tests to determine

1. *Gau. Dh.* S, XII. 6-8, 19; *Vas. Dh.* S, V. XIX, 21.
2. *Uttarā,* 20. 42. Also see CHARANDAS CHATTERJEE's article on some Numismatic data in Pāli literature, Buddhistic Studies, pp. 383 ff.
3. WALSH, Memoir No. 59 of the 'ASI.
4. JNSI, II; N. S. No. XLVII of JASB.
5. JBROS, 1919, pp. 16-72.
6. Ibid, 1939.
7. Memoir No. 62 of the ASI, 1940.
8. JBORS, 1939, pp. 91-117.
9. J. Ar—A Review, 1961-62.

the chronology of some of these coins. It may be presumed that the larger and thinner punchmarked coins belong as a general rule to an earlier date than the smaller and thicker ones. D.D. Kosambi has shown that generally the number of reverse marks on the early coins increases with their age while their weight decreases correspondingly.

A six-armed symbol with three arrow heads and three ovals was found on the coins in the Golakhpur hoard. It has therefore been suggested with great probability that this particular variety of the six-armed symbol belongs to the pre-Mauryan age. On the coins of the Bhir Mound hoard, we find the symbols of the Sun, the six arms, a hill above a tank with two fish, and a peculiar symbol surrounded with five taurineess. The coins with these symbols were current just before the foundation of the Mauryan empire. Coins having a hare on a hill and a bull on a hill were widely current in northern India on the eve of the Mauryan empire, and may have been issued by the kings of the time of Bimbisāra and some by the rulers of the Nanda dynasty.

The number of symbols on the obverse is generally five. On some coins, there is a sixth symbol, but it probably represents an authentication mark punched later; 19 coins in the Bhir Mound hoard (1924) had a sixth mark. One coin in the Patrāha hoard had also a sixth mark. There are also some coins having four symbols. Such for instance is the case with thc coins of the Paila hoard. The bent bar coins have only two symbols along with a third one which may have been added later. The obverse symbols on ardha-*Kārshāpaṇas* and pāda-*Kārshāpaṇas* were naturally fewer. The tiny *māshaka* pieces could with difficulty accommodate only one symbol.

The reverse side, which was originally blank, began to be punched haphazardly at different times with a number of symbols. On the coins of the later period, their number is reduced to one or two, and they seem to have been impressed on a definite plan and probably at one time. The symbols on the reverse are generally smaller in size than those on the obverse. Some of them are square, some rectangular, some oblong, some polygonal, some elliptical, and some circular. Some coins have become cupshaped owing to the punching of a number of symbols on their thin flans. Some are of the shape of a bent bar.

The punchmarked coins are usually found in silver and copper. Silver pieces are more numerous than the copper ones. Gold *Kārshāpaṇas* may also have been issued like the silver and copper ones. Their non-discovery is not a decisive argument against their existence.

The vast majority of the silver punchmarked coins follow the standard of 16 *māshakas* of 32 *ratis*. The average weight of well-preserved punchmarked coins is approximately 56 grains. In ancient Kośala, we have found a number of punchmarked coins weighing only about 42 to 43 grains. It is, therefore, clear that ancient Kośala was following lighter-weight standard of 12 *māshakas* or about 42 grains. The province of Gandhāra was issuing silver punchmarked coins known at present as Bent-bar coins and probably called *Āyatākāra Kārshāpaṇas* in ancient times. The largest denomination coins of this series weigh about 175 grains. This weight is equal to that of 100 *ratis* or double *sigloi* of the Achaemenian standard.

Dvi-Kārshāpaṇas of this weight standard are also found. Large Kośala coins, which weigh about 79 or 80 grains, are most probably *dvi-Kārshāpaṇa* pieces of the 12 *māshaka* standard. *Ardha-Kārshāpaṇas* are frequently referred to in the *Tripiṭakas*, the *Jātakas*, and in the grammatical works. Quarter *Kārshāpaṇas* were often known as *pādas*. The *chaturmāshaka*, *Trimāshaka*, *Dvi-māshaka*, *Eka-māshaka*, *Ardha-māshaka*, and *Kākaṇikā* were also known. To carry on daily transactions, currency of small denominations was also issued.

THE SYMBOLS ON THE PUNCHMARKED COINS

The reverse marks on the earlier coins occur haphazardly. Usually, the more worn out a coin is the larger is the number of its reverse marks. The principal marks on the obverse appeared not haphazardly, but they had a definite significance. The most common symbols are the Sun and six arms. It is quite possible that this Sun symbol had a mythological significance. Solar dynasties were ruling at Ayodhyā and in Videha. It is, therefore, not improbable that the Sun symbol was originally intended to denote the Solar origin of the dynasty of the issuer, and when once it had become popular, it may have been mechanically copied on the coinage of other dynasties as well. This is also the tone of the coins bearing an elephant and a bull as symbols.

The symbols had probably some conventional, local or religious significance. The bull may denote Vatsa dynasty of Kośāmbī. The hill and tank marks in their different varieties may be different places or region marks.

On most of the punchmarked coins, there are five symbols on the obverse which have occasioned a number of conjectures to explain them. Two of these symbols, the Sun and the six-armed symbol, are constant and do not carry much significance. Durga Prasad had suggested that the third symbol probably changed with the king, the fourth with the year, and the fifth with the locality. According to D.D. Kosambi, they may refer to the names of the ruling king, his father, and his grandfather. It is equally possible that one of the symbols may have stood for the Governor, the other for the mint master and the third for the place or province of issue.

D.D. Kosambi has also suggested that the symbol of the hill may denote descent. Thus the peacock and the elephant on the hill would denote descent of the dynasty of the issuer from the peacock or elephant or gods, having them as their mounts. G.H.C. Walsh has suggested that all coins having elephants upon them may be taken to have been issued by kings as distinguished from those issued by *Saṁghas*. Elephants are almost universally associated with royalty.

PRICES

In early Buddhist literature, we find the prices of every vendible commodity mentioned, prices of a dead mouse too as well as fees, pensions, fines, loans, stored treasures and incomes stated in figures of a certain coin or its fractions.[1] In most cases, prices given are fantastic and fabulous. Only a few references may be regarded as mentioning the actual market-price of certain commodities. It appears that articles of food were cheap. According to the *Vinaya* texts, a small quantity

1. For details of prices, see JRAS, 1901, pp. 882 f.

of ghee or oil could be bought for a *Kahāpaṇa* only.[1] Meat for a chameleon could be bought for a *Kākiṇī* or an *Addha-Māsaka*,[2] and a fish cost only seven *Māshakas*[3]. A jar of liquor was available for one *Māshaka*.[4] It is further said that a *Māshaka* was sufficient for an ordinary wage-earner to buy a garland, perfume, and some strong drink.[5]

Animals of inferior quality were cheap while those of superior quality were costly. A thoroughbred horse cost 1,000 *Kahāpaṇas*[6] a donkey only eight *Kahāpaṇas*[7] a pair of oxen 24 *Kahāpaṇas*[8], a nice plump dog one *Kahāpaṇa*, and a cloak[9] and a dead mouse only one *Kākiṇī*[10]. As far as the price of land is concerned, a monastic cell (*vihāra*) could be purchased for 500 *Kahāpaṇas*.[11] A play-hall for 600 boys constructed by voluntary labour is estimated to have cost 1,000 *Kahāpaṇas*.[12] We are told that a partridge could be bought for one *Kāhāvaṇa*[13] and a cow for fifty coins ;[14] the price of a blanket varied from 18 *rūpakas* to a hundred thousand *rūpakas*.[15]

There are numerous references that show how prices were determined by haggling.[16] The act of exchange between the producer and dealer during this period was a free bargain, a transaction unregulated by any system of statute-fixed prices.[17] There was no authority which could fix prices and force the traders to sell at the rate fixed. No doubt, there was an official of the state known as the court-valuer (*Agghakāraka*,

1. *Vinaya*, IV. 248-50.
2. *Jā*, VI. 346.
3. Ibid, II. 424.
4. Ibid, I. 350.
5. Ibid, III. 446.
6. Ibid, II. 306.
7. Ibid, VI, 343.
8. Ibid, VI, 343.
9. Ibid, II. 247.
10. Ibid, I. 120.
11. *Majjh*, (No. 52) I. 553.
12. *Jā*, VI. 332.
13. *Das. chū*, p. 58.
14. *Āva. chū*, p. 117.
15. *Bṛh, Bhā*, 3. 3890.
16. *Jā*, I. 111-13, 195; II, 289. 424-55; III, 126-27; VI, 113.
17. JRAS, 1901, p. 874.

Agghāpanaka, Agghāpanika)[1] whose duty was to fix prices of the articles bought for the royal household, but he was not concernd with the whole society.

FEES AND SALARIES

Like prices, we find generally exaggerated statements about fees and salaries, but a few references do appear to be authentic. Thus the *Mahāvagga* tells us that a courtesan's fee for one night was 50 to 100 Kahāpaṇas.[2] A teacher's honorarium for the whole course was probably 1,000 silver *Kahāpaṇa*.[3] A labourer earned only 1½ *Māshaka* daily according to a *Jātaka* story.[4] There are references to show that the earning of the labourer was not sufficient enough to ensure him a happy life, and that he lived in stark penury and misery.[5]

LOANS AND INTEREST

Loans and debts could be taken on interest. There was a money-lender Ānanda of Vāṇijyagāma.[6] Money lending was looked upon as an honest calling. Letters of credit as substitutes for money were known. It is noteworthy that the *Gautamadharmasūtra*[7] prescribes a limit to the interest chargeable by the creditor. The lawful limit is 1¼% per month or 15% per year. The interest cannot exceed the principal howsoever long the debt may remain unpaid.[8]

WEIGHTS AND MEASURES

Because of the repid progress in the sphere of trade and commerce, weights and measures were properly maintained. Pāṇini[9] mentions them as *Āḍhaka, Achita, Patra, Droṇa*, and *Prastha*. According to the *Vasishṭha Dharmasūtra*[10], right measurement is necessary and the king should arrange for it. False weights and measures were considered to be crimes. According

1. *Jā*, I. 124.
2. *Mv*, VIII. 1. p. 1-3.
3. *Jā*, II 47; 278; IV. 38; V. 128.
4. Ibid, III. 326.
5. Ibid, 1. 475; *Jā*, III. 446.
6. Uvā, I, p. 6.
7. *Gau. Dh.* S, XII. 26.
8. Ibid, XII. 28.
9. *Pā*, 5, 4-102; 5. 1. 53.
10. *Vas. Dh.* S, 19. 23,

to Āpastamba,[1] if any one uses wrong measure, he should not be invited to a *Śrāddha*. The Buddha says that if a person earns money by weighing less, he is a liar.[2] In the *Mahānārada Kassapajātaka*,[3] there is a reference to a Weighing House. Weights made of steatite and jasper of different denominations discovered in excavations at Eran, Vaiśālī and Chirand also prove that commodities were weighed and sold.

1. *Ap. Dh.* S. 2.6.19.
2. *Dīgha*, 8. 3. 48. Vol, 3, p. 136.
3. *Jā*, Vol. VI, p. 119.

CHAPTER IX

ART AND ARCHITECTURE

It is somehow difficult to give a detailed account of art and architecture during the age of Lord Mahāvīra, primarily because no sufficient specimen are surviving. It is not unlikely that being made of perishable materials like wood, they have vanished. It is also likely that some of them might still be lying buried under the soil. The noteworthy feature of this period is the revival of urb an life and coming into existence of a number of towns, the remains of some of which have been excavated. Along with the urban life, several new arts and crafts started. This period is noteworthy also for the introduction of a new fabric in pottery known as the North Black Polished Ware. Many a literary work throws abundant light on the art and architecture of this period.

ARCHITECTURE

1. *Secular Architecture*

(a) *Town architecture*

Even before Lord Mahāvīra, there were towns and cities during the period of the Indus Valley civilization. The traces of such towns have been discovered at Mohenjodāro, Harappā, Rūpar, Ālamgirpur, Sarasvatī Valley in Rajasthan, Lothal, and Raṅgpur. Vedic literature offers evidence of the existence of such towns as Āsandīvant,[1] Kāmpīla,[2] Ayodhyā,[3] and Kaūśāmbī.[4] The word *Pura* denoting rampart, fort, or stronghold

1. Vedic Index, Vol. I, p. 72.
2. *Taitt. Saṁ*, VII. 4. 9; *Maitra. Saṁ*. III. 12. 20.
3. *Ait. Br*, VII. 3. 1.
4. *Śat. Br*, XII. 2. 2. 13; *Gop: Br*. 1. 2. 24; *Śat. Br*, VIII. 14.

frequently occurs in Vedic literature.[1] Deities like *Indra* and *Agni* are involved in destroying enemy's forts,[2] many of which were wide and broad and had ramparts of mud or unbaked bricks, probably also a stone facing.[3] The word *Dehī*, referring to defences or ramparts of hardened earth with palisades and a ditch, occurs in the *Ṛigveda*[4]. A passage in the *Śatapatha Brāhmaṇa* shows that the moat or ditch was also known in the period of this Brāhmaṇa.[5]

Archaeological excavations reveal that in about 1025 B.C, Kauśāmbī developed as a town fully equipped for its protection by the magnificent defences built on the Harappan pattern. The discovery of Harappan site at Ālamgirpur (District Meerut, U.P.) has established definite evidence of the penetration of the Harappan culture into the Gaṅgā-Yamunā Doab. Similarly the fortification of Kauśāmbī built after the Harappan pattern is obvious. A rampart of mud with sloping sides revetted with a burnt brick wall, battered back to about 30° to 40°, of which the coarses are laid in the so-called English bond, leaving footings in successive courses, reinforced by bastions and towers, square in plan, are elements of construction strongly reminiscent of the Harappan citadel. The defences, built on this model, continued for some time, and they also made use of a curved entrance, enclosing an underground passage built on corbelled arch. In about 885 B.C., the concept of defence was revolutionized by the construction of a moat round the rampart, a feature not yet recorded from any Harappan city.[6]

Literary works of the days of Lord Mahāvīra contain the names of the principal cities of India. Some Jaina canonical works[7] refer to ten capital cities of India—Rāyagiha, Champā, Mahurā, Vārāṇasī, Sāvatthi, Sākeya, Kampilla, Kośāmbī, Mihilā, and Hatthināura. The Buddhist canon[8] testifies to the

1. *RV*. I. 53. 7; I. 131. 4; III. 15. 4; *Ait. Br*, IV. 6. 23; *Śat. Br.* III. 4. 4 3; V. 3. 3. 24.
2. *RV*. I. 89. 2.
3. Ibid. II. 35. 6.
4. Ibid. VI. 47. 2; VII. 6. 5; Vedic Index, Vol. I. pp. 379, 539.
5. *Śat.* Br, VII, 1. I. 13.
6. The excavations at Kauśāmbī. p. 41.
7. *Thā*, 10. 718; *Niśī. Sū*, 9. 19.
8. *Mahāparinibbāna Sutta* (SBE. XI), 99.

existence in India of populous cities with large buildings long before the time of the Buddha. Pāṇini[1] refers to some important towns of his time: Kāpiśī, Takshaśilā, Hastināpura, Śāṁkāśya and Kāśī. T.W. Rhys Davids gives a list of the principal cities existing in India in the seventh century B.C.: Ayojjha, Baranasi (Benares), Champa, Kampilla, Kosambi, Madhura, Mithila, Rajagaha, Roruka, the capital of Sauvīra, Sagala, Saseva, Savatthi, Ujjeni, and Vesali.[2]

The existence of these cities shows progress in the art of town-planning (*Nagara-māpana*) and architecture (*Vāstuvidyā*). From different literary sources of this period, it is known that a well laid-out city was equipped with a multitude of buildings, both for its defence and for the practical needs of residence and business. The fortification consisted of moat, parapet wall, and gateways, while the civil architecture had its residential buildings, business quarters (*Āpaṇa*), intersected by streets (*Saṁchara*), royal store-houses (*Koshṭhāgāra* and *Bhāṇḍāgāra*), king's council-hall (*Rājasabhā*), and a number of other buildings comprised under the general term *Śālā*, *e.g.*, places of dramatic performance, dancing, music, concerts and sports.

It is known from Jaina canonical literature that the city of Champā was solidly built and hard to enter. Its moat (*Phalihā*) was broad on top and cut deep down; it had discs (*Chakka*), clubs (*Gaya*), maces (*Musuṇḍhī*), barriers (*Graha*), war-machines (*Sayagghi*), and double doors (*Jamalakavāḍa*); it was surrounded by a wall (*Pāgāra*) bent in a curve like a bow, and decorated with cornices (*Kavisīsa*) arranged in circles; its bastions (*Aṭṭālaya*), rampart paths (*Chariya*), door-ways (*Dāra*), gates (*Gopura*), and arches (*Toraṇa*) were lofty, its high roads (*Rāyamagga*) duly divided; its gate bars (*Phaliha*) and bolts (*Indakīla*) were strong and fashioned by skilful artificers.[3]

It is said that Mahāgovinda planned the city of Rājagṛiha and several other capitals of Northern India and that he also designed palaces.[4] The city of Vaiśālī was surrounded by

1. *India as known to Pāṇini*, p. 137.
2. RBI, p. 21.
3. *Ovā*. 1; also *Uttarā*, 9. 18-24.
4. *Vimānavatthu* commentary, p. 82.

three walls at a distance of a *Gāvuta* from one another, each provided with gates and watch towers.[1] It was rich in a variety of buildings, *chaityas*, and palaces of its 7707 chiefs.[2] There were beautiful parks, gardens, and lotus ponds. The city has also been described as 'opulent, prosperous and populous.'[3] It looked 'like the loka of Śakra' in the magnificence of its appearance and the happiness of its inmates who had continual festivities.[4] The city comprised three districts.[5] The first district had 7,000 houses with golden towers; the middle one had 14,000 houses with silver towers, and the last district possessed 21,000 houses with copper towers. These houses were under the possession of the upper, the middle and the lower classes, according to their positions.[6] Jaina traditions inform us that *Kshatriyas, Brāhmaṇas, and vaṇiks* occupied their respective *Upanagaras* in Vaiśālī.[7]

The existence of some of these cities in the sixth century B.C. is confirmed even by the archaeological evidence. The planning of the city of Girivraja[8] or Rājagṛiha[9] in the sixth century B.C. was the work of a genius. It is surrounded on all sides by hills and its surviving city walls and fortification still show the architectural standard reached during that period. These city walls were built in cyclopaean fashion, of massive unheaven blocks of stone pierced by gateways, each flanked on either side by a semi-circular bastion, over which probably rose the watch-tower, an almost invariable feature of these fortress cities. The fortification hitherto believed to be built of rubble is supposed to have been founded by Ajātaśatru. Originally, there was a mud rampart. The top of this rampart was hardened by yellowish mud and brick-

1. *Jā*, Vol. I. No. 149.
2. Ibid, p. 316. According to the *Mahāvagga*, there were 7707 pinnacled buildings.
3. LEFMANN : *Lalitavistāra*, Chap. III, p. 21.
4. W. W. ROCKHILL : *The Life of the Buddha*, p. 63.
5. Ibid, p. 62.
6. Ibid, p. 62.
7. Vaiśālī Excavations, 1905, p. 1.
8. Girivraja or the city of hills is said in the *Mahābhārata* to belong to the Bārhadrathas in which time Jarāsandha was a great ruler.
9. The new Rājagṛiha was founded by Bimbisāra.

bats. Associated with it was a moat, the full width and depth of which has not been so far determined. The original rubble fortification wall was strengthened gradually by brick wall in course of time.[1]

At Rajghat[2] near varanasi, an enormous clay rampart dating back to the first quarter of the first millennium B.C. has been discovered. Built directly over the natural soil and available to a height of about 10 metres, the rampart has a pronounced slope towards the river. It has been breached several times by heavy floods, but it was in existence in 600 B.C. That a large urban population existed at Mathura in the sixth century B.C. is proved by the vast Katra mound. Furthermore, an exploratory survey revealed the existence of two rings of mud-ramparts—the first elliptical in shape and the second quadrangular and comprised within, the first, as if signifying a citadel.[3] From the excavations at Śrāvastī, it is clear that there was habitation in the sixth century B.C. and the mud rampart was erected in the fourth century B.C.[4]

At Eran,[5] a moat and a mud-defence wall built in the late phase of the chalcolithic occupation have been discovered. They continued even during the sixth century B.C.

The excavations at Ujjain[6] reveal a continuity of occupation on the site from a date prior to 600 B.C. The massive rampart with a moat can be traced back to the earliest period of occupation on the site, which coincides with the Pradyota period. This type of fortification was of mud and belonged to a citadel, but the humbler habitations were situated undefended in the outside area. The rampart enclosed an area approximately two kilometers with a basal width of a little over two hundred feet and a maximum extent height of forty-two feet. The contours of the area occupied by the rampart show several openings of varying dimensions, suggesting gateways. The rampart was built by the dumping of

1. I. Ar.—A review 1961-62.
2. Ibid, 1960-61, p. 37.
3. Ibid, 1954-55, p. 15.
4. Ibid, 1958-59, p. 47.
5. Ibid, 1963-64, p. 15.
6. Ibid, 1956-57, p. 20; 1957-58, p. 32,

dug-up yellow and black clays to form a thick wall, with a gentle slope on the inner side and a less pronounced on the interior.

The rampart was surrounded on the west, and distantly on the north, by the river Siprā, while a moat on the eastern side, formed to be filled with greenish water-borne silt, added to it a line of defence in that direction, and presumably on the south side as well, completing the circuit of a water-barrier. The moat was found to have been at least eighty feet wide and twenty-two feet deep. The fortification on the riverside was breached by floods on at least three occasions during this period but it was repaired from time to time.

(b) *Building Architecture.*

The actual remains of the buildings of this period are few because of the frail or perishable nature of the material used. In order to get information on the building activity during this period, we must depend upon literary works, both Jaina and Buddhist, some of which have preserved a record of traditional forms as current in memory and folk-lore. Sometimes the description given of these buildings in these literary works is exaggerated, but still after critical examination and sifting the evidence, we can infer some of the general features of art during this period. These literary works mention a number of architectural terms and various forms of particular structures which show the extensive development of this science in those days. The main types of building found in those days were royal buildings, lofty mansions for rich and well-to-do people, houses of the ordinary people, huts of the poor, and religious buildings.

The palaces were known as *Pāsāda* and *Vimāna* to distinguish them from ordinary dwellings. In the Jaina *Āgama* literature, the most illustrative example of palace architecture occurs in the *Rāyapaseniya Sutta*[1] in an account of the *Vimāna* of Sūryābha Deva. It was surrounded on all sides by a rampart, and embellished with beautiful cornices. There were gates with cupola opening on all sides. Gates, pillars and doors were decorated with various kinds of figures and motifs.

1. *Rāya.* Sū, 97 f.

There is also a description of a big theatre hall (*Pekkhā-ghara-maṇḍava*) which was supported on many columns and was furnished with a terraced railing, gateways with architrave and *Śālabhañjikā* figures. It was decorated with many other motifs and ornamental figures. At the centre of the theatre hall was a stage.[1]

In the *Nāyādhamma Kahā*[2] is a description of the bed-chamber of a queen which had an outer courtyard, an assembly hall polished and well set with pillars, endowed with statues (*Śāla-bhañjiyā*), latticed windows, moon-stone at the foot of the stairways, projecting ledges, and a room upon the roof called *Chandra-śālikā*. Its interior was lined with paintings; the floor was inlaid with semi-precious stones and the ceiling had a canopy painted with designs of lotus flowers and creepers.

In a description of the palace of the *Chakravartī* king Mahā-Sudassana, some details of palace architecture are found. Its height was equal to three *Purusha* measures, it had bricks of four kinds, pillars 84,000 in number, wooden planks of four colours, staircases, cross-bars, copings, rooms with beds of gold, silver, ivory and crystal; doors with palm trees on two sides, a double railing round the palace, a net work of jingling bells and several lotus-ponds provided with staircases and platforms.[3]

A Jātaka[4] gives a vivid account of the palace of the *Mahā-Ummagga*. It had big dimensions worthy of a royal palace. There were gateways in the palace wall, one of which opened towards the city. On both sides of the long corridor of the palace were one hundred niches for lamps closed and opened by mechanically operated shutters. It was provided with hundreds of rooms. In each room was laid a great couch overhung with a white parasol and a throne placed near the couch. The principal hall of this palace was decorated with ten motifs of divine character. There were also courtyards, one of which was known as the Assembly Hall. The pillars and walls were decorated with a number of painted motifs.

1. *Rāya. Sū*, 100, p. 164.
2. P. L. Vaidya's edition, para 208.
3. *Mahā-Sudassana* Sutta, Dīgha Nikāya.
4. *Jā*, IV. p. 431.

At Nālandā, Lepa who was a rich householder, had a beautiful bathing hall called *Śeshadravyā* containing many hundreds of pillars.[1]

From the description of different royal palaces in literary works, it is possible to form an idea of the general architectural features of these palaces. The royal palace was constructed at the centre of the capital town along with other royal buildings. The palace was divided into courts of which there were usually three in the early stages. The first court had a *Dvārakoṭṭha* leading to open grounds for stables for horses and elephants and also barracks for soldiers. In the second court on the ground floor was the great pillard hall which was used for public audience of the king.

The royal palace had two distinct parts, the ground floor and the upper floor. On the ground floor were located the palace garden, kitchen, bath-rooms with fountains of flowing water, wells, step-wells, lotus-ponds, temple, etc. The upper floor was meant for the members of the royal family. There were stairways going up into or coming down from a palace. The king's own chamber was known as *Sirigabbha*. A separate building was provided for the crownprince, and it was spoken of as *Upaṭhāna* and located in a portion of the king's palace. The quarters meant for the queens, princesses and other ladies were collectively called *Antepurikā*, and they were properly guarded. The palace was surrounded by an outer wall (*Prākāra*), having a main gate or perhaps four gates. The outer gate-house lay at some distance from the actual palace, and sometimes the guests were received at the outer gate. The pillars and walls of the palace were overlaid with many beautiful motifs.

The palace had one or more storeys, but a building of three storeys was more common. Sometimes each storey of the palace consisted of a number of rooms known as *Kūṭāgāras* with a peaked top, usually a pavilion with a gabled end and vaulted room bearing small *Stūpīs* over it. The *Kūṭāgāra* room was provided with a latticed window or screen, and a ventilator. It could be closed from inside by drawing

1. SBE, XLV, p. 420.

across the doorleaves, a transverse bar, and also from outside by locking.

Different kinds of palaces (*Kokanāda Pushpaka* etc.) are mentioned as having different forms. Some were constructed with only one pillar (*Ekathunakam*)[1] and such buildings were of the shape of round towers'. Palaces with many columns were not unknown.[2] In one *Jātaka*, there is a mention of a palace with a thousand columns.[3] Palaces were surrounded by various kinds of wall having gateways. Verandah or porticoes were attached to buildings and were called *Alindaka*. The term *Uparipāsādatala*, or the upper storey of a palace with a roof surmounted by a pinnacle called *Kannika* is an indication of the development that took place in the science and art of architecture. Many-storeyed palaces with many pinnacles are also mentioned in some of the tales.

There were lofty mansions for rich and well-to-do people, costly buildings with a large number of rooms and halls. The walls and pillars were profusely decorated, and the houses were provided with all kinds of comfort and luxury.

The *Vinaya Texts*[4] gives us an idea of the common dwelling houses, which were made of stone, brick or wood, and had roof of five kinds—brick, stone, cement, straw and leaves. The walls and roof were plastered from within and without. The sleeping rooms were whitewashed, the floors were coloured in black, and the walls in red. They were overlaid with paintings and engravings such as human figures, and motifs such as wreaths and creepers. Provision was made for windows with shutters and curtains, elaborate doors with key-holes, verandahs covered terraces, inner verandahs and overhanging caves, dwelling rooms, retiring rooms, store-rooms, closets, and wells with lids under sheds made of hide-skin. Hygienic arrangements were kept in view while constructing privies. The house had sometimes two or more storeys, and it was fashionable to have verandahs supported on pillars with capitals in the form of heads of animals.

1. *Jā*. Nos 121, 451 and 465.
2. Ibid, No 465
3. Ibid, No. 543.
4. Sixth *Khandhaka*.

Generally, the bulk of the people at this time lived in flimsy huts, often thatched with leaves and grass and having walls made of reed or wood. This does not mean that sturdier structures of wood, brick and stone were unknown. In order to assure greater stability, wood was used for constructing posts, walls, doors, and also for laying foundations of the huts. One *Jātaka*[1] describes a *Pannaśālā* (a thatched hut) in which trunks of fig wood were used to construct, and obviously to strengthen, its foundation. Its walls, however, were made of interwoven reeds.

There were also cellars and big underground tunnels. The description of an *Ummaga* or an underground tunnel which a certain person, named Mahosadha, had constructed in order to elude the pursuit of his enemies is an instance which shows that underground structures were also not unknown in those days. The entrance of the great tunnel was provided with a door eighteen cubits high, fitted with a mechanical device so that it could be manipulated by pressing a peg. On either side, the tunnel was built up with bricks and worked with stucco ; it was roofed over with planks, smeared with cement and whitened.[2]

There were different types of public building. The *Svayaṁvara* halls rested on hundred columns and were embellished with sportive *Śālabhañjikā* statues.[3] We also come across references to *Uvaṭṭhāṇasālā*[4] (attendance hall), *Posahasālā*[5] (Fasting hall), *Kūḍāgārasālā*[6] (pinnacled hall) and square tanks[7] (*Pokkhariṇī*). There were also *Aṭṭaṇasālā* (hall for gymnastic exercises), *Majjaṇaghara* (bathing house) and *Nhāṇamaṇḍapa*[8] (bath room).[9]

2. *Religious Architecture*

Some literary sources refer to *Devakulikas* or *Chaityas*, the worship of which was very popular during the time of

1. *Jā*, No. 489.
2. Ibid, No. 546.
3. *Nāyā*, pp. 179-82.
4. *Kalpa*, 4 61 f.
5. *Nāyā*, I, p. 19.
6. *Rāya*, 94. p. 150.
7. *Nāyā* 13, p. 142 f
8. Hot-air baths are described in the *Chullavagga*.
9. Kalpa. 4. 61 f.

Lord Mahāvīra. A *Chaitya* or *Devakulikā* was some sort of sacred enclosure containing a garden, grove or park and a shrine. Mahāvīra, Buddha and many other religious ascetics are represented as halting or resting in these shrines. From the *Uvāsaga-dasāo*, it is known that Mahāvīra visited the shrine of Pūrṇabhadra at Champā, the shrine called Dvipalāśa of Vaṇijagrāma, the Koshṭhaka shrine of Bāraṇasī, the garden called Saṅkhavana of Ālabhī, the garden called Sahasrāmravana of Kāmpilyapura, Sahasrāmravana of Polāsapura, the shrine called Gunasila of Rājagṛiha and the Koshṭhaka shrine of Rājagṛiha.

In the *Mahāparinibbānasutta*,[1] Buddha spoke of the efficiency of erecting *dhātu-chaityas*, and he himself visited *Chaityas* like Udena, Gotama and Sattambaka of Vaiśālī while the *Dīghanikāya* bears testimony to the fact that the Buddha lived at the Ānanda-Chaitya in Bhojanagara. In the *Āśvalāyana Gṛihya Sūtra*, we find for the first time the mention of a *Chaitya* sacrifice. Whether the reference to the *Chaitya* by Āśvalāyana is a reference to the Vedic *Chaitya* or *Yajñasthāna* or to something else is, of course, a matter of dispute.

Some of these shrines had the form of a temple equipped with doors, hall, etc. We hear of a shrine (*Deuliyā*) about the size of a man's hand and built of one block of stone.[2] The images were of wood. There was a hall (*Sabhā*) attached to the shrine which was besmeared with cow-dung. We hear of the Puṇṇabhadda shrine of Champā which was decorated with umbrella, standards, bells, flags, peacock-feather whisk and railing; the interior floor was coated with cow-dung and the walls white-washed; it bore palm impressions in red *Gosīsa* or *Dardara* sandal-wood; it was beautified with *Chandana kalaśas* and on the doors were erected *Toraṇas* with *Chandanaghaṭa* decorations. The floor was sprinkled with perfumed water and garlands were hung, and it was fragrant with flowers of five colours, *Kālāguru*, *Kundurukka* and *Turukka*; it was haunted by actors, dancers, rope-walkers, wrestlers, boxers, jesters ballad-singers, story-tellers, pole-dancers, picture-showmen, pipers,

1. Chap. III. Secs. 36-47 and especially 47.
2. *Uttarā. Ṭī* 9, p. 142.

flute-players and minstrels. Many people came to worship at this shrine.[1]

The evidence of early structures of *stūpas* is available in the archaeological remains discovered at some places. At a village Lauria Nandangarh in Champaran District of Bihar, three rows of earthen barrows or huge conical mounds of earth have been discovered. These were identified by A. CUNNINGHAM as sepulchral mounds, and they belonged too 600 B.C. or earlier. Their character as burial mounds, seems to be supported by the wooden post found in the centre of one of them known as lofty *Chaitya-yūpa*. Two of the mounds are formed of whitish clay. T. BLOCH actually found a *repousse* gold plaque depicting the earth goddess in the characteristic pose of the ancient Mother-Goddess figurines, also depicted on ancient small rectangular metallic pieces from Rajgir.

The remains of a very early *stūpa* have been discovered at Piprahwa (District Basti) on the Nepal border, 16 km from Kapilvastu. The *stūpa*, 116 feet in diameter at the base and 21.5 feet in height at present, was built in brick (16″/11″/3″) as a solid cupola, with excellent masonry, well and truly laid, containing a great sandstone coffer, made out of a huge monolith with a lid fixed by clamps having perfect edges which confirm a high standard of craftsmanship. According to an inscription, the *stūpa* was built by the Śākyas, relatives of Buddha, to enshrine a part of his original relics. The stone box contained, in a casket, not only some scraps of bone as relics but several hundreds of other articles of high artistic value, *e.g.* ornamental forms, flowers and leaves wrought in various semi-precious stones as carnelion, amythist, topaz, garnet, coral, crystal, shell and metal and gold, all in exquisite designs. They included a square gold leaf stamped with a lion, gold leaf stars, dedicately carved miniature leaves of crystal and other substances, *Tri-ratna* gold leaf cross, a coil of fine silver wire, *Svastika* stamped on gold leaf, taurine symbols stamped on gold leaf, small pearls, beads of beryl; topaz etc. a small bird in red-carnellion carved with great skill, an elephant in gold leaf; a figure of the Earth-

1. *Ovā*, 2.

Goddess stamped on gold foil closely resembling Earth-Goddess from Lauriā Nandangarh; another standing female figure heavily draped, having an elaborate fan-like coiffure, marked by some auspicious symbols fixed in the hair. A remarkable decorative design is found on a large disc of gold leaf, consisting of rows of whorls with six wavy arms going round a centre, an intricate form of *Āvarta*, covering the whole field in a symmetrical way of forming an intricate *Vyūha*.

Amongst other relics are pots, covered bowls, round relic-caskets, including one made of cut and polished crystal with a lid beautified on the top of a fish-design, most minutely worked and highly polished, which gives an indication of the extremely fine workmanship of the lapidarists, who lived and worked in the sixth or fifth century B.C.

The Jaina stūpa of Mathurā is known to be the work of the gods, from the inscription of the second century A.D.[1] It was probably, therefore, erected several centuries before the Christian era. Jinaprabhasūri, an author of the fourteenth century, has preserved the legend of the foundation and repair of this 'stūpa built by the gods' in his work *Tīrthakalpa*[2] which is based on ancient materials. This account confirms the belief that the original *stūpa*, a small one, was a mound of earth which concealed a miniature *stūpa* of gold and gems. Later on, it was encased by larger *stūpas* of bricks and stones. Some scholars ascribe the original one to the third century B.C. while others go as far back as to the sixth century B.C. If the ascription of the original stūpa to the sixth century B.C. is right, it would be the oldest known specimen of religious architecture.

MATERIAL

As very few structures of so early a period are surviving, a fair idea of the materials used may also be formed from

1. V. A. Smith: The Jain *Stūpa* and other Antiquities of Mathura, p. 12.
2. According to this work, the *Stūpa* was originally of gold, adorned with precious stones, and was erected in honour of the seventh Jina, Supārśvanātha; by Kuberā Yakshī at the desire of two ascetics named Dharmaruchi and Dharmaghosha. During the time of the twentythird Jina, Pārśvanātha, the golden stūpa was encased in bricks, and a stone temple was built outside. The Sanctuary was restored in honour of Pārśvanātha by Bappa Bhaṭṭasūri, thirteen hundred years after the Lord Vīra had reached perfection.

these literary works. The material employed in constructing even ordinary dwelling houses was wood. References to bricks, both burnt and unburnt, are found. Rhys Davids is of opinion that in earlier times "the superstructure of all dwellings was either of wood-work or brick-work."[1] The *Vinaya Piṭaka*, compiled not long after the *Parinirvāṇa* of Buddha, makes mention of Buddha's permission that his disciples might use bricks in the basement of their halls, stairs and roofings of palaces.[2]

The use of stone for architectural purpose during this period is a controversial matter. Scholars generally believe that stone was not used in Indian architecture before the third century B.C. as no definite archaeological evidence is now available in this connection. Rhys Davids[3] notices that "in the books referring to this earlier period, there is no mention of stone except for pillars or staircases. A palace of stone is only once mentioned and that is in a fairy land. This palace of stone has been referred to in connection with a *Jātaka* story".[4]

This view does not seem to be reasonable. There are some literary references to a few stone buildings which may safely be accepted as reliable evidence of the fact that the ancient Indians knew how to use stone in architecture even in the sixth century B.C. Direct references to the use of stone may be found in the *Jātakas* also. We read of bases of pillars like mortars of stone[5], thrones of yellow marble,[6] hill forts or *Giridurga*,[7] stone cutters and stone pillars.[8] In the *Vinaya* rules, the Buddha allowed his disciples to make use of stone not only in the basements of their halls, stairs, flooring and walls but also in the roofing of their houses.[9] This literary evidence proves the existence of stone buildings in the sixth

1. RBI. p. 68.
2. *Chv*, V. 11. 6; VI.; 3.11.
3. RBI, p. 68.
4. *Jā*, No. 545.
5. Ibid. No. 514.
6. Ibid. 519.
7. Ibid 516.
8. Ibid, 476.
9. *Chv*. VI. 3. 11.

century B.C. *Jarāsandha-ki-Bāiṭhaka* at Rājagṛiha, the approximate date of which was the sixth century B.C., if not earlier, and which was built wholly of blocks of stone neatly fitted together without mortar supplies an instructive archaeological proof. Structures of this kind must have been few and far between in the earliest times because wood was generally used for building purpose. This may account for the rarity of stone-building in that age.

During this period, there was a tendency to bid good bye to the age-old building materials like mud and mud-bricks, but a complete switch-over to the more durable material—*i.e.* burnt bricks, had not been made. It seems that the use of the kiln bricks was largely confined to the structures of public utility. The perplexing discovery of 250 ft. long wall at Rupar,[1] probably an enclosure of a big edifice, a barn and chain from Hastināpura and remains of tank and well at Ujjain testify to this fact. Structures made of mud and mud-bricks still persisted, and they are found at Nagda, Atranjikherā, Hastināpura, Mathurā and Rājghāṭ. While at Ujjain and Awra, the use of dressed stones with mud for building purposes is also noticed. Small hearths of bamboo and reed have been discovered at Chandraketugarh[2] and Mathura.[3] The discovery of terracotta ring-wells, soakage jars at close intervals, brick and pottery drain[4] in the habitual areas reflect, in a way, the high civic sense and sanitation arrangements.

PAINTING

We have no extant specimen of painting because walls, pillars and roofs made of wood and bricks used for purpose of decoration perished in course of time. But it is clear from both the earliest Jaina and Buddhist canonical literature that painting, both secular and religious, was considered an important form of artistic expression and was widely practised by the classes and masses alike. A number of motifs illustrating

1. I. Ar. A Review, 1953-54, p. 6.
2. Ibid, 1959-60, p. 50.
3. Ibid, 1954-55, p. 15
4. Ibid. 1959-60, p. 60.

scenes from heavenly life, mythical beliefs and Nature are found mentioned.

The *Saṁyukta Nikāya* refers to a method of preparing pigments, and the *Chullavagga* refers to a kind of plaster on which colours were to be painted. In the *Chullavagga*[1], Buddha is further said to have instructed his disciples on the rules of building and painting on their walls. In some Jaina literary works,[2] the painters are mentioned along with brushes and colours ; first they divided the wall surface and then prepared the surface. There were painters who were adepts in their profession. One painter is mentioned who could portray the complete figure of bipeds (*duvaya*), quadrupeds (*Chauppaya*) and objects without feet (Apaya) even if he saw a part of their body. Pictures were drawn on walls as well as on panels.

Portrait-painting was very much in vogue. According to the *Vinaya Piṭaka*, Āmrapālī invited painters from various countries and asked them to paint on her walls the figures of kings, traders and merchants seen by them; and it was by seeing the portrait of Bimbisāra so painted that she fell in love with him. We are told that a *Parivvāiyā* painted the portrait of the princess Sujeṭṭhā on a board and showed it to king Seṇiya who fell in love with her. Similarly, prince Sagarachanda became enamoured of Kamalamālā when her portrait was shown to him.

The patronage given to painting by kings and wealthy persons during this period is clear from the mention of picture-galleries. The *Vinaya Piṭaka* also makes several references to the pleasure-houses of king Prasenajit, containing *Chittāgāras* or picture-halls or galleries. One such picture-gallery was built by a banker of Rājagiha in the forest adjoining the city which was decorated with wooden (*Kaṭṭha-kamma*), earthen (*Pottakamma*) and plaster decoration (*Leppa*), wreaths (*ganthima*), images (*Vaḍhima*), and dolls (*purima*) which were stuffed and made of cloth (*Saṅghāim*).[3] We are

1. *Chv*, VI. 3. 11.
2. *Nāyā* 8, p. 106 f; Uttarā 35. 4.
3. *Nāyā*, 13. p. 142.

told that in the picture-gallery of prince Malladina, the pictures were imbued with coquettish sentiments and feelings (*Hāvabhāva*), the play of the eyes (Vilāsa) and amorous gestures (*Bibboya*).[1] Jiyasattu is mentioned as another king who owned a picture-gallery. We are told that when the construction of this gallery was in progress, a painter's daughter formed the design of a peacock feather in the mosaic floor. The king, under a false impression of its being natural, was tempted to pick it up but in this attempt, the nails of his fingers scraped against the floor, and he hurt his hand.[2] Dummuha is mentioned as still another king to have a picture-gallery.[3]

Besides portraiture and mural paintings, we also find mention of such widely-known practices as *Lepya-chitras*, *Lekhya-chitras*, *Dhūli-chitras*, etc. *Lepya-chitras* are nothing but continuous narratives in lines and colour on textiles, and partook of the nature of *paṭa-chitras* of later tradition. *Lekhya-chitras* are probably line-drawings of a decorative nature like *Ālimpanas* or *Ālpanās* of later tradition, while *Dhūli-chitras* are also of the same nature and character, but the material used is powdered rice, white or coloured.

Trees, mountains, rivers, seas, houses, creepers, full vessel and *Sovatthiya* etc. were painted. The *Rāyapasaniya Sutta*[4] describes that the *Vimāna* of Sūryābha Deva was decorated with many kinds of figures and motifs (*Bhatti-chitra*), *e.g.* fabulous animals (*Īhāmiga*), bulls (*Usabha*), horses (*Turaya*), Yakshas or Atlantes figures (*Nara*), crocodiles (*Magara*), birds (*Vihaga*), serpents or dragons (*Vālaga*), Kinnaras (*Centaurs*), deer (*Ruru*), Śarabha (lion-like figures), Yak (*Chamara*), elephants (*Kuñjara*), wild creepers (*Vanalayā*) and lotus-creepers (*Paumalayā*). Some of these figures as listed in Jaina texts are almost the same as we find elsewhere, from the stone railings and gateways of Bharhut and Sāñchī painting to pre-existing wooden prototypes.

An interesting list of motifs illustrating scenes from

1. *Nāyā*. 8, p, 106 ff
2. *Uttarā*, *Ṭī*, 9, p. 141.
3. Ibid, p. 135.
4. *Rāya. Sū* 97 f.

heavenly life and mythical beliefs on the walls of the Great Hall of the Mahā-Ummaga palace is also given :[1]

1. *SAKKA-VILĀSA* : Scenes of Indra enjoying dance and music with his heavenly nymphs in Sudharmā Assembly Hall.

2. *SINERU-PARIBHAṆḌA* : The beautiful designs on the vertical faces of the terraces round the mountain Sumeru.

3. *SĀGARA-MAHĀ-SĀGARA* : Small and big ponds with lotus and other flowers and a number of watery birds and aquatic animals.

4. *CHATU-MAHĀDVĪPA* : The four continents which faced the four cardinal points of Sumeru.

5. *HIMAVANTA* : The great Himālaya mountain shown with its Kailāsa peak, especially Lake *Mānasarovara* or *Anavatapta* with the four great rivers flowing in the four directions.

6. *ANOTATTA* : This was the same as *Mānasarovara*, the ideal holy lake described in Jaina, Buddhist, and Brahmanical literatures, as the holy lake of Brahmā. The *Saptarshis*, gods and other divine beings, take their bath in the *Anotatta* in which the Buddha also is said to have taken his bath.

7. *MANO-SILĀTALA* : The great throne made of red stone which was placed near a pond or in the main Assembly Hall of the palace for the king to sit and rest.

8. *CHANDA-SŪRIYA* : The motif of the Moon and the Sun who were drawn as gods in human form or in natural form.

9. *CHĀTUM-MAHĀRĀJIKA* : The four Mahārājika Gods with their courtly attendants, *viz.*, Vaiśravaṇa, king of Yakshas in the north ; Dhṛitrāshṭra, king of Gandharvas in the east ; Virūḍhaka, king of the Kumbhāṇḍas in the south; and Virūpāksha, king of the Nāgas in the West.

10. *CHHA-KĀMA-SAGGA* : *i.e.* the six heavens of sensuous pleasures, popularly conceived as abodes of happiness and longevity, same as *Kāmāvachara Deva-loka*.

1. *Mahā Ummaga Jā*, VI, 432.

Some paintings of this period seem to have been preserved in rock shelters discovered at Mahadeo Hills round Pachmarhi, Singhanpur and Kabra Pahar, Bhim Baiṭhaka, near Bhopal, Mori in District Mandsor, Likhunia, Kohbar, Mehraria, Bhaldaria and Bijaigarh in Mirzapur area, and Manikpur in Banda District. The paintings both of prehistoric and historic periods have been found. During the historic period, the cultural scene changed from that of primitive hunters to that of well-armed warriors and mounted horsemen in the battle field where archers and swordmen are engaged in fierce action. Armed cattle raiders are also seen. Besides, the home life of the people is also depicted, *e.g.* a man playing on a harp; a woman pounding roots and grinding grain; huts with women inside; men and women dancing in groups and pairs; men playing drums and a double pipe, entertained by a performing monkey and a dancing bear. Cattle and birds of various kinds, including geese and peacocks and also pigs and dogs, are represented—virtually a cross-section of the life of the people. In Mahadeo Hills, near Pachmarhi, we find bun hair-dressing, loin-cloth ending in a tail between the legs, bows and quivers, straight swords, leaf-shaped daggers and round shields. There are a few mythological figures as well—a heroic personage in a *vimāna* or sky-chariot and a giant leading a tiger with a rope as if he were a pet dog. Another subject shows a male person resisting a lion or tiger on one side and a wild bull on the other while the cattle thus protected are moving below. Cave paintings at Manikpur show mounted archers and a person seated in a wheelless bullock cart. The Mori rock paintings depict animals, dancing human figures, and pastoral scenes.

SCULPTURES

Even before the time of Lord Mahāvīra, there were traces of image-worship. The Indus-valley civilization revealed innumerable sculptures in terra-cotta, stone, and bronze. Image-worship must have existed in the Vedic period among the lower stratum of society, even if not among the followers of the *Vedas*. The custom of image-worship was definitely in vogue in India in the later Vedic period.[1] The *Maitrāyaṇi-Saṁhitā*, while referring to the names of several gods and goddesses, also describes the iconographic features of some of them. Thus the names *Karaṭa Hastimukha* and *Chaturmukha Padmāsana* of Gaṇeśa and Brahmā respectively indicate the iconography of those deities. Similarly, the *Taittirīya Āraṇyaka* refers to the traits of some of the gods such as *Vakratuṇḍa-danti i.e.* Gaṇeśa), *Mahāsena Shaṇmukha* (Kārttikeya), Suvarṇa-paksha Garuḍa. Vajranakha-Tīkshṇadaṁshṭra-Narasiṁha. The *Mahānārāyaṇa Upanishad*[2] further elaborates iconography of some of these gods who were, according to J.N. BANERJEE, mostly folk-gods absorbed in the Vedic society. The iconographic traits of the folk-gods, such as Yakshas, also arose in the later Vedic age.

The earliest materials for constructing images seem to have been wood. The *Vyavahāra Bhāshya* refers to the sage Vārattaka whose wooden figure was built and worshipped by his son.[3] We also hear of images made of plaster, ivory, and stone.[4] During the time of Mahāvīra, the worship of Yakshas was popular. Both Mahāvīra and the Buddha are known to have stayed in these Yaksha temples.

The images of these Yakshas were made of wood. Jaina traditions tell us that Pradyota, the king of Ujjain, installed the *Jivanta Svāmī* (life-time) images of Mahāvīra at Ujjain, Daśapura, and Vidiśā.[5] The *Jātaka* stories refer to the statues of Indra (Sakka)[6]. One *Jātaka*[7] story refers to a boy "as lovely as Brahmā" which indicates the beauty of the image of Brahmā of that period. The Siri-kālakanni *Jātaka*[8] offers a description of the goddess Kālakanni which may be regarded as containing the iconographic features of a prototype of the goddess Kāli in her dreadful form.

1. J. N. BANERJEA : The Development of Hindu Iconography, pp 576-78.
2. Vya. Bhā IV. 1-18.
3. Ibid, 2. 11.
4. *Bṛh. Bhā* 1. 2469.
5. *Jaina Tīrtha Sarva Saṁgraha*, p. 322.
6. *Jā*. No. 541.
7. Ibid, No. 118.
8. Ibid, No. 382.

In the *Sūtra* period, we find definite references to icons. The iconographic features of many gods seem to have been fixed in this period. The *Baudhāyana Gṛihyasūtra* refers to Jyeshṭhā; the Āpastamba to Īśāna Mīḍhuṣī and Jayanta; the Pāraskara to Īśāna, Mīḍhuṣī, Jayanta, Śrī., Dhanapati, Bhadrakālī, Kshetrapāla, etc. Pāṇini's Grammar also contains reference to images.[1] The *Āśvalāyana Gṛihyasūtra* Pariśishṭa[2] describes the inconography of many Vedic and Puranic gods.

TERRACOTTAS

The art of terra-cottas known as clay-figurines outlived the art of sculptures. The earliest female figures, all hand-modelled and belonging to the Indus-Valley civilization (2500 B.C.), are (1) female figures and (2) animal figures. The female figurines, though rudimentary as specimens of art, are marked by bold expression. The animal figurines, on the other hand, both of faience and clay, are much more finished and realistic. In the figurines of a bull and a tiger, the vigour and charm of animal life are seen at their best. The terra-cotta objects of the Chalcolithic period are human and animal figures, pottery discs, wheels, etc. Among the animal figures, those of bulls are in large number.

About the terracotta figurines during the time of Mahāvīra, we get some knowledge both from literary and archaeological sources. In the *Bhaddasāla Jātaka*, reference is found to princes receiving presents of elephants, horses, and other toys from their mother's father.[3] We come across a mechanical image (*Jantapadimā*) of a human being which could walk, open and shut its eyes.[4] Another specimen of fine workmanship in mechanical toy is supplied by the mechanical elephant (Jantamayahatthi) manufactured by king Pradyota to capture Udayana of Kauśāmbī.[5]

1. *India as known to Pāṇini*, pp. 361-364.
2. Ch. I. Sec. VI and Ch. II. Sec. V.
3. *Jā*, No. 465.
4. *Bṛih. Bhā*, 4. 4915.
5. *Āva Chū* II, p. 161.

The terra-cotta figurines belonging to this period like those of the preceding cultures are hand-made, but they are important for their modelling, surface treatment, details and continuity of the tradition in a developed form. The figurines are better modelled than the specimens of the preceding cultures. Production of human and animal models in grey, N.B.P and red ware is evident in the period. The occurrence of human models is comparatively more than the preceding post-Harappan chalcolithic cultures. The use of a pedestal for the figurine disappears.

The terra-cotta figurines of this age are obtained from such sites as Hastināpura, Mathurā, Ahichchhatra, Rajghat, Prahladpur, Sarai Mohana, Masaon, Śrāvastī, Sonepur, Pāṭalīputra, Chiranda, Kayatha, Burar, Sugh, and Noh.[1] They are decorated by incision, circles, and stamping. The circlets became common in this period for expressing, along with the old technique, anatomical details and decoration on the body. It was probably a development over 'applique' and pinch' technique. It introduced a new trend in the tradition which involved less time, lively execution, and, lastly quick production of the figurines. This idea of punching the circlets on the figurines was probably borrowed from punch-marked coins. The stamping of the figurines with *Chakra* and leaf symbol seems to have been a later development in the period.

From the specimens discovered at Rājghāt, it is clear that there is closer similarity in the slip, polish, and painting with the black slipped and N.B.P. ware pottery. This clearly indicates that the artist modeller was inspired by the potter's technique. The figurines discovered from Pāṭalīputra are important in exhibiting the composite technique. In the figurines, the eyes, breasts, and genitals are clearly shown by punched circlets, while hair and fingers are indicated by incision. The use of the composite technique for modelling can be further attested by the Nāga figurines discovered at Sonepur; the breasts and eyes of the specimens are shown by the applique method while other details are depicted by punched circlets and incision. The animal figurines discovered at

1. Journal of the Oriental Institute, Baroda, XXII, p. 390.

Mathurā and Masaon are stamped with *Chakra* and leaf. Similar symbols along with circlets have also been noticed on the elephant figurines at Hastināpura. Painted terra-cottas have been discovered at Noh and Buxar (Charitravan).

CERAMICS

That this period witnessed a great boom in the ceramic activities is clear both from literary and archaeological evidences. From the *Uvāsagadasāo*[1], it is learnt that Saddālaputta, a *Śrāvaka* of Mahāvīra, owned, outside the town of Polāsapura, five hundred pottery shops where people prepared a large number of bowls, pots, and pitchers and jars of different sizes. At Rajagṛiha, there was a Magadhan potter, Bhagava, in whose workshop the Buddha spent a night.[2] Maṅkhali Gośāla also had his headquarters at Sāvatthi in the workshop of the potter woman, Hālāhalā.[3] The archaeological excavations conducted at different sites give us an idea of the ceramics used by the people. This period was noteworthy for the introduction of some new fabrics, the most important of which was the North Black Polished Ware. Black slipped Ware, Red and Black Ware, Grey Ware and Red Ware were the associate potteries of this age which met the increasing demand of the people.

Smoothness and lustre are the characteristics of the North Black Polished Ware. We may describe it as the prince of Indian potteries. As it was a costly ware and used by aristocrats, it was praised as a ware de luxe. It is made of well levigated clay and fired under very high temperature. It is of various shades and colours, such as golden, silvery, pinkish, gold-blue, brown-black, and steel-blue. The chief earthenware vessels produced by this pottery include dishes with incurved sides, bowls with straight convex, corrugated or tapering sides, lids, and rimless carinated handiwork.

This Northern Black Polished Ware seems to have originated in Magadha in the seventh century B.C., and became very popular in the Gangetic valley in the sixth century B.C.

1. Uvā, p. 119.
2. ABORI 1926-27, p, 165.
3. Bhag, XV.

This ware has been obtained from several sites in Bihar such as Bodha-Gaya, Vaiśālī, Rajgir, Chirand and Sonpur. At Sarnath, Kauśāmbī, Rajghat and Śrāvastī, large quantities of this ware in various shades and in fine fabric have been found, though not as frequently as that found in Bihar. At Taxila, Rupar, Atrañjikheda, Hastināpura, Tamluk, Śiśupālagarh, and Amaravati, it has been found in a small quantity, and that also in one or two sherds only. Ujjain was a separate centre of this pottery, but here it was of a poorer quality. The political expansion of Magadha is responsible for the spread of this ware in different parts of the country, but commerce and religion are also no less important factors.

METAL OBJECTS

Different kinds of metal objects recovered from early historical sites in the excavations give an idea of the state of art during this period. Some objects were used for ornaments, while others served domestic and other purposes. Such ornaments as ear-lobes, torques of different shapes, necklaces, bangles, pendants and rings made of different materials like terracotta, precious stones, glass, ivory, bone, and copper began to be used by women for adornment. Those who could not afford to have precious ornaments made of stone or copper, contented themselves with earthen beads, bangles, and ear-studs, while on the other hand, the rich section adorned themselves with ornaments of precious stones like shell, agate, carnelian, amethyst, soapstone, and glass.

Beads of different shapes, sizes and designs, have been obtained from Ujjain, Nagda, Maheśvara, Avra, Eran, Bharoch, Sonpur, etc. They are of different shapes barrel-like, spherical, and triangular. These are made of agate, carnelian, faience, steatite, terracotta, shell, glass, paste, etc. Nagda and Sonpur have offered pendants made of ivory and crystal respectively. The finding of unfinished beads at Avra and Ujjain proves the existence of local industries for their manufacture.

The toiletry included antimony rods of copper, hair pins of bone, combs of ivory, terracotta flesh rubber, and nail-parer.

The extensive use of iron during this period bears testimony to the advancement made in the technical knowledge of smelting and forging iron implements. The excavations at Ujjain serve as evidence of it. The manufacture of weapons like lances, spears, javelines, arrow-heads and daggers proves that people were better equipped for war purposes than before. For both war and domestic purposes, pans, lamps, nails, knife blades, clamps, etc. began to be prepared from iron. Further, the use of iron implements brought momentum into the field of agriculture, as a result of which ploughing and harvesting became easy with iron plough, sickle, and hoe. Tools, such as drills, adze, and chisel which boosted the woodcraft of the period, began to be manufactured.

While the use of iron increased, that of copper became limited. It was now used in the production of punchmarked and cast coins and also for manufacturing antimony rods, toys, rings, and beads. The use of silver is also attested by the discovery of silver punchmarked coins.

BONE AND STONE OBJECTS

A large number of bone objects have been unearthed from different archaeological sites. These are points, styluses, arrow heads, etc. Perhaps bone points and arrow heads were used in hunting small birds. Some polished stone celts have been discovered from Sonpur, Chirand, Vaiśālī, and Oriup in Bihar, Jaugada and Śiśupālagarh in Orissa and Taxıla in the North West. These were employed to cut dowu forests and bring wider areas under cultivation and settlement in the neighbourhood of urban centres.

SYMBOLS ON COINS

Punchmarked coins in the sixth century B.C., such as *Kārshāpaṇas*, have a number of symbols punched upon them by different punches one after another. These symbols are important from the artistic point of view. They are known to us from the coins of Bihar mound hoard of Taxila, Paila hoard, Ahaura hoard, and Golakhpur hoard. The Sun, the six-armed symbol, a hill above a tank with two fish, a peculiar symbol surrounded with five taurines, a hare and a bull on a hill—these were the current symbols on the punchmarked coins in the sixth and fifth century B.C. The Sun is represented as a rayed figure with a circle in the centre having a point or pellet within it. The rays are both thick and thin, straight and curved. The six-armed symbol consists of six spokes crossing at the centre, the six arms being tipped with ovals, globes, tridents, taurines, arrow-heads, triangles, balls, heart-shaped signs, dumbles, etc.

MISCELLANEOUS OBJECTS

There are some miscellaneous objects also which give an idea of the art of this period. These include seals and sealings, potter's dabbers, potter's stamps, stone pestles and querns, stone discs, and dice made of terracotta and bone. Clay spundles prove that weaving was practised. Ring wells recovered from the excavations at Ujjain, Hastināpura and Kauśāmbī reveal that they were used for storing grain and other domestic purposes.

CHAPTER X

EDUCATION, LITERATURE AND SCIENCES

The period of Lord Mahāvīra can justly be regarded as the most creative epoch in the spheres of education, literature and the sciences. Education acquired greater complexity and exactitude, and produced specialists in the form of private teachers in different branches of learning. Another development was the art of writing, which proved to be instrumental in the advancement of learning and the diffusion of knowledge. Prakrits (Vernaculars) grew as literary languages. Different religious teachers contributed to the growth and development of literature of their respective sects. As a result, there was a prolific output of religious literature in which instruction was imparted through oral methods. The *Sūtra* (a short rule) style was devised to memorise this type of literature, and it became a special feature of the age. This literature survived for considerable time in the form of oral traditions, and was codified in local dialects with habitual interpolations.

EDUCATION

When there was neither any printing press nor an easy means of communication from one place to another, the religious teachers, who wandered from place to place propagating their doctrines, proved to be potential media of mass education. True education was not understood as comprising merely of reading books, but as self-culture and self-development. It was regarded as a process of illumination which brought about harmonious development of physical, intellectual and spiritual faculties of man. Education was understood as the acquisition of knowledge by which a person achieves an understanding of words and their meaning and thus finds his way in the forest of the fourfold *Saṁsāra*; like a needle with its thread, the soul possessing sacred knowledge will not be lost in the *Saṁsāra*. If one performs all prescribed actions relating to knowledge, discipline, austerities and conduct, and is well-versed in his own as well as heterodox creeds, he will become invincible.[1]

AIMS AND IDEALS OF EDUCATION

As this age is characterised by the rise of different religious sects and schools, it was natural that the infusion of piety and religiousness among students was regarded as the first and foremost aim of education. Different religious rituals, observances, prayers and festivals tended to foster piety and religiousness in the mind of young students. The formation of character by the proper cultivation of the moral feeling was the second aim of education. Character was considered to be more important than learning. He alone was learned who was righteous. During this period, students lived in hermitages (*Āśramas*) under the direct and personal supervision of their teacher who was not only responsible for their intellectual progress but also looked after their moral conduct.

The development of personality was the third aim of educational system. This was sought to be realised by eulogising the feeling of self-respect, by encouraging the sense of self-confidence, by inculcating the virtue of self-restraint and by fostering the powers of discrimination and judgement. The feeling of self-respect was developed among students by giving them honourable place in society. Self-confidence was fostered by emphasising self-reliance. For the attainment of self-restraint, simplicity in life and habits was insisted upon. The different branches of learning such as Logic, law and philosophy, bristling with controversies, helped to develop the powers of discrimination and judgement.

The inculcation of civic and social duties was the fourth aim of education. After finishing his studies, the student was not to lead a self-centred life but had to work for the good of the whole society. The promotion of social efficiency and happiness was the fifth aim of education. A large number of professions and industries came into existence during this period and the society accepted the theory of division of work. Each trade, guild and family trained its

1. *Uttarā*, XXIX, 59.

members in its own profession. Differentiation of functions and their hereditary specialisation in families naturally heightened the efficiency of trades and professions.

The preservation and transmission of cultural heritage was another important aim of education. It was incumbent on the religious teachers to commit their respective sacred books to memory in order to ensure their transmission to unborn generations. Members of the professions were also to train their children along their own lines. These religious and professional teachers were not only preserving the knowledge of the ancients in these branches, but constantly increasing its boundaries by their own contributions. For the preservation of cultural traditions, special methods were adopted. The theory of three debts was propounded. First of all, one owes a debt to gods, and one can liquidate it only by learning how to perform proper sacrifices and by regularly offering them. Religious traditions of the race were thus preserved. Secondly, one owes a debt to *Rishis* or savants of the bygone ages and one can discharge it only by studying their works and continuing their literary and professional traditions. This enabled one to master and maintain the best literary and professional traditions. The third debt was to ancestors, which could be rapaid only by raising progeny and by imparting proper education to it. There were also practices of *Svādhyāya* and *Ṛṣitarpaṇa*; the former enjoined a daily recapitulation of at least a portion of what was learnt during student-life and the latter required a daily tribute of gratitude to be paid to the literary giants of the past at the time of daily prayers.

SOME EDUCATIONAL PRINCIPLES AND POSTULATES

The aim of the educational system was not to impart general education but to train experts in different branches of learning. It took particular care to train and develop memory. Education was available to all those who were qualified to receive it. The *Upanayana* ritual, which marked the beginning of religious and literary education, was made obligatory both for males and females. Teaching was considered to be a pious duty which was to be discharged without any consideration for fee. In order to bring education within the reach of the poorest, it not only permitted students to beg but elevated begging itself into the highest duty of student-life.

Education was a serious proposition. At the time of study, students had to lead a celibate life. Long, continued and laborious preparation was necessary to acquire real grounding and efficiency in a subject.

Both the rich and the poor had to submit to stern discipline in order to become learned. The fifth year and the eighth year were considered to be the proper time for the beginning of primary and secondary education respectively.

The *Gurukula* system was one of the most important features of the pattern of education during this period. The student began to live under the supervision of his teacher after his *Upanayana*. Direct, personal and continuous contact with a teacher produced a powerful effect on students. The general belief that *Gurukulas* (hermitages) were founded in forests, away from the din of city life, is only partly correct. In majority of cases, *Gurukulas* were located in villages or towns. The famous *Gurukulas* during this period, as known to us from Buddhist literature, were situated at Rājagṛiha, Champā, Vaiśālī, Nālandā, Śrāvastī, etc.

TEACHER AND STUDENT

The teacher was held in high reverence in society. He was to lead the pupil from darkness of ignorance to the light of learning.[1] He was considered to be a spiritual and intellectual father because he used to offer a new life, and no education was possible without his help and guidance.[2] During this period, sacred learning was transmitted orally from one generation to another. Great importance was attached to proper accent and pronunciation in its recitation and it could be correctly learnt only from the speech of a properly qualified teacher. Spiritual salvation also depended upon the proper guidance by the teacher. Books being rare and costly, the student had generally to rely upon his teacher alone. In the case of professions, a good deal had to be learnt from the teacher.

1. *Āp*. Dh. S, i, 10, 11.
2. Ibid, 1.1. 1. 12-17.

There were different classes of teachers such as *Āchārya*, *Pravaktā*, *Śrotriya*, *Upādhyāya* and *Adhyāpaka*. There was no course of teacher's training prescribed for these different categories of teachers. During the course of study, brilliant students acquired sufficient experience of teaching. They participated in debates, and discussions, and they were also provided opportunities for teaching.

The teacher was an ideal person of high character and was to treat his students impartially. He was well grounded in his own branch of knowledge and was to continue its study throughout his life. In the *Sūtrakṛitāṅga*[1], the ideal teacher has been described as follows: "He is not to conceal or contradict the truth, not to show any pride and not to denounce teachers of other religions. He is to be a genuine scholar having complete knowledge of all other religions. His life is to be full of penances and his speech should be chaste." Baudhāyana[2] insists that the teacher should teach his student the sacred science with whole-hearted attention without withholding from him any part of the whole Law. The generosity and large-heartedness of teachers can be judged from the conduct and exclamation of Alāra Kalāma, when the future Buddha had finished his education under him :

"Happy friends are we in that we look upon such a venerable one, such a fellow ascetic as you. The doctrine which I know, you too know, and the doctrine which you know, I too know. As I am, so you are, as you are, so am I. Pray, Sir, let us be joint wardens of this company".[3]

The teacher was to adopt and love the pupil as his own son.[4] Though it was the duty of the pupil to render services to the teacher to please him, the teacher must be careful to see that the pupil is not exploited for his own purposes to an extent detrimental to his studies. Such services were meant for the pupil's own moral improvement and not solely for the practical benefits of the teacher. In times of distress,

1. *Sūtra*, I. 14; 19-27.
2. *Bau. Dh. S*, i. 2. 48.
3. Further Dialogues of the Buddha, *Ariyaparivesana Sutta*, p. 116
4. *Bau. Dh.* S, i. 2. 48.

however, the teacher was permitted to accept the assistance of his pupil.

The teacher had no fixed income. It consisted partly of offerings obtained by him on occasions of rituals and sacrifices and partly of voluntary gifts given by his students either during or after their course of study. The respectable status of a teacher depended not on his wealth but on his scholarship and character.

The relations between the teacher and the student were direct and not merely institutional. They were very cordially intimate, united, to quote the words of the Buddha, 'by mutual reverence, confidence and communion of life.'[1] A good pupil never disobeyed his teacher or behaved rudely with him; he never told a lie and always carried out his command like a thorough-bred horse. If he perceived the teacher in an angry mood, he pacified him by meekness, appeased him with folded hands and avowed not to do wrong again. It is stated that a pupil should not sit by the side of the teacher, not before him, nor behind him; he should never ask questions when sitting on a stool or his bed, but always rising from his seat and coming near, he should ask him with folded hands.[2]

There were bad pupils too. They received kicks and blows from their teachers. They were also beaten with sticks and addressed with harsh words.[3] Bad students are compared with bad bullocks who break down through want of zeal. Such pupils, if sent on an errant, did not do what they were asked to do, but strolled about wherever they liked. Sometimes, teachers were tired of such pupils, left them to their fate, and retired to the forest.[4]

It does not mean, however, that the student was to follow blindly even his teacher's misconduct. Both Buddha and Āpastamba, who enjoin high reverence for the teacher, lay down that the student should draw his teacher's attention in private to his failings, dissuade him from wrong views if he happened to be inclined towards them; the duty of obedience

1. *Mv* I. 32. I.
2. *Uttarā*, I. 13 f, 12, 41, 18, 22.
3. Ibid, 38; ibid, 3, 65a; also *Jā*, II, p. 279.
4. *Uttarā*, 27. 8, 13, 16.

comes to an end if the teacher transgresses the limits of *Dharma*. His commands were to be regarded as ultravires, if they were likely to jeopardise the student's life or were against the law of the land.

PRIVATE TEACHERS AND OTHER AGENCIES

As education became more complex and exact during this period, specialists started appearing in the form of private teachers. They were to be found scattered all over the country, but they used to congregate in large numbers in certain places on account of the facilities they received. Such places were usually capitals of kingdoms and famous holy places. Taxila and Banaras became well known educational centres where a number of famous scholars imparted education in their individual capacity but did not as a rule combine to form any colleges. If the number of pupils under any teacher happened to be large, he would either engage an assistant teacher, or assign part of the work to brilliant advanced students.[1]

Besides these private teachers, the followers of different *Vedas* had formed their own Academies of learning called the *Charaṇas*. These *Charaṇas* were merely loose organisations based upon a fellowship of teachers and students working at different centres but promoting the study of particular Vedic *Śākhā*. At different centres of learning, there were Councils of learned men known as *Parishads* which also worked as agencies of education. After completing their education, students were to present themselves for a test of their knowledge.

EDUCATIONAL CENTRES

Taxila became a widely known seat of learning during this period. It had many famous teachers to whom hundreds of students flocked for higher education from distant places like Rājagṛiha, Vaiśālī, Banaras, Ujjayinī and Mithilā. These teachers were not members of any organized institution like college or University but every teacher, assisted by his advanced students, formed an institution by himself. One such institution under a world-renowned teacher had five

1. *Anabhirati Jā*, II p. 185 and *Mahādhammapāla Jā*, IV, p. 447.

hundred students under his charge.[1] From the *Sutasoma Jātaka*, it is known that one of the archery schools at Taxila had on its roll 103 princes from different parts of India.[2] Heir-apparents of Banaras came to this place for higher studies.[3] King Prasenajit of Kośala, a contemporary of Mahāvīra, was educated here. Prince Jīvaka, an illegitimate son of Bimbisāra, spent seven years at Taxila in learning medicine and surgery. As Pāṇini hailed from Śalātura near Attock, he also must have been on the alumni of Taxila University.

Generally, students used to go to Taxila for higher studies at the age of sixteen. As a general rule, they stayed with their teachers. Those, who were rich like prince Juṇha from Banaras, used to have separate special houses for their residence.[4] The well-to-do students used to pay their lodging and boarding expenses along with their fees, sometimes even at the beginning of their course. Poor students, who were unable to pay fees, used to work in their teacher's house by day, Special classes were held for them at night.

Next to Taxila, Banaras was an eminent seat of learning. In the earlier period, one of its kings, Ajātaśatru had been a great philosopher and a patron of learning. Many of the teachers of this place had been students of Taxila.[5] It seems that Banaras, as a seat of learning, was largely the creation of the ex-students of Taxila. In the course of time, the teachers of Banaras began to attract scholars from far and wide. *Kosiya* and *Tittiri Jātakas* refer to the famous teachers of Banaras maintaining schools for the teaching of three *Vedas* and eighteen *Sippas*, and *Akitta Jātaka* describes how students used to flock to Banaras for higher education, when they were about 16 years of age. The son of a Brāhmaṇa magnate worth eighty crores was educated in Banaras.[6] There were again certain subjects in the teaching of which Banaras seems to have specialized. There is a reference, for instance, to a school of

1. *Jā.* I, No. 239, 317, 402; III, 18. 235, 143, 171 etc.
2. Ibid, V, p. 407.
3. Ibid, No. 252.
4. *Jā*, No 456.
5. Ibid, No. 150, See also No. 80.
6. *Jā*, Vol, IV, 237,

Music presided over by an expert who was "the chief of his kind in all India."[1] Buddha selected this place for the first promulgation of his gospel because it became the famous seat of learning in eastern India. It it stated that prince Agaḍadatta of Saṅkhapura went to Banaras for study. He stayed in the house of his teacher, and returned home after completing the course of study. Sāvatthi[2] is mentioned as another centre of education.[3]

Mahāli[4] a native of Vaiśālī, is known to have gone to Takshaśilā for learning *Śilpa* or *arts*. After the completion of his studies, when he came back home, he trained five hundred Lichchhavīs. These five hundred again, after finishing their courses, instructed many in different parts of the country. Vaiśālī itself was a centre of learning.[5] The Lichchhavīs were so much interested in high religious and philosophical discussions that they built a Kūṭāgāra Hall,[6] where such discussions took place. The Buddha gave many of his discourses at this place.

HERMITAGES AS CENTRES OF LEARNING

The educational system of this period produced men of affairs as well as those who renounced the world in the pursuit of Truth. The life of renunciation indeed claimed many an ex-student of both Taxila and Benaras. In the sylvan and solitary retreats away from the busy life of cities, the hermitages served as schools of higher philosophical speculation and religious training. These special schools of spiritual study are also referred to as being consisted of 500 ascetics gathering round the personality of an individual hermit of established reputation to impart instruction as his disciples.[7] Such hermitages were generally established in the Himālayas.[8] Sometimes,

1. *Jā*, No. 243.
2. *Uttarā. Ṭī*, 4, p. 83.
3. Ibid. 2, p. 22.
4. FAUSBOLL : *Dhammapadam* (Old edition), p. 211.
5. *Chullakāliṅga Jā*, No. 301.
6. RHYS DAVIDS : *Sumaṅgalavilāsinī*, Pt. I, PTS, London, 1886.
7. *Jā*, Vol. I, 141.
8. Ibid, Vol. I, 406, 431; III, 143; IV, 74.

however, they were built near the centres of population in order to have facilities for attracting recruits.

SUBJECTS OF STUDY

In the *Bhagavatisūtra*,[1] eighteen subjects—six *Vedas*, six *Vedāṅgas* and six *Upāṅgas* have been mentioned for study. In the *Uttarādhyayana Ṭikā*,[2] we find the following fourteen subjects of study—4 *Vedas*, 6 *Vedāṅgas*, *Mīmāṁsā*, *Nyāya*, *Purāṇa*, and *Dharmmasattha*. Seventy two *Kalās* are frequently mentioned in Jaina texts. The list contains the *Sippa*s and also the list of traditional knowledge and sciences. These *Kalās* may be classified under thirteen heads—1. Reading and writing; 2. Poetry; 3. Sculpture; 4. Music; 5. Clay-modelling; 6. Gambling; sports and indoor games; 7. Personal hygiene, toilet and food; 8. knowledge of various marks and signs; 9. The science of omens; 10 Astronomy; 11. Alchemy; 12. Architecture and 13. Art of fighting.[3]

The three *Vedas*, Grammar, Philosophy, Law and eighteen *Sippas* were the principal subjects selected for specialisation at Taxila. Among the latter were included Medicine, Surgery, Archery and allied military arts, Astronomy, Astrology, Divination, Accountancy, Commerce, Agriculture, Conveyancing, Magic, Snake charming, the art of finding treasurers, Music, Dancing and Painting. Jīvaka had gone to this place for studying medicine and surgery and two youths from Banaras went there for studying Archery and Elephant Lore. Two Chaṇḍāla boys from Ujjayinī in the disguise of young Brāhmaṇas visited Taxila for the study of law.[4] There were no caste restrictions on the choice of subject; Kshatriyas used to study the *Vedas* along with Brāhmaṇas and the latter used to specialise in archery along with the Kshatriyas. A Brāhmaṇa royal priest of Banaras had once sent his son to Taxila not to learn the *Vedas* but to specialise in Archery.[5] Similar subjects were also taught at Banaras and other educational centres.

1. *Bhag*, 5, 3. 3. 185.
2. *Uttarā*, *Ṭī*. 3, p. 56.
3. JLAIDJC, pp. 172-173.
4. *Jā*, No. 498.
5. Ibid. 522.

HOLIDAYS

A systematic list of holidays has been given in the Brahmanical literature.[1] Interruptions of study were allowed for a variety of causes and circumstances. The principal cause of such interruption was the occurrence of certain natural phenomena—untimely clouds, thunder, heavy showers, frost, dust-storms etc. Secondly, the standing list of holidays included the following : four in the month at an interval of a week, the new and full moon days and the eighth day of each fortnight; certain other days were set apart for religious ceremonies and festival days. Thirdly, study was forbidden in the event of certain political or other incidents taking place, *e.g.* when the peace of the settlement was disturbed by an invasion or by incursions of robbers or cattlelifters, or when the king or a Brāhmaṇa had met with an accident or died. Arrival of distinguished guests led to the suspension of studies. Fourthly, study was to be stopped when certain sounds were heard, *e.g.* howling of jackals, barking of dogs, braying of donkeys, grunting of camels, cry of a wolf, screeching of an owl; the sound of an arrow, of a large or small drum; the noise of a chariot and the wail of a person in pain or weeping.

ORGANIZATION AND DURATION OF COURSES

There was no clear cut course of a definite duration in different subjects because education was mostly imparted by private teachers without any government control. The duration and contents of the course were therefore largely determined by the will, capacity and convenience of the student. Those, who were content with a superficial knowledge, used to return home in six or even three years. Persons desiring higher education had to spend about 15 or 16 years subsequent to the time of his *Upanayana* at the age of eight or nine. Usually one could finish education and become an expert in one particular subject at about the age of 24 which was regarded as the ideal age for marriage. Actuated by spiritual motives, some persons used to observe life-long celibacy

1, *Gau. Dh. S,* II. 7; *Bau. Dh. S,* I. 11. The works of Vasishṭha, Vishṇu and Vikhānas a hardly add anything new regarding interruption of study.

and devote their time entirely to religion and education. They were known as *Naishṭhika Brahmachārins.* Their primary motive was spiritual salvation, but they set out to achieve this not by penance or meditation, but by the dedication of a life of celibacy to the cause of the sacred lore.

FEMALE EDUCATION

The permission granted by Mahāvīra and the Buddha for the admission of women into their respective Orders, provided an impetus to the spread of education and philosophy among the ladies. Some of them distinguished themselves as teachers and preachers. They used to lead a life of celibacy, with the aim of understanding and following the eternal truths of religion and philosophy. Ajita Chandanā became the first disciple of Mahāvīra under whom a large number of nuns practised the rules of right conduct and attained salvation.[1] Another famous lady Jayantī, the sister of king Sayāṇīya of Kośāmbī, abandoned her royal robe and became a devout nun.[2] Some of the nuns well-versed in the knowledge of the sacred texts became teachers of the junior nuns.

The ladies who entered the Buddhist order were known *Theris*, some of whom *made themselves off.* The most distinguished of them was Dhammadinnā who brought about her husband's spiritual salvation. She solved all difficult metaphysical problems with the ease of 'one who severs the stalk of a lotus with the sword.' Mahāprajāpati, the sister of the Buddha's mother, who entered the Order with a following of 500 other Śākya ladies constituting the Order of Nuns, was hardly inferior to any of the monks in piety and learning. Kisā Gotamī was known for her progress in virtue and philosophical learning. Sukkā was such a successful speaker and preacher that, to hear her speak, people would flock out of the city and not feel tired of listening to her.[3]

When a large number of ladies were receiving higher education and were making their own contributions to the growth of knowledge, it is but natural to suppose that some of them

1. *Anta*, 8; *Kalpa*, 5. 135.
2. *Bhag*, 12 2.
3. C. A. Foley's article in the Ninth Oriental Congress Report Vol. I, pp, 340 f. See also A. S. Altekar: Ancient Indian Education, pp. 464-466.

must have followed the profession of teaching. *Āchāryā*[1] and *Upādhyāyā* were the titles of female teachers. Pāṇini refers to female students as *Chhātrī* and their hostels *Chhātrīśālā.*[2] These hostels were probably under the superintendence of lady teachers, who had made teaching their profession.

Women students were divided into two classes—*Sadyodvāhas* and *Brahmavādinis*. The *Sadyodvāhas* used to prosecute their studies until their marriage at the age of 15 or 16. Girls could remain unmarried until the age of 16 and the *Upanayana* was as common in the case of girls as it was in the case of boys. During the eight or nine years, they used to learn religious-hymns prescribed for daily and periodical prayers and for those rituals and sacraments in which they were to take active part after marriage. Like men, women used to offer their prayers regularly in the morning and in the evening. *Brahmavādinīs* aimed at high excellence in scholarship. They were lifelong students of Theology and Philosophy.

ART OF WRITING

The period of Lord Mahāvīra is noteworthy for the evolution of the art of writing. G.H. OJHA[3], R.B. PANDEY,[4] and D.R. BHANDARKAR[5] are of the opinion that a system of writing was prevalent even earlier during the Vedic period. But, most of the indologists do not ascribe to this view. Since no positive evidence regarding writing has been found in Vedic literature, it is not possible to hazard any final conclusion.

The definite traces of writing hail from the sixth century B.C. The Pāli *Tripiṭakas* give numerous references to writing and the material used for it. *Piṭaka* means 'basket' which implies something to hold or contain—a written document. References to writing occur in the *Vinaya Piṭaka* at many places. The terms *Lekhaka*[6] and *Lekhāpeti*[7] are used for 'writer' and 'caused to be written' respectively. Further, a 'letter-game' known as *Akkharikā* clearly indicates that some

1. India as known to Pāṇini, p. 288.
2. *Pā*, VI. 2. 86.
3. *Prāchīnalipimālā*, p. 12.
4. Indian Palaeography, p. 15.
5. Sir Asutosh Mookerjee Silver Jubilee Volumes, Vol. III, p. 494 ff.
6. *Vin*, IV-8.
7. Ibid, II-110.

sort of writing was known to the people. A prescribed thief is called *Likhitaka chora* which means literally 'registered thief.'[1] The word *Akkhara* occurs in the *Aṅguttara Nikāya*,[2] the *Saṁyutta Nikāya*[3] and the *Dhammapada*.[4] The word *Lekhanī* (pen) is mentioned in the *Aṅguttara Nikāya*.[5] The prose-*Jātakas*, which were admittedly compiled later, possess a number of references to writing, writing material and several kinds of written documents. All these Pāli evidences prove that some sort of writing definitely existed during the sixth century B.C. or even earlier, but unfortunately we do not know its name or character.

The *Ashṭādhyāyi* of Pāṇini contains the terms denoting the existence of the art of writing—*Lipi*[6] and *Libi* (script), *Lipikāra*[7] (a writer or scribe), *Yavanānī*[8] (Greek script), *Grantha*[9] (a book) and *Svarita*[10] (a mark in writing).

For the first time we meet two scripts, Brāhmī and Kharoshṭhī, in cursive and advanced forms of letters during third century B.C. in the Aśokan inscriptions. This fact also leads us to infer that writing had a long history before the epigraphs of Aśoka were engraved.

Brāhmī and Kharoshṭhī are the two most important scripts mentioned in the Jaina and Buddhist texts. In the Jaina *sūtras*—the *Pannavaṇā*, the *Samavāyāṅga* (Ch. XVIII) and the Bhagavatī (Ch.V), the names of scripts are mentioned. The first two contain a list of eighteen scripts and the last one refers to only one—Brāhmī.[11] The Buddhist work *Lalitavistāra* contains the names of 64 scripts, both Indian and foreign, known to or imagined by the Indians during the

1. *Vin*, I-2.
2. *Aṅgu*, I-72, III-107.
3. *Saṁ*, II-267, 1-38.
4. Dhp, (*Taṇhāvagga*-19)
5. *Aṅgu*, II-200.
6. *Pā*, 13. 2. 21.
7. Ibid.
8. Ibid, 4. 1. 49.
9. Ibid, 1. 3. 75.
10. Ibid, 1. 3. 11.
11. According to Jaina traditions, this script was given by the first Tīrthaṅkara Ṛishabha to his daughter Brāhmī, from whom it derived its name.

period when these lists were compiled. Out of these, only two, the Brāhmī and Kharoshṭhī seem to have been current in the sixth or fifth century B.C. The Brāhmī was written from left to right and it was popular in eastern India. G. BUHLER[1] has adopted the designation Brāhmī for the characters in which the majority of the Aśoka edicts were written. He and his followers like W. JONES,[2] A WEBER, and ISAAC TAYLOR[3] advocated that Brāhmī originated from a Semitic alphabet. The theory of the indigenous origin of Brāhmī has been propounded by many modern scholars, mostly Indians. Some of them like R.B. PANDEY[4] and D.C. SIRCAR[5] even think that Brāhmī alphabet seems to have been derived from the pre-historic Indus Valley scripts.

The Kharoshṭhī script was written from right to left. It was introduced in the extreme north-west of India in about the sixth or fifth century B.C. and was used locally in Gandhāra. G. BUHLER[6] suggested that it originated from the Aramic alphabet because there is resemblance of letters in these two scripts. During the Achaemenian rule, Aramic script was used for official and other purposes in India and adjacent countries. Kharoshṭhī alphabet was the result of the intercourse between the offices or the Satraps and the natives. The Indians probably used at first the pure Aramic characters, and they introduced in the course of time the modifications observable in the Kharoshṭhī alphabet. On the other hand, R.B. PANDEY[7] does not agree with the theory of Aramic origin of the Kharoshṭhī and has proved that it was invented by Indian genius.

LANGUAGE

The most remarkable feature of this age is that Sanskrit lost its position as the medium of expression and its place was soon taken by the Prakrits (Vernaculars) which also grew

1. BUHLER : Indian Palaeography, pp. 9-11.
2. TAYLOR ; The Alphabet, Vol. II, p. 304.
3. Ibid, Vol. I. pp. 335-346.
4. R. B. PANDEY: Indian Palaeography, p. 50.
5. D. C. SIRCAR : Inscriptions of Aśoka, p. 25.
6. BUHLER : Indian Palaeography, pp. 19-20.
7. R. B. PANDEY : Indian Palaeography, pp. 57-58.

as literary languages. It is for this reason that both Mahāvīra and Buddha propagated their faiths among the masses with the help of the Prakrits and not Sanskrit. It is probable, though not definitely proved, that both Mahāvīra and Buddha preached their doctrines in old Ardha-Māgadhī dialect, but the extant canonical texts of their sects are written in a language which is quite different. The original scriptures are lost, but the language of the preserved Jaina canons has undergone considerable changes and shows a strong influence of the Mahārāshṭrī Prakrit. As regards Buddhist canon, the best preserved is that of the Hīnayāna school (Theravāda) in Pāli. The particular prakrit dialect from which pāli was derived is a matter of dispute among scholars and no unanimous conclusion has yet been arrived at. While some derive it from the Prakrit dialect current in Magadha, others find a closer association between it and the dialects of Kauśāmbī or Avanti *i.e.* the Midland or Madhyadeśa.

From the different *Sūtra* works (600-400 B.C.) and Pāṇini's *Ashtādhyāyi*, we know about the contemporary position of Sanskrit Language. This language had now become widely differentiated from the Vedic idiom. These *Sūtras* are written in a peculiarly terse style which may be traced to the prose of the Brāhmaṇas. They, however, employ long compounds and gerunds to economize the use of syllables. The language of the *Sūtras* comes very close to the norm set up by Pāṇini. Occasionally, we find words and forms belonging to the Vedic period and also some Prākritisms and solecisms. The contact of the Aryans with the aboriginal tribes may have hastened to a certain extent the process of simplification of the older language. The language of these works was the spoken language as was current among the hieratic classes. Sanskrit language ceased to be the language of the masses and its use was restricted only to the highly educated class.

LITERATURE

There was a general efflorescence of literary activity during this age. Because of the rise of different religions, religious and philosophical literature proliferated in context and diversity. Most of this rich literature was lost because it was handed down by the religious teachers orally in the form of traditions and was not committed to writing. Even those preserved orally took literary form after considerable time, and it underwent many changes in language and subject matter. Hence, it is not possible to offer a definite and true picture of literature. The achievements in some branches of technical literature also were of high order.

THE JAINA CANON

Originally, there were two kinds of Jaina sacred books—the fourteen *Pūrvas* and the eleven *Aṅgas*. The fourteen *Pūrvas* are said to be coming down from the time of Pārśva, the illustrious predecessor of Mahāvīra. Traditionally, the eleven Aṅgas based on the teachings of Mahāvīra are said to have been composed by his immediate disciples but actually they do not belong to one period. The fourteen *Pūrvas* were reckoned to make up a twelfth *Aṅga* called the *Dṛishṭivāda*. Mahāvīra preached his religion in Ardha-Māgadhī which is said to be the language of the canon. The language of the available canon, however, shows a great influence of Mahārāshṭrī Prakrit. Besides, the present canon has undergone considerable modifications and interpolations and at the same time, certain canons or parts of the canons have become totally obsolete. Different names are ascribed to one and the same canon and the number of canons varies considerably.

The *Āgama* or Canonical literature, according to the Śvetāmbara Jains consists of the eleven *Aṅgas*, twelve *Upāṅgas*, ten *Paiṇṇas* (*Prakīrṇas*), six *Chhedasūtras*, *Nāndī* and *Anuyogadvāra* and four *mūlasūtras*. The eleven *Aṅgas* are the oldest part of the Canon. On the other hand, according to the Digambar tradition, not only the *Drishṭivāda* but also eleven *Aṅgas* were lost by degrees in course of time. They do not know of other works grouped as *Upāṅgas*, *Chhedasūtras*, etc., which are found in the present canon of the Śvetāmbaras. A list of these texts according to the usual enumeration is as follows :—

1. *Eleven Aṅgas* : *Āchāra*, *Sūtrakṛita*, *Sthāna*, *Samavāya*, *Bhagavatī*, *Jñātādharmakathās*, *Upāsakadaśās*, *Antakṛiddaśās*, *Anuttaraupapātikadaśās*, *Praśnavyākaraṇa Vipāka* (Dṛishṭi-vāda, no longer extant).

2. Twelve *Upāṅgas* : *Anupapātika*, *Rājapraśnīya*, *Jīvābhigama*, *Prañāpanā*, *Jambūdvīpaprajñapti*, *Chandraprajñapti*, *Sūryaprajñapti*, *Nirayāvali* (or *Kalpika*), *Kalpāvataṁsikā*, *Pushpikā*, *Pushpachūlikā* and *Vṛishṇidaśīs*.
3. Ten *Paiṇṇas* (*Prakīrṇas*) : *Chatuḥśaraṇa*, *Saṁstāra*, *Āturapratyākhyānam*, *Bhaktāparijñā*, *Taṇḍulavaiyālī*, *Chandavīja*, *Devendrastava*, *Gaṇivija*, *Mahāpratyākhyāna*, and *Vīrastava*.
4. Six *Chhedasūtras*: *Niśitha*, *Mahāniśītha*, *Vyavahāra*, *Daśāśrutaskandha*, *Bṛihatkalpa* and *Pañchakalpa*.
5. Two *Sūtras* without a common name : *Nandi* and *Anuyogadvāra*.
6. Four *Mūlasūtras* : *Uttarādhyayana*, *Āvaśyaka*, *Daśavaikālika* and *Piṇḍaniryukti*.[1]

Among these different *Aṅgas*, only the *Āchārāṅga*, the *Sūtrakṛitāṅga* and the *Uttarādhyayana* contain the oldest part of the canon from linguistic and literary points of view.[2] The same may be true to some extent of the *Bhagavatī Sūtra*. The *Sāmāyika* prayers, like the Buddhist formulae of confession, obviously formed the very beginning of the sacred writings, but unfortunately we do not have them in their authentic form. The older parts of the canon contain many archaic forms. The older prose works generally abound in endless repetitions but some contain systematic expositions. Of the twelve *Upāṅgas*, only the first two perhaps contain some early material, the rest being 'systematic' and exaggerated dogmatic, scientific and mythological treatises. Of the first two *Upāṅgas*

1. During the course of three recensions, the Jaina *Sūtras* have undergone considerble changes. The first attempt was made by convoking the council at Pāṭaliputra 160 years after Mahāvīra's death (*i. e.* about 307 B C) and the sacred lore which was in a state of decay, was put in order. This is known as the Pāṭaliputra version (*Vāchanā*) of the Jaina Canons. Another council was summoned at Mathurā under the presidentship of Ārya Skandila between the years 827 and 840 after the death of Mahāvīra (*i. e.* 350-373 A. D.) and the Scriptural texts were brought into order. This is known as the Māthurī version (*Vāchanā*) of the Canons. Lastly the council of Valabhi met under Devardhi Gaṇin Kshamāśramaṇa (Vīra 980=A. D. 513) and the Jaina Canon was written down in book form. This is known as Valabhi version (*Vāchanā*) of the Canons.
2. SBE, XXII, pp. XI-XLIII.

the *Rājapraśniya*, in particular, seems to be based on an old tradition, since the *Pāyāsisutta* in the *Dīghanikāya* is either an adaptation of it or draws on the same source. The *paiṇṇas*, as their title indicates, are miscellaneous pieces and their list is in reality quite indefinite. Of the *Chhedasūtras*, according to M. WINTERNITZ, only the *Bṛihatkalpa*, with its supplement —the *Vauhāra*—and the *Āyāradasāo*, can be considered early.

THE BUDDHIST CANON

It seems that Gautama Buddha, like Mahāvīra, preached his doctrines in Old Ardha-Māgadhī, but he enjoined upon his disciples that his teachings should be studied by the people in their own dialects. We have definite evidence that Buddhist canon was redacted in Pāli, Māgadhī and other dialects. of these, the Pāli version alone has survived in its entirely. Of the rest, only very small fragments have so far come to light.

The Pāli canon consists of three *piṭakas* (baskets) known as the *Tripiṭaka*. These are *Vinaya*, *Sutta* and *Abhidhamma Piṭakas*. There is yet another division of the canon into nine *Aṅgas*. They are—sermons in prose only (*Sutta*), sermons in prose and verse (*Gavya*), explanations (*Veyyākaraṇa*), stanzas (*Gāthā*), epigrams (*Udāna*), short saying beginning with "Thus spoke the Buddha" (*Itivuttaka*), stories of previous incarnations (*Jātaka*), miracles (*Abbhutadhamma*), and teachings in the form of question and answer (*Vedalla*).

The *Vinaya Piṭaka* comprises the following texts : *Pātimokkha*, *Sutta Vibhaṅga*, *Khandhakas* and *Parivāra*. The *Sutta Piṭaka* comprises the following five collections called *Nikāyas* : (1) *Dīgha*, (2) *Majjhima*, (3) *Saṁyutta*, (4) *Aṅguttara* and (5) *Khuddaka*. The *Abhidhamma* comprises seven books commonly known as *Sattapakaraṇa* which belong to a later date containing a more elaborate and classified exposition of the *Dhamma* than given in the *Nikāyas*.

CHRONOLOGY OF THE BUDDHIST CANON

Like the Jaina canon, the Buddhist canon too was not compiled at one particular time. The quotations from scriptures in Aśokan edicts, references to persons well-versed in sacred texts in inscriptions of the second century B. C. and scriptures, reliefs and inscriptions on the railings and gateways at Bhārhut and Sanchi, suggest that the works on *Dharma* and *Vinaya* were current before the rise of the Maurya dynasty. The *Mahāvagga* and *Chullavagga* are evidently assignable to the period of Aśoka, as they are silent about the third Council. The *Sutta Vibhaṅga* and the five *Nikāyas* which are referred to in the *Chullavagga* are certainly much older. There is no reference to the *Abhidhamma*, which is the latest of the *Piṭakas*. As the *Nikāyas* know no place in the east, south of Kaliṅga, and no place in the west, south of the Godāvarī, the Geography of the *Nikāyas* points to their age being much earlier than Aśoka. Therefore, it appears that the bulk of the *Vinaya Piṭaka* and the first four *Nikāyas* of the *Sutta Piṭaka* were compiled before 350 B.C.

After discussing the chronology of the Pāli canonical texts from different points of view, B. C. LAW places them in the following groups in their chronological order.[1]

1. The simple statements of Buddhist doctrine now found in identical words in paragraphs or verses recurring in all the books;

2. Episodes found in identical words in two or more of the existing books;

3. The Sīlas, the *Pārāyaṇa* group of sixteen poems without the prologue, the *Aṭṭhaka* group of four or sixteen poems, the *Sikkhāpadas*;

4. Dīgha Vol. I, *Majjhima*, *Saṁyutta*, *Aṅguttara* and earlier *Pātimokkha* with 152 rules;

5. Dīgha Vol. II, III, *Thera-Therī-gāthā*, 500 *Jātakas*, *Suttavibhaṅga*, *Paṭisambhidāmagga*, *Puggalapaññatti* and *Vibhaṅga*;

6. *Mahāvagga*, *Chullavagga*, *Patimokkha* with 227 rules, *Vimānavatthu*, *Petavatthu*, *Dhammapada*, *Kathāvatthu*;

7. *Chulla-and Mahā-niddesa*, *Udāna*, *Itivuttaka*, *Sutta Nipāta*, *Dhātukathā*, *Yamaka*, *Paṭṭhāna*;

8. *Buddhavaṁsa*, *Chariyāpiṭaka*, *Apadāna*;

9. *Parivārapāṭha*;

10. *Khuddakapāṭha*.

Vaṅgīsa, a native of Magadha, is known to have been the celebrated poet during the time of Buddha. He repeated

1. History of Pāli literature I, 42.

many beautiful stanzas before the Buddha who praised him much.[1]

THE ĀJĪVIKA CANON

That the Ājīvikas had a canon of sacred texts in which their doctrines were codified, is clear from the Pāli and Prakrit texts of Buddhism and Jainism. The Ājīvika canon consisted of eight *Mahānimittas* and two *Mārgas*, which are at least partially based upon the *Pūrvas* coming down from the time of Pārśva. B.M. Barua, on the other hand, interprets the word *Pūrva* in the text not in the specialised Jaina sense, but merely as past traditions.[2] His view is strengthened by the fact that the eightfold *Mahānimitta* of the Ājīvikas bears no resemblance to the titles of the fourteen lost *Pūrvas* of the Jaina tradition. In spite of this, it can be said that the scriptures of the Ājīvikas may have had something in common with the earliest scriptures of the Jainas.

In the *Bhagavatīsūtra*,[3] it is described that the six Disāchāras "extracted the eight-fold *Mahānimitta* in the *Puvvas* with the *Maggas* making the total up to ten, after examining hundreds of opinions", and that this was approved by Gośāla maṅkhaliputta after brief consideration. The eight *Aṅgas* of the *Mahānimitta* are as follows—

1. *Divyam*, "of the Divine",
2. *Autpātam*, "of Portents",
3. *Āntariksham*, "of the sky",
4. *Bhaumam*, "of the earth",
5. *Āṅgam*, "of the body".
6. *Svāram*, "of sound",
7. *Lākshaṇam*, "of characteristics"; and
8. *Vyāñjanam*, "of indications".

The *Mahānimittas* are listed in the *Sthānāṅga Sūtras*,[4] with the variation *Suviṇe* (dreams) for *Divyam*. The *Uttarādhyayana Sūtra*[5] gives a similar list, and adds that the Jaina *Bhikkhu* should not live by such means. The two *Maggas* are described

1. *Sam.* I, p. 185.
2. JDL, II, p. 41.
3. *Bhag*, XV. *Sū.* 539, Fol. 658-9.
4. *Sthānā*, VIII, 608.
5. *Uttarā*, XV, 7.

by the commentator Abhayadeva to have been those of song and dance. The *Maggas* may represent texts containing Ājīvika religious songs and directions for ritual dances respectively.

VEDĀṄGA LITERATURE

The *Vedāṅga* literature composed during this period does not form part of the Vedic literature, but is in close association with it. It is not the *Veda*, a divine revelation, but the *Vedāṅga*, "the limbs of the *Veda*", constituting works of human authorship. These *Vedāṅgas* include a number of exegetical sciences like *Śikshā* (phonetics), *Kalpa* (ritual), *Vyākaraṇa* (Grammar), *Nirukta* (etymology), *Chhandas* (metrics), and *Jyotisha* (astronomy). These six *Vedāṅgas* refer to the six subjects that help the proper understanding, recitation, and the sacrificial use of the *Vedas*. As a whole, these have been written in a *Sūtra* style. A *Sūtra* has come to mean a short rule, in as few words as possible, giving a clue to the learning of a particular topic. The voluminous increase of knowledge along with the oral system of instruction necessitated this peculiar fashion of *Sūtra* style so that it might be easier to memorize. The intricacies of Vedic ritual, which were to be scrupulously observed in every small detail, contributed to a certain extent to the development of this form of literature.

In course of time, each of the original Vedic *Aṅgas* gave rise to a number of allied sciences through its specialized and scientific study in special schools. The sacrificial ritual itself led to the growth of some of the sciences. Geometry and Algebra arose out of the elaborate rules for the construction of altars. Astronomy and Astrology grew out of the necessity of finding out the proper times and seasons for sacrifice and other purposes. The foundation of Anatomy was laid in the dissection of sacrificial animals. Grammar and Philology had their origin in the care to preserve the sacred texts from corruption and fix the methods of their proper pronunciation.

CLASSES OF SŪTRA WORKS

The first branch of the *Sūtra* literature is called *Śrauta*. The *Śrauta Sūtras* deal with the rites and sacrifices which involve the services of a number of priests. The second branch is the *Gṛihya Sūtras* which are concerned with the numerous ceremonies applicable to the domestic life of a man and his family from birth to death. The third is the *Dharma Sūtras* dealing with the customary law and practice. They enumerate the duties of the castes and stages in life (*Āśrama*). They lay the foundation of civil and criminal law. The last is the *Śulva Sūtras* giving minute details regarding the measurement and construction of the fire-altars and the place of sacrifice. They may thus be regarded as the oldest books of Indian geometry.

The dates of the principal *Śrauta Sūtras* and some of the *Gṛihya Sūtras* have been decided between 800 and 400 B.C. G. BUHLER and J. JOLLY have placed them between the sixth and fourth (or third) centuries B.C., though others assign to them a somewhat later date. Although none of the extant *Dharma Sūtra* is older than 600 B.C., there is no doubt that there were works of this class belonging to an earlier period.[1]

PHILOSOPHICAL LITERATURE

In the sixth century B.C., there was a rise of new philosophical tenets often of a revolutionary character. Many of these philosophical dogmas had a merely temporary phase and gradually faded away but a few, however, came to stay. Besides Mahāvīra and Buddha, the chief heterodox religious teachers of this age were Pūrṇa Kassapa, Pakudha Kachchāyana, Makkhali Gośāla, Ajita Keśakambalin and Sañjaya Belaṭṭhiputta. They were renowned philosophers of their times and propounded independent views on different philosophical subjects. Their works are not available, but we know about their views from the Buddhist and Jaina literature.

The six systems of Indian Philosophy are distinguished as orthodox systems from the heterodox systems of the Buddhists, Jainas and Chārvākas, because they are all somehow reconcilable with the Vedic system, though they mutually differ in their relations to the same. The six systems are known as (1) the Sāṁkhya of Kapila, (2) Yoga of Patañjali (2) Nyāya of Gautama, (4) Vaiśeshika of Kaṇāda, (5) Pūrva Mīmāṁsā of Jaimini, and (6) Vedānta of Bādarāyaṇa.

1. KHDS, I. pp. 8-9; SBE, II, XIV, Introduction.

These systems of philosophy certainly had their beginning much earlier, earlier perhaps than even Lord Mahāvīra, but the texts of the *Sūtras* which embody their conclusions were composed later. There is a great controversy among scholars about the chronology of these *Sūtras*. The proposed dates for the different *Sūtras* vary over a wide range of more than a thousand years between the fifth century B.C. and fifth century A.D. Generally, Vaiśeshika and Nyāya *Sūtras* are regarded as the earliest and Sāṅkhya as the latest.

It is to be noted that the philosophers to whom these systems are ascribed were not necessarily their originators. They gave the final form to the *Sūtras* which themselves refer to older philosophers. Some of the *Sūtras* refer to the opinions of other *Sūtras* and their refutations which show that the different philosophical schools were already in existence before the final redaction of the *Sūtras* took place. It may further be noted that the extant literary works in which the doctrines of the six systems are embodied are themselves much later in date than their original founders. It is possible that these systems of philosophy originated much earlier but they were composed in *Sūtra* style much later.

TECHNICAL AND SCIENTIFIC LITERATURE

Another noteworthy feature of this age is that separate schools of *Kalpa*, *Vyākaraṇa*, and *Jyotisha* apart from Vedic schools, came into existence. These subjects were not taught as auxiliary branches of the Vedic lore to the students of a common school, but each of these subjects was attaining independent development through treat. ıent in a special school. Independent works were written on these branches of knowledge.

(A) *Grammar*

The earliest existing work, dealing with the Grammar of the contemporary spoken language is Pāṇini's *Ashṭādhyāyī*. The author refers to his predecessors like Śākaṭāyana and Śaunaka but their works are not available. It indicates the existence of a long tradition of grammatical studies before the days of Pāṇini. Pāṇini was the native of a village called Śālātura in N.W.F. Province. His work consists of some 4,000 *Sūtras* divided, as the title suggests, into eight chapters.

The date of Pāṇini is not definite, and he has been placed between the seventh and fourth centuries B.C. It is to be noted that the subject, as treated by Pāṇini, is no longer subservient to the needs of mere *Veda*-study but has an independent life and destiny of its own, though it does not exclude the *Veda* from its purview. It is no longer a mere handmaiden of the *Vedavidyā*. It is a distinct science laying down the laws applicable to the entire Sanskrit language, of which the typical form assumed is what we call classical Sanskrit.

(B) *Metrics*

There are many scattered references to metre in the Brāhmaṇas, but it is in the *Sūtras* (e.g. the *Śāṅkhāyana Śrauta Sūtra*, the *Ṛigveda Prātiśākhya* and the *Nidāna Sūtra* that an attempt is made to arrange the archiac metres systematically. The earliest existing work on Metrics is Piṅgala's *Chhandaśāstra*. He started the practice of measuring a metrical line with the help of the *Tṛikas* or the eight groups of three letters each. From very old times, the Sanskrit metres in the *Vedas* were distinguished from each other by the number of letters contained in each line of a stanza. Piṅgala's date is uncertain but he may be assigned to the first or second century B.C. Piṅgala himself mentions earlier authorities like Rāta, Māṇḍavya, Kāśyapa and others while defining the classical metres, which shows that the development of the classical metres had begun long before Piṅgala.

(C) *Science of Polity*

It is only after the rise of the well organized states in the age of Mahāvīra that the Science of Polity seems to have originated. Both the *Mahābhārata* and the *Arthaśāstra* give us information about the early writers of Hindu Polity and the theories propounded by them. These two works represent independent traditions and sources. Kauṭilya refers to nineteen teachers who precede him—Manu, Bṛihaspati, Parāśara, Uśanas, Bharadvāja, Viśālāksha, Piśuna, Kauṇapadanta, Vātavyādhi, etc. The *Mahābhārata* mentions some common names besides five others.

Unfortunately, the works of these authors have been lost, but their opinions quoted in the *Mahābhārata* and the *Artha-*

śāstra give us some idea of their contents. One of them named Uśanas went to the extent of advocating the extreme view that politics was the only science worth study. They believed in the monarchical form of government. They seem to have devoted considerable space to the discussion of the training of the prince and the qualifications of an ideal ruler. The relative importance that he should attach to the difficulties and calamities in connection with the treasury, forts and army were also exhaustively discussed. The constitution and functions of the Ministry were described at length by most of them and they widely differed from one another about the number of the Ministers and their qualifications. Principles of foreign policy were also debated upon, Bhāradvāja advocating submission to the strong when there is no alternative and Viśālāksha recommending a fight to finish, even if it meant annihilation. Vātavyādhi did not ascribe to the theory of *Shāḍguṇya* but advocated that of *Dvaiguṇya*. The questions of the control over revenue and provincial officers were discussed. These early works contain important sections dealing with civil and criminal law and laid down a scheme of fines and punishments, theft, robbery, misappropriation, etc.[1]

Thus, these different schools of political thought before Kauṭilya definitely prove that they were not confined to a mechanical repetition of each other's views but they ceaselessly endeavoured to ascertain how far the end of the state could best be realized within the ambit of the ancient *dharma*.

MATHEMATICS, ASTRONOMY AND ASTROLOGY

The early Jaina texts provide ample evidence of progress made in Mathematics, Astronomy and Astrology. It is said that Mahāvīra was versed in Arithmetic and Astronomy.[2] *Gaṇita* is also described as one of the four expositions of the principle (*anuyoga*) in the Jaina text.[3] The *Ṭhāṇāṅga* mentions ten kinds of science of numbers, viz., *parikamma* (fundamental operation), *vavahāra* (subject of treatment), *rajju* ("rope" meaning geometry) *rāsi* ("heap" meaning measurement of

1. State and Government in Ancient India, pp. 8-9.
2. *Kalpa*, 1. 10.
3. *Das. chū*, p. 2.

solid bodies), *Kalāsāvanna* (fractions), *jāvaṁtāvam* ('as many as' meaning simple equations), *vagga* ("square" meaning quadratic equation). *ghaṇa* ("cube" meaning cubic equation), *vaggavagga* (liquidratic equation) and *vikappa* (permutation and combination).[1]

The *Suriyapannatti* and the *Chandapannatti*, the fifth and the seventh *Upāṅgas* of the Jaina canon respectively deal with Astronomy. The *Suriyapannatti* deals with various astronomical views of the Jainas such as the orbits which the Sun circumscribes during the year, the rising and the setting of the Sun, the speed of the course of the Sun through each of its 184 cubits, the light of the Sun and moon, the measure of the shadow at various seasons of the year, the connection of the moon with lunar mansions (*nakshatra*), the waning and the crescent of the moon, the velocity of the five kinds of heavenly bodies (the Sun, the Moon, planets, *nakshatras* and *tārās*), the qualities of the moon-light, the number of Suns in Jambūdvīpa, etc.[2]

The *Joṇipāhuḍa*[3] and the *Chūḍāmaṇi*[4] deal with astrology. *Vivāhapaḍala* was another work of astrology. The knowledge of astrology was considered necessary for fixing the time of religious ceremonies.

It seems that the eight *Mahānimittas*, the early scriptures of the Ājīvikas contained considerable sections on the subject of Astrology because the Ājīvika mendicant often acted as an astrologer or reader of omens.[5] The Jaina saint Kālaya or Kālaka is said to have learnt the *Mahānimittas* from the Ājīvikas.[6] That the Jainas, despite the veto of the *Uttarādhyayana*, also employed the eightfold *Mahānimitta* is shown by Kālaka's knowledge of it, and by an inscription at Śravaṇa Belgolā, which states that the pontiff *Bhadrabāhu* knowing the eightfold *Mahānimitta*, seeing past, present and future, foretold in Ujjayinī a calamity of twelve years' duration.[7]

1. *Ṭhā*, 10. 747.
2. M. Winternitz : History of Indian Literature, Vol. II, p. 457, JASB, Vol. 49, Pt. I, 1880.
3. *Bṛih Bhā*, I. 1303.
4. Ibid. 1. 1313.
5. *Jā* I, p. 257. *Nakkhatta Jātaka*.
6. *Pañchakalpa chūrṇi*.
7. *Epi. Carn*, II, No 1.

That the Brāhmaṇas also acted as the fortune-tellers by reading symbols of men and by interpreting the dreams and other omens is known by the evidence of the *Jātakas*.[1]

SCIENCE OF MEDICINES

The science of Medicine (*tegichchhaya* or *Ayuvveya*) is said to have been discovered by Dhannantarī[2] (Dhanvantari). He was well versed in the medical science which comprises eight branches.[3] It is not possible to fix the date of Dhannantarī.

In the days of Mahāvīra, the medical science was in the stage of advancement because Taxila was famous for the medical school which must have been the best of its kind in India. It is for this reason that prince Jīvaka spent seven years there, learning medicine and surgery.[4] The practical course in Medicine included a first hand study of the plants to find out the medicinal ones. The *Jātakas* also refer to the medical students at Taxila treating for cranial abscesses and intestinal displacement.

On his return to Magadha after completing education, Jīvaka was appointed the royal physician because he was successful in operating on the fistula of king Bimbisāra. He had also to treat the *Bhikshu* patients suffering from leprosy, goitre, asthma, dry leprosy and *apasmāra*. He cured the head trouble of the wife of a banker of Sāketa, the skin disease of a banker of Banaras and jaundice of king Pradyota.[5] There was also another physician at Rājagṛiha named Akāsagotta who operated on the fistula of a *bhikkhu*.[6]

The *Āchārāṅga* mentions the following sixteen diseases : boils (*gaṇḍī*), leprosy (*kuṭṭha*), consumption (*rāyaṁsī*), epilepsy (*avamāriya*) blindness (*kāṇiya*), stiffness (*jhimiya*), lameness (*kuṇiya*), humpback (*khujiya*), dropsy (udari), dumbness (*mūya*), swelling (*sūṇiya*), over-appetite (*gilāsaṇi*), trembling (*vevai*), disablement (*piḍhasappi*), elephantiasis (*silīvaya*) and diabetes

1. FSONB, pp. 229-234.
2. *Niśī. chū*, 15, p. 944; *Ayoghara Jā.* (No. 510), IV, pp. 496, 498.
3. *Vivā*, 7, p. 41.
4. *Jā*, No. 498.
5. *Vinaya* Texts of the *Mūlasarvāstivādins* (Gilgit Manuscripts, Vol. III, part 2, pp. 1-52.
6. *Vinayapiṭaka*, I, p. 215.

(*madhumeha*).[1]

Hospitals (*tigichchhayasālā*) are freely mentioned. The *Nāyādhammakhā* mentions that a hospital was built on hundred pillars where a number of physicians and surgeons were employed who treated various kinds of patients with various kinds of medicines and herbs.[2] There were state physicians and hospitals as well.[3] The physicians carried their bage of surgical instruments and gave various treatment according to the nature of the disease.

SCIENCE OF ENGINEERING

The science of Engineering seems to have become very popular and well-developed. The construction of cities, forts palaces, buildings, tanks, canals, etc. would not have been possible without a proper study of the subject. Even the *Bhikshus*, who now-a-days are seen only having a life of ease and comfort and engaging themselves merely in religious and philosophical studies and meditations, were then enthusiastically concerned with the work of superintending the construction of fine buildings.[4]

1. *Āchā*, 6 1. 173.
2. Nāyā, 13, p. 143.
3. *Bṛih. Bhā*, P. 1 376; *Vya. Bhā*, 5 21
4. *Chū*, VI (Tr. by Rhys Davids and Oldenberg SBE,XX), pp. 189-90.

GENERAL BIBLIOGRAPHY

I. *ORIGINAL SOURCES*

(A) Texts and Translations

1. *BRAHMANICAL*

(a) *VEDIC*

Aitareya Brāhmaṇa : Ed. K.S. Agashe, Poona, 1896.
Trans. by A.B. Keith,
Hos, Vol. XXV, Cambridge, Mass., 1920.

Atharvaveda : Ed. with Sāyaṇa's Comm. by S.P. Pandit, Bombay, 1895-8.
Trans. in part, M. Bloomfield,
SBE, Vol. XLII, Oxford, 1897.

Bṛihadāraṇyaka Upanishad : Ed. with trans. by O. Bohtlingk, Leipzig, 1889.

Chhāndogya Upanishad : Ed. with trans. by O. Bohtlingk, Leipzig, 1889.

Gopatha Brāhmaṇa : Ed. by Rajendra Mitra and H. Vidyabhushan, Calcutta, 1872.

Kāṭhaka Saṁhitā : Ed. by Von Schroeder, Leipzig, 1900-11.

Kaushitaki Brāhmaṇa : Ed. by E. B. Cowell, Calcutta, 1891.
Trans. by A. B. Keith, HOS, XXV, Cambridge, Mass., 1920.

Maitrāyaṇī Saṁhitā : Ed. by Von Schroeder, Leipzig, 1881-6.

Pañchaviṁśa Brāhmaṇa : Ed. by A. Vedantavagisa, Calcutta, 1869-74.

Ṛigveda : *Saṁhitā* and *Pada* text with Sāyaṇa's Comm. Ed. by F. Max Muller (Second Edn.) 1890-2. *Saṁhitā and Pada* text with Sāyaṇa's Comm. Critically edited by Vaidika Saṁśodhana Maṇḍala, Poona, Four Vols. 1933, etc.

Śatapatha Brāhmaṇa : Ed. by A. WEBER, London, 1885. Trans. by J. EGGELING, SBE, XII, XXVI, XLI, XLIII, XLIV, Oxford, 1882-1900.

Taittiriya Saṁhitā : Ed. by A. WEBER, Berlin, 1871-72; with the Comm. of Mādhava, Calcutta, 1854-99.

(b) *SŪTRAS, EPICS, PURĀṆAS AND GRAMMAR*

Āpastamba Dharma-Sūtra : Ed. by G. BUHLER (Bombay Sanskrit Series), 1892-1894.

Āpastamba Gṛihya-Sūtra : SBE, Vol. XXX.

Ashṭādhyāyī of Pāṇini : Tr. by S. C. VASU, Vārāṇasī, 1891-1898.

Āśvalāyana Gṛihya-sūtra : Ed. A. G. STENZLER, Leipzig, 1864.

Baudhāyana Dharma sūtra : Ed. by W. CALAND, Calcutta, 1904-23.

Baudhāyana Gṛihya-sūtra : Ed. by R. SHAMA SASTRI, Mysore, 1920.

Bhagavadgītā : Ed. by K.S. AGASHE, ĀSS, Poona, 1909. Eng. Trans. by K. T. TELANG, SBE, 2nd Ed. Oxford, 1908.

Bhāgavata Purāṇa : Ed. by V. L. PANSIKAR, Bombay, 1920, Eng. trans. by J. M. SANYAL, Calcutta, 1930-34.

Gautama Dharmasūtra : Text ĀSS, Tr. SBE, II.

Mahābhārata : Eng. trans. by M. N. DUTT, Calcutta, 1985-1905.

Matsya Purāṇa : Eng. trans. by A. Taluqdar of Oudh. SBH. 2. Vols. Allahabad, 1916-17.

Pāraskara Gṛihyasūtra : Ed. by GOPAL SHASTRI NENE, Benares, 1926.

Rāmāyaṇa : Trans. into English prose by M. N. DUTT, Calcutta, 1892-94.

Śāṅkhāyana Gṛihya Sūtra : SBE, Vol. XXIX.

Sarvadarśana Saṅgraha : Trans. by COWELL and GOUGH.

Śrīmālapurāṇa athavā Śrīmāla Māhātmya : Ed. by Jatashankar Liladhar and Keshavaji and Vishvanath, Ahmedabad, 1899, V. S. 1955.

Vasishṭha Dharmasūtra: Ed. by A. A. Fuhrer, Bombay, 1916.

Vedāntasāra : Ed. Cowell.

2. *JAINA*

(a) *CANONICAL*

Āchārāṅga : *Niryukti*, Bhadrabāhu.
: *Chūrṇi*, Jinadāsagaṇi, Ratlam, 1941.
: Com. Śīlāṅka, Surat, 1935.
: Trans. H. Jacobi, SBE, XXII.

Antagaḍdasāo : Com. Abhayadeva, Ed. by M. C. Modi, Ahmedabad. Ed. P. L. Vaidya, Poona, 1932. Trans. L. D. Barnett, London, 1907.

Anuttarovavāiyadasāo : Com, Abhayadeva, Ed. by M. C. Modi, Ahmedabad, 1932.
: Ed. P. L. Vaidya, Poona, 1932.

Anuyogadvāra : *Chūrṇi*, Jinadāsagaṇi, Ratlam, 1928.
: Com. Haribhadra, Ratlam, 1928.
: Com. Maladhārī Hemachandra, Bhavanagar, 1939.

Āupapātika : Ed. by N. G. Suru, Poona, 1936.

Āvaśyaka : *Niryukti*, Bhadrabāhu
: *Bhāshya*
: *Chūrṇi*, Jinadāsagaṇi, Ratlam, 1928.
: Com. Haribhadra, Āgamodaya Samiti, Bombay, 1916.
: Com. Malayagiri, Āgamodaya Samiti, Bombay, 1928.
: *Niryukti Dīpikā*, Māṇikyaśekhara, Surat,
: 1939.

Bhagavatī : Com. Abhayadeva, Āgamodaya Samiti, Bombay, 1921, Ratlam, 1937.
: Ed. by Jozef Deleu with introduction,

	Critical analysis, commentary and indexes 'De Tempel' Tempelhof 37, Brugge (Belgie).
Bṛihatkalpa	: *Bhāshya*, Saṅghadāsagaṇi.
	: Com. Malayagiri and Kshamākīrti,
	: Ātmānanda Jaina Sabhā, Bhavanagar, 1933-38.
Dasaveyāliya	: *Niryukti*. Bhadrabāhu.
	: *Chūrṇi*, Jinadāsagani, Ratlam, 1933.
	: Com. Haribhadra, Bombay, 1918.
	: Introduction and notes W. SCHUBRING, Ahmedabad, 1932.
Jīvābhigama	: Com. Malayagiri, Bombay, 1919.
Kalpasūtra	: Trans. H. JACOBI, SBE, XXII, 2nd Reprint, Delhi, 1968.
Mahāniśītha	: Ed. W. SCHUBRING, Berlin, 1918. Guj. trans. NARSIMHA BHAI (Mss).
Nandi, Devavāchaka	: *Chūrṇi*. Jinadāsagaṇi Ratlam, 1928.
Kshamāśramaṇa	: Com, Haribhadra, Ratlam, 1928. Com, Malayagiri, Bombay, 1924.
Nāyādhammakahā	: Ed. N. V. VAIDYA, Poona, 1940. Com. Abhayadeva, Āgamodaya, Bombay 1919.
Niryāvaliyāo	: Com. Chandrasūri, Ahmedabād 1938. Ed. GOPANI and CHOKSHI, Ahmedabad, 1934, Ed. P. L. VAIDYA, Poona, 1932.
Niśītha	: *Bhāshya*
	Chūrṇi Jinadāsagani, Ed. VIJAYA PREMA SURISVARA, V. S. 1995.
	Eka Adhyayana by D. S. MALAVANIA.
Ogha Nijjutti	: Com. Droṇāchārya, Bombay, 1919.
Ovāiya	: Com. Abhayadeva, Second Ed. Surat V. S. 1914.
Painnas (ten)	: Bombay, 1927.
Paṇhavāgaraṇa	: Com. Abhayadeva, Bombay, 1919.

A critical introduction to the Paṇhavāgaraṇāim. by Amlyachandra Sen, Wurzburg, 1936.

Pannavaṇā : Com. Malayagiri, Bombay, 1918-19.
: Guj. trans. Bhagavandas, Ahmedabad, V. S. 1991.

Piṇḍanijjutī : Com. Malayagiri, Surat, 1918.

Rāyapaseṇiya : Com. Abhayadeva, Ahmedabad V. S. 1994.
: Eng. Trans. by N. V. Vaidya, Ahmedabad, 1938.

Samavāyāṅga : Com. Abhayadeva, Ahmedabad, 1938.

Sūtrakritāṅga : *Niryukti*, Bhadrabāhu.
: *Chūrṇi*, Jinadāsagaṇi, Ratlam, 1941.
: Bom. Śīlāṅka Āgamodaya Samiti, Bom-
: bay, 1917.
: Eng. Trans. by H. Jacobi, SBE, XLV, Delhi, Reprint 1964.

Tandulaveyāliya : Com. Vijayavimala, Devachandra Lalabhai.

Ṭhāṇāṅga : Com. Abhayadeva, Ahmedabad, 1937.

Uttarādhyayana : *Niryukti* Bhadrabāhu.
: *Chūrṇi* Jinadāsagaṇi, Ratlam, 1933.
: Eng. Trans. by H. Jacobi, SBE, XLV, Delhi, Reprint 1964.
: Ed. J. Charpentier, Upsala, 1922.

Uvāsagadasāo : Eng. Trans. by A. F. R. Hoernle, Calcutta, 1888, Ed. P. L. Vaidya, Poona, 1930.

Vavahāra : Bhāshya
: Com. Malayagiri, Bhavanagar, 1926.

Vivāgasuya : Com. Abhayadeva, Baroda, V. S. 1922.
: Ed. A. T. Upadhye, Belgaum, 1935.

(b) *NON-CANONICAL*

Ārādhanā Kathākosha of Nemidatta with Hindi Trans. Bombay 1915

Darśanasāra of Devasena, Ed. by N. R. Premi, Bombay, V. S. 1974.

Daśabhaktyādi-saṁgraha of Pūjyapāda, MS

Harivaṁśapurāṇa of Jinasena Sūri, Bombay, 1930, with Hindi Trans. Bhāratīya Gyānapīṭha, Kashi, 1962.

Jīvandhara Champū of Harichandra, with Hindi Trans. Bhāratīya Gyānapīṭha, Kashi, 1958.

Kasāya-Pāhuḍa (*Jayadhavala*) of Vīrasena and Jinasena, Vols. I & II, Mathura, 1944.

Mahāpurāṇa (*Ādipurāṇa and Uttarapurāṇa*) of Jinasena and Guṇabhadra, Indore, V. E. 1973-75, with Hindi Trans. Bhāratīya Gyānapīṭha, Kashi, 1951-54.

Mahāvīrachariya of Guṇachandra, Bombay, 1929, with Gujarati Trans. Bhavanagar, V. S. 1994.

Mahāvīracharita of Nemichandra Devendragaṇi, Jaina Ātmānanda Sabhā, Bhāvanagara, 1933.

Pariśishṭa-Parvan of Hemachandra, Ed. by H. JACOBI, Calcutta, 2nd edition, 1932.

Paum-chariu (*Rāmāyaṇa*) of Vimalasūri, Ed. H. JACOBI, Bhavanagar, 1914.

Tiloyapaṇṇati of Yativṛishabha Ed. A. N. UPADHYE & H. L. JAIN, Solapur, 1951.

Trilokasāra of Nemichandra, Bombay.

Trishashṭiśalākāpurushacharita, trans. by H. M, JOHNSON, Baroda, 1930.

Varāṅga-charita of Jaṭāsiṁhanandi, Ed. by A. N. UPADHYE, Bombay, 1933.

Vardhamāna-charita of Asaga, Solapur, 1931.

Vāsudevahiṇḍi of Dharmadāsa, Bhavanagar, 1930.

Vividha-tīrtha-kalpa of Jinaprabha, Ed. by JINAVIJAYA, Bombay.

3. *BUDDHIST*

(a) *CANONICAL*

Aṅguttara-Nikāya : Ed. R. MORRIS and E. HARDY, PTS. London, 1885-1900.
Tr. F. L. WOODWARD and E. M. HARE. The Book of the Gradual Sayings, 5 Vols. P.T.S. London, 1932-36; I & II Vols. 1951.

Apadāna : Ed. Mary E. Lilley, PTS, London, 1925-27

Buddhacharyā : (Being a Hindi translation of selected portions from the *Tripiṭaka* and *Aṭṭhakahā* Tr. by Rahula Sankrityayana, 2nd Ed. Sarnath, 1952.

Dhammapada : Text. Ed. by Rahula Sankrityayana, Rangoon, 1937.
Eng. Trans. by F. Max Muller, SBE, Oxford, 1898. Ed. and trans. by Mrs. Rhys Davids, SBE, London, 1931.

Dīgha Nikāya : Ed. T. W. Rhys Davids and J. E. Carpenter, 3 Vols. PTS, London, 1890, 1903, 1911. Eng. trans. (Dialogues of the Buddha) by T. W. Rhys Davids. 3 Vols. SBB. London, 1899-1910, 1921.
Tr. Rahula Sankrityayana in Hindi *Dighanikāya*, Mahābodhi Sabha, Sarnath, 1936.

Jātaka : Ed. V. Fausboll. 7 Vols. London, 1877-97. Eng. trans. under the Editorship of E. B. Cowell, 7 Vols. Cambridge, 1895-1913.

Mahāvagga : Ed. by N. K. Bhagat, 2 Vols, Bombay 1944-1952.

Majjhima Nikāya : Ed. by V. Trenckner and R. Chalmers, PTS, London, 1888-1902.
Eng. Trans. (Further Dialogues of the Buddha by Ford Chalmers, 2 Vols. SBE, London, 1926-27.
Tr. Rahula Sankrityayana in Hindi, Mahabodhi Sabha, Sarnath, 1933.

Niddesa. : *Mahāniddesa*, Ed. by L. DE La Vallee Poussin and E. J. Thomas. PTS, London, 1916-17. *Chullaniddesa*, Ed. by W. Stede. PTS, London, 1918.

Petavatthu : Ed. by J. Minayeff, PTS, London, 1888.

Saṁyutta Nikāya : Ed. by Leon Freer, PTS, London, 1884-98. Indexes by Mrs. Rhys Davids, London, 1904. Eng. trans. (Book of the kindred sayings or Grouped Suttas) by Mrs. Rhys Davids and F.L. Woodward, PTS, London, 1917-30.

Sutta Nipāta : Ed. by D. Andersen and H. Smith, PTS, London, 1913.
Eng. trans, by V. Fausboll, SBE, Oxford, 1898.Ed. by Rahula Sankrityayana, Rangoon, 1937.

Therī-gāthā : Ed. by H. Oldenberg, PTS, London, 1883.Eng. trans (Psalms of the Brethren) by Mr. Rhys Davids, PTS, London, 1913.

Thera-gāthā : Ed. by R. Pischel, PTS, London, 1883. Eng. trans. (Psalms of the Sisters) by Mrs. Rhys Davids, PTS, London, 1909.

Udāna : Ed. by P. Steithal, PTS, London, 1885. Eng. Trans. by D. M. Strong, London, 1902.

Vimānavatthu : Ed. by Rahula Sankrityayana, Rangoon, 1937.

Vinaya Piṭaka : Eng. trans. (Vinaya Texts) by T. W. Rhys Davids and H. Oldenderg. SBE, Oxford, 1881-85. Tr. by Rahula Sankrityayana in Hindi, Mahabodhi Sabha, Sarnath, 1935.

(b) *NON-CANONICAL*

Dhammapada Commentary Ed. by H.C. Normal, 5 Vols. PTS, London. 1906-15.
Eng. trans. (Buddhist Legends) by E.W. Burlingame, 3. Vols. HUS. Cambridge, Mass. 1921.

Dīpavaṁśa : Ed. and trans. by H. Oldenberg, London, 1879.

Divyāvadāna : Ed. by E.B. COWELL and R.A. NELL, Cambridge, 1886.

Lalitavistara : Ed. by R. MITRA, Calcutta, 1877.
: Ed. by S. LEFMANN, HALLE, 1902-08.

Mahāvaṁsa : Ed. & Tr. Geiger, PTS., London, 1912.

Mahāvastu : Ed. by E. SENART, Paris, 1882-97.

Milindapañho : Ed. by V. TRENCKNER, London, 1880.
Eng. trans. by T.W. RHYS DAVIDS, SBE, Oxford, 1890-94.

Sumaṅgala Vilāsinī- : Commentary on the Dīgha Nikāya.
Ed. by T.W. RHYS DAVIDS, PTS, London, 1886.

II. *MODERN WORKS ON HISTORY AND LITERATURE*

(A) *ENGLISH*

AGRAWALA, V.S. : India as known to Pāṇini, Lucknow, 1953. Indian Art, Varanasi, 1965.

ALLAN, J. : Catalogue of Coins, Ancient India, London, 1936.

ALTEKAR, A.S. : State and Government in Ancient India, 2nd ed. Benaras, 1955.
The Position of Women in Hindu Civilization, Benaras, 1938.
Education in Ancient India, Varanasi, 1957.

BANDOPADHYAYA, N.C. : Economic Life and Progress in Ancient India, Calcutta, 1945.

BANERJEA, J.N. : Development of Hindu Iconography, Calcutta, 1956.

BANERJEE, S.C. : Dharma Sūtras, A Study in their Origin and Development, Calcutta, 1962.

BARUA, B.M. : A History of Pre-Buddhistic Indian Philosophy, Reprint 1970, Delhi. Gaya and Bodha-Gaya, Calcutta, 1934.

BASHAM, A.L. : History & Doctrine of the Ājīvikas, London, 1951.

BEAL SAMUEL : Buddhist Records of the Western World from the Chinese of Hiuen Tsang, London, 1884.

BHANDARKAR, D.R. : Lectures on the Ancient History of India (Carmichael Lectures, 1918), Calcutta, 1919.

BUHLER, J.G. : *Uber die indische Secte der Jainas*, Viena, 1887.
(Eng. trans. The Indian Sect of the Jainas by J. BURGESS, London, 1903).
: On the Indian Origin of the Brāhmī Alphabet.

CUNNINGHAM, A : Ancient Geography of India, Calcutta, 1924.
: Coins of Ancient India, London 1891.

DEO, S.B. : History of Jaina Monachism, Poona, 1956.

DEVA KRISHNA and MISHRA, VIJAYAKANTA : Vaiśālī Excavations, Vaiśālī, 1961.

DIWAKAR, R.R. : (General Editor) : Bihar through the Ages, Calcutta, 1959.

DUTTA, S.K. : Early Buddhist Monachism, London, 1924.

FICK, R. : Social Organisation in North-East India in Buddha's Time, Tr. S.K. MAITRA, Calcutta, 1920.

FORLONG, J.G.R. : Short Studies in the Science of Comparative Religions, London, 1897.

GHOSHAL, U.N. : History of Hindu Political Theories, London, 1923.
Studies in Ancient Indian History and Culture, Calcutta, 1957.

JAIN, B.C. : Lord Mahāvīra (A study in Historical Perspective), Benares, 1948.

JAIN, C.L. : Jaina Bibliography, Calcutta, 1945.

JAIN, J.C. : Life in Ancient India as depicted in the Jain Canons, Bombay, 1947.

JAIN, J.P. : The Jaina Sources of the History of Ancient India, Delhi, 1964.

JAIN, K.C. : Jainism in Rajasthan, Sholapur, 1963.
Malwa Through the Ages, Delhi, 1972.

JAYASWAL, K.P. : Hindu Polity, 3rd ed. Bangalore, 1955.

KANE, P.V. : History of Dharmaśāstra, 3 Vols., Poona, 1941.

KERN, H. : Manual of Indian Buddhism, Strassburg, 1896.

LAW, B.C. : India as Described in Early Texts of Buddhism and Jainism, London, 1941.
History of Pāli Literature, 2 Vols, London, 1933.

: Mahāvīra, His Life and Teachings, London, 1937.

: Geography of Early Buddhism, London, 1932.

: Some Jaina Canonical Sūtras, Bombay, 1949.

: Indological Studies, I & II, Calcutta, 1962.

MAJUMDAR, R.C. : Corporate Life in Ancient India, Calcutta, 1918.

: History of Bengal.
Suvarṇadvīpa, Parts 1 & 2, Dacca, 1937-38.

MAJUMDAR, R.C. and PUSALKER, A.D. : Ed. The Age of Imperial Unity, 2nd ed. Bombay, 1953.

: Ed. The Vedic Age, 2nd Impression, London, 1932.

MAJUMDAR, R.C. RAYCHAUDHURI, H.C. and DATTA, K. K. : An advanced History of India, 2nd ed. London, 1950.

MARSHALL, SIR JOHN : Mohenjo-Dāro and the Indus Civilization, 3 Vols., London, 1931.

MATHUR, J.C. and MISHRA, YOGENDRA : Ed. Homage to Vaiśāli, Vaiśālī, 1948.

MAX MULLER : Hibbert Lectures.

MEHTA, RATILAL N. : Pre-Buddhist India, Bombay, 1939.

MISHRA, YOGENDRA : An Early History of Vaiśālī, Delhi, 1962.

MITTAL, A.C. : Early History of Orissa, Banaras, 1962.

MOOKERJI, R.K. : A History of Indian Shipping, London, 1912.

: Ancient Indian Education, London, 1951.

: Hindu Civilization, London, 1936.

PANDEY, G.C. : Studies in the Origins of Buddhism, Allahabad, 1957.

PANDEY, R.B. : Indian Palaeography, Banaras, 1952.

PARGITER, F.E. : Ancient Indian Historical Tradition, London, 1922.

PRADHAN, S.N. : Chronology of Ancient India, Calcutta, 1927.

RAPSON, E.J. Ed. : Cambridge History of India, Vol. I : Ancient India, Cambridge, 1922.

RAYCHAUDHURI, H.C. : Political History of Ancient India, Sixth edition, Calcutta, 1953.

ROCKHILL, W.W. : The Life of the Buddha, Second Edition, London, 1884.

RHYS DAVIDS, T.W. : Buddhist India, ninth edition, Delhi, 1970.

: Buddhist Birth Stories, London, 1880.

SANKALIA, H. D. : Ed. Indian Prehistory, Poona, 1964.

SEN AMULYACHANDRA : Schools and Sects in Jaina Literature, Calcutta 1931.

SHAH, C. J. L. : Jainism in North India, London, 1932.

SHARMA, G. R. : The Excavations at Kauśāmbī, Allahabad, 1960.

SINGH, M. M. : Life in North-Eastern India in Pre-Maurya Times, Delhi, 1967.

SIRCAR, D. C. : Inscriptions of Aśoka. Delhi, 1967.

SMITH, V. A. : Jaina Stūpa and other Antiquities from Mathura, Allahabad, 1901.

STEVENSON, Mrs. SINCLAIR : The heart of Jainism, first Indian Edition 1970.

TAYLOR, ISAAC : The Alphabet, 2 Vols.

THOMAS E. J. : History of Buddhist Thought, London, New Delhi, 1953.

TULSĪ : Pre-Vedic Existence of Śramaṇa Tradition.

UPASAKA, C. S. : The History and Palaeography of Mauryan Brahmi Script, Varanasi, 1960.

WINTERNITZ, M. : A History of Indian Literature, Calcutta, 1933.

H. ZIMMER : Philosophies of India.

(B) *VERNACULAR*

HASTIMAL : *Jaina Dharma* Kā Maulika Itihāsa, I, Jaipur, 1971.

JAIN, H. L. : *Bhāratīya Saṁskṛiti me Jaina Dharma Kā Yogadāna*, Jabalpur, 1962.

: *Jaina Tīrtha Sarvasaṁgraha*, Ahmedabad, 1953.

KALYAN VIJAYA : *Śramaṇa Bhagavān Mahāvīra*, Jalor, V. S. 1998.

: *Vīra Nirvāṇa Saṁvata aura Jaina Kāla Gaṇanā*, Jalor, 1930.

MUKHTAR, JUGALKISHORE : *Jaina Sāhitya aura Itihāsa para Viśada* : *Prakāśa*, Delhi, 1956.

NAGARAJA : *Āgama aura Tripiṭaka eka Anuśīlana*, 1969.

OJHA, G.H. : *Prāchīna Bhāratīya Lipimālā*, Ajmer, 1919.

PREMI, N.R. : *Jaina Sāhitya aura Itihāsa*, Bombay, 1956.

SHASTRI, K.C. : *Jaina Sāhitya kā Itihāsa*, Varanasi, V.N.S. 2489.

VIJAYENDRA : *Tīrthaṅkara Mahāvīra*, Bombay, V.S. 2017

GENERAL

B. C. LAW Volume : Bhārata Kaumudī, Allahabad, 1945.

DE, N. L. : Geographical Dictionary of Ancient and Medieval India, London, 1927.

Encyclopaedia of Religion and Ethics.

Imperial Gazetteer of India, Vols. 12 and 15, New Edition, Oxford, 1908.

JAYANTA VIJAYA : Ed. Arbudāchala pradakshiṇā Jaina Lekha Saṁdoha, V. S. 2005.

MACDONELL, A. A. and : KEITH, A. B. : Vedic Index of Names and Subjects, 2 Vols. London, 1912.

MALASEKHARA, G.P. : Dictionary of Pali Proper Names, 2 Vols. London, 1237-1938.

Sir Asutosh Mookerjee Silver Jubilee Volume.

Vaiśālī Abhinandanagrantha.

JOURNALS, REPORTS and *MEMOIRS*

Annals of the Bhandarkar Oriental Research Institute, Poona.

Annual Reports of the Archaeological Survey of India.

Epigraphia Carnatica.

Epigraphia Indica, Otacamund.

Indian Antiquary, Bombay.

Indian Archaeology—A Review, Delhi.

Indian Culture.

Indian Historical Quarterly, Calcutta.

Jaina Siddhānta Bhāskara (Hindi- English).

Journal of the Asiatic Society of Bengal, Calcutta.

Journal of the Bihar Research Society, Patna.

Journal of the Department of Letters, Calcutta University, Calcutta.

Journal of Indian History, Trivandrum.

Journal of the Numismatic Society of India, Banaras.

Journal of the Oriental Institute, Baroda.

Memoirs of Archaeological Survey of India.

Nāgarī Prachāriṇī Patrikā, Banaras.

Numismatic Chronicles.

Proceedings of the All-India Oriental Conference.

INDEX

C

L

M

O

P

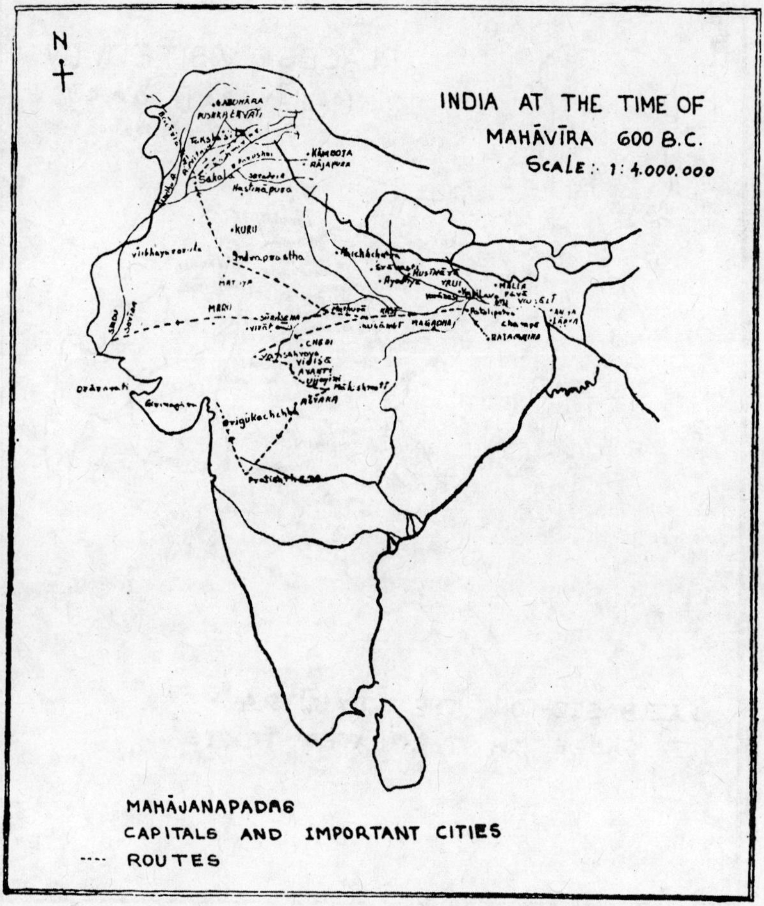
N
INDIA AT THE TIME OF
MAHĀVĪRA 600 B.C.
SCALE: 1: 4.000.000
KURU
MAGADHA
CHEDI
AVANTI
MAHĀJANAPADAS
CAPITALS AND IMPORTANT CITIES
---- ROUTES

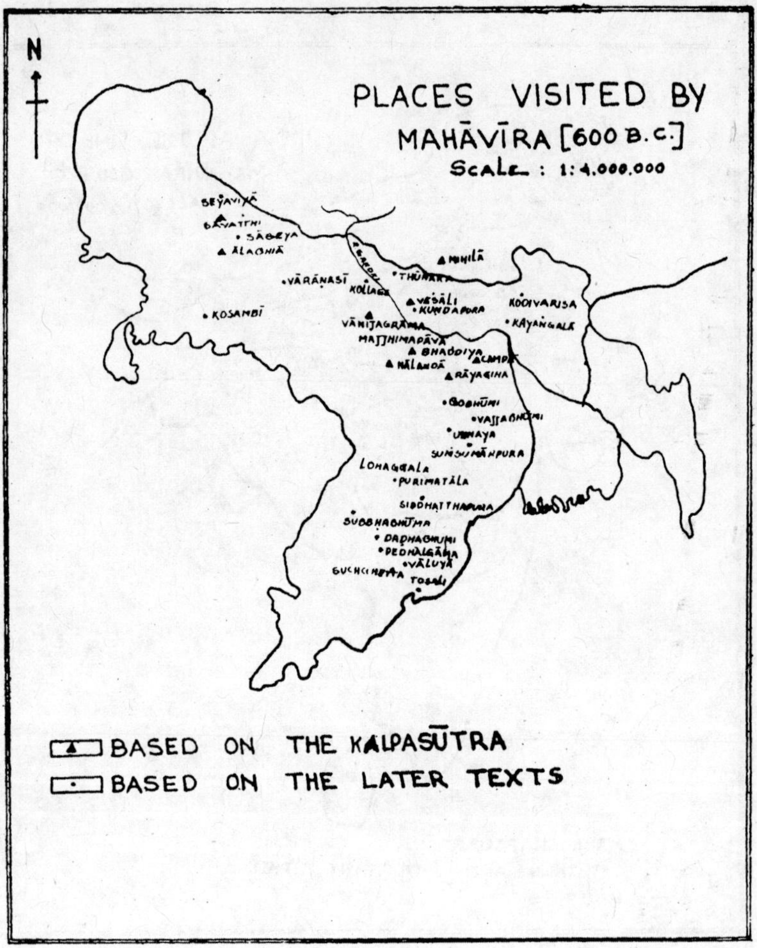
N
PLACES VISITED BY
MAHĀVĪRA [600 B.C.]
Scale : 1:4.000.000
SEYAVIYĀ
SĀGEYA
ĀLABHIĀ
VĀRĀṆASĪ
KOSAMBĪ
KOLLAGA
VĀṆIJAGRĀMA
MAJJHIMAPĀVĀ
BHADDIYA
NĀLANDĀ
CAMPĀ
RĀYAGIHA
KUṆḌAPURA
KODIVARISA
KAYAṄGALĀ
GOBHŪMI
LOHAGGALA
PURIMATĀLA
SIDDHATTHAPURA
SUBBHABHŪMA
DAḌHABHUMI
PEDHĀLGĀMA
VĀLUYĀ
SUCHCHHETTA
TOSALI
BASED ON THE KALPASŪTRA
BASED ON THE LATER TEXTS